THE
COMPLETE
PET BIRD
OWNER'S
HANDBOOK

GARY A. GALLERSTEIN D.V.M.
with Julie Rach

Avian Publications

6380 Monroe St. NE
Minneapolis MN 55432

Bruce Burchett Publisher/Owner
www.avianpublications.com
bruce@avianpublications.com
Phone & fax 763-571-8902

National Library of Canada Cataloguing in Publication

Gallerstein, Gary A., 1952-
The complete pet bird owner's handbook / Gary A. Gallerstein.

Includes biblipgraphical references and index.
ISBN 1-895270-25-1
1. Cage birds. 2. Cage birds - Health.
I. Title. II. Title: Pet bird owner's handbook.

SF461.G354 2003 / 636.6\8   C2003-902806-2
$\qquad$ GAL

Production and Design
Silvio Mattacchione and Co. / Peter A. Graziano Limited
1251 Scugog Line 8, RR#1.
Port Perry, ON, Canada L9L 1B2
Telephone: 905.985.3555
Fax: 905.985.4005
silvio@primus.ca
pgraziano@sympatico.ca
www.silvio-co.com

Printed in Singapore by A-R Bookbuilders

Dedication

Dedicated with love,

to my wife,

Laura and

my children,

Laura,

Eric and

Mitchell

Gary A. Gallerstein DVM

For Sindbad and all the other "second-hand birds" and the owners who've found how very special these birds can be--

Julie Rach

Contents

Contents

Acknowledge

More than 20 years ago, the first edition of this book was in its conceptual and developmental stages. It began as a series of informational handouts for our clients and evolved into first a booklet and then into a "real" book. The first edition was called *The Bird Owner's Home Health and Care Handbook*, the second edition, *The Complete Bird Owner's Handbook* and now this third edition, *The Complete Pet Bird Owner's Handbook*. It has taken a mere 20 years, but I think we have finally gotten the title right!

The scope, character and quality of this book is the result of the efforts of multiple authors. My time constraints and the ever-expanding knowledge base of avian husbandry and medicine required the input from other avian experts in the field. The result, is once again, almost a complete revision with an abundance of new material. The new topics and new insights have benefited greatly from the writings of these individuals.

Julie Rach, created the most of the new chapters and general layout, and wrote and/or re-edited the non-medical chapters. Julie is a professional writer and editor with multiple bird books to her credit. Her creative writing and organizational skills radiate throughout the pages of this new edition. Julie, it was a privilege to work with you.

Pat Mulloy, R.V.T., avian/exotic veterinary nurse and avian behavior consultant for the writing of the new behavior chapter and help with many of the new photographs. Pat has worked very hard and passionately over the last several years to distinguish herself as an accomplished avian nursing technician and avian behavior consultant.

Charisse Davidson, D.V.M., for being the contributing author for the *Emergency Medicine and Medical Problems Chapters*. She has the wonderful ability to take complex medical concepts and express them in clear and simple to understand English.

Acknowledgements

Stacy Stephens, D.V.M., with a strong interest in avian medicine, for her section on *Avian Complementary Veterinary Medicine*. In the last edition, only a brief paragraph was written on this subject. However, in both human and veterinary medicine, all forms of alternative medicine have continued to grow in popularity. It was time to collaborate with an expert who understands avian medicine and the alternative approaches to their health care.

Nicole Perretta, artist extraordinaire, for her wonderful illustrations. This includes drawings carried over from the previous edition and new ones specially created for this new edition. Nicole, it's always a pleasure to work with you. Thank you very much!

Leo Burrell, for contributing the home cooking recipes. These have been carried over from the previous edition and have met with much approval from many bird owners.

I want to also thank our professional and expert staff at the Acacia Animal Health Center. Thank you for allowing me the time and peace of mind to complete the new edition of this book. I could not have done it without all of your support.

Wayne Zucker, Bernie Feldman, Stuart Yasgoor, and Butch Hiller for their continued support and encouragement. Old friendships are the best!

The Association of Avian Veterinarians and many fellow colleagues for their numerous contributions to the advancement of avian medicine and avian behavior. I have indeed been privileged to learn from, work with, and develop many friendships with so many dedicated individuals.

Although not a living and breathing person, I have to also thank computers and word processing software. My first book was written "longhand" with pencil, eraser and paper. This was the era when "cutting and pasting" really meant using scissors, tape and glue! Let us never take for granted the ease, speed and creativity this new technology provides.

Bruce Burchett and the editors of Avian Publications for being my partners on this writing adventure. Thank you for your confidence and support.

My mother, Sally, and sister, Sue, for teaching me well.

My wife, Laura, who has been wonderfully understanding and always encouraging during the time it takes to create a new book. My children, Laura, Eric and Mitchell, for sharing their dad with the computer. It was a team effort!

Gary Gallerstein

7

About the Authors

Gary A. Gallerstein, D.V.M.

Dr. Gallerstein is a practicing veterinarian and owner of Acacia Animal Health Center in Escondido, California. At Acacia, he and his associates take care of more than 15,000 patients, including birds, dogs, cats, rabbits, ferrets, reptiles and other family pets. Dr. Gallerstein's primary interest is birds, their medical and surgical needs as well as the education of their owners.

Graduating from the School of Veterinary Medicine at the University of California, Davis, in 1978, Dr. Gallerstein began developing his avian medical expertise at a large group practice in San Francisco. He has never looked back. His dedication to avian medicine has been a source of inspiration to many young students. He is an active member of many professional organizations, bird clubs and other animal-related groups. A widely requested speaker at both local and national seminars, as well as all levels of public schools, Dr. Gallerstein stays very involved in his profession.

8

Dr. Gallerstein realized very early that many bird owners lacked informative, educational material about their birds. He took their needs very seriously, and that concern led to his becoming an author. His first book, *The Bird Owner's Home Health and Care Handbook*, published in 1984, has been considered the standard in the bird care field since it first appeared. The goal he had of creating a practical, easy-to-read, complete guide for bird owners had been met.

Rapid advancements in the field of avian medicine, nutrition and husbandry dictated the need for a more current reference source. Dr. Gallerstein's second book, *The Complete Bird Owner's Handbook*, is even more complete, yet remains as practical and "user friendly" as the first.

In his spare time, Dr. Gallerstein, his wife, Laura, and three children enjoy the numerous outdoor activities available in southern California.

Julie Rach

Julie has been fascinated by birds for more than 30 years, beginning with pigeons that her father used to feed outside the kitchen window at the family's home in Culver City, California. She owned a budgie named Charlie when she was a child and has been owned by an African grey named Sindbad for more than 10 years. Julie is a former editor of *Bird Talk* magazine and is the author of six books and numerous magazine and online articles on bird care.

Pat Mulloy, R.V.T.

Pat is a registered veterinary technician and is the avian/exotic nursing supervisor at Acacia Animal Health Center. She is also the instructor for Acacia's "Well-Mannered Parrot" classes. She has spent the last ten years developing the facilities and systems needed to care for birds at the hospital. She is a member of the Association of Avian Veterinarians and the California Veterinary Medical Association.

About the Artist
Nicole Perretta

Nicole has been drawing and keeping birds since she was 9 years old. She has kept many types of birds and currently raises pheasants and other gamebirds. Nicole works as a wildlife painter and illustrator. She is also a full-time mom of her young son, Anthony. Nicole is a master falconer and it is her passion to be out in the field with a free-flying hawk or falcon. She is also involved with research and is currently working with the San Diego Natural History Museum's Bird Atlas project.

Note to the Reader

Your bird should thank you for taking the time to read this book. It will help your pet live a longer, healthier life.

The general care recommendations are those most commonly agreed upon by avian health care professionals, and the first aid recommendations provide safe and simple guidelines to follow when your bird is sick. These recommendations have been reviewed and agreed upon by several avian veterinarians. However, they will not work in every case. Your veterinarian should always be consulted first, before any home treatment is attempted and at the earliest signs of illness.

If your veterinarian's advice is contrary to that found in this book, be sure to follow his or her prescription for the care of your bird. Your veterinarian will know best because he or she will have the benefit of a thorough history of your pet and a hands-on physical examination.

Introduction

Welcome to the third edition of
The Complete Pet Bird Owner's Handbook.
Not only has this book undergone several title changes over
the years, but the three editions provide an insight into what
was important to pet bird owners when the books were being
written. The first edition focused primarily on the needs of
wild-caught birds, which is what most of the birds being
offered as pets 15 to 20 years ago were. Bird owners at that
time were most concerned with simply keeping their pets
alive. At that time, pet birds ate seed-based diets, and some of
them had behavioral problems, but issues such as nutrition
and behavior weren't being examined in depth by many people at that time.

The focus of the second edition changed somewhat to
reflect the needs of bird owners about 10 years ago. Bird
owners at that time could choose from either wild-caught or
domestically-raised pets, and knowledgeable owners selected
the domestically raised birds because they often had better
health and fewer behavioral problems than their wild-caught
cousins. Avian nutrition and behavior were being studied by
experts in the field as well as pet bird owners, and the focus
shifted from keeping the birds alive to maintaining their health
and paying attention to their nutritional and emotional needs.

As this book goes to press, wild-caught birds are only
occasionally available as pets. Pet stores or private owners
sometimes sell wild-caught adult birds that have been long-
time pets, but no young wild-caught birds are offered for sale
any more. Domestically raised birds have proved to be much
more suitable as companion animals, and now that pet bird
owners know about the importance of a balanced diet; daily
interaction with their pets in a safe, interesting environment;
and regular veterinary care, the focus shifts again. This time
around, we're interested in helping our birds be the best pets
they can possibly be, which means that this book will focus

on selecting the bird that best suits an owner's personality and lifestyle and will offer an expanded section on bird behavior in addition to the most up-to-date information on nutrition, caging, home safety, emergency care and avian medical information.

We hope you will find this book a useful guide to life with your feathered friend. Please use it as that -- a guide, rather than a substitute for an avian veterinarian. The relationship you form with your avian veterinarian is vital to your bird's long-term health and well-being. Choose your avian veterinarian as soon as possible after bringing your bird home (in fact, it's ideal if you have a veterinarian selected before you bring home your bird). Together, you and your avian veterinarian are your bird's best defense against serious illness, and you both can help your pet live a long, healthy life!

Gary Gallerstein

Julie Rach

Chapter 1

Selecting Your Bird

Eenie, Meenie, Miney...

You've decided you want a bird, but you don't know where to begin your search. Maybe you find yourself drawn to the aviaries at the zoo and unable to leave until you've stopped at each cage to talk to the residents, or a friend's cockatoo amuses you with his antics every time you visit. Perhaps you have cherished memories of a childhood budgie or the canaries your grandmother raised in her spare bedroom.

Before you begin your search, you need to understand a bird is more than a beautiful, animated creature. It has certain characteristics and quirks, along with requirements for care and maintenance. To ensure the best possible match between owner and bird, you must consider all these factors before you purchase a pet bird.

Zoological gardens are one place that people first fall in love with parrots. This macaw is on display at the San Diego Zoo.

Although it's easy to put your needs and wants first when selecting a pet bird, stop and think about what your bird needs and what benefits it will derive from living with you. Will its life be interesting and content? Will it be well cared for? If so, your bird will be a lucky animal. If not, perhaps a bird is not the pet for you.

Simply put, bird owners need to be animal advocates. This means that the needs of a pet bird come before the needs of the owner. Will you be able to take care of the pet bird you've chosen for its entire life? Will you be willing to put up with a bird's constant demands on your time and your lifestyle? Remember, birds aren't like children--they won't grow up and move out someday. You will need to fix meals for, clean up after, and spend time with this pet for 10, 20, 50, or more years, depending on the species you select.

If you become bored with your pet and neglect it as a result, you'll probably feel somewhat guilty, but such a situation

Do your part to help ensure the long-term survival of all our magnificent birds. This umbrella cockatoo was domestically bred and raised. Take the time to learn how to provide pet birds with a safe and healthy home environment. (Bonnie Jay)

can become much more serious for your pet. It may develop behavioral problems or it may be put up for adoption and shuffled from home to home. Neither is an ideal situation for a sensitive, intelligent creature like a pet bird.

In addition to considering the unique needs of their feathered friends, bird owners should join avicultural and conservation groups and act as ambassadors for bird ownership.

The goal of this book is to help you make the most of your relationship with your pet bird and to help you avoid some common pitfalls many owners fall into.

Like many relationships, the level of satisfaction you derive from owning a pet bird will be largely determined by how much you put into that relationship. If you are willing to devote a significant amount of time each day to feeding, caring for, and playing with your bird, you will be rewarded many times over with affection and amusement.

First, Do Your Homework

Becoming a bird owner is a process requiring a lot of consideration on your part. This is not the time to be impulsive, so take your time and think through this decision carefully. Pet birds are living creatures that should receive a lifelong commitment to good care and a safe, loving home from their owners, so before you start visiting bird stores to pick the perfect pet for you, you need to think long and hard about the following questions:

Why do you want a bird? People select birds as pets for all sorts of reasons. A good reason for choosing a pet bird is that you want an intelligent companion animal. Other, not-so-great reasons for selecting a pet bird include saving a picked-upon animal from cagemates at a pet store, the gratification of having a pet that can say your name, the high price of the bird, or the fact that the bird's coloration matches the decor in your living room.

Do you have long-standing hobbies and interests, or do you bounce from fad to fad and from trend to trend? If having a pet bird around for the next 10, 20, or even 50 years sounds like a lot of fun, you're a good candidate for bird ownership. If, on the other hand, it sounds like an awful chore, you may want to select a different type of pet or consider not getting a pet at all.

Do you have time to care for a pet bird properly? If you're a busy executive who travels out of town frequently, or if your family already has several other pets, it may not be fair to a pet bird to bring it into your home right now. If you are undergoing a major life change, such as getting married or divorced or starting college, getting a pet bird may not be a good idea right now. You may want to wait until your life is a bit more settled. If, however, you have some time in your day that isn't completely spoken for, a pet bird may help you fill that time enjoyably.

Here are some things you'll need to have time for when adopting a pet bird:

- *cleaning the cage and the area around the cage daily*
- *playing with the bird daily*
- *cuddling the bird several times a day*
- *preparing food at least twice a day*
- *feeding the bird at least twice a day*
- *washing bird dishes daily*
- *bathing and grooming the bird daily*
- *visiting the veterinarian annually*
  (and when problems arise)
- *visiting the pet store regularly for supplies*
- *cleaning, changing, and replacing toys and other cage on a regular basis*
* *learning more about the bird and bird care by reading magazines and books, watching videos, and attending bird club meetings, bird shows, or conferences*

Canaries and finches will require a shorter time commitment than parrots because canaries and finches often remain in their cages or aviaries, whereas parrots require regular periods of out-of-cage time to interact with their owners.

If you have a parrot, you should allow time in the morning for interacting with your pet and allow it time out of its cage and for preparing its meals. You can allow time for meal preparation and time together in the evenings. Time together can be as simple as having your parrot sit on its playgym near you as you watch television, or it can involve cuddling and scratching (if your parrot allows this type of interaction). If you're lucky enough to work at home, or if you come home for lunch, your parrot will probably come to expect attention throughout the day *(and it will probably get it, too!)*.

Are you being pressured into purchasing a bird by a spouse, child, or roommate? Spouses, roommates, or children may be gung-ho for a pet bird initially, but the novelty may wear off. In other cases, a pet bird can be an enjoyable addition to a household. You and the other people with whom you live will have to make the best decision about whether or not a pet bird is for you.

Can you have pets where you live? Although many property owners don't consider birds to be pets, it's difficult to sneak a macaw or cockatoo into an apartment building without the neighbors noticing.

Do you have space in your home for a bird? Cage size is an important consideration, and it's often directly related to the size of the bird that will live in the cage (although purchasing a good-sized cage is recommended for smaller birds, too). If you live in a small apartment or condominium, you may want to consider a smaller species of bird than if you live in a single-family detached home.

Do you mind a little mess (seed hulls, feathers, occasional droppings, and discarded food) in your home? If you're a meticulous housekeeper, having a pet bird around may not be ideal, but if you don't mind cleaning up after your feathered friend regularly, then a pet bird might be for you.

Can you tolerate parrot noise, such as squawking, singing, whistling, talking, or screaming? Potential bird owners need to realize all birds, even those species that are described as quiet, are noisy some of the time. Many parrot species like to vocalize at sunrise or sunset, while other pet birds may sing or whistle at different times during the day. Some people find a budgie's chattering distracting, while others take the screams of a macaw or cockatoo in stride. You need to determine the level of noise with which you're comfortable, before adopting a pet bird and make your choice accordingly.

Can you afford a bird right now? Remember, there's more to owning a bird than just the price you pay for your pet. You'll need to factor in a cage, toys, other accessories (a play-gym, extra perches, additional food and water bowls), food, treats, regular veterinary care, and grooming into your budget. Say you have set aside $500 for your pet bird. Don't rush out and buy the first $500 bird you see. Take some time to determine the size of bird that will suit you best (the species information section later in this chapter will help you decide which bird is best for you). Are you attracted to a cockatoo but find that it's too noisy? Consider a cockatiel. Do you find macaws appealing, but you can't see how you'll fit a bird that big into your studio apartment? Think about a conure.

Once you've determined the type of bird that's best for your situation, comparison shop for cages and other accessories before selecting a bird. Have the cage set up and ready for your new bird before you actually bring the bird home to minimize stress on the bird and on you, the new owner. Be sure to set aside some of your money for a new bird examination at an avian veterinarian's office in your area to ensure that your new pet is healthy. Your avian veterinarian is also a good resource for questions about proper nutrition and housing, and he or she can help you stay up-to-date regarding avian health information.

Young or Old?

A very important question to consider when shopping for your pet bird is whether you want a young bird or an adult bird. Young birds are usually more easily tamed and trained. They are more likely to accept a wider variety of foods, which will ensure good health. However, young birds take a lot of time.

Adult birds are usually more calm and sedate, and their personalities are more predictable. However, their previous history may be unknown and adult birds can be more set in their ways. Determining age in mature pet birds is often impossible.

Look for Weaned Birds

First-time parrot owners may believe that they need to purchase a baby bird that is still being hand-fed to ensure that the bond between parrot and owner develops properly. Although parrot experts touted this theory for years, and although the theory is still frequently included in bird care books and magazine articles, it has been proven largely to be untrue.

The American Federation of Aviculture (AFA), an organization that promotes the advancement of aviculture through educational programs that support improved husbandry, conservation, research, and legislative awareness, has adopted the following position on unweaned baby parrots:

The Bottom Line
Some things you'll want to think about as you become a pet bird owner are:
- the cost of the bird itself
- the cost of a cage and accessories
- the cost of bird food (formulated diets and fresh foods)
- the cost of toys
- the cost of veterinary care
- the amount of time you can devote to your bird each day
- how busy your life is already
- who will care for the bird if you go on vacation or are called out of town unexpectedly
- how many other pets you already own
- the size of your home

- *AFA recognizes that tragic results are likely to occur when unweaned baby birds are placed with those individuals who lack the necessary skills.*
- *AFA recognizes that successful hand-rearing involves a multitude of skills and that there is no substitute for experience.*
- *AFA finds the transfer of unweaned baby birds to parties unable to provide proper care is a problem of undocument ed and unknown magnitude.*
- *AFA finds there is no PRACTICAL way to determine or define qualifications indicating that a particular party is or is not able to provide proper care for an unweaned baby bird.*
- *AFA finds the issue of whether or not an individual is able to provide proper care in a particular hand-rearing situation to be a matter of personal responsibility between the parties involved in the transfer of the bird or birds.*
- *AFA opposes the transfer of unweaned baby birds to parties unable to provide proper care.*
- *AFA opposes any legislative or regulatory intrusion on issues of personal responsibility surrounding the transfer of unweaned baby birds by attempting to define or qualify who can or cannot provide proper care or hand-feeding.*
- *AFA THEREFORE opposes any legislation or regulatory limitations on the sale of unweaned baby birds.*

Experts now believe hand-feeding and weaning baby parrots are processes best left to people who are experienced in these areas. When a parrot chick is newly hatched, hand-feeding is a round-the-clock process, and it often doesn't fit easily into a schedule that includes a full-time job or other time constraints.

During weaning, a baby parrot learns to eat solid food rather than the food it receives from its parents or from a hand-feeder. It is a stressful time for both bird and owner as the bird makes the adjustment to a grown-up diet. Weaning is different from fledging, when a chick starts flying, although some people use the terms interchangeably.

Before their owners wean them from hand-feeding formula, chicks will often decide to stop on their own, and most will wean between the ages of 5 and 12 weeks. Smaller species, such as "budgies" and cockatiels, wean more quickly than the larger species, such as macaws and cockatoos.

These weaning ages will give new bird owners an idea of when young birds should be eating solid food and be able to go to pet homes.

New bird owners should try to purchase young birds that have been weaned. These blue-and-gold macaws may be too young to be cared for by inexperienced owners.

About three weeks before weaning time, breeders will place small chunks of fruits and vegetables in low-sided bowls in the chick's brooder to encourage it to play with (and hopefully eat) some of these interesting new foodstuffs. Cheerios™ and other unsweetened cereals are also popular weaning foods. The chick may play with these foods more than it eats them, but at least the bird is being introduced to foods that look, feel, and taste different from the hand-feeding formula.

The breeder will change the foods frequently because the environment in the brooder is warm and moist, which may cause food in the brooder to spoil more quickly. During this transition, the breeder will continue to offer the chick feedings of formula, and the breeder will monitor the chick's weight carefully. Expect the bird to lose weight--between 10 and 15 percent of its body weight--as it weans.

Approximate Weaning Ages

These weaning ages will give new bird owners an idea of when young birds should be eating solid food and be able to go to pet homes.
- budgerigar 6 weeks
- cockatiel 7 weeks
- conures 8 weeks
- miniature macaws 9 weeks
- Amazons 11 weeks
- African greys 13 weeks
- cockatoos and macaws 14 weeks

Breeders eliminate the midday hand-feeding first. If the bird seems to be okay without its midday meal, the breeder will most likely eliminate the morning feeding next. The chick will be offered seeds, pellets and fresh foods during the day to encourage it to eat solid food, but the breeder will still give it an evening feeding of formula so it will have something in its stomach to sleep on.

As parrot chicks grow up in the wild, their parents gradually and gently force them to become self-sufficient. From the moment they come out of the egg, chicks are conditioned to beg for food from their parents. They improve their begging skills while their parents are feeding them so they are true experts by the time they should be weaned. In the wild, young parrots often harass their fathers mercilessly with begging and chasing as they approach the time they are to be weaned. However, the parent birds gradually stop giving in to the chicks' begging, which forces the chicks to be self-sufficient.

Before the parent birds wean their chicks, they encourage their chicks to explore their surroundings, and many parent birds give their chicks a gentle nudge that gets the young birds started on their first flights. The parent birds continue to encourage their chicks to explore as the chicks are weaned and as they continue to grow. The parent birds teach the chicks where to find food, which foods are good to eat, how to protect themselves against predators and other important life lessons.

In the home environment, parrot owners either don't know or forget to give their young birds gentle nudges toward self-sufficiency. They often make huge fusses over their baby birds when the birds first come into their homes. Couples or family members may compete, in fact, to see who will hold the little bird while it's being hand-fed. If a parrot is cuddled and held all the time without ever having a chance to learn how to entertain itself, it will soon learn how to beg for attention, which may create behavior problems later on.

The young bird will also not know how to entertain itself, which can cause it to become confused later when it's not such a cute little baby bird and

Currently there are a few bird breeders who incorporate "co-parenting" techniques into their aviculture practices. With co-parenting everyone participates in raising the chicks, the parents and the aviculturist. This technique requires that the parents be tame enough to tolerate humans near the nest. The aviculturist handles the baby birds daily, weighing them and returning them to the nest.

There are even a few aviculturists who allow the parents to totally raise the babies from hatching through fledging. This technique requires a large aviary and areas where the parents can hide from the chicks to avoid over-dependence.

During the later stages of weaning, birds should be fledged. Fledglings are baby birds that are learning to fly and fend for themselves. This stage is critical in the mental, emotional and physical development of the bird. A bird learns to think, how to land, how to handle their bodies, how to determine a safe landing site and many other physical and mental skills. By purchasing a fully-fledged bird, an owner may be preventing a lot of unwanted problems later. Non-fledged chicks may be more easily frightened, less confident, less able to handle the challenges life sends it's way.

its owners have gone back to their lives, leaving the poor parrot to fend for itself. In such cases, the stage may be set for this poor, confused little parrot to become a screaming, feather-pulling, attention-craving problem pet that may get bounced from home to home, and the saddest part of the story is this doesn't have to happen.

What About an Adult Bird?

Many pet bird owners start with young, hand-fed birds, but some people start right off with an adult parrot. You may be wondering which option is the right one. As in so many instances in life, there isn't one right answer. If you have the time to devote to a young parrot's needs, then that should be the option you should explore. If you don't want to start with a young bird, then by all means you should look into adopting an adult parrot.

Keep in mind that adopting a young parrot may be easier because the bird hasn't had a chance to develop many bad habits. In some cases, bringing home an adult bird could be a great mistake (if the bird has a number of behavioral problems), while in other instances an adult bird could turn out to be the best pet you'll ever have.

People put adult birds up for sale for many reasons. Perhaps the bird has detected stress in the home and has begun to pull its feathers, and the owners have neither the time nor the patience to solve the problem. The owners may have a child and suddenly no longer have time for the parrot, or they may be moving out of the country and cannot take their pet with them. Some people simply lose interest in their birds and sell them after a few years.

If you do consider an adult bird, ask its current owner a lot of questions. Has the bird been moved from home to home, or is the current owner the bird's first owner? Why is the bird being put up for adoption? Has the bird seen a veterinarian recently? What does the bird like to eat? Does it like to come out of its cage regularly?

Pay attention to the bird and its actions during your visit. Is the bird fully feathered? Does it scream constantly during your visit? Does it cower in the corner of its cage? Does it seem to want to make your acquaintance, or does it seem uninterested in its surroundings?

Listen to what your heart and your head tell you when you see this bird. Don't adopt it because you feel sorry for it— that's the worst reason to become a pet owner. If you and the bird seem to have a bond, consider adopting it. If, however, the bird shows all its problem behaviors in a single visit, look elsewhere for your chosen pet.

Where Will You Get Your Bird?

Pet birds can be purchased through several sources, including pet stores, bird breeders, classified advertisements found in

Bird specialty stores are a good place to look for a pet bird. Not only do they offer birds, but they also provide a source for bird-care supplies and a knowledgeable staff to answer questions and offer advice to owners.

newspapers, bird specialty magazines, or through the Internet; and bird shows and marts.

Most people will probably select a good pet store or bird specialty store as the place from which to purchase their bird because a good pet store will offer an experienced staff that is also able to provide follow-up advice and care on subjects such as grooming or boarding. A good pet store should also provide buyers with a health guarantee or have a return policy in case the bird has a health problem.

Buying a bird from a pet store is not the same as buying a cat or a dog from a pet store. Some pet stores received a bad reputation in the late 1980s for selling puppies and kittens that came from "mills" or breeders that bred unhealthy, inferior stock, which may have lead people to think that all livestock sold in pet stores is inferior. With pet birds, this is not the case. Pet bird stores usually deal with small local breeders, and it's in the store's best interest to deal with breeders who keep their birds healthy so pet bird owners receive the benefits of healthy stock.

When you find a bird store in your area, visit the store and make sure it's clean and well kept. Walk around the store a bit. Is the store neat and orderly? Do the cages look and smell like they're cleaned regularly? Do the animals in the cages appear alert and well-fed? Are measures in place to ensure the health of birds on the premises, such as spray-on disinfectant to clean your hands before and after handling the birds? Are the cages crowded or do the birds have some room to move around?

Did someone greet you when you walked into the store? Did the store's staff seem to care that you came in to shop? Remember you will be visiting a pet store every week or two to purchase food, toys, and other items for your bird, so you might want to select a store with helpful, interested people behind the counter.

If something about the store, staff, and livestock doesn't feel quite right, choose another establishment. If the store and its livestock meet with your approval, then it's time to get down to the all-important task of selecting your pet bird.

Look at the birds that are available for sale. If possible, sit down and watch them for a while, or even visit the store several times before making your final decision. If you decide to return, let the store staff know which birds you're interested in so they can let you know if some-one else wants to adopt that particular bird. Don't rush the selection process--it's very important.

A well-stocked bird specialty or pet store will offer a wide variety of bird toys and other accessories.

Do some birds seem bolder than the others? Consider those first--you want a curious, active, robust pet, rather than a shy animal that hides in a corner. Are some birds sitting off by themselves, seeming to sleep while their cagemates play? Reject any birds that seem too quiet or too sleepy because these signs can indicate illness.

Remember healthy birds spend their time doing three main activities--eating, playing, and sleeping--in about equal amounts of time. They should also eliminate regularly. If you notice that a bird seems to only want to sleep, for instance, reject that bird in favor of another whose routine seems more balanced.

25

You may think saving a small, "picked-upon" bird from its cagemates seems like the right thing to do, but please resist this urge unless you're willing to take on a "work in progress" that may have health or behavioral problems.

If possible, let your pet bird choose you. If one bird waddles right up to you and wants to play, or if one comes over to check you out and just seems to want to come home with you, that's the bird you want!

What to Look for

Here are some of the indicators of a healthy pet bird. Keep them in mind when selecting your pet.
• bright eyes
• clear nares (nostrils)
• upright posture
• a full-chested appearance
• active movement around the cage
• clean legs and vent
• smooth feathers
• good appetite

If the decision has been made to purchase a new bird from a bird breeder, the following questions should be considered:
• Ask for references from former customers, local bird veterinarians and local bird behavior consultants.
• Are the aviaries clean and not over-crowded?
• Ask about the method used to hand-raise baby birds
• Is the facility overly careful and conscientious about introducing new birds to their established collection?

Classified advertisements are usually placed in newspapers by private parties who want to place pets in new homes. If the advertiser offers young birds, chances are you've found a private breeder who wants to place a few birds in good homes. Some breeders may also offer older birds for sale from time to time. These are most likely breeder birds that are too old to produce chicks but are still good candidates for pet situations.

Bird breeders also advertise birds for sale in bird specialty magazines and on the Internet. In some cases, the breeders will ship a bird to you by air, while in other situations, they will only deal with buyers in their local area. Discuss delivery options with the breeder.

The downside of purchasing a bird through a classified advertisement is you can't be sure of the health and temperament of the bird you're buying, and you will likely have no recourse if the bird turns out to have health or behavioral problems once the sale has been completed.

Bird shows and marts offer bird breeders and bird buyers an opportunity to get together. Bird shows can provide prospective bird owners with the chance to see many different types of birds all in one place (usually far more than many pet

shops would keep at a time), which can help you narrow your choices if you're undecided about which species to keep. At a bird show, you can watch to see which birds win consistently, then talk to the breeder of these birds after the show to see if he or she expects to have any chicks in the near future.

A bird mart is a little different than a bird show. At a bird mart, various species of birds and a wide variety of birdkeeping supplies are offered for sale, so you can go and shop to your heart's content. Some bird marts even offer new bird checkups from an on-site avian veterinarian.

Bird rescue groups sometimes host adoption fairs to help place birds in their care in new, loving homes. (Parrot Education and Adoption Center)

Open leg bands identify a bird that has been legally imported into the United States.

Closed leg bands, such as this one, are used to indicate a bird that has been domestically bred.

The Adoption Option

Another possible source for finding a pet bird is a bird rescue group. These organizations take in unwanted birds and find new homes for them. Ask avian veterinarians and humane societies if such an organization exists in your area or use the Internet to locate such a group. Have your Web browser search for "parrot rescue groups."

Leg Bands: What Are They for?

Most birds sold commercially will have a metal band around the lower part of one of their legs. This is a leg band, and it's found in a variety of shapes, colors, and sizes. It's a very simple identification system.

Closed bands ("seamless" bands) form a continuous circle, like a ring, and denote a domestically bred bird. These bands are placed on the legs of very young birds. The numbers, letters, or design engraved on the band indicates, in code, the breeder and sometimes the birthdate of the bird. The law already requires all parakeets be banded, but some states now require all domestically raised birds to be closed-banded. In addition, these same states require all birds for sale be closed-banded.

Open bands have a small break in the circle. Before 1992, all legally

Beware of Smuggled Birds

Although many species of pet birds have not been legally imported into the United States since 1992, birds are still smuggled into the United States from Mexico. These birds are often offered for sale at swap meets or from the backs of cars or trucks in southern California, Arizona, New Mexico, and Texas. Smuggled parrots, usually Amazons, lack leg bands, and many have their head feathers dyed yellow. If someone offers you a deal on a parrot and it seems too good to be true, it probably is. Do not buy birds under these conditions, and report people who are trying to sell birds under these circumstances to the authorities.

imported birds had to pass through federal quarantine procedures, and during this time a band was placed on one of the legs. Each quarantine station had its own identifying marks, and this was noted on the band. Since no birds have been legally imported into the United States since 1992, open leg

bands aren't seen very frequently, but they can still show up on adult birds that are being re-homed.

Leg bands serve a useful purpose. However, they can also cause occasional problems (see chapter 14, "Medical Emergencies").

Until the early 1990s, imported birds were the primary source of birds for the pet trade. In those days, as this photo demonstrates, birds were kept in overcrowded conditions that often led to outbreaks of disease. Since 1992, domestically raised birds have been the mainstay of the pet industry.

Health Assurance

To ensure your new pet's health, arrange to take it to an avian veterinarian as soon as possible after purchasing it. Ask the person from whom you purchase your pet if a health guarantee is available on the bird, and try to get that guarantee in writing.

Granted, a veterinary examination is going to cost money, but it will be money well spent to ensure the health of your new pet. Pet birds often hide signs of illness until they are gravely ill, so a veterinary examination can help head off health problems before they become serious. A new bird examination of a healthy pet can also provide your avian veterinarian with good baseline information that can be used for comparison purposes in the future. It also gives you a chance to learn about the latest advances in avian health care, to discuss nutritional concerns you may have, or to learn about safe toys and cages from the veterinarian and the clinic's knowledgeable staff.

If you have other birds at home, a new bird exam is a must to protect your existing pets

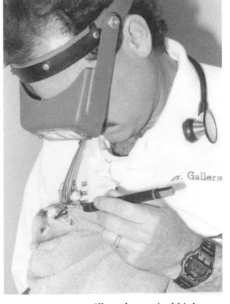

from the possibility of disease. Quarantine your new pet away from your existing flock for at least a month, and feed and water your new bird last with separate bowls to prevent any diseases your new pet may have from being spread to the other birds.

All newly acquired birds, such as this Amazon, should be examined by an avian veterinarian within the first week after purchase.

Because they are easy to care for, zebra finches often make good first-time pet birds.

The Bengalese finch is a completely domesticated animal. No wild specimens of this bird exist because the species was created by breeders.

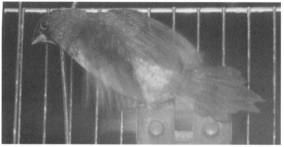

Which Bird Do I Want?

A potential bird owner has a wide variety of species to choose from, and a number of decisions to make based on those species. Notice the use of the word species, and not breed. Most pet birds are considered genetically separate and distinct species of animals, as opposed to dogs and cats, which humans, using a single species (Canis familiarus for dogs and Felis catus for cats), have developed over thousands of years into different breeds. Canary fanciers may speak of different breeds within their aviaries, but parrots and many other commonly kept pet birds are described as species by breeders and scientists.

Although many first-time bird owners are captivated by the striking appearance of a macaw or cockatoo, it's often best to start with a smaller species. Many of the appealing characteristics of macaws can be found in their smaller cousins, the conures, and cockatiels offer many of the same charming attributes as cockatoos.

Avian behavior consultant Layne David Dicker offered the following suggestions about noise, cuddliness, and calmness in his article, "The Parrot Connection" in the Birds USA 1999/2000 annual:

Quieter species:

Some pet birds, such as Brotogeris, like to snuggle in their owners' clothing.

Rose-breasted cockatoos; Pionus parrots; Meyer's, Jardine's, or Senegal parrots; smaller Amazon parrots; and green-cheeked, maroon-bellied or painted conures.

Louder species:

Miniature macaws, African grey parrots, yellow-fronted Amazons and Eclectus parrots.

Cuddliness:

Cockatoos and macaws
(all-over scratches)
African greys, Amazons, cockatiels, lovebirds, budgies, conures, and parrotlets
(head scratches)
Eclectus *(beak rubs)*

Although lorikeets are considered parrots, their diets differ dramatically from those of other psittacine birds. Lorikeets and lories need a diet of nectar, fruits and a powdered diet to fulfill their nutritional requirements.

Toucanettes and other softbilled birds appeal to some pet keepers because of their exotic looks. The term soft-bill doesn't apply to the birds' bills, but rather to their diets, which are primarily composed of fruits.

Macaws are popular pet birds because of their large size and bright colors. They are also outgoing parrots that enjoy learning tricks.

African grey parrots are noted for their talking ability. These medium-sized parrots are popular pet birds.

Eclectus parrots are an example of sexual dimorphism. Male birds are green, while female birds are red and purple. When early explorers first discovered these birds, they thought they had located two separate species because their plumage was so markedly different.

Amazons are among the most popular pet parrots. Owners enjoy their outgoing personalities and their talking ability.

Calmer species:

Yellow-fronted and mealy Amazons, hyacinth and green-winged macaws, Eclectus, and Pionus.

More active species:

Caiques, yellow-collared macaws, Hahn's macaws, grey-cheeked parakeets, budgies, and lories.

Before beginning to shop, consider what's important to you: Do you want a bird that's cuddly? Do you want one that will do tricks readily? Do you want one that will talk up a storm?

Few pet birds fill all of these traits completely, and no bird is guaranteed to talk. Use the personality profiles that follow to help you decide which species is best suited to your ideal pet bird.

The profiles have been divided into small, medium, and large birds and are presented in alphabetical order under those categories. Because prices differ around the country, a scale of dollar signs will be used to indicate costs of the different types of pet birds: a single $ indicates a relatively inexpensive bird, two $$ indicate a mid-priced bird, and three $$$ indicate an expensive bird.

SMALL PET BIRDS

Budgerigars

The budgerigar or "budgie," also commonly called a parakeet, is the most popular pet parrot in the world. This Australian bird has been kept in captivity since the 1840s and has been raised in captivity for more than 100 years because Australia stopped exporting these perky little parrots in the 1890s. Budgies can be kept singly or in pairs. You can often tell male birds from females by the color of the cere (the bare area immediately above the beak). Adult male birds have blue ceres, while adult females have brownish or tan ceres. Budgies are good candidates for first birds because of their small size and their relatively uncomplicated care regimens. They are also recommended for apartments and other small living spaces.

Budgies can develop sizable vocabularies. Sparkie, a budgie with a 531-word, 383-sentence repertoire, was written up in *The Guinness Book of World Records*. Owners of these small birds may have to listen carefully to hear their pets' tiny voices.

Budgies can be prone to obesity, so they need regular exercise. Provide your budgie with a good-sized cage and a variety of interesting, safe toys. You can also give your pet supervised out-of-cage time every day on a playgym.

Scientific name:	*Melopsittacus undulatus*
Where from:	Australia
Size:	7 inches in length; 30 to 60 grams in weight
Minimum cage dimensions:	12 inches long by 14 inches wide by 12 inches high
Age at maturity:	Between 6 and 8 months
Suitable for apartments?:	Yes
Behavioral quirks:	None noted
Activity level:	High
Noise level:	Low
Playfulness:	High
Destructiveness:	Low
Cuddliness:	Moderate
Talking potential:	High
Biting potential:	Low
Recommended for first-time owners?:	Yes
Initial cost of bird:	$
Require regular interaction with owners?:	If kept as single pet, yes

Caiques

Caiques (ky-EEKs) are small, highly active South American parrots. These intelligent birds are likely to chew on almost anything and everything around them. They can be quite vocal, too. Commonly kept species are the white-bellied and the black-headed caiques.

Caiques love to play, so a playgym and a large cage with a regular supply of interesting, safe toys are necessary to keep these birds healthy and happy. Caiques can be strong-willed and may get out of control quickly without guidelines set by their owners.

Caiques need good-sized cages and time to interact regularly with their owners outside of the cage.

Scientific name:	*Pionites sp.*
Where from:	South America
Size:	9 inches in length; 170 to 190 grams in weight
Minimum cage dimensions:	24 inches long by 24 inches wide by 36 inches high
Age at maturity:	About 1 year
Suitable for apartments:	Yes
Behavioral quirks:	Some birds can be noisy. Caiques can also become bonded to a single person in the household, which can lead them to act aggressively toward other people in the home. All caiques are highly active.
Activity level:	High
Noise level:	Low to moderate
Playfulness:	High
Destructiveness:	Low to moderate
Cuddliness:	Moderate
Talking potential:	Low
Biting potential:	Low
Recommended for first-time owners:	Maybe
Initial cost of bird:	$$
Require regular interaction with owners:	Yes

Canaries

Canaries are small cage-birds that have been kept in captivity since the 1400s and are thoroughly domes-ticated. Commonly kept varieties include the American singer, the Border fancy, and the red fac-tor.

Breeders concentrate on different attributes in their canary lines. Some breed type canaries for shape and stance, while others want color canaries that are developed for their colorful feathers (along with the familiar yellow, canaries can also come in white, red, orange or brownish feathers). Still others breed song canaries for their lovely singing abilities.

Canaries are not noted for being interactive pets. They are content to remain in their cages most of the time. Because they spend so much time in their cages, a good-sized cage is recommended. Rectangular cages with perches placed on either end are preferred to provide a canary with optimal exercise opportunities.

If you want a singing canary, you will have to locate a male. Make arrangements with the breeder or store to return the bird if it proves to be a non-singer. Keep in mind males sing to attract females. If canaries are kept in pairs, males won't sing. Males won't sing during the summer because this is the molting period. If your bird stops singing at any other time, contact your avian veterinarian for an evaluation because this can indicate illness.

Scientific name:	*Serinus canarius domesticus*
Where from:	Canary Islands, but all pet birds available today are domestically bred
Size:	4 to 8 inches in length; 12 to 29 grams in weight
Minimum cage dimensions:	18 inches long by 12 inches wide by 12 inches high
Age at maturity:	About 1 year
Suitable for apartments:	Yes
Behavioral quirks:	Most canaries do not like to be handled
Activity level:	Low to moderate
Noise level:	Low
Playfulness:	Low
Destructiveness:	Low
Cuddliness:	Low
Talking potential:	Low
Biting potential:	Low
Recommended for first-time owners:	Yes
Initial cost of bird:	$ to $$, depending on type
Require regular interaction with owners:	No

Cockatiels

Cockatiels are small Australian parrots and are second only to budgies in popularity as pet parrots. These slender, crested parrots are available in a wide variety of colors, including gray, lutino, albino, pied, pearl, cinnamon, and charcoal. They are known for their whistling ability and their gentle natures. The cockatiel's small size and fairly quiet voice make it a popular choice with apartment dwellers.

A cockatiel's cage should be roomy enough to accommodate the bird's long tail and to allow the bird to exercise.
These active little birds also require regular out-of-cage time,
and many enjoy spending time on playgyms.

Scientific name:	*Nymphicus hollandicus*
Where from:	Australia
Size:	12 inches in length; 80 to 100 grams in weight
Minimum cage dimensions:	18 inches long by 18 inches wide by 18 inches high
Age at maturity:	Between 7 and 12 months
Suitable for apartments:	Yes
Behavioral quirks:	Some cockatiels can become biters if not given appropriate guidance from their owners
Activity level:	Moderate to high
Noise level:	Low to moderate
Playfulness:	Moderate to high
Destructiveness:	Low
Cuddliness:	Moderate
Talking potential:	Low
Biting potential:	Moderate
Recommended for first-time owners:	Yes
Initial cost of bird:	$ to $$, depending on whether or not bird is a "normal gray" or a special color mutation
Require regular interaction with owners:	If kept as single pet, yes

Finches

Finches are small, active cage-birds that come from
Asia, Africa, and Australia. They are well suited to
community aviaries or flights, although a pair can
easily be kept in a cage. Keeping a single pet finch is
not recommended because these small birds enjoy
each other's company and because finches rarely
interact well with people.

Some species are noted for their colorful feathers, while others sing pleasant songs. Although some birds have been known to enjoy sitting on their owners' shoulders, most finches are admired from afar.

Because finches spend most of their time inside their cages, a large rectangular cage or an aviary is recommended. Place perches on opposite ends of the cage to provide maximum flying distance for your finches.

Scientific name:	*Chloebia sp., Poelphila sp., Zonaeginthus sp., Stizoptera sp., Lonchura sp.*
Where from:	Asia, Africa, Australia
Size:	3 to 8 inches; 10 to 20 grams in weight
Minimum cage dimensions:	36 inches long by 10 inches wide by 14 inches high
Age at maturity:	Between 2 and 6 months
Suitable for apartments:	Yes
Behavioral quirks:	Some birds can be high strung
Activity level:	High
Noise level:	Low
Playfulness:	Low
Destructiveness:	Low
Cuddliness:	Low
Talking potential:	Low
Biting potential:	Low
Recommended for first-time owners:	Some species, yes
Initial cost of bird:	$ to $$, depending on species
Require regular interaction with owners:	No

Grass Parakeets

Grass parakeet is a term used to describe small, colorful Australian parrots, such as the Bourke's parakeet, the Princess of Wales parakeet, the elegant parakeet, the splendid parakeet, and the red-rumped parakeet, that make good candidates as pets. Many species are sexually dimorphic, which means males and females look different. Male birds generally display brighter, more colorful plumage than the females.

Grass parakeets are noted for their quiet, sweet voices and their gentle, active natures. They do not need regular interaction with people to feel content, although some birds will learn to tolerate regular handling. Grass parakeets need to live in large cages or aviaries because they are strong fliers and need to exercise their wings.

Scientific name:	*Neophema sp.* and *Polytelis sp.*
Where from:	Australia
Size:	7 to 10 inches in length; 50 to 60 grams in weight
Minimum cage dimensions:	36 inches long by 24 inches wide by 24 inches high
Age at maturity:	About 1 year
Suitable for apartments:	Yes
Behavioral quirks:	None noted
Activity level:	High
Noise level:	Low
Playfulness:	Low
Destructiveness:	Low
Cuddliness:	Low
Talking potential:	Low
Biting potential:	Low
Recommended for first-time owners:	Maybe
Initial cost of bird:	$$
Require regular interaction with owners:	No

Kakarikis

Kakarikis (kak-uh-REE-kees) or "kaks" are small, highly active parrots from New Zealand whose name comes from a Maori word for "little parrot." "Kaks" are bold, highly curious birds that enjoy exploring their environment. Close supervision is required when these birds are out of their cages to ensure their safety.

"Kaks" are predominantly green, with either red or yellow feathers on their heads. The color of the head feathers depends upon the species of kakariki you own. Two species are available in the United States: the red fronted and the yellow crowned.

"Kaks" are notorious chewers, so provide them with an ample supply of toys. Be aware these birds may try to chew on your clothing or jewelry if it gets too close to their beaks.

Because of their active natures, kakarikis need large cages. Unlike other parrots, they need to have their food bowls placed on the bottom of their cages because kakarikis will dig around in their food bowls.

Scientific name:	*Cyanoramphus sp.*
Where from:	New Zealand
Size:	9 inches in length; about 100 grams in weight
Minimum cage dimensions:	36 inches long by 24 inches wide by 24 inches high
Age at maturity:	About 1 year
Suitable for apartments:	Yes
Behavioral quirks:	Kakarikis are highly active parrots
Activity level:	High
Noise level:	Moderate
Playfulness:	High
Destructiveness:	Moderate
Cuddliness:	Low
Talking potential:	Low
Biting potential:	Low to moderate
Recommended for first-time owners:	No
Initial cost of bird:	$$
Require regular interaction with owners:	No

Lovebirds

Lovebirds are energetic little parrots from Africa and Madagascar. They are available in a variety of colors, including blue, green, yellow, and pied. Commonly kept species include the peach-faced, Fischer's, and the masked.

Despite their seemingly cuddly name, lovebirds can be downright aggressive toward other birds and people. Lovebirds do not need to be kept in pairs to be happy, but owners of single pet birds should spend time with their birds daily. Hand-fed birds, which are easier to tame than parent-raised birds, require daily handling to retain their sweet pet qualities.

Lovebirds like to climb and exercise, so even though they

are small birds, they require good-sized cages. They are prone to chewing, and paper is one of their favorite things to rip up. Lovebirds need lots of toys, and they can also learn to perform tricks.

Scientific name: *Agapornis sp.*
Where from: Central and Southern Africa, and Madagascar
Size: 6 inches in length; 50 to 70 grams in weight
Minimum cage dimensions: 18 inches long by 18 inches wide by 18 inches high
Age at maturity: Between 4 and 8 months, depending on the species
Suitable for apartments: Yes
Behavioral quirks: Some lovebirds can become feather pickers. Some birds can also be noisy.
Activity level: High
Noise level: Low
Playfulness: Moderate to high
Destructiveness: Low
Cuddliness: Low
Talking potential: Low
Biting potential: Moderate
Recommended for first-time owners: Yes
Initial cost of bird: $ to $$, depending on species
Require regular interaction with owners: If kept as single pet, yes

Parrotlets

Parrotlets are small, mostly green birds from Latin America. These intelligent, spunky little birds have large personalities and are well suited to living in small spaces, such as apartments or mobile homes.

    Commonly kept species include the Pacific, the Mexican, and the spectacled.

    Parrotlets are bold little birds and need close supervision when out of their cages to ensure their safety. They enjoy human companionship and are very active. If allowed out of their cage, the birds will play actively on a playgym, or they will exercise inside their cages. They can be housed in medium-sized cages.

Scientific name:	*Forpus sp.*
Where from:	Mexico, South America
Size:	5 inches in length;
	20 to 30 grams in weight
Minimum cage dimensions:	18 inches long by 18 inches
	wide by 18 inches high
Age at maturity:	About 1 year
Suitable for apartments:	Yes
Behavioral quirks:	Parrotlets can learn to bite
	in order to get their way.
	Some birds can become
	feather pickers.
Activity level:	High
Noise level:	Moderate
Playfulness:	Moderate
Destructiveness:	Low to moderate
Cuddliness:	Moderate
Talking potential:	Low
Biting potential:	Moderate
Recommended	
for first-time owners:	Maybe
Initial cost of bird:	$$
Require regular interaction	
with owners:	If kept as single pet, yes

MEDIUM-SIZED PET BIRDS

Brotogeris

The *Brotogeris* (bro-toe-JER-us) genus, which includes grey-cheeked and canary-winged parakeets, are small green birds from Mexico and South America. Birds of this genus are sometimes called "pocket parrots" because of their small sizes and their fondness for hiding in the pockets of their owners' shirts.

Brotogeris are intelligent, affectionate pets. They can become very attached to their owners and can learn to be noisy if this behavior is reinforced by their owners. Brotogeris like to climb and are strong fliers, so be sure to keep a pet *Brotogeris'* wings clipped. Brotogeris also enjoy frequent baths, and some birds will take a dip in their water bowls.

These active parrots need medium-sized cages and ample time out of their cages to interact and play with their owners.

Some birds can become nippy if they aren't handled regularly.

Scientific name:	*Brotogeris sp.*
Where from:	Central and South America
Size:	9 inches in length; 55 to 70 grams in weight
Minimum cage dimensions:	18 inches long by 18 inches wide by 18 inches high
Age at maturity:	About 1 year
Suitable for apartments:	Yes
Behavioral quirks:	Some *Brotogeris* can become overly bonded to a particular person in the home, which can cause them to behave aggressively toward other members of the household. Brotogeris can also be quite noisy.
Activity level:	Moderate
Noise level:	Moderate to high
Playfulness:	Moderate to high
Destructiveness:	Low
Cuddliness:	Moderate to high
Talking potential:	Moderate
Biting potential:	Moderate
Recommended for first-time owners:	Maybe
Initial cost of bird:	$$
Require regular interaction with owners:	Yes

Conures

Conures are small parrots from South America and come in a variety of colors, ranging from muted greens to brilliant oranges. Commonly kept species include jendays, nandays, half moons, suns, and cherry heads. Conures are inquisitive little birds that offer something for almost everyone. Some species can be quite talkative, while others are known to be cuddlers, and still others are playful clowns.

Conures are notorious chewers, and many have quite loud voices. They enjoy regular baths, and some species sleep on their backs with their feet in the air. Some species may pick their feathers.

Conures need roomy cages in which to exercise and play. Of course, they need out-of-cage time, too, which can be spent on a playgym or with their owners.

Scientific name:	*Aratinga sp., Pyrrhura sp., Nandayus sp., Cyanoliseus sp., Enicognathus sp.*
Where from:	Central and South America, Caribbean Islands
Size:	9 to 18 inches in length; 80 to 130 grams in weight
Minimum cage dimensions:	18 inches long by 18 inches wide by 18 inches high for most species. Larger birds, such as the Patagonian or the slender bill, will require larger cages.
Age at maturity:	Between 1 and 3 years, depending on species
Suitable for apartments:	Maybe
Behavioral quirks:	Some conures can be quite noisy. All have the potential to be destructive chewers. Some birds can be aggressive.
Activity level:	High
Noise level:	Moderate to high
Playfulness:	Moderate to high
Destructiveness:	Moderate to high
Cuddliness:	Moderate
Talking potential:	Low
Biting potential:	Moderate
Recommended for first-time owners:	Some species, yes
Initial cost of bird:	$$ to $$$, depending on the type of conure.
Require regular interaction with owners:	Yes

Hawkheaded Parrots

Hawkheaded parrots are colorful, medium-sized parrots from South America. They are affectionate, lively birds with unusual plumage. Hawkheads have brown faces, green wings, and red chest and neck feathers that are tipped in blue. The neck feathers can be raised so that the feathers form a ruff around the bird's face. The ruff can be raised to intimidate another bird or a person, or when the birds are exceptionally happy.

Hawkheads are capable of mimicking sounds and whistles, and some may learn to say a few words. They require daily attention and a variety of toys to be contented pets.

Scientific name:	*Deroptyus accipitrinus*
Where from:	South America
Size:	12 inches in length; about 250 grams in weight
Minimum cage dimensions:	24 inches long by 16 inches wide by 28 inches high
Age at maturity:	About 1 year
Suitable for apartments:	Maybe
Behavioral quirks:	Some hawkheads can be noisy
Activity level:	Moderate
Noise level:	Moderate to high
Playfulness:	High
Destructiveness:	Moderate
Cuddliness:	Low to moderate
Talking potential:	Low to moderate
Biting potential:	Moderate
Recommended for first-time owners:	No
Initial cost of bird:	$$$
Require regular interaction with owners:	Yes

Lories

Lories are active, brightly colored parrots from the South Pacific. Commonly kept species include the blue streaked, the chattering, the Goldie's, and the Swainson's.

Some lory species are likely to talk, and all are willing and eager to play. A playgym or a cage-top play area is recommended for these

acrobatic birds. Some lories can be quite vocal, and nippiness can be a problem with some species as they mature.

Lories enjoy frequent baths and may bathe in their water bowls. These active parrots need large cages and plenty of toys. Because of their specialized diet requirements, lories are not recommended for first-time bird keepers.

Scientific name:	*Chalcopsitta sp., Eos sp., Lorius sp., Pseudeos sp., Trichoglossus sp.*
Where from:	Indonesia, New Guinea, Australia
Size:	7 to 12 inches; about 250 grams in weight
Minimum cage dimensions:	24 inches long by 24 inches wide by 36 inches high
Age at maturity:	1 to 2 years
Suitable for apartments:	No
Behavioral quirks:	Some lories can be quite noisy. Many love to take frequent baths. All produce messy liquid droppings. Some birds can be high strung.
Activity level:	Moderate to high
Noise level:	Moderate
Playfulness:	High
Destructiveness:	Low to moderate
Cuddliness:	Low
Talking potential:	Moderate
Biting potential:	Moderate
Recommended for first-time owners:	No
Initial cost of bird:	$$
Require regular interaction with owners:	Yes

Mynahs

Mynahs are social, vocal birds that are capable of imitating a wide range of voices, intonations, and sounds. Some birds can be quite loud.

As a softbill, a mynah relies on a large amount of insects and fruits in its diet, supplemented with mynah pellets. Mynahs are messy eaters and require diligent clean-up by their owners to ensure their health.

Mynahs cannot tolerate extremes of heat or cold for long periods of time, so they must be housed in draft-free enclosures in the winter and provided with adequate shade in the summertime. Mynahs also need a nest box or other private area in which to retreat from time to time (even a paper bag in the cage will fill the bill).

Mynahs require regular human interaction to be contented pets. Many like to sit on their owners' shoulders and preen their owners' hair and faces. They can also learn to sit on an owner's open hand.

Scientific name:	*Gracula sp.*
Where from:	India, Southeast Asia, Indonesia
Size:	12 inches in length; 180 to 240 grams in weight
Minimum cage dimensions:	24 inches long by 24 inches wide by 18 inches high
Age at maturity:	About 1 year
Suitable for apartments:	No
Behavioral quirks:	Some mynahs do not enjoy being handled. All produce liquid droppings. Some birds can be high strung and may hop nervously about their cages.
Activity level:	Moderate
Noise level:	High
Playfulness:	Moderate
Destructiveness:	Low
Cuddliness:	Low
Talking potential:	High
Biting potential:	Low

Recommended
for first-time owners: No
Initial cost of bird: $$
Require regular interaction
with owners: Yes

Poicephalus

The *Poicephalus* genus includes small- to medium-sized African parrots, such as Senegals, Jardine's, Meyer's, and red-bellied parrots. Some birds may learn to talk and some can perform tricks. Some have the habit of sleeping or lying on their backs with their feet in the air, appearing to play dead. Poicephalus are also noted for their chewing ability.

Poicephalus parrots are lively, affectionate pets; however, some can become nippy or strong-willed if they are not given guidance and guidelines by their owners. Their size and noise level make them good candidates for apartment living. *Poicephalus* parrots need good-sized cages and a wide variety of toys.

Scientific name: *Poicephalus sp.*
Where from: Africa
Size: 8 to 13 inches; 90 to 300 grams in weight, depending on species
Minimum cage dimensions: 18 inches long by 18 inches wide by 24 inches high
Age at maturity: About 1 year
Suitable for apartments: Yes
Behavioral quirks: Some birds can become overly bonded to one person, which can cause them to act aggressively toward other people in the home.
Activity level: Moderate to high
Noise level: Low to moderate
Playfulness: Moderate to high
Destructiveness: Moderate
Cuddliness: Moderate

Talking potential: Moderate
Biting potential: Moderate
Recommended
for first-time owners: Some species, yes
Initial cost of bird: $$ to $$$, depending on
                                 species

Require regular interaction
with owners: yes

Quaker Parakeets

Quaker or monk parakeets are small South American parrots that come in a variety of colors, including green, lutino (yellow), and blue. One of the Quaker's most unusual habits is the fact that these birds build nests, unlike other parrots, which are cavity nesters. Some nests in the wild can become quite large because Quakers constantly add to and remodel their nests.

Quakers can develop good vocabularies and can learn to do tricks. They are chunky, active little birds that need adequate space in which to exercise.

Quakers have become well established in some areas of the United States and in feral or wild colonies of escaped pet birds. They are outlawed in some states because of a perceived threat to agriculture from escaped pet birds. Quakers should be housed in large cages and given plenty of toys. Some birds can become accomplished escape artists, so additional cage locks may be required.

These birds can become aggressive toward other birds and humans who invade their space. They can also become possessive of their favorite person in the home.

Scientific name: *Myiopsitta monachus*
Where from: South America
Size: 11 inches in length; about
                                 150 grams in weight
Minimum cage dimensions: 18 inches long by 18 inches
                                 wide by 24 inches high
Age at maturity: About 1 year
Suitable for apartments: Maybe
Behavioral quirks: Some Quakers can become
                                 expert escape artists. Some
                                 birds can also become

aggressive toward other birds and people, while oth ers may become possessive of a favored person.

Activity level:	Moderate to high
Noise level:	Moderate to high
Playfulness:	Moderate to high
Destructiveness:	Moderate
Cuddliness:	Moderate
Talking potential:	Moderate to high
Biting potential:	Low to moderate
Recommended for first-time owners:	Yes
Initial cost of bird:	$$
Require regular interaction with owners:	Yes

Ringnecked Parakeets

Ringnecked parakeets are slender, long-tailed birds and hail from Africa and Asia. They take their name from a thin ring of feathers that encircles their necks. Most birds are bright green, but color mutations of lutino, blue, gray, albino, and pied are available.

The personalities of the ringnecked parakeets differ. Indian ringnecks are comical showoffs, while Alexandrines are more serious. Plumheads are talkative little rascals, while slatyheads are sweet, quiet birds. Some species are sexually dimorphic, which means the males and females look different, while others are not. Adult plumage develops when the birds are about 18 months old.

Ringnecks can develop sizable vocabularies, and they can learn to perform tricks. These active parrots need large cages in which to exercise and to protect their plumage from damage, and they like to play with toys as well as interacting with their owners.

Scientific name:	*Psittacula sp.*
Where from:	Africa and Asia
Size:	16 inches in length; 105 to 115 grams in weight
Minimum cage dimensions:	18 inches long by 18 inches wide by 18 inches high.

Larger cages may be recommended for some species because of their long tail feathers.

Age at maturity:	About 18 months
Suitable for apartments:	Maybe
Behavioral quirks:	Psittacula can be noisy pets.
Activity level:	Moderate to high
Noise level:	Moderate to high
Playfulness:	Moderate
Destructiveness:	Moderate
Cuddliness:	Moderate to high
Talking potential:	Moderate to high
Biting potential:	Moderate
Recommended for first-time owners:	No
Initial cost of bird:	$$ to $$$, depending on species
Require regular interaction with owners:	Yes

Rosellas

Rosellas are small, sometimes aggressive parrots from Australia. They are most often kept in aviaries, but they can also be kept as single pet birds. Commonly kept species include the crimson, the eastern, and the western.

Rosellas need to be housed in large cages or aviaries. They are active fliers and need regular opportunities to exercise. These birds also need a regular supply of chewable toys. Rosellas have independent natures and are not naturally cuddly, so owners should give these colorful birds their space. Some can learn to sit on their owners' shoulders or arms. Rosellas are noted for having melodic voices and for their whistling ability.

Scientific name:	*Platycercus sp.*
Where from:	Australia and Tasmania
Size:	10 to 14 inches in length; 180 to 200 grams in weight
Minimum cage dimensions:	18 inches long by 18 inches wide by 24 inches high
Age at maturity:	About 1 year
Suitable for apartments:	Yes

Behavioral quirks:	Some rosellas can be quarrelsome if kept in an aviary
Activity level:	Moderate
Noise level:	Low
Playfulness:	Moderate
Destructiveness:	Low
Cuddliness:	Low
Talking potential:	Moderate
Biting potential:	Low
Recommended for first-time owners:	Maybe
Initial cost of bird:	$$
Require regular interaction with owners:	Yes

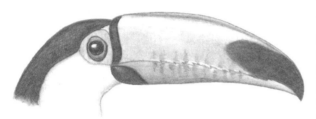

Toucans and Toucanettes

Toucans and toucanettes are medium-sized, Latin American softbills with distinctive beaks. Despite their large size, their beaks are surprisingly lightweight. Toucans are unable to use their beaks to chew, and even crushing grapes can be difficult for them. However, they can use their beaks to inflict painful bites.

These birds need to live in large aviaries or flights because they need a lot of exercise. Toucans are incredibly curious and will try to eat almost anything they can get their beaks on, so their aviaries or flights will need to be toucan-proofed for their safety. Commonly kept species include the toco, the keel-billed and the Swainson's. They are not recommended for first-time bird keepers.

Scientific name:	*Ramphastos sp.*
Where from:	Mexico, Central and South America
Size:	13 to 26 inches in length; 175 to 1,000 grams in weight
Minimum cage dimensions:	A large outdoor flight or aviary is required
Diet requirements:	Diced fruit supplemented with softbill pellets. Some species require live food, such as newborn mice or insects.

Age at maturity:	About 1 year
Suitable for apartments:	No
Behavioral quirks:	Some toucans can become quite territorial. All produce loose, messy droppings. Some birds can be high strung.
Activity level:	High
Noise level:	Moderate to high
Playfulness:	Low
Destructiveness:	Low
Cuddliness:	Low
Talking potential:	Low
Biting potential:	Low
Recommended for first-time owners:	No
Initial cost of bird:	$$ to $$$, depending on species.
Require regular interaction with owners:	No

LARGE PET BIRDS

African Greys

African greys are predominantly grey birds with red tails that come from Africa. Three subspecies are commonly kept: the Congo, which is a light gray bird with a black beak and a bright red tail; the Ghana, which is a dark gray bird with a black beak and a bright red tail; and the Timneh, which is also a dark gray bird with a reddish cast to its beak and a maroon tail.

African greys are well known for their talking abilities. A grey named Prudle even made *The Guinness Book of World Records* with its 1,000 word vocabulary. Some greys can become quite good mimics of household sounds, such as microwave timers, garbage disposals, telephones, answering machines, and other pets.

Unfortunately, some greys can be high strung. African greys can sometimes become bonded to one person in the home. Greys also produce powder down, which can cause allergic reactions in some people.

Greys need good-sized cages, plenty of toys, and ample time out of their cages with their owners.

Scientific name:	*Psittacus erithacus*
Where from:	Africa
Size:	13 inches in length; 275 to 600 grams in weight, depending on the sub species
Minimum cage dimensions:	24 inches long by 24 inches wide by 36 inches high. Young greys need slightly smaller cages because these birds have a tendency toward clumsiness when young.
Age at maturity:	About 3 years
Suitable for apartments:	Maybe
Behavioral quirks:	Many greys are described as nervous, high strung, or shy. A grey can easily become "a one-person bird," bonding closely with a chosen person in the home.
Activity level:	Moderate
Noise level:	Moderate
Playfulness:	Moderate
Destructiveness:	Moderate
Cuddliness:	Moderate to high
Talking potential:	High
Biting potential:	Moderate
Recommended for first-time owners:	Maybe
Initial cost of bird:	$$ to $$$, depending on subspecies
Require regular interaction with owners:	Yes

One Amazing African Grey

In 1977, Irene Pepperberg, Ph.D., purchased an African grey parrot at a Chicago pet store as part of a research project to examine animal intelligence and communication skills. That bird, named Alex (for Avian Learning EXperiment), has proved be an exceptional research subject. He not only uses human language to communicate, but he uses language appropriately, noting differences and similarities in objects that are shown to him and telling researchers the colors and materials these objects are made from.

Dr. Pepperberg became interested in animal intelligence in 1973, while completing her doctorate in chemical physics at Harvard. After seeing the success others had in teaching chimps to use sign language, she began studying animal intelligence with a special emphasis on vocal communication. She spent about 40 hours a week researching animal intelligence, while devoting another 40 hours a week to wrapping up her doctorate.

Within two years of beginning her study, Alex used language with meaning to identify objects. He could identify more than 30 items by name, shape, and color and had averaged 80 percent accuracy on tests administered to chart his progress. Alex now knows the names of almost 100 items, he can count to six, and he can name about seven colors and about seven different types of materials.

At the beginning of the study, Alex was approximately a year old and had received no prior speech instruction. He was domestically bred, but he was not a hand-raised parrot. The chicks that joined the study in 1992 were domestically bred and hand-raised.

In 1997, research involving Alex was discussed at the annual American Veterinary Medical Association meeting. After administering intelligence tests frequently used on chimps and dolphins, Dr. Pepperberg announced that Alex scored as well as they did on many of the tests and better than the mammals on some tests. This means that Alex is capable of mastering complex intellectual concepts that humans cannot achieve until they are about five years of age.

Although the term "birdbrain" is not usually a compliment, Alex has demonstrated that a bird's brain is really capable of quite amazing feats.

Amazons

Amazons are chunky green parrots from Latin America. They are noted for their talking and singing skills and can be quite outgoing birds, singing opera or performing tricks for people outside of the family flock. Popular species include the yellow nape, double yellow head, blue front, lilac crown and red lored.

Amazons are playful birds that enjoy human companionship, and they will tolerate cuddling on their terms. Some birds can be quite vocal at sunrise and sunset.

Amazons may be aggressive during breeding season. They can also bond to a single person in the home. They can be strong-willed and stubborn.

These parrots need roomy cages with interesting toys and time out of their cages on playgyms or with their owners to be mentally and physically fit.

Scientific name:	Amazona sp.
Where from:	Mexico, Central and South America
Size:	10 to 15 inches in length; 240 to 600 grams, depending on species
Minimum cage dimensions:	24 inches long by 36 inches high by 24 inches wide
Age at maturity:	Two years or more, depending on species
Suitable for apartments:	No
Behavioral quirks:	Many Amazons are not fond of cuddling. Some species can be aggressive during breeding season. Amazons can also be quite vocal, particularly at sunrise and sunset.
Activity level:	High
Noise level:	Moderate to high
Playfulness:	High
Destructiveness:	Moderate to high
Cuddliness:	Low to moderate

Talking potential: Moderate to high

Biting potential: High to extremely high, depending on the species. Biting by mature birds is particularly likely during breeding season.

Recommended for
first-time owners: No

Initial cost of bird: $$ to $$$, depending on species

Require regular interaction
with owners:
Yes

Cockatoos

Cockatoos come from Australia and the islands of the South Pacific. These crested white or pink birds are sure to attract attention with their striking looks and cuddly personalities. Commonly kept species include the Goffin's, the rose breasted, the sulphur crested, the umbrella, and the Moluccan.

The pet qualities that most owners find appealing in cockatoos are that they are cuddly, comical parrots. With these charming qualities comes aggressive behavior, particularly during breeding season. Some birds may scream, pick their feathers or mutilate their skin. Most cockatoos are not recommended for small apartments because of the size of their cages and their potential for making noise.

A cockatoo owner must provide an adequate amount of attention to his or her pet, and the owner must also make sure that the bird has consistent guidance and opportunities to play quietly in its cage. Otherwise, the bird may become downright unmanageable. First-time bird owners may be surprised or even disappointed in the amount of attention cockatoos demand. Cockatoos produce powder down, which can cause allergic reactions in some people.

Cockatoos need large, secure cages, and they may require additional locks on their cages because these clever birds can often learn how to open cage doors. These birds are notorious chewers, so they must receive a regular supply of toys and perches.

Scientific name:	Cacatua sp., Eolophus roseicapillus (rose-breasted cockatoo)
Where from:	Australia, Indonesia, Tasmania, New Guinea
Size:	10 to 20 inches in length; 220 to 1200 grams, depending on species
Minimum cage dimensions:	24 inches long by 24 inches wide by 36 inches high. Some species may require larger cages.
Age at maturity:	About 2 years
Suitable for apartments:	No
Behavioral quirks:	Cockatoos can become highly bonded to their owners, demanding constant attention. Some birds can be aggressive during breeding season. Cockatoos have the potential to be destructive chewers, and many are quite loud. Some species are highly active. Cockatoos require constant mental stimulation because these intelligent birds can become easily bored.
Activity level:	High
Noise level:	High to extremely high
Playfulness:	High
Destructiveness:	Moderate to high
Cuddliness:	High
Talking potential:	Low
Biting potential:	High

Recommended for
first-time owners: No
Initial cost of bird: $$ to $$$, depending on type
                                       of cockatoo

Require regular interaction
with owners: Yes

Eclectus

Eclectus are large, solid, sexually
dimorphic parrots. Unlike many other
parrot species, males and females can
be distinguished by their different
color feathers. Males are bright green
with yellow-orange beaks, while
females are red and violet with black
beaks. When early explorers first saw
these parrots in the South Pacific,
they thought they had discovered
two different species because males
and females looked so different.

    Eclectus are usually not cuddly
and seem to prefer sitting on their owners' hands or on a
perch near their owners. They are not noted for their talking
ability, but some birds can learn to say a few words or phrases.

    Females become sexually mature at about four years of
age and can be aggressive during breeding season.
Provide these parrots with large cages and time out on a
playgym or with their owners to keep them content.

Scientific name: Eclectus sp.
Where from: Indonesia, Australia,
                               New Guinea
Size: 14 inches in length; 380 to
                               525 grams in weight
Minimum cage dimensions: 24 inches long by 36 inches
                               wide by 48 inches high
Age at maturity: About 4 years
Suitable for apartments: Maybe
Behavioral quirks: Eclectus are not particularly
                               cuddly birds, and some may
                               appear downright lethargic.
                               Females can become aggres
                               sive during breeding season,
                               and females are generally
                               moodier than males. 59

Activity level: Low to moderate
Noise level: Moderate
Playfulness: Low
Destructiveness: Moderate
Cuddliness: Low
Talking potential: Low to moderate
Biting potential: Moderate
Recommended for
first–time owners: No
Initial cost of bird: $$ to $$$, depending on type
                         of Eclectus

Require regular interaction
with owners: Yes

Macaws

Macaws are the largest cage birds, with a length of up to three feet and a weight of around two pounds for larger varieties. They hail from South America and are available in a rainbow of colors, including green, blue and red. Commonly kept species of larger macaws include the scarlet, the blue and gold, and the greenwinged, while commonly kept species of miniature macaws include the noble and the severe.

Macaws are highly intelligent, outgoing birds that can learn to talk or to perform tricks. They enjoy chewing and can become quite destructive, so be sure to provide plenty of destroyable toys. Macaws can also be prone to fits of screaming that makes them unsuitable for apartment living. These large birds require large cages, so they can be difficult to accommodate in a small apartment or home.

Macaws can be aggressive during breeding season. They can intimidate some owners with their beaks and their strong wills. These traits make larger macaws unsuitable for most first–time bird owners.

Scientific name:	Ara sp., Anodorhynchus hyacinthinus (hyacinth macaw)
Where from:	Central and South America
Size:	12 to 36 inches in length; 220 to 1550 grams in weight, depending on species
Minimum cage dimensions:	18 inches long by 18 inches wide by 24 inches high for miniature macaws, 5 feet long by 5 feet high by 3 feet wide for larger macaws.
Age at maturity:	2 years for miniature macaws, 5 years for other species
Suitable for apartments:	No
Behavioral quirks:	Macaws can be destructive chewers. They are often noisy birds. Some macaws can bite hard enough to require medical attention, and many become aggressive during the breeding season. Some birds are high strung.
Activity level:	Moderate to high
Noise level:	High
Playfulness:	High
Destructiveness:	High
Cuddliness:	Moderate to high
Talking potential:	Low to moderate
Biting potential:	High
Recommended for first-time owners:	No
Initial cost of bird:	$$ to $$$, depending on type of macaw
Require regular interaction with owners:	Yes

Pionus

Pionus (pie-OH-nus) are generally quiet, curious Latin American birds. These predominantly green, chunky parrots enjoy bathing and climbing, and they are noted for their chewing abilities. Pionus have gentle, even temperaments. Commonly kept species include: blue headed, Maximilian's, and white capped.

Pionus enjoy human companionship, but they do not need to be handled and cuddled in order to be content. Their size and quiet natures make them ideal for apartment dwellers.

Pionus may wheeze when excited, and they can be high strung and somewhat nervous. They do not tolerate heat and/or humidity well and may become stressed easily. Pionus socialize well and are good choices for first parrots. They need to be housed in large cages.

Scientific name:	Pionus sp.
Where from:	Central and South America
Size:	9 to 12 inches in length; 240 to 280 grams in weight
Minimum cage dimensions:	24 inches long by 36 inches high by 24 inches wide
Age at maturity:	Between 18 months and 3 years, depending on species
Suitable for apartments:	Yes
Behavioral quirks:	When distressed, some Pionus wheeze. Some birds are quite high-strung.
Activity level:	Low
Noise level:	Moderate
Playfulness:	Moderate
Destructiveness:	Low to moderate
Cuddliness:	Moderate
Talking potential:	Low
Biting potential:	Low
Recommended for first-time owners:	Maybe
Initial cost of bird:	$$ to $$$, depending on species.
Require regular interaction with owners:	Yes

Beware of Bird Burnout!

When you first start visiting bird stores, it's easy to fall in love with many of the birds you see, and it's tempting to want to own a virtual Noah's Ark of pet birds. Before you end up with more birds than you can handle, set some reasonable and realistic limits on the number of birds you will purchase or adopt.

Birds whose owners have become "burnt out" on bird-keeping suffer from neglect, and they may end up being bounced from home to home, and burnt-out owners don't derive much pleasure from their pets. A pet bird deserves a home in which it can be loved and appreciated for the special animal that it is, so don't allow yourself to acquire more birds than you really have time for.

Just How Long Do Birds Live?

With good care, a pet bird can easily fulfill Mr. Spock's blessing on *Star Trek*, "Live long and prosper." Although the potential life spans of many companion birds are still being studied, avian veterinarians Branson Ritchie and Greg J. Harrison provided the following information in their book
Avian Medicine: Principles and Application:

Zebra finch	17 years
Canary	20 years
Mynah	8 years
Budgerigar	18 years
Lovebird	12 years
Neophema	10 years
Cockatiel	32 years
Rainbow lorikeet	15 years
Rosella	15 years
Eclectus parrot	20 years
Galah	20 years
Bare-eyed cockatoo	40 years
Sulphur-crested cockatoo	40 years
African grey parrot	50 years
Pionus parrot	15 years
Amazon parrot	80 years
Macaw	50 years
Conure	25 years
Grey-cheeked parakeet	15 years

Use these numbers as general guidelines for your bird's potential life span. Because almost all birds kept as pets today have been captive-bred and because avian nutrition has improved tremendously in the last few years, the potential for longer and longer avian life spans now exists.

Other reports of long-lived parrots include the story of King Tut, a Moluccan cockatoo who served for many years as the official greeter at the San Diego Zoo. King Tut was brought to the zoo in 1926 by explorer Frank Buck and was on display near the zoo's main gate each day until 1989 when he was retired. King Tut died a few years later after more than 60 years in captivity. The London Zoo's records indicate that a vasa parrot lived in the zoo's Parrot House for 54 years, and a blue-and-gold macaw spent 64 years there. An Amazon named Polly whose story was told in *Bird Talk* magazine was reported to be 106 years old when she died in Alaska in the early 1990s, and two Muller's parrots that were kept in Europe lived 81 and 85 years, respectively.

Do You Still Want a Bird?

Birds can make wonderful pets, but much thought and time must be put into the selection process. If it's the right bird for you, the bird will bring you many years of companionship and happiness. Be especially careful when buying a so-called "bargain bird." The best bargain is a healthy bird with a good temperament.

Chapter 2

Your New Bird

The Do's and Don'ts

Now that you've read about avian personalities and made some decisions about which type of bird you want, let's look at the type of care your new friend will require. We'll look first at what's required when you initially bring your bird home, followed by daily, weekly, monthly, and annual care recommendations.

When You First Bring Home Your Bird

When you bring your pet bird home, please keep in mind all the changes your new friend has undergone and all the changes it will experience as it adapts to life in your home. Adjusting to all these stresses is a lot to ask of any living creature.

Introducing a bird into a new environment means new sights, sounds, and smells. A whole new world of sensory perceptions opens up. Each bird will react differently to its new surroundings, and it will take time for your pet to adjust to these changes. Some birds adapt to new situations quickly, while others take more time. During this period of adjustment, allow for your bird to just be itself. When you first bring home your bird, try to minimize changes in its environment (see "Stress Reduction Do's and Don'ts" below for tips on this). Allow the bird's normal behavior to develop. Take the time to become familiar with your bird's unique personality.

When transporting your bird, place its cage or carrier in the back seat for added safety, and use a seat belt to secure the cage in place.

Remember to be very careful moving around your new bird. During this early adjustment time, a loud noise or quick hand movement could startle your pet and delay the confidence building you must now establish. Also, your bird may bite if frightened or startled. You can

Finches can be flighty and nervous when they first arrive in your home. Move slowly and cautiously around these birds to avoid startling them.

see how important these early contacts are to the future of your relationship with your new pet.

A common mistake new bird owners make is expecting too much of their new pet too soon. It takes time to get to know your new friend, and vice versa. Birds tend to be conservative. The period of adjustment can range from a day or two for domestically raised young birds to several weeks or months for a previously owned, wild-caught adult bird.

Stress

Stress, as defined by *Webster's Dictionary*, is "a physical, chemical, or emotional factor that causes bodily or mental tension and may be a factor in disease causation." It's important to understand that all new birds are stressed to some degree. The degree of stress is highly dependent on the individual bird, and many factors play a significant role in the amount of stress an individual bird will be under at any given time. Nature has given all animals, including birds and humans, a "fight or flight" response. This allows them to cope with stress and avoid danger. When confronted with a stressor (something that causes stress), certain changes occur in the chemical makeup of the body. This assists the animal in running faster to get away from the stress, or it helps protect the body if a fight ensues. Thus, "fight or flight!" This is truly a phenomenal occurrence. Providing the stressor goes away, the body can return to normal. In animals, if the stressors never go away, they will have to live with these chemical, physical, and/or emotional changes.

Just how do these changes affect a bird? Stress causes decreased resistance to disease. This is due to the immune system being suppressed during periods of stress. It can also lead to other problems throughout the body.

Minimizing your bird's exposure to stress will play an important part in its overall health. Stress is part of everyday life; however, the key is to lessen it.

Let's look at some of the most common causes of stress in a pet bird and see which ones we can work on to eliminate or at least reduce significantly.

Causes of Stress

- *New home/new owners*
- *Separation anxiety from cagemate or previous owner*
- *Temperature extremes*
- *Overcrowding*

- *Daylight/darkness excesses
  (about 12 hours per day of each is ideal)*
- *Inadequate caging*
- *Loud noises*
- *Harassment from other animals (including people)*
- *Poor nutrition/dietary changes*
- *Molting*
- *Breeding*
- *Disease*

Stress Reduction Do's and Don'ts

Do strive to create a stress-free environment for your pet. Listen to what it wants and use common sense to help it get there. For instance, if your bird chirps and squawks at you if you continue to watch television after you've covered its cage in the family room for the night, perhaps the bird needs a sleeping cage in a quieter room.

Do obtain as much basic information on your new bird as possible. For example, what has the diet been, what type of cage has been used, how much human interaction is the bird accustomed to, what toys does it like or dislike? These questions will help you create an environment that is as similar as possible to your new bird's previous home. This is not to say that those circumstances cannot be changed, but remember change is stressful, and during these first few weeks, minimizing stress is an important priority. Of course, if the bird was being kept in unhealthy or unsafe conditions in its previous home, immediate change is for the better. Remember, there are no set rules--each situation is different.

Zebra finches and other finch species do not need to come out of their cages and interact with their owners to be contented pets.

Do get a health checkup for your bird. Detecting any physical problems early will help minimize the long-term effects of illness. Many bird health guarantees require a new bird exam by a veterinarian.

Do allow time for the bird to acclimate to its new environment. This varies with each individual bird. If your new bird has been well socialized and likes attention, then continue to give it. This is where a good history can help ("He likes to be scratched on the back of his head, but he hates to have his wings touched"). Knowing what type of attention the bird likes will help minimize stress. If your bird is unaccustomed to people and not well socialized, give it "space." During this period, keep handling and interruptions to a minimum.

Do ensure plenty of rest and relaxation. Quiet time is very important. Allow maximum time for sleeping, and realize that total darkness is important for sleep. A cage cover can be used if needed, but only if your bird is accustomed to one. Otherwise, you may be adding a new stress.

Do isolate the new bird for at least a 30-day period from any other birds you might have. Keep the newcomer in a separate room and avoid cross-contamination of food and water bowls. This will help prevent the spread of disease if there is a hidden problem. Bird diseases can be transmitted to an owner's clothing, hair, or shoes, so it's important to take care of the new bird after you care for your other birds in order to prevent diseases from being spread to the other birds in your home.

Do provide the ideal cage environment (see chapter 3, "Proper Caging and Furnishing," for information on caging). Introduce new toys and other accessories slowly over time. Do keep the new bird's diet similar to what the bird has been eating. Try to introduce new foods slowly, but always keep an adequate supply of the previous diet available unless it was very deficient.

Do keep the cage area warm. Birds can expend tremendous amounts of energy trying to stay warm. Provide warmth and the bird can conserve energy for other essential life functions. An ambient temperature of 75 to 80 degrees Fahrenheit is ideal, and avoid cold drafts and the consequences they may bring, such as stress and illness.

Do consider having your bird's wings trimmed if the bird will be allowed out of its cage. This will prevent the bird from flying away, and it will also prevent flying accidents, which happen frequently.

Don't expect too much too soon. New bird owners are frequently unrealistic in their expectations of a new bird. Untamed birds cannot be "gentled" overnight, and birds cannot always adjust quickly to new foods. Birds also can't be trained to talk overnight. These desired behaviors require time, effort, and trust. Once again, have patience. Create a lasting relationship based on trust, not fear.

Don't create too many changes at once. Remember, everyone is a stranger to your new bird. Avoid parading your friends and neighbors in front of its cage right now. Wait until the adjustment period is well underway and then slowly introduce the bird to new people.

As your bird gets comfortable around you and your family, establish a routine for it that's fairly regular. Feed it at about the same time each day, and clean its cage on a regular basis. Although you shouldn't create a rigid, inflexible regimen, a certain amount of routine is comforting to your pet, and having an established mealtime and cage–cleaning time may make bird keeping more enjoyable for you.

Spending time with your bird doesn't have to be restricted solely to meals and cage cleaning. In fact, you and your bird will both enjoy time spent away from the cage. Consider setting up a playgym in your TV room so your bird can perch in the evenings as your family watches television. Let your bird sit in your lap as you read a magazine or enjoy a cup of tea after dinner, or add a portable perch to your home office or computer room so your feathered friend can keep you company as you work or surf the Internet.

Daily Care

Once your pet bird has settled into its new home, it will require a certain level of care each day to ensure its health and well-being. Here are some of the things you'll need to do each day for your pet:

- *Take the time to learn not only what is normal behavior for your bird's species, but also what is normal behavior for your bird. Perhaps you have a shy cockatoo or a quiet macaw--these are not usual characteristics of these species, but they could be completely normal, routine behavior for your pet. Watch for anything out of the ordinary in your pet's routine, appetite, or behavior, and report the changes to your avian veterinarian promptly. Your daily observations and prompt action when you detect something out of the ordinary can be one of your bird's best defenses against illness.*

Spend some time with your bird each day, as this Amazon's owner is doing. Not only will you be able to check its appearance and observe its activity level, but you'll develop a closer relationship with your pet by taking the time to play with and cuddle it.

- *Remove old food and offer fresh food (ideally twice a day). Wash food dish thoroughly with detergent and hot water. Rinse thoroughly and allow to dry.*
- *Provide fresh water in a clean dish. Wash dish as above.*
- *Change paper in cage tray.*
- *Allow your bird regular opportunities to bathe. Regular baths encourage your bird to preen and help keep its feathers in top condition. Some smaller birds enjoy bathing*

71

in birdie bathtubs that sit on the floor of their cages, while others like to roll in damp lettuce leaves or other greens. Still others like to be misted with a spray bottle, and some birds even enjoy taking a shower with their owners.

• Let the bird out of its cage for supervised playtime.

• Finally, you'll want to establish a bedtime routine for your pet. Some birds benefit from having their cages covered to indicate bedtime, while others merely need the lights in the bird room turned out. If your bird is prone to episodes of thrashing, it may require a night-light in its room. Keep in mind that your pet

Some pet birds, such as this African grey parrot, enjoy bathing on top of their cages. Regular bathing can promote good grooming, and it can also help reduce a bird's tendency to pick its feathers.

will require 10 to 12 hours of sleep a day, but you can expect that it will take naps during the day to supplement its nightly snooze.

As part of your daily cage cleaning and observation of your feathered friend, look at its droppings carefully. Learn what is normal for your bird in terms of color, consistency, and frequency, and report any changes to your avian veterinarian promptly.

Weekly Care

Some of your weekly chores will include:

• *Removing old food stuck to cage bars and from the corners of the cage, where it invariably falls.*

• *Removing, scraping, and replacing the perches to keep*

Give your pet bird four or five toys in its cage, and rotate the toys regularly to ensure your pet doesn't become bored with them. This African grey has a good selection of toys from which to choose.

them clean and free of debris (you might also want to sand wooden or PVC perches lightly with coarse grain sandpaper per to clean them further and improve perch traction for your pet).

• *Rotating toys in your bird's cage to keep them interesting. Remember to discard any toys that show excessive signs of wear (frayed rope, cracked plastic, or well-chewed wood).*

- *You can simplify the weekly cage cleaning process by placing the cage in the shower and turning the shower on full blast with hot water. Be sure to remove your bird, its food and water dishes, the cage tray paper, and its toys before putting the cage into the shower. You can let the hot water run over the cage for a few minutes, then scrub any stuck-on food with an old toothbrush or some fine-grade steel wool. After you've removed the food and other debris, you can disinfect the cage with a bird-safe disinfectant. Ask your avian veterinarian for recommendations.*

- *Rinse the cage thoroughly and dry it completely before returning your bird and its accessories to the cage. If you have wooden perches in the cage, you can dry them more quickly by placing the wet wooden dowels in a 400-degree oven for 10 minutes. Let the perches cool before you put them back in the cage.*

- *In addition to these daily and weekly chores, you'll need to pay attention to the length of your pet's wing feathers and have them trimmed regularly to prevent your pet from injuring itself or from flying away. You'll also have to schedule regular visits with your avian veterinarian to ensure your pet's continued good health.*

Time-Saving Tips

Many pet bird owners soon learn that taking care of a pet bird can take quite a bit of time. However, daily and weekly bird care don't have to become daunting chores. With a little planning and some basic time management, you can combine some tasks and make birdkeeping easier and more enjoyable. For instance, instead of preparing your bird's fresh foods each day, spend a little more time on the weekend or in the evening making up a week's worth of fresh foods and store each day's portion in plastic bags or plastic containers in your refrigerator. Remember to allow your bird's daily serving of food to warm to room temperature before serving it to your pet. Room-temperature food seems to be more appealing to a bird than food fresh out of the refrigerator.

You can also group chores, such as changing the cage paper when you offer your bird its breakfast food and water bowls, rather than changing the paper at a different time of day. Line the bird's cage tray with several layers of newspaper so you only need to remove the soiled top sheet when cleaning. Put a plastic runner or other easily cleaned material under your bird's cage to make cleanup quicker and easier. Use special bird-dropping-removal solutions to make cleaning up after your pet easier. You can also keep a roll of paper towels near your bird's cage to wipe up droppings and spills. Make it a habit to clean up after your bird each day to keep cleanup easy and manageable.

Keep a checklist near your bird's cage, or write birdkeeping chores on an erasable white board near the cage so you know what's been done and what still needs to be done. If the bird is a family pet, delegate care responsibilities among family members. This will help keep one family member from feeling overwhelmed by birdkeeping chores, and it will also foster a better relationship between all family members and the bird. Keep all your bird supplies in one place so you'll have everything handy and organized. By keeping everything together, you can also easily tell when you're running out of a particular item.

When the Weather Turns Warm (or Cold)

Significant temperature changes may require a change in your bird-care routine. Warm weather requires a little extra vigilance on the part of a pet bird owner to ensure that your pet remains comfortable, even in hot weather. To help keep your pet cool, keep it out of direct sunlight, provide shade with an awning or shadecloth, watch for panting and other signs of heatstroke (see chapter 14, "Medical Emergencies"), offer your bird lots of fresh, juicy vegetables and fruits (be sure to remove these fresh foods from the cage promptly to prevent your bird from eating spoiled food), and mist it lightly with a clean spray bottle (filled with water only) that is used solely for birdie showers.

By the same token, pay attention to your pet's needs when the weather turns cooler. You may want to use a heavier cage cover, especially if you lower the heat in your home at bedtime, or you may want to move the bird's cage to another location in your home that is warmer and less drafty.

At least once a year, your pet bird will lose some of its feathers. Don't be alarmed, this is a normal process called molting (see chapter 6, "Grooming," for more information on molting). Many pet birds seem to be in a perpetual molt, with feathers falling out and coming in throughout the summer. You can consider your bird in molting season when you see a lot of whole feathers in the bottom of the cage and you notice that your bird seems to have broken out in a rash of stubby little aglets (new feathers that resemble those plastic tips on the ends of your shoelaces). These are the feather sheaths that help new pinfeathers break through the skin, and they are made of keratin (the same material that makes up our fingernails). The sheaths also help protect growing feathers from damage until the feather completes its growth cycle.

You may notice that your bird is a little more irritable during the molt; this is to be expected. Think about how you would feel if you had all these itchy new feathers coming in all of a sudden. However, your pet parrot may actively seek out more time with you during the molt because owners are handy to have around when a bird has an itch on the top of its head that it can't quite scratch! (Scratch these new feathers gently because some of them may still be growing in and may be sensitive to the touch.) Some canaries and other pet birds may benefit from special conditioning foods during the molt; check with your avian veterinarian to see if your bird is a candidate for these foods.

Pay attention to the length of your bird's wing feathers immediately after a molt and be sure to keep the feathers trimmed to ensure your pet's safety and reduce its chances of flying away. Also make sure to trim your bird's toenails (you can learn to do this yourself or have your veterinarian do it) on a regular basis to keep them from catching on toys or getting tangled in the cage floor, either of which can result in injury to your pet.

Holiday Hazards

The holidays bring their own special set of stresses, and they can also be hazardous to your pet bird's health.

Chewing on holiday plants, such as poinsettia, holly, and mistletoe, can make your bird sick, as can chewing on tinsel or ornaments. Round jingle-type bells can sometimes trap a curious bird's toe, beak, or tongue, so keep these holiday decorations out of your bird's reach. Watch your pet around strings of lights, too, as both the bulbs and the cords can prove to be great temptations to curious beaks.

Keep in mind that the kitchen is the least desirable room in the house in which to have a pet bird. Marathon cooking sessions may result in overheated cookware or stovetop drip pans, which could kill your bird if the cookware or drip pans are coated with a nonstick finish (see chapter 14, "Medical Emergencies," for more information on the hazards of nonstick cookware for pet birds). You may want to consider replacing your nonstick cookware with stainless steel pots and pans or glass cookware, which you can treat with a nonstick cooking spray to make cleanups safe and easy.

By the same token, the self-cleaning cycle on some ovens can create harmful fumes for pet birds. Use this cycle only if you've opened the windows around your bird's cage to let in fresh air (make sure your pet's cage is closed securely before opening a window), or after you've moved your bird's cage to a part of the house that's far away from the kitchen.

Visitors may upset your pet's routine by offering it richs foods, alcohol, or other unhealthy treats, or by leaving a window open near your bird's cage, which could prove an inviting escape route.

The holidays can bring both joy and additional stress to a bird owner's life. Take precautions to protect your pet against household hazards, and take time to enjoy the season, too!

Fumes from fireplaces or simmering pots of holiday potpourri may overcome your pet, and flickering candles or glowing embers from the hearth can tempt a pet bird right into an open flame or a serious burn if its cage is open.

Other Special Situations

If you're considering a remodeling or home improvement project, think about your pet bird first. Fumes from paint or formaldehyde, which can be found in carpet backing, paneling, and particle board, can cause pets and people to become ill. If you are having work done on your home, consider boarding your pet at your avian veterinarian's office or at the home of a bird-loving friend or relative until the project is complete and the house is aired out fully. You can consider the house safe for your pet when you cannot smell any trace of any of the products used in the remodeling.

Having your home fumigated for termites or other pests poses another potentially hazardous situation to your pet. Ask your exterminator for information about the types of chemicals that will be used in your home, and inquire if pet-safe formulas, such as electrical currents or liquid nitrogen, are available. If your house must be treated chemically, arrange to board your bird at your avian veterinarian's office or with a friend before, during, and after the fumigation to ensure that no harm comes to your pet. Make sure your house is aired out completely before bringing your bird home, too.

Daily care is required to ensure your pet's continued good health, and certain situations, such as home improvement projects and the holidays, require a little extra care on the part of bird owners to protect pets from harm.

Chapter 3

Proper Caging and Furnishings

Home Sweet Home

Your bird's cage is one of the most important purchases, beside your bird, that you'll make as a bird owner. The cage must be spacious, secure, comfortable, and safe. It will be your pet's home for years to come and it will likely be a sizable investment, since many cages cost almost as much as the birds that live in them. The cage must also be easy to clean and service. Although these requirements don't seem overwhelming, it can be difficult to find a cage that fulfills all of them.

In this chapter, we'll look at some of the criteria you'll need to consider when selecting a cage for your pet, accessories your bird will need in its cage, and how to set up the cage to make your pet feel most secure.

Choosing a Cage

When you walk into a large pet supply store or look through the pages of a bird specialty magazine, you're sure to see a wide variety of cages on display. Which one is the right one for your pet bird? Some of the things you'll need to consider are the size of the cage, the width of the bar spacing within the cage, the cage material, its design, the mobility of the cage and its doors, flooring, and feeder design. We'll look first at cages for parrots and then consider the special needs of canaries, finches, and softbills.

Size

First, let's consider cage size. The dimensions of the cage must be adequate for the size of the bird. For instance, a macaw wingspan can be 36 inches. In order to provide enough space to live, a macaw cage should have opposing sides that are more than 36 inches apart. An ideal rule of thumb is that

Cage Questions to Ask

When shopping for the perfect cage for your pet bird, ask yourself the following questions:
- Is the cage big enough for my bird?
- Is the cage rectangular or square?
- Is the cage stable?
- Is the door safe and secure?
- Is the cage made of strong, safe material?
- Is the bar spacing appropriate for my bird?
- Does the cage have some horizontal bars?
- Does the cage have a pull-out tray?
- Does the cage have a grate above the tray?
- Can the food and water bowls be accessed easily from outside the cage?
- Is the cage certified to be free of zinc, which can make a bird ill?

at an absolute minimum the cage should allow the bird to at least extend its maximum wingspan in all directions.

If your bird has a crest or an extremely long tail, you will need to take these things into consideration when selecting a cage. Make sure that your bird has adequate head room if it has a crest, or that its long tail won't be caught between the cage bars.

Notice the length of this macaw's tail feathers. When selecting a cage for a macaw or other long-tailed parrot, remember to keep the length of its tail feathers in mind to ensure your pet won't be cramped in its new home.

Smaller birds, such as budgies and lovebirds, are more flight oriented, and their cages should be designed to allow for this. Long, rectangular cages that offer horizontal space for short flights are preferable to high, tall cages that don't provide much flying room.

A bird's activity level must also be considered when selecting the size of its cage. Small, highly active birds, such as parrotlets or caiques, need plenty of room to roam and run around inside their cages so they can expend some of their seemingly boundless energy.

You may also want to take into account the shape of the cage you're considering. Cages that come in unusual shapes or styles may provide special cleaning challenges, which may make you less likely to keep your pet's home clean.

You must also consider the size of the room in which you'll be setting up your bird's cage; pay special attention to the width of your doorways. Some large cages may need to be brought home "knocked down" and assembled in the room in which they'll be used because they may not fit through a narrow doorway any other way.

Bar Spacing

Next, consider bar spacing. The spaces between the bars present a major safety concern for the occupant. While your goal is to provide the largest cage practical, be very aware of the bar spacing. With the larger cages, the bar spacing is generally wider. *No bird should be able to fit its head through the bars of its cage*. If it can, it is in a potentially life-threatening situation.

Reject any cages that have bar spacing that is too wide for your pet bird. Here are the recommended bar spacings for commonly kept pet birds:

- budgies and lovebirds,   3/8 inch
- cockatiels and small conures,   1/2 to 3/4 inch
- Amazons, African greys,
  and other medium-sized parrots,   3/4 to 1 inch
- macaws and large cockatoos,   3/4 to 1 1/2 inch.

Cage Material

This is an example of inappropriate bar spacing. For its own safety, this hyacinth macaw should not be able to squeeze its head through the cage bars.

The material used to manufacture the cage should also be a major consideration when purchasing this important piece of equipment. Metal is the most common material used to make birdcages.

Stainless-steel cages are the "gold standard"--they are the top of the line in terms of quality. These cages are very durable and easy to keep clean, and stainless steel will not make a bird ill if a bird chews on it. However, make sure the welds are not accessible to the bird's beak. Some of the larger birds will enjoy gnawing until a soldered joint breaks. The main drawback of stainless steel cages for most owners is their cost.

81

Powder-coated or baked-enamel finishes are also frequently found on cold-rolled steel birdcages. Powder coating is a durable finish, and it cleans easily. A wide variety of colors are available, which can make them appealing to owners who want their bird's cage to coordinate with their home decor. Many smaller birdcages are plated with brass or nickel, then coated with a clear epoxy to seal the finish. When the epoxy seal wears away, the metal finish may become dull and some rust may develop on the cage. If a bird is a determined chewer, it may become ill from these cages because the metal under the plated finish contains zinc, which can be toxic to birds if ingested. (See "Zinc Poisoning" in chapter 14 for more information on this subject.)

Wrought iron is another often-used cage material. Because these are generally the least expensive, they have traditionally been the cage of choice for larger birds. They are usually painted with a flat black paint; unfortunately, the color can rub off and soil the bird. Contrary to past beliefs, these cages are no longer painted with lead-based paints. A popular option is to have the cage sandblasted and powder-coated for durability and ease of cleaning.

Examine the cage finish carefully before making your final selection. Make sure that the finish is not chipped, bubbled or peeling, because a curious bird may find the spot and continue removing the finish. This can cause a cage to look old and worn before its time, and some cages may start to rust without their protective finishes, which can mean that a cage needs repainting or replacement before its time. Finally, if your bird ingests any of the finish, it could become ill.

The life span of a cage finish depends upon several factors: the climate in which you live, the bathing habits of your bird, and its interest in chewing on the cage finish. Some birds don't mar the finish on their cages at all, while others make a determined effort to test every joint from the inside out. In most cases, though, you'll notice wear and tear of the cage finish on the cage bars upon which your bird frequently climbs to get from perch to perch.

Although you may be tempted to purchase a galvanized wire cage, such as a rabbit hutch, for your bird, please resist this temptation. Some small-animal cages are made from galvanized metal, which contains zinc.

Bird cages are traditionally made of metal. However,

acrylic cages enjoyed a brief reign of popularity in the early 1990s, especially for small birds, and they are again rising in popularity in the new millennium. These cages are quite good at containing seed hulls, loose feathers, and other bird debris. Acrylic cages clean up easily with a damp towel and regular changing of the tray that slides under the cage itself. If you choose an acrylic cage for your pet, make sure it has numerous ventilation holes drilled in its walls to allow for adequate air circulation. Be particularly careful about not leaving your pet bird in direct sunlight if you choose to house it in an acrylic cage, since these cages can get warm rather quickly and your bird could become overheated.

Wood cages are also available, but they are not recommended. They cannot be adequately cleaned and disinfected. They can also be chewed on and destroyed by your fine, feathered friend. A wood cage is not a good choice for any bird--regardless of its size.

Design

Cage design should be both pleasing to the eye and functional. There are several important reasons for this.

Cages can be fashioned in squares, rectangles, rounds, pyramids, and other exotic shapes. Make sure the cage you are considering has parallel bar spacing in all areas accessible to the bird. Bars with spaces that narrow at the ends, such as some on the top of a dome-shaped cage, can catch wings, feet, and toes and lead to serious injury. Also be sure that the design incorporates both horizontal and vertical bars so that your bird can get a little exercise climbing on the walls of its cage.

Cage designs have been developed to allow maximum enjoyment for both owner and pet. They should also provide maximum convenience for cleaning, feeding, and access to your bird. Newer models can be found with a skirt or extension around the base to catch food and droppings before they reach the floor. Playpens that attach to the top of the cage are another option. In addition, many have special feeder-cup

designs to make feeding birds more convenient with less waste and with less possible contamination from the droppings.

Remember, no matter what shape cage you choose, you will have to place newspaper, computer paper, or other similar paper on the cage floor. The easier the paper is to change, the more often you will be likely to change it. Make sure the basic cage design will accommodate the standard newspaper shape so you don't have to cut the paper.

Mobility

Most cages for smaller birds are portable, but many cages for larger birds can be rather immobile. Wheels or casters on the bottom of the bigger cages can be of real value because you may need to move a larger cage for cleaning, as well as when you want to give your bird a change of scenery. Make sure the casters can be locked so that your bird's cage doesn't roll every time someone brushes past it.

Doors

The size of the cage door, its location on the cage, and the type of latch it has are also factors to consider. The larger the door, the easier the cage is to clean, but a large doorway also increases the chance of a bird escaping. The doorway should be large enough for an owner to get his or her hand in easily, it should accommodate "birdie bathtubs" or other items that may be placed in the cage, and it should allow your bird to exit the cage easily and comfortably.

Well-designed cages should provide maximum enjoyment for the bird as well as convenience and eye appeal for owners. Just as birds come in a variety of sizes, from cockatiels to macaws, so do their "homes!" (Animal Environments)

The latch should be human friendly as well as birdproof. Remember, larger birds can be masters of figuring out how to open all different types of latches. It is not uncommon to see padlocks on larger cages, not as a deterrent to theft, but to prevent the bird from escaping! However, if this is necessary, make sure the cage can be opened quickly in an emergency.

Because some birds have been severely injured when a cage door dropped on them unexpectedly, watch out for guillotine-style doors that slide up and down over the cage entrance.

Flooring

The design of the cage floor is important for ease of cleaning, decreasing contamination, and helping to keep the bird clean. The easier the floor is to clean, the more frequently it will probably be cleaned. Many cages come with a pull-out cage tray designed for quick cleaning and paper changing.

Birds, such as this cockatoo, love to spend time working on their cage locks. Make certain the latch or lock is "bird-proof."

Placing a grate along the bottom of the cage will allow food and droppings to pass through to the pan below. A grate will also prevent the bird from being able to track through its droppings or pick up spoiled or contaminated food. Use of a grate helps decrease the potential for spread of disease and will keep your bird cleaner. Remember, in the wild birds never come into contact with their own droppings.

Newspaper, computer paper, and butcher paper are the best and least-expensive cage tray liners. Multiple layers of paper can be placed in the tray and removed a few layers at a time when they become soiled. Having paper in the cage tray can also help you easily monitor the appearance of your bird's droppings, which is an excellent indicator of its health. If chewed on, the ink in newspaper will not cause problems. Other products, such as dried corn cobs, crushed walnut shells, pelletized grasses, sawdust, cat litter, or artificial grass, are **not** recommended for cage floor liners. There is a danger that birds may ingest them and become ill. In addition, owners cannot evaluate a bird's droppings after they have fallen on these products, and such cage flooring is changed less frequently, creating an excellent medium for the growth of disease-causing organisms.

Feeders

The arrangement of feeders has also been taken into account on newer cage designs. Some cages have the food cups outside the cage to maximize interior space, while others have a separate door to access the food cups, which is especially

Special features that help keep a cage clean include a grille to keep the bird separated from its droppings and other debris that falls into the cage tray, a pullout tray with raised "ribs" to prevent the cage paper from sticking to the tray, and a "skirt" that helps control loose feathers and seed hulls. (Animal Environments)

useful with an aggressive or untamed bird. This type of feeder design will also make it easier for pet-sitters to feed your bird.

If the cage you choose has rings to hold food and water bowls in place, make sure that bowls are always in these rings because some birds have been injured when they tried to climb into or through the empty rings.

The Special Needs of Canaries and Finches

Although canaries and finches are fairly small birds, they require large (at least 30 inches long) rectangular cages in order to feel secure. The larger cage is a necessity in part because many finches and canaries spend all their time inside their cages, as opposed to parrots that receive out-of-cage time on a regular basis. The recommended bar spacing for a finch or canary cage is 3/8 inch.

Rectangular cages also encourage finches and canaries to fly and exercise regularly. The corners provide adequate places for shy birds to hide and feel secure, and the length of the cage provides ample space even for a pair of birds. Flights are often preferred to cages for finches. A flight is a large enclosure (between 4 and 6 feet in length) that allows a bird to fly with outstretched wings. These can be constructed either indoors or outdoors, and many often contain nontoxic plants to provide lots of hiding and nesting spots for finches. Prefabricated flight kits are available, or you design and build your own to meet the needs of your finches.

Some pre-made indoor flights are quite ornate, with dec-

orative cabinetry available in different styles to match your decor. Air filtration systems and full-spectrum lighting are available on some models. You can get more information on these indoor flights at your pet supply store or you can locate manufacturers by consulting advertisements in bird specialty magazines.

The Special Needs of Softbills

Because toucans, touracos, and other medium- to large-sized softbills need lots of room to hop about and exercise daily, large outdoor flights or aviaries are most often recommended for housing them. Toucanettes can sometimes be kept as indoor pets, but macaw-sized cages are required. However, make your cage selection with care because macaw-sized cages may have bar spacing that is too wide for toucanettes to be housed safely. The maximum recommended bar spacing for toucanettes is one inch.

Food and water bowls that can be serviced from the outside can be very convenient for owners of small birds, such as these canaries. Owners of larger pet birds may also find these out-side-access feeders handy, especially if petsitters occasionally come in to care for the bird. (Animal Environments)

Cleaning and Disinfecting

Keeping your feathered friend's home environment clean and sanitary is often an overlooked part of birdkeeping. Remember, organisms found in a dirty environment cause the majority of health problems. Therefore, the health of both owner and bird benefit from a clean and sanitary home for your bird.

Birds in the wild are accustomed to living in

Sometimes, a finch or canary cage has a decorative base (left), while other times the base can be used as a storage area for bird supplies (right). (Animal Environments)

a clean, fresh environment. For example, as they move around in the trees, their droppings immediately falls to the ground, well below where they are perched. They rarely, if ever, come in contact with their own droppings. When pets are kept in a caged environment, they are exposed to potential health problems arising from their small, confined living arrangement and forced proximity to their own wastes. Since bird droppings have no odor, they can be overlooked easily when general housecleaning chores are performed. Therefore, it is essential that you remember to clean and disinfect your pet's "home sweet home."

What does disinfecting mean? It is the act of destroying infective agents, namely bacteria, viruses, and fungi. These are the germs that cause disease.

Metal, plastic, tile and cement are easiest to disinfect. Wood, bamboo, and wicker caging should not be used because germs can penetrate their surfaces, and they cannot be disinfected adequately. Wooden perches and toys can be used but require frequent, thorough cleaning.

An ideal cleaning schedule is outlined below.

Daily:

*   *Change the food and water.*
*   *Soak the water dish in diluted bleach solution (one part chlorine bleach to 30 parts water) or hot water and dish soap.*
*   *Wash the food dish.*
*   *Change the cage paper.*

Weekly:

*   *Clean the cage.*
*   *Clean all accessories.*

Every Two Weeks:

*   *Thoroughly disinfect the cage and all accessories.*

Cleaning

Cleaning can be done with mild soap and lots of hot water. Use a scrub brush (or nonabrasive cleaning pad) and lots of elbow grease! Perches can be soaked in hot water and scrubbed with an abrasive brush or wire-bristle brush. Rinse all items well, and if possible, allow the cage and all accessories to dry in the sun. The sun's rays also act as a disinfectant. Wooden items should be completely dry before putting them back in the cage. Two sets of cups, perches and accessories are ideal. This allows one set to be drying while the other is in use.

Disinfecting

Disinfecting is an important part of maintaining a clean, sanitary environment. Many different types of disinfectants are available, each having its own unique characteristics. It is important to realize that a degree in chemistry is not a prerequisite to doing a good job. A good disinfectant must fulfill two basic requirements. First, it must be effective against most of the common germs found in a bird's environment. Second, it must be able to be used safely around both birds and humans.

Many good disinfectants fit these requirements. Consult your avian veterinarian or other pet bird professionals for product recommendations. Many disinfectants are rendered useless in the presence of organic debris (dirt)! Therefore, thorough cleaning of all surfaces with soap and water is essential prior to disinfecting. Once all the surface debris has been removed, the disinfectant can go to work killing germs.

Safety is critical when using disinfectants. Birds are especially sensitive to chemicals and fumes, so use caution when disinfecting. Rinse all items well and let them air dry. Here are some additional safety tips:

- *Remove your bird from the area where chemicals are being used.*
- *Use gloves and protective eye wear when mixing solutions.*
- *Read all product labels fully before beginning.*
- *Follow all manufacturer's instructions carefully. Exact dilutions must be used--more is not usually better!*
- *Always add water first and chemicals last to avoid splashing of the chemicals.*
- *Work in a well-ventilated area. Open the windows or set up fans to remove fumes as quickly as possible.*

Cage Accessories

In addition to the cage itself, many accessories are needed to round out your pet's environment. Each part of the cage must be customized for your bird's size, strength, and activity level. Not every bird needs every accessory mentioned, just as a child doesn't need every toy on the market.

Perches

Perches are not always included with new cages. Therefore, you may need to be purchase them separately. Birds spend most of their lives standing on two feet. Many parrots eat with their feet, and some birds even chew on or play with their perches. Birds should have a variety of places to sit in the cage so they don't have to hang on the bars.

When you are selecting perches, it is important to vary their thickness and shape. For this reason, natural wood branches work best. Natural hardwood perches are best for large birds and ideal for any birds that like to chew. For smaller birds, softer wood branches made from fruit and eucalyptus trees work well. Of course, branches treated with pesticides should never be used.

Recommended perch diameters are as follows:

- *3/8 inch for finches and canaries*
- *1/2 inch for budgies*
- *5/8 inch for cockatiels*
- *3/4 inch for conures*
- *1 inch for Amazons and other medium-sized parrots*
- *2 inches for cockatoos and macaws*

Perches can easily become soiled and must be cleaned frequently. Also, in order to prevent droppings from falling into food and water bowls, perches should not be placed over them.

When choosing perches for your pet's cage, try to buy two different diameters or materials so your bird's feet won't get tired of standing day after day on a perch of the same size and made of the same material. Birds spend almost all of their lives standing, so keeping their feet clean and healthy is important. Also, foot problems are much easier to prevent than to treat after they've become a problem.

Braided, colorful rope perches provide an option to the traditional wood perch. Check rope perches regularly for signs of fraying. Also, keep your bird's nails trimmed to prevent them from getting caught up in the threads.

When you walk down the bird-care aisle at your local pet store, you'll probably notice that a variety of perch materials are available to bird owners. Along with the traditional wooden dowels are manzanita branches, PVC tubes, rope perches, and terra cotta or concrete grooming perches. Each has its advantages.

Manzanita offers birds varying diameters on the same perch, along with chewing possibilities, while PVC is virtually indestructible. (Make sure any PVC perches you offer your bird have been scuffed slightly with sandpaper to improve traction on the perch.)

Rope perches also offer varying diameters and a softer perching surface than wood or plastic; terra cotta and concrete provide slightly abrasive surfaces that birds can use to groom their beaks without severely damaging the skin on their feet in the process. Some bird owners have reported that their pets have suffered foot abrasions with these perches; however, if you choose to use these perches in your pet's cage, watch your bird carefully for signs of sore feet, such as an inability to perch or climb, favoring a foot, or raw, sore skin on the feet. If your bird shows signs of lameness, remove the abrasive perches immediately and arrange for your avian veterinarian to examine your bird.

To further help your bird avoid foot problems, do not use sandpaper covers on its perches. These sleeves, touted as nail trimming devices, really do little to trim a bird's nails because they don't usually drag their nails along their perches. What the sandpaper perch covers are good at doing, though, is abrading the surface of your bird's feet, which can leave them vulnerable to infections and can make moving about the cage painful for your pet.

When placing perches in your bird's cage, try to vary the heights slightly so your bird has different levels in its cage. Don't place any perches over food or water dishes, because birds can and will contaminate food or water by eliminating in it. Finally, place one perch higher than the rest for a nighttime sleeping roost. Parrots like to sleep on the highest point they can find to perch, so please provide this security to your pet.

Feed Cups

Feed cups are available in a variety of sizes, shapes, textures, and colors. Most importantly, they must be easy to clean and be able to withstand the ravages of being chewed. Some cups are hooded or covered to help prevent food from being tossed out. However, they are also more difficult to clean, and some birds may be reluctant to eat from them. For large birds, metal or heavy-duty plastic cups are recommended; pottery crocks are also frequently used. Unfortunately, these can develop small cracks, which will harbor disease-producing organisms. Discard them if they become cracked.

Most feeder cups can be washed in a dishwasher. Again, make sure that you place cups in areas of the cage that are not as likely to become contaminated with droppings.

Swings

Swings provide a wonderful source of entertainment for many birds. A large variety of different shapes and sizes are available. These range from a very simple plastic swing for canaries or budgies to the elaborate "activity centers" for larger birds.

Toys

Toys will help turn a cage into a home. They bring fun and exercise into a bird's environment and can help to minimize boredom. However, they must be safe in order not to risk possible injury. The size, shape, and durability of toys selected must be based on the type of bird; very simply, larger birds need more durable toys.

When selecting toys for your pet, keep a few safety tips in mind. First, is the toy the right size for your bird? Large toys can be intimidating to small birds, which makes the birds less likely to play with them. On the other end of the spectrum, larger parrots can easily destroy toys designed for smaller birds, and they can sometimes injure themselves severely in the process. Next, is the toy safe? Good choices include sturdy wooden toys (either undyed or painted with bird-safe vegetable dye or food coloring) strung on closed-link chains or vegetable-tanned leather thongs and rope toys. If you purchase rope toys for your bird, make sure its nails are trimmed regularly to prevent them from snagging in the rope; discard the toy when it becomes frayed to prevent accidents from happening.

Toys can be made from a variety of materials, including metal, plastic, wood, rock, leather, and even food items such as nuts. These toys are size-appropriate for this sun conure, but remember that larger birds require stronger toys! (Animal Environments)

Mirrors are found on many bird toys, and most smaller birds are fascinated with and enamored of that handsome pet in the reflection. Some birds become so infatuated with "the other bird" that they seem to lose interest in their owners, so you might want to wait until your bird is settled in its surroundings and comfortable with you before adding a mirrored toy to its cage. Mirrored toys are not recommended for larger pet birds because larger birds may break the mirrors and injure themselves.

Watch out for unsafe toys: brittle plastic toys that can be shattered into fragments easily by a bird's busy beak; lead-weighted toys that birds can crack open and ingest the lead;

loose link chains that can catch toenails or beaks; ring toys that are too small to climb through safely; or jingle-type bells that can trap toes, tongues, or beaks. To protect your pet from possible lead or zinc poisoning, replace C-clamps and wires used in toys. Stainless steel C-clamps are available at ship's chandlery stores, and toys can be restrung on vegetable-tanned leather or yarn.

This spiral rope toy does double duty, serving as both a perch and a chew toy.

Some safe and entertaining toys can be made from items you already have at home. Some birds like to hide in or chew on paper bags, while others enjoy chewing on empty paper-towel rolls (these are also good for playing tug-of-war with their owners). Nuts in their shells, dog biscuits, or cinnamon sticks can also make good birdie chew toys.

When you're putting toys or other items in your bird's cage for the first time, you might want to leave the item next to the cage for a few days before actually putting it in the cage. Some birds accept new things in their cages almost immediately, while others may need a few days to size up a new toy, dish, or perch before sharing cage space with it.

Cage Covers

Birds seem to prefer darkness when sleeping. Cage covers can provide this in a dimly lit room. They can also serve to protect birds from drafts. The cover should be washable.

You can purchase a cage cover or you can use an old sheet, blanket, or towel that is clean and free of holes. Be aware that some birds like to chew on their cage covers through the cage bars. If your bird does this, replace the cover when it becomes too full of holes to do its job effectively. Replacing a well-chewed cover will also help keep your bird from becoming entangled in the cover or caught in a ragged clump of threads. Some birds have injured themselves quite severely by being caught in a tattered cage cover, so help keep your pet safe from this hazard.

Playpens

Playpens are wooden, acrylic, or metal activity centers outside the cage. They help keep a pet parrot in one area while providing a variety of fun and games. Playpens can be located on top of the cage or be a freestanding "gym." Playpens usually consist of perches, ladders, and swings with food and water cups on a flat base and are designed for total enjoyment. Toys can also be added to the playpen.

Quality workmanship is important when selecting a playpen for your pet bird. Sharp edges, protruding nails, or flimsy construction can injure birds. An untamed bird may not be able to enjoy its playpen for awhile, so this is one accessory that can be purchased later.

You will want to set up your bird's playpen in a secure location in your home that is safe from other curious pets, ceiling fans, open windows, and other household hazards. You will also want to place it in a spot frequented by your family so your bird will have company while it plays and supervision to keep it from getting into trouble.

T-stands

T-stands are another type of activity center for parrots outside of the cage. The T-stand usually consists of a single perch that stands six inches to three feet off the ground, with food and water cups attached. Toys can be hung from T-stands for additional entertainment. The T-stand is an ideal place to begin training your bird. Because the T-stand can be moved easily from room to room, it allows birds to participate in family activities. A bird that frequently flies off its T-stand can get into trouble. Therefore, birds using T-stands must learn to stand on them until you take them off.

T-stands can be either elaborate or very simple; both can work well for this macaw. (Animal Environments)

Where to Put the Cage

Now that you've picked the perfect cage for your pet, where will you put it in your home? Before you bring your feathered friend home, consider where it will live in your house or apartment. Selecting where your bird's cage will be located in your home is as important a decision as the one you made when you selected your pet's cage. Don't wait until your bring your bird home to think this through; you'll want your new pet to settle in to its surroundings right away, rather than adding to its stress by relocating it several times before selecting the right spot for its cage.

Your bird will be happiest when it can feel like it's part of

the family, so the living room, family room, or dining room may be among the best places for your bird. If your bird is a child's pet, it may do well living in its young owner's room. (Parents should still check on the bird, though, to ensure that it's being fed and watered regularly and that its cage is clean.) Whatever room you choose, keep the cage out of direct sunlight and make sure that the cage is placed against a solid wall so that your bird doesn't become stressed by feeling that its home is exposed on all sides.

Avoid keeping your bird in the bathroom or kitchen because sudden temperature fluctuations or fumes from cleaning products used in those rooms could harm your pet. Another spot to avoid is a busy hall or entryway, because the activity level in these spots may be too much for your pet.

Your bird's cage is its home, and the selection of an appropriate cage requires as much time and consideration as the selection of your bird. Cage accessories, such as perches, bowls, and toys, help make a cage more comfortable and interesting for a bird.

Proper Caging and Furnishing

Travel carriers come in many different styles for pet birds. This acrylic carrier allows this African grey to see what's going on around it, and the numerous holes in the carrier provide adequate ventilation.

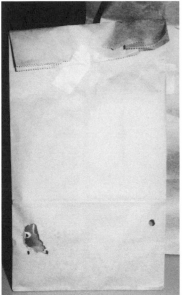

Lovebirds and other parrots enjoy playing with paper bags. Keep in mind that a paper bag is not a suitable carrier for confining or transporting your pet.

A Bird Owner's Shopping List
When you go to the pet supply store to pick out your bird's accessories, take a copy of this list along so you won't forget any of the important items your new pet will need to feel right at home!
• a cage
• open food and water bowls (at least two sets of each for easier dish changing and cage cleaning)
• perches of varying diameters and materials
• a sturdy scrub brush to clean the perches
• food (a formulated diet, such as pellets or crumbles)
• a powdered vitamin and mineral supplement to sprinkle on your pet's fresh foods
• a variety of safe, fun toys
• a cage cover (an old sheet or towel that is free of holes and ravels will serve this purpose nicely)
• a playpen to allow your bird time out of its cage and a place to exercise
• a travel cage or carrier to bring your new bird home from the pet store or breeder (travel cages can also be used to take a bird to the veterinarian or on a trip)

Chapter 4

Nutrition

Feeding for Health, Vitality, and Longevity

Good nutrition is the most important element in the health, vitality, and longevity of your pet bird.

Your bird is what it eats! Most people now understand the importance of a good diet for themselves. Birds are no different. Unfortunately, the actual nutritional requirements necessary to create a well-balanced diet for many species of pet bird are not yet known. This is complicated by the fact that, to some degree, each species has its own unique set of essential nutrients. Eventually these requirements will all be known. Until then, diets will continue to evolve based on years of experience and trial and error.

In the past, birds have been classified into two groups-- seed eaters and meat eaters. This is why parrots were origi- nally fed mostly seeds. Over time, fruits and vegetables were added to better round out the diet. Today, the combination of commercial diets, home cooking, fresh fruits and vegetables, and possibly a few seeds have proved to produce the happi- est and healthiest pet birds.

In birds, the rate at which life-sustaining chemical reac- tions occur in the body is the fastest of all animals. The ener- gy required to generate these vital activities is known as metabolism. Due to their high metabolic rate, birds require large amounts of food relative to their body size. In fact, if a 175-pound person, pound for pound (or gram for gram), were to eat the same amount of food each day as a hum- mingbird, he or she would have to eat 175 pounds of pota- toes, 28 eggs, 100 slices of bread, 50 cups of milk, and 17 pounds of hamburger! Remember, this is compared to a hummingbird. Larger pet birds, such as parrots, have consid- erably slower metabolisms. However, it still illustrates the incredible high-energy requirements needed to sustain birds' daily activities. Any lack of proper nutrients, including a decreased food intake, will affect them very quickly.

Malnutrition is the result of an improper balance between what a living creature eats and what is required to maintain optimal health. Malnutrition is usually associated with eating too little (under-nutrition), but don't forget that it can also be associated with an incorrect balance of basic foods and by

99

dietary excess (over-nutrition). In many instances, in an attempt to provide pet birds with the best diet possible, they have been over-supplemented with "too much of a good thing." This, too, will cause health problems.

Remember, just provide a variety of good wholesome foods to eat. Commercially formulated pet bird food is now available and is highly recommended. In addition, you can throw in some freshly cooked foods as described in this chapter, some fresh fruits and vegetables and, of course, plenty of fresh water. Now, if all bird owners had time to prepare this wonderful food on a daily basis and if all birds ate everything they're offered, life would be very easy. This chapter will explain in much more detail all the factors involved in providing the very best diet for pet birds.

Natural Feeding Behaviors
Habitat

The native habitat for each species of bird is not usually taken into account when selecting a proper diet. For instance, the seasonal changes in the native habitat will affect the availability of the various foods. What a parrot eats in the Amazon jungle is different from what a cockatoo eats in Australia. Even though this chapter does not distinguish between the native diets of the various species, it attempts to meet the general nutritional needs of all parrots.

For those interested in finding out more about the diets of birds in their native habitat, additional research can be done, as follows. For information on a bird's country or region of origin, see the species profiles in chapter 1, "Selecting Your Bird." Next, consider finding the answers to some of these questions:

- *What seed- or fruit-producing plants would likely be the primary food source?*
- *What foods available locally most closely match those in the wild?*
- *What kinds of trees are used for nesting? Knowing the tree types will help determine food availability.*
- *When do the seasons change in the country of origin?*
- *What climate changes occur there? Countries of origin below the equator have seasons opposite to those above the equator. Seasonal molting, reproduction, and food availability can all be affected.*

Foraging

In the wild, it is common for birds to spend the morning foraging for food. They move from place to place seeking, probing, tearing, and discovering edible foods. In other words, they work for their meal. They must also be on the lookout for predators during their food searches. To minimize exposure to danger, many birds have evolved a food–holding sac called a crop. This allows them to ingest large amounts of food in a short time and move on to a safe haven to digest it. The day is left for other activities, but the food search begins again in the afternoon.

All parrots and passerines (mynahs, canaries and finches) have crops. Other groups of birds, such as penguins and gulls, do not have crops.

Pet birds, on the other hand, usually have food provided for them all day long. Foraging and twice-daily feeding behaviors are eliminated. What can result is boredom, lack of natural curiosity, and "fussy" feeding behaviors.

To help ensure a pet bird's emotional and physical well-being, an attempt should be made to modify the environment to stimulate natural feeding behaviors. It may require time for birds to adjust to new routines and toys, but persistence pays off!

The list below provides some ideas on how to eliminate feeding boredom and stimulate interest. These are only some suggestions--creativity and imagination can supply the rest.

Food/toy combinations can be used to stimulate natural foraging behaviors. This is just one of the many possibilities. (Animal Environments)

- *Hang vegetables and fruits on a rod-type feeder. Birds must hold the feeder to keep it from mov - ing while they eat.*
- *Weave foods into the bars of the cage. The bird must climb to the spot and "unweave" them.*
- *Provide cooked chicken leg bones to larger parrots. It will require considerable effort to strip the meat and crack the bone to reach the rich marrow.*
- *Stuff food in the "nooks and crannies" of pine cones. This encourages food-seeking and probing behaviors. Treats will reward the bird for its effort.*
- *Commercially prepared or homemade food-toy combina tions can combine nuts, dried fruits, and vegetables. This combines playtime with food-gathering activities.*

- *Put your bird on twice-daily feedings. Remove food after 20 or 30 minutes. This stimulates active feeding twice a day and provides the thrill of anticipation.*

"Life Stages" and Nutrition

Growth, reproductive status, environmental changes (stress), and sickness will all affect dietary needs. Therefore, during these times, diets should be modified to reflect the body's new demands.

Following is a chart indicating the types of changes that occur and how the diet must be modified to adjust to the body's changing needs.

Life Changes Requiring Dietary Modifications

Growth	increased calories from all food sources, increased protein
Temperature extremes	increased fats, carbohydrates for the cold; increased fruits, lots of water for higher temperatures
Exercise increase	increased calories from carbohydrates and other food sources
Reproduction	increased calories, protein, calcium intake, increased fruits and vegetables
Stress	increased carbohydrates and fruit
Disease	increased nutritional need, (feed your bird its favorite foods, increase calories and protein, and follow veterinarian's advice)

The Basic Nutrients

A complete diet consists of a balance of certain key food elements. These are the nutritional building blocks that sustain life.

Water

The body is composed of approximately 80 percent water! Every cell is dependent upon water for its very existence. It is necessary for energy production, transportation of nutrients, and to help regulate body temperature. It is well known that a body can survive longer without food than without water. Under extreme conditions, it is possible to lose 50 percent of muscle mass and almost 100 percent of fat stores, but a 15 percent fluid loss could lead to death!

A constant source of clean, fresh water is essential for your bird's well-being. Be sure to keep water containers clean and to change the water at least daily. More frequent changes are needed if the bird drops its food in the water, since food will contaminate the water quickly. Also, place food and water cups in areas where droppings will not fall into them. For example, keep them out from under perches.

Proteins

Proteins are essential for the health and mainte-nance of all body tissues. They play a key role in normal growth, reproduction, and resistance to infection. Proteins are made up of small sub-units called amino acids. Every species has its own requirements for certain amino acids. These essen-tial amino acids cannot be manufactured by the body and must be provided by the diet.
Common sources of proteins include beans, nuts, eggs, meat, and dairy products.

*Average Daily Water Intake**	
Finch or canary	1/2 teaspoon
Budgie	1 teaspoon
Cockatiel	2 to 3 teaspoons
Amazon parrot	5 to 8 teaspoons
Macaw or cockatoo	10 to 15 teaspoons

These amounts are only guide-lines; diet and other environmen-tal factors will influence water intake greatly.

Carbohydrates

Carbohydrates are the body's primary fuel. They are found in plants and include starches and sim-ple sugars. Carbohydrates that are not immediately needed by the body are stored in the liver and muscles. Fiber, often found in carbohydrates, helps maintain normal intestinal function and prevent constipation.
Common sources of carbohydrates include fruits, vegetables, and cereal grains.

Fats

Fats are the most concentrated energy source. They provide more than twice as much energy per unit than either protein or carbohydrates. Fats insulate and store energy for the body and are also required for the normal absorption of fat-soluble vitamins A, D, E, and K.
Common sources of fats include nuts, seeds, and many dairy products.

Minerals

Minerals play a crucial role in the maintenance and strength of bone, normal cell function, nerve conduction, and muscle contraction. They are also important in maintaining the prop-er balance of body fluids.
Minerals are required in only minute amounts, but the balance between different minerals is crucial. If this balance is

disrupted, it can lead to serious problems. Therefore, supplementation, if needed at all, is best done with a complete, balanced, mineral supplement.

Common sources of minerals include egg shells, cuttlebone, oyster shells, fish and bone meal, mineral blocks, and commercial vitamin-and-mineral supplements.

Vitamins

Vitamins promote and regulate a wide variety of body functions. They are essential for normal development, growth, and maintenance of good health. Without them, the utilization of protein, carbohydrates, and fats would be impossible.

Birds require approximately 13 essential vitamins. They appear to be able to only partially manufacture three of them--vitamins C, D3, and niacin. Vitamins are found naturally in the food supply.

Common sources of vitamins include a good diet and commercial vitamin and mineral supplements.

What to Feed

There is no such thing as a "perfect diet." To come closest, feed your bird a fresh, balanced variety of foods. On the surface, this seems easy to accomplish. However, birds are not always cooperative. They may not be willing to taste new foods. Therefore, first learn what constitutes good nutrition. There are many ways to achieve an optimal diet. It is most important that birds eat something from each of the food groups rather than multiple items from a single group.

Commercially Formulated Diets

Commercially formulated diets should form the "main course" of a complete and balanced diet. They provide a combination of nutrients from all the food groups and have been developed through research and years of field observations. Formulated bird foods have eliminated much of the guesswork bird owners face when trying to provide a balanced, nutritious diet.

The many formulated diets commercially available are manufactured in a variety of forms such as pellets, crumbles, and cakes; ask your avian veterinarian or local bird shop for a recommendation. Switching birds to this type of diet may present some challenges; see the discussion later in this chapter.

A wide variety of formulated diets are made by many different manufacturers. Please note that no study has yet been undertaken to determine which brand is best. Avian veterinarians, bird breeders, and others with a long-time interest in birds all have their favorite brands, but the brand that is best for your bird may well be the one that your bird will eat. You'll have to experiment with different brands to discover which one your bird likes best.

This is a small sampling of the variety of commercially formulated bird diets available. Note the different sizes, shapes and textures. Birds, like people, have food preferences. One brand may actually be preferred over another.

Note that while commercially formulated diets can be fed as the sole source of nutrition, to stimulate natural feeding behaviors, consider adding a small percentage of foods from other categories.

Some birds, such as these Amazons, like to pick up food with their feet. Large pieces allow for easier "self service." (Lafeber Company)

Home-Cooked Diets

Home-cooked diets can be offered as "side dishes" in your bird's menu. They can be visually appealing, provide a good variety of food sources, and are usually well accepted by birds. Most commonly, foods such as beans, rice, corn, pasta, and whole grains are cooked and combined to form a fresh, healthy diet. It's important to remember variety. Be sure to include an assortment of beans, grains, and vegetables.

Most bird owners cook a large amount of food, divide it into smaller quantities and freeze the portions. This allows the food to be fed fresh. It is commonly fed twice daily: in the morning and in the evening. Cooked foods spoil quickly, so you'll need to keep the following in mind:

Rule No. 1 (the 30-Minute Rule): Never leave cooked foods, fruits and most vegetables in the cage longer than 30 minutes. Bacterial, fungal, and mold contamination can begin this quickly.

Later in this chapter you'll find an assortment of recipes your bird will enjoy.

Note: Home-cooked diets should not be fed as the sole source of nutrition. They need to be supplemented with foods from the other categories.

Nutritional Deficiencies Of A Seed Diet*

Protein (amino acids):
Lysine, methionine

Vitamins:
A, D, riboflavin, B12, possibly E, K, pantothenic acid, niacin, biotin and choline

Minerals:
Calcium and possibly sodium

Trace minerals:
Possibly iron, copper, zinc, manganese, iodine, and selenium

Seeds

Long considered the standard diet for pet birds, seeds now play a very limited role in a healthy pet bird's diet. Consider them as the "dessert" course or use them as rewards during training sessions.

The problem with seeds is that they are high in fat (up to 50 percent), lack many important nutrients, and can cause finicky eating habits.

During certain times of the year, especially in warmer climates, seeds can be "buggy." Some insects will hatch among seeds, regardless of how well they are handled and stored during processing. Moths or other small bugs will not hurt your pet birds, but many owners find the bugs annoying. To eliminate moths and other insects, freeze the seed mix for 24 hours after purchase. Afterward, refrigerate seeds to maintain their freshness.

Vegetables

Vegetables are a marvelous source of carbohydrates and vitamins. However, they are not a complete diet. There are a
tremendous variety of vegetables and all are safe for birds.
They do, however, vary in their nutritional content. In general,
light-colored vegetables with a high water content, such as
iceberg lettuce and celery, are low in nutrients and also take
up a lot of room in the stomach. A good source of information regarding the nutritional content of 470 vegetables is the
*U.S. Government book Composition of Foods: Vegetables and
Vegetable Products. It is available from the U.S. Government
Printing Office, Washington, D.C. 20402.*

Most vegetables can be offered uncooked. However, for a
change of pace and perhaps for greater acceptability, try
cooking them, but remember the 30-Minute Rule for cooked
foods given earlier in the chapter. The size of the pieces
offered may affect whether the bird will eat vegetables or not.
Some birds prefer diced foods, while others prefer to tear the
pieces themselves. Uncooked corn on the cob, carrots, and
other firm vegetables can be hung in the cage as an edible
toy.

*Fresh vegetables,
fruits, and nuts can
all play a role in an
avian diet. Ask your
veterinarian for more
information on these
tasty "side dishes."*

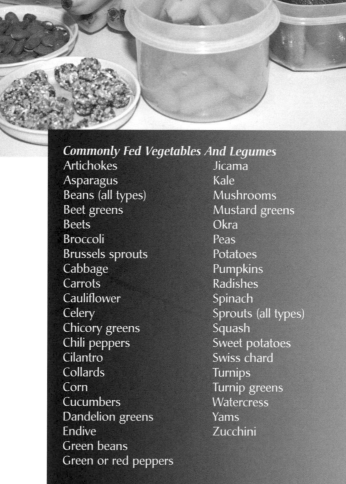

Commonly Fed Vegetables And Legumes

Artichokes	Jicama
Asparagus	Kale
Beans (all types)	Mushrooms
Beet greens	Mustard greens
Beets	Okra
Broccoli	Peas
Brussels sprouts	Potatoes
Cabbage	Pumpkins
Carrots	Radishes
Cauliflower	Spinach
Celery	Sprouts (all types)
Chicory greens	Squash
Chili peppers	Sweet potatoes
Cilantro	Swiss chard
Collards	Turnips
Corn	Turnip greens
Cucumbers	Watercress
Dandelion greens	Yams
Endive	Zucchini
Green beans	
Green or red peppers	

Nutrition

Consider vegetables as a "side dish" for your bird's diet--between 10 and 25 percent of the diet. Be sure to vary the selection of vegetables to maximize their benefits.

Fruits

Fruits are a valuable addition to the diet and provide a quick energy source. Virtually all pet birds eat fruit in the wild. Most fruits are safe; however, the pits of apricots, cherries, and peaches, along with apple seeds, should be avoided because they can cause problems. Avocado should also be avoided because it has been toxic to some birds. There is also a government publication about fruits and their nutritional content. Order a copy of *Agriculture Handbook No. 8-9 from the U.S. Government Printing Office, Washington, D.C. 20402.*
Fruit is high in sugar, making it very palatable to birds. This also makes it attractive to ants and other insects, and it is prone to bacterial contamination. Therefore, remove all uneaten fruit within 30 minutes to avoid these problems. Fruits can also create a sticky mess in the cage, so be sure to keep the cage clean.

Fruits are also considered "side dishes"--between 5 and 10 percent of your bird's diet can be fruit. Use seasonal varieties to your best advantage. Make sure all fruit is fresh and washed thoroughly.

Commonly Fed Fruits	
Apples	Oranges
Apricots	Papayas
Bananas	Peaches
Berries	Pears
Cantaloupe	Persimmons
Figs	Pineapple
Grapefruit	Plums
Grapes	Pomegranates
Guava	Raisins
Honeydew melon	Tangerines
Kiwi fruit	Watermelons
Kumquats	
Mangoes	

Meat and Dairy Products

Small amounts of meat and dairy products can be fed as occasional treats. Surprisingly, pet birds enjoy meat and dairy products. In small amounts, all types of these foods are safe and nutritious. Common choices include eggs, cheese, yogurt, and well-cooked chicken or beef. Remember the 30-Minute Rule.

Birds are deficient in the enzyme lactase, which is necessary to digest dairy products. Therefore, most birds can only tolerate small amounts. Yogurt is an especially good choice for birds because the cooking process makes it easier to digest than other dairy products.

Supplements

Vitamins and Minerals

A vitamin and mineral supplement is usually not necessary when feeding a commercially formulated diet. For any other diet plans, this is a good product to use. Use only a balanced supplement made exclusively for pet birds and follow manufacturer-recommended amounts. Too much of a good thing can also cause problems.

Use powdered vitamin and mineral supplements sprinkled on soft foods or mixed in with home-cooked diets. Parrots have dry tongues, and powdered supplements on seeds mostly fall to the ground rather than being consumed. Do not use supplements that must be added to water. They will increase the rate at which bacteria contaminate the water. Note: Many brands of vitamin and mineral supplements are available for birds. Consult your avian veterinarian for a recommendation.

Grit

Grit consists of small pieces of sand and stones once thought to be crucial for digestion of food in the bird's gizzard. The notion of feeding grit to pet birds was borrowed from poultry. Chickens and turkeys eat whole seeds and require small bits of sand to grind off the coating of the seed in order to digest it. Parrots, on the other hand, crack their seeds before they eat them. This eliminates the need for "grinding stones" in the gizzard. Canaries and finches do require extremely small amounts of grit in order to digest their food. Two pieces per week is probably adequate for these birds.

A danger exists in overfeeding grit to birds. From boredom or sickness, birds sometimes eat too much grit, and they can develop an impaction in the digestive tract. For the same reason, you should not use sand-covered cage liner even if it's not called "grit." Birds can eat this sand as well.

Foods to Avoid

Birds can eat almost everything we can. If it's healthy for people, it should be perfectly safe for pet birds. Except for avocado, common sense should indicate that the foods below are not ideal for pet birds:

Avocados: Surprisingly, avocados have caused severe digestive problems, even death, in some birds. Even though many parrots seem to tolerate this food well, it is not recommended.

Alcohol: Alcohol can obviously cause problems in birds. Even in small amounts, it can cause sickness, shock, and even death. During a party, make sure your guests do not playfully offer alcohol to your bird.

Junk Food: Junk food is not healthy for people, and it certainly should be avoided in your bird's diet. Potato chips, cookies, candy, salted popcorn, and other fatty or highly salted or sweetened foods fall into this category.

Chocolate: In large amounts, chocolate is poisonous to dogs. It can also cause serious problems, including death, in birds. Therefore, don't take any chances and don't feed your bird chocolate.

Pesticides and herbicides: Obviously, no one would choose to feed these to a bird. However, in today's hectic life, it is important to remember to take the time to wash all fruits and vegetables thoroughly. Parrots are especially sensitive to environmental toxins. You may want to consider purchasing organically grown produce for your pet.

Getting Finicky Eaters to Accept New Foods

The best food in the world won't help if it isn't eaten! What is fed is not as important as what your bird actually eats! If your bird is finicky about its diet, make an effort to widen the variety of food your pet accepts. Your reward will be a healthier, happier pet. Young birds should be offered a wide variety of foods from the very beginning, which should help eliminate "fussy eater" problems.

Adult birds can be resistant to dietary change, especially those that are "seed junkies." This section is written for them. On the other hand, a few birds readily accept new foods. They are the exception and not the rule. Remember, a bird's food preferences have probably evolved over a number of years.

Don't expect change to occur immediately. Above all else, have patience and be persistent. Most birds can be converted to a new and healthier diet over time.

With any of the suggested methods, food will be wasted. It will either become spoiled sitting around uneaten in the cage or playfully tossed to the floor. During the conversion process, offer only small amounts and learn to recognize your bird's food preferences. That way, less food will need to be discarded.

Regardless of the method used, monitor your bird's weight during the diet conversion. If your bird loses more than 10 percent of its weight during this time, consult your avian veterinarian.

Introducing New Foods

Because no single method works for all birds, a wide variety of methods are given below to encourage birds to try new foods. If one method doesn't work with your bird, try another. Remember, persistence pays off in a healthier pet!

One Step at a Time: The new diet is slowly increased while seeds are gradually decreased. This continues until the bird accepts the new food. It may take weeks or even months for this to occur. Be sure the bird never has quite enough seeds in its bowl to satisfy its hunger because this helps force the bird to try the new food. Monitor weight every few days by weighing your pet on a gram scale. Ask your avian veterinarian for suggestions on where to purchase such a scale, or check with kitchen specialty stores in your area because many food scales are calibrated to weigh items in grams as well as ounces.

Cold Turkey: As the name implies, simply remove the seeds and immediately replace them with the new diet. This method is not recommended for novice bird owners because some birds will go without eating for several days. Monitor weight daily. If weight loss becomes a problem, return the old diet to the bird's food bowl.

Cold Turkey in the Morning: Remove the seeds at night, before bedtime. In the morning, offer only the new food. You can even sprinkle a few seeds on the new diet. In the evening, offer the bird its regular diet. Continue this "on again, off again" adventure until the bird eats its new diet with no resistance.

Search and Recovery: Continue to feed the regular diet, but mix in the new foods. The bird will have to pick around the unfamiliar food to reach its favorites. In this way, some of the new food will at least be tasted. This method works especially well with home-cooked foods.

Change is Good: Commercially formulated diets come in a variety of shapes, colors, smells, and textures. Perhaps a change of scenery can help convert a bird to a new diet. Try different brands of pellets until you find one that your bird will eat. This method can be tried with or without the old diet being in the cage.

La Salsa: Lightly flavor the formulated diet with your bird's favorite sauces, broths, or fruit juices to make them more palatable. Once your bird readily eats the pellets, discontinue the sauces.

Copycat: Let your bird watch you eat. At mealtime, bring the cage or perch alongside the dinner table. If you want to, let the bird have its own plate of whatever you're eating. Also, to help show the bird just how good the food really is, express your pleasure with phrases such as, "Mmmm, good!" Birds have a natural curiosity and a desire to mimic, so sometimes this method works well.

Birds of a Different Feather: Try feeding new foods in different forms: chopped vs. whole, cooked vs. uncooked, cold vs. warm, but always fresh. Also try placing the food in different locations--attached to the cage wall, placed at the end of a perch, or served in favorite areas outside the cage.

Changing a pet bird from a seed-based diet to a formulated or pellet-based diet along with healthy side dishes is very important. Here are two more nutritional rules to consider:

Rule No. 2: If a bird is sick, don't change its diet.
Sick birds are usually eating less at a time when they need the most nutrition. This is not the time to create more stress for them by forcing them to make new food choices. However, even sick birds need complete, balanced diets.

Rule No. 3: Where there's a will, there's a way.
Who's training whom? We are supposed to be smarter than our birds. Be imaginative in the ways you present new foods. Also, ask experienced bird people for suggestions. Persistence pays off. Even having the bird accept one or two new foods is a big accomplishment.

Time and Nutrition

If everyone had unlimited time, this discussion would be unnecessary. In the real world, time is at a premium. Even people who are passionate about their birds may not always have time to prepare the very best diets. This section provides suggestions on how to combine foods for a well-balanced diet, regardless of the amount of time available.

"LOTS OF TIME":
- Commercially formulated diets
- Home-cooked diets
- Fresh vegetables and fruits
- Fresh water

"SOME TIME":
- Commercially formulated diet
- Home-cooked diet when time permits
- Fresh vegetables and fruits
- Fresh water

"NO TIME":
- Commercially formulated diet
- Fresh fruits and vegetables
- Fresh water

Recipes You Can Make at Home for Your Bird

Vegetable Medley

1/4 cup paddy rice (available at Asian food markets or natural food stores) or long-grain brown rice
1/4 cup hulled millet
1/4 cup red lentils
1/4 cup small-type pasta, such as acini pepe, tubettini or orzo (optional)
1 1/4 cups water
1 cup frozen vegetables

Combine rice, millet, lentils (and pasta, if included) with water and microwave on high for 15 minutes or until soft. Drain excess water and mix in vegetables. Stir to thaw vegetables and cool rice mixture.

Refrigerate leftovers or freeze. This recipe is also good for softbills by adding chunks of apple, banana, papaya, or other fruit.

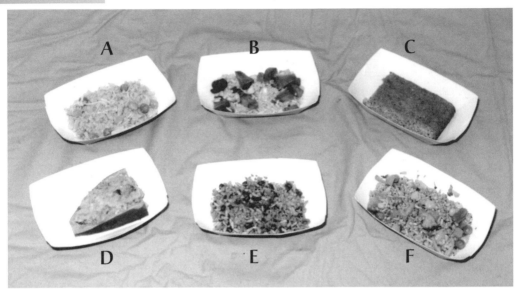

Mini Chili

1/4 cup adzuki beans (found in natural food stores)
1/2 cup long-grain brown rice
1/4 cup quinoa (KEEN-wah, found in health food stores)
2 3/4 cups water
3 whole green chiles
1 bay leaf
pinch of dried oregano

    Place all ingredients in 1 1/2-quart microwave casserole (or 11- by 7- by 2-inch ovenproof glass dish) and stir to distribute evenly. Cover with wax paper and microwave on high for 35 minutes. Let cool before serving. One-quarter cup is an average serving for a medium-sized parrot.

    Refrigerate or freeze leftovers. This is a good recipe for small birds.

Luv That Stuffing

1/4 cup stuffing mix (try cornbread)
1/4 cup defrosted mixed vegetables or grated carrots,
chopped broccoli or diced bell pepper
1 tablespoon almonds
1 tablespoon shredded mozzarella cheese
1/4 cup cooked pasta (optional)

Place all ingredients in microwave-safe dish. Add just enough water to make slightly moist and stir. Heat in microwave on high until warm, about 30 seconds. Be sure cheese is not too hot before serving. This provides two servings for medium-

Home-cooked foods are an excellent addition to a bird's diet. Recipes for these "goumet meals" can be found in this chapter:
A) Luv That Stuffing
B) Vegetable Medley
C) Nutri-Birdie Bar
D)Parrot Tater Melt
E) Mini Chili
F) Birdie "Power Lunch"

sized parrots.
Refrigerate or freeze leftovers.

Parrot Tater Melt

1/2 baked potato (sweet, white or yam)
3 tablespoons chopped raw broccoli
2 tablespoons shredded mozzarella cheese

Scoop out potato and mix with broccoli and cheese in microwave-safe dish. Microwave on high until broccoli is bright green and cheese has melted (about one minute). Place mixture back into potato skin. Cool before serving (be sure cheese is not too hot). You may serve as is or cut up into pieces.

Refrigerate or freeze leftovers.

Birdie "Power Lunch"

1 cup long-grain brown rice
1/2 cup quinoa
1/2 cup hulled millet
1/2 cup almonds
1 tablespoon dried oregano
1 tablespoon dried basil
3 cups water
1 teaspoon chicken bouillon

Place all ingredients in 8- by 8- by 2-inch microwave-safe dish or 1 1/2-quart glass bowl and mix well. Cover with wax paper and microwave on high for 25 minutes. Add to this fresh cut-up vegetables, such as tomatoes, celery, bell pepper, or squash, or defrosted mixed vegetables. Serve warm. One-quarter cup is an average serving for a medium-sized parrot. Refrigerate or freeze leftovers. This recipe is also enjoyed by smaller birds.

Nutri-Birdie Bar

2 eggs (shells optional)
1/4 cup raisins
1/4 cup walnuts
18 1/2-ounce box cornbread mix
1/3 cup apple juice
1/4 cup applesauce
1/2 cup defrosted mixed vegetables
1/2 cup chopped kale leaves, broccoli, or shredded carrot

Put eggs, walnuts, and raisins in blender and blend until egg shells are chopped very fine. Place this mix into bowl with remaining ingredients. Stir until well blended.

Put into greased 8- by 8- by 2-inch pan and bake at 400 degrees Fahrenheit for 20 minutes. Cool 10 minutes on rack, loosen edges with a knife or spatula, and turn out to finish cooling.

This bread can be left in a bird's cage all day. Discard uneaten portions at day's end.

Diets for Lories and Softbills

Up to this point, the nutritional information contained in this chapter has been concerned with the diet of parrots. However, softbills eat only soft foods, such as fruits. Their special dietary needs make them unique in the bird world. In the wild, fruit, along with some insects, makes up the majority of their diet. Depending on which softbill you own, the dietary recommendations will vary slightly. Before deciding on one of these types of birds as a pet, be aware that they do require additional time for food preparation and cleanup. Since the bulk of the diet is either soft or liquid foods, the birds' droppings will be similar in nature.

Lories and Lorikeets

Lories and lorikeets can make wonderful, loving companions. In the wild, these birds feed on fruit, flowers, nectar, pollen, and an occasional insect. They have brushlike tongues that are ideally suited for eating these types of foods. Lories and lorikeets appear to have lower protein needs than other types of pet birds. Health problems could result if protein levels are too high in their diet.

A lory or lorikeet diet should consist of commercial lory diet, fresh fruit, nectar and fresh water.

Commercial lory diet: These special diets have been created to supply a balanced and nutritious food source. They are available in a wet form, where water needs to be added, or as a dry powder. Both are good; however, with the dry diet, a bird's droppings are a little less watery.

Fruits: All fresh fruits are good to feed. Feed them diced, or at least sliced. In a pinch, canned fruit with no sugar added can be considered an acceptable alternative.

Nectar: Even if your birds are on a commercial lory diet, consider adding a little nectar to the diet each day.

Mynahs, Toucans, and Touracos

A mynah bird, toucan, or touraco diet should consist of mostly fruit, a few vegetables, a good protein source, and fresh water.

Fruit: Most any fruit will do, but feed citrus sparingly because of potential problems with iron storage disease (see note below). Fruits such as pears, apples, grapes, and papaya are good choices. They should be offered diced, since the birds usually swallow them whole.

Vegetables: Some of these birds also enjoy vegetables. Raw mixed vegetables can be added to the fruit mix.

Protein: Since fruits and vegetables are low in protein, a good source needs to be added to the diet. Commercial mynah bird pellets are recommended and can be soaked in water or fruit juice prior to serving. A few insects, such as mealworms or crickets, can also be offered.

Fruits, vegetables and the protein source can all be blended together in a food processor. Even tofu, carrots, and some cheese can be added. Mynah bird pellets can be used to control the texture of this mixture, which should be moist and a little crumbly. Pound cake soaked in fruit juice or nectar is a much-enjoyed treat for many softbills.

Note: Some of these birds have a tendency to store abnormally high amounts of iron in their livers (iron storage disease). Therefore, a good protein source with a low iron content is essential. The iron content of the food should be less than 150 parts per million. Because of their iron content, dog food, cat food, monkey chow, dried fruits, raisins, and spinach should not be fed to softbills.

Chapter 5

Bird Restraint

Catch 'em and Hold 'em Safely

A bird that is easy to handle is a wonderful pet, and an owner who knows how to handle his or her pet safely will gain more enjoyment from the bird-owner relationship. In this chapter, we'll look at some basic handling techniques every bird owner should know.

Picking Up Your Pet

One of the most important techniques bird owners need to know is the up/down command. You can teach your bird to step up by gently pressing your finger up and into the bird's belly. This will cause the bird to step up. As it does so, say "step up" or "up." Before long, your bird will respond to this command without much prompting--many birds take their cue from having a hand placed in front of them and step up without the verbal prompt.

When you put the bird down on its cage or playgym, simply say "down" as the bird steps off your hand. These two simple commands offer you a great deal of control over your bird because you can use "up" to put an unruly bird back in its cage or you can tell a parrot that needs to go to bed "down" as you put the bird in its cage at night.

Are Gloves Necessary?

Some people may try to tell you that you need to wear gloves while taming your parrot. Don't do this because wearing gloves will make your hands appear more frightening to your bird. If your pet is scared, it will take more time to tame, which may make the process less enjoyable for you.

Keep Your Pet Close to Your Heart

To help protect yourself from possible injury and to prevent your bird from developing behavior problems, don't allow it to ride on your shoulder. Birds consider you an equal if they can look you in the eye, and they may also perceive the rest of your body as a tree on which to perch. If something threatening comes along, your bird may bite at your face to encourage you to flee.

When Not to Handle a Bird

- it "flashes" its eyes (pupils dilate and contract quickly)
- it fans its tail feathers
- it strikes at you with its beak
- it drums its wings or stamps its feet
- it crouches tightly on its perch and fluffs its nape and back feathers

In bird body language, all of these gestures indicate aggression, and an unwary owner who approaches his or her pet at these times may be bitten. Learn to read your bird's body language and you'll know when it's safe to pick up your pet.

121

In addition to the potential for serious injury to your face, this situation also results in a bird that can be difficult to handle. By holding your bird at the level of your heart, you may also help soothe it because it can hear your heart beat.

If your bird is used to being on your shoulder, you can train it to perch on your knee or to sit on the arm of your chair. If your bird tries to climb up to your shoulder, place your hand

in front of your bird and tell it to step up, then place the bird back where you want it to sit. Eventually, your bird will get the idea that your shoulder is now off limits. When you have your bird on your arm, remember to keep your arm bent at the elbow and tucked close to your ribcage. This way, your bird will not be able to run up your arm to your shoulder.

Safe Restraint Techniques

Catching or holding a bird will probably become necessary. The reasons for physical restraint include grooming, medicating, and some emergencies. Injuries to both the holder and the bird are the primary concerns when restraining your bird.

Tips to Remember When Restraining:

Work quickly to minimize handling time. Stress and overheating problems will be reduced.

Keep your bird, such as this umbrella cockatoo, on your wrist, hand, or forearm, keeping the top of its head at the level of your heart. (Bonnie Jay)

Plan ahead. Have all tools, equipment, medications, and anything else you may need ready prior to restraining your bird.

For small birds especially, a net would be helpful to catch the bird if it escapes.

Towel selection is based on the size of the bird. It will be chewed on, so choose an old one!

With parrots, it's their beaks that can cause injuries. Respect your bird and protect yourself. (Hawks and other raptors inflict injuries with their feet.) Parrot nails may scratch and cause minor skin punctures, especially with people who have delicate skin. However, the nails are unlikely to cause serious injury.

Birds have very fragile bones. Their legs and wings are most susceptible to injury.

Don't put any pressure on the chest while holding a bird. It will interfere with breathing.

It may help to darken a room just prior to catching birds. The darkness temporarily "freezes" them.

Supplies for Restraint

Towels are the best tool to catch and hold birds. Use small washcloths for canaries, parakeets, and lovebirds; kitchen or hand towels for medium-size birds; and bath towels for larger birds. Towels work best for two reasons. First, they protect and hide the hands. The bird does not see a human hand approaching, only a towel. The thicker the towel, the more finger protection available. Secondly, the towel allows the bird's body to be wrapped up once it is caught. Wing flapping is avoided.

Contrary to popular belief, gloves are not a good way to catch and hold birds. They imitate the shape of the human hand and don't provide any "wrapping material."

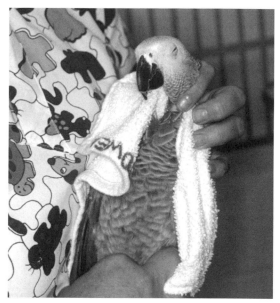

The "Catch"

When done properly, the "catch" is performed slowly, smoothly and even lovingly. An improper "catch" could physically harm your bird, and even cause some psychological trauma as well. Remember, you are not an eagle trying to catch prey. Rather, you are a loving owner trying to maintain a close bond and trusting relationship with your fine feathered friend. Therefore, the goal is to safely and gently "towel" the bird.

Toweling a bird is an important part of being able to handle it safely. Birds such as this African grey often direct their energies toward chewing on the towel, which means that owners are less likely to be bitten during handling.

Introduce your bird to "Mr. towel" slowly and gently. Some suggestions to do this:

- Lay a towel near the cage for a few days. Then gradually move it closer to the cage and eventually into the cage.
- Shower with your bird and wrap yourselves together in a large towel to dry.
- Select a towel the same color as a familiar bedspread or room color.
- Lay the towel on the bed and lay the bird on the towel. Over a period of time gently cover the bird with the towel.
- Play peek-a-boo with the towel.

Very importantly, if you can get your bird to readily accept toweling one of the most significant stress factors can be eliminated. If possible, smaller birds are best caught inside the cage or, if "finger tame," directly from the hand. Tamed larger birds are usually best captured outside the cage in a confined area such as a corner of a small room. In a large area, it's easier for birds to get away. Untamed larger birds usually need to be caught in their own cages.

Inside the Cage

A darkened room makes it much easier to catch smaller birds; the sudden darkness temporarily "freezes" them. If needed, the cage can be carried to a room that can be easily darkened, and a small flashlight can be used to determine the bird's location so it can be grabbed quickly. If you use this technique with larger parrots, be very careful. The restrainer also has limited vision, and even friendly parrots will bite when frightened.

To capture the bird inside the cage, first remove toys and perches. Depending on the size and temperament of the bird, place either one or both hands behind the towel. The "writing hand" takes charge of the head, while the other hand holds and wraps the body. For example, if you are right-handed, use your right hand to hold the bird's head. Second, bring the towel into the cage and quickly drape it over the bird. Next, grasp the bird by the head, with the thumb and index finger protected by the towel. The fingers should be pressing directly on the bird's jawbone. The palm of the hand should rest on the back of the neck. The opposite hand quickly wraps the towel around the bird's body. After this, remove the bird from the cage. The two-hand technique works well for medium-size and larger birds. A modification involving only one hand is used with small birds.

Once the bird is out of the cage, adjust the towel as needed and uncover the bird's face. Allow the bird to chew on the towel. This keeps the bird occupied, and it can blame the towel, not the holder, for the indignity.

Outside the Cage

The technique for catching a bird outside the cage is very similar to catching a bird inside a cage. Remember to coax the bird into a corner. The kitchen or another room with a tile or linoleum floor works best. Carpeting can catch toes, and it's not as easy to clean up messes. Show your bird the towel and in a soft and loving voice tell them what you are going to do. Then slowly and gently lay the towel over the bird and grasp the head. Frequently, you will miss the head on the first try and you will need to repeat the entire process.

Unfortunately, some birds will roll over on their backs when approached with a towel. If this should happen, the risk of being bitten is greater. First, reach for a thicker towel or fold the towel you have in half. You must then use both hands to "pin" the head against the floor. Immediately slide one hand around and in back of the head. Be sure to continue to gently press the head toward the floor with the other hand.

As soon as the head is under control, lift the bird up and rearrange the towel. There will be more wing flapping, so it might help to press the bird's body against your chest during the towel arranging. This is going to be the most difficult situation you encounter during restraint.

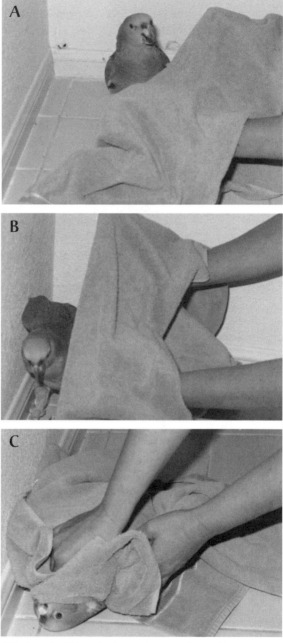

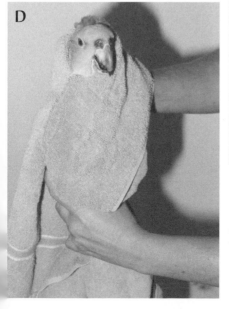

"The Catch": (A) Position hands beneath the towel and coax the bird into the corner of a room. (B) Begin to position one hand above and behind the bird's head. (C) Gently and carefully grasp the bird's head from behind; the other hand then works to control the body. (D) This is a well-restrained Amazon.

125

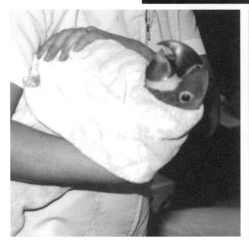

Towels are the best way to catch and hold a bird. The larger the bird, like this macaw, the larger the towel needed.

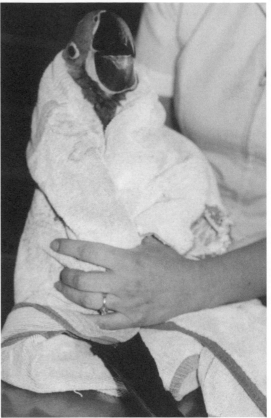

Once the bird has been caught, reposition the towel to cover both wings and fold the towel back to uncover the bird's face. Cradle the bird against your body for added restraint.

Bird Restraint

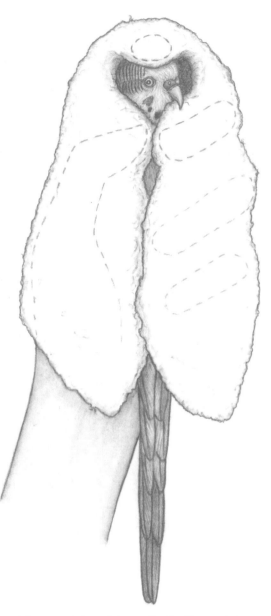

The "Three-Point" Hold

For more control of the head, which you might need when administering oral medications, try this technique. The only difference is that three fingers are restraining the head instead of two.

Begin by using the same capture method as described previously, but once you have safely restrained the bird in the towel, you will change the finger positions on the head. Instead of holding the head with the thumb and index finger only, also use the middle finger, for additional restraint. Simply slide the index finger up and around to the very top of the head. Move the middle finger up to the same place that the index finger was and keep the thumb in the same spot.

Some Other Tidbits to Remember

• It is important to remember that there is a fine line between too little and too much restraint. There is a need to be firm, but also gentle. Pressure can easily be applied to the jawbones with the fingers holding the head. On the other hand, very light pressure is sufficient around the body. The towel will help to cushion the hold around the bird.

• With parrots remember, only the beak "bites." Therefore, when catching a bird, always take control of the head first, and then follow by gaining control of the body. When releasing the bird, let go of the body first and the head last.

Try the "three-point hold" when more control of the bird's head is needed.

Practice restraining your bird before there is a need to do so. It's easier to learn in a calm and relaxed setting than under the pressure of having to do it. A second person may be helpful, not only for moral support, but also for adjusting the towel around flapping wings. Practice makes perfect!

127

Bare-hand restraint can be used for small birds such as this budgerigar.

Chapter 6

Grooming

Maintaining the Wings, Nails, and Feathers

We humans have always been fascinated with birds' ability to fly. Free of any mechanical aids, they soar the skies, peering down at us from lofty heights. Our envy for easy flight can be traced back thousands of years to the tale of Icarus in Greek mythology, who built the ill-fated flying suit of wax and feathers.

The radiance, beauty, and function of feathers is truly one of the wonders of the world. When birds live in their natural setting, their feathers are the key to their survival and are maintained in near perfect condition. Caged birds, on the other hand, often need help keeping their feathers in clean and healthy condition.

This chapter will assist bird owners with the care and maintenance of feathers, nails, and beaks.

Feathers

Most bird owners would never dream that their beautiful feathered friends are closely related to reptiles. In fact, the feathers of birds actually evolved from the scales of reptiles. Scales protect a reptile's skin, just as feathers protect a bird's skin. Feathers play many different roles. They enhance a bird's beauty, sexual attraction, warmth, waterproofing, and ability to protect itself. And, not least of all, feathers give a bird the ability to fly. Feathers allow a bird to cover enormous areas in search of food and to escape from predators quickly.

The condition and appearance of the feathers can be an excellent window to a bird's overall health. A well-nourished, healthy bird will have a magnificent coat of shiny, glossy feathers to show off. Birds with dull, off-colored, broken, or tattered feathers may be malnourished or sick.

Preening is work a bird does on its feathers to maintain their beauty and function. Birds have 2,000 to 3,000 feathers, and each of these must be cleaned of dust and dirt, untangled, fluffed, lubricated, and properly replaced in its special position every day. This is work. A healthy bird will spend much of its waking hours caring for its feathers. Owners can help encourage this very important activity by following the suggestions below.

131

Bathing

Bathing is an excellent way to encourage preening. In the wild, birds are often seen splashing in puddles or playing on wet grass and leaves.

In captivity, birds can bathe in many ways. Every bird will have its own preference when it comes to bathing. If your bird does not appear to like bathing, chances are you simply have yet to discover the method it prefers. Here are some bathing suggestions:

• A shallow bowl filled with water

• A clean plant mister filled with warm, clean water. This is an ideal method for larger birds. Try experimenting with different spray settings.

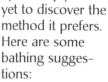

• A water faucet, making sure the water doesn't get too hot

• Wet foliage, such as lettuce leaves. This is great for budgies and other small birds.

• Sprinklers outside on a warm day

• A steamy bathroom

These Moluccan cockatoos are enjoying a shower outside. Let your pet bird outside only if its wings have been trimmed and someone is available to supervise the bird at all times.

Bathing can play an important part in good grooming. Some birds, such as this cockatiel in the shower, bathe with their owners,

(Animal Environments)

• A shower with a buddy (larger birds usually love this!)

Bathe your bird during the warmest part of the day. Daily bathing is ideal, but a realistic schedule is two to three times per week.

Commercially prepared bird-bathing solutions are available. However, fresh tap water works best. Soap or other cleaning agents should not be used. Even in small amounts,

these products could damage the protective oil coating on the feathers.

Others, such as this cockatoo, prefer to be misted with clean water.

(Animal Environments)

Molt

Molting is the term given to the shedding or loss of old feathers that occurs simultaneously with the growth of new ones. Molting is a very stressful time in a bird's life, and there are several reasons for this. For birds flying free, molting is the time when they are most susceptible to predators. This lack of security carries over to pet birds, as well.

Growing new feathers requires considerable energy. If the bird is already on a good diet, no change is necessary. However, a marginal diet may need to be improved during this time. See chapter 4, "Nutrition," for general dietary recommendations.

Some birds, such as red factor canaries, emerald toucanettes, and Pekin robins, require certain color foods to maintain the proper colors in their plumage. These color foods are available in natural (beta carotene) and synthetic (canthaxanthin) forms. Canaries should be fed color foods immediately before they begin to molt, while softbills should receive the color foods after they begin to molt.

Recommendations During Molting

- Minimize stress: Allow for rest and relaxation, increase the feeling of security.
- During a heavy molt, increase the room temperature; 75 to 80 degrees Fahrenheit is ideal.
- Good nutrition is essential.
- Encourage preening.

Wing Trimming

If we love our birds and want to keep them safe, their wings must be trimmed regularly to ensure their safety and well-being. A wing trim, properly done, will prevent a pet bird from flying away. It will also prevent injuries commonly associated with flying and make training easier. Several methods have been described for trimming wings. Some birds will retain the uncanny ability to fly, regardless of the trimming method used. The preferred method is to trim both wings. By trimming the flight feathers of both wings instead of just one, a bird can still have a safe, controlled glide to the floor. When only one wing is trimmed, the bird's balance will be poor and it will lose its directional ability, which can result in dangerous crash landings.

Ideally, pet bird owners will have their birds' wings trimmed professionally. Although, in and of itself, wing trimming is not difficult, properly restraining a bird to accomplish the task is. People who own one or two pet birds simply don't practice restraint techniques often enough to become proficient at them, which is why professional grooming is recommended. The wing trimming process will be described below for those owners with a number of pet birds, but professional grooming is strongly recommended for owners of single pet birds.

The size of a pet bird is another important consideration in determining whether or not an owner should trim his or her pet bird's wings. Smaller birds, such as budgies or cockatiels, can be restrained fairly easily, while larger birds, such as macaws or cockatoos, can be more difficult to restrain. Larger birds can also suffer greater harm than smaller species from blood loss if a blood feather is cut during wing trimming. The first step in wing trimming is to assemble all the things you will need and find a suitable place to groom your pet before you catch and trim them. Because grooming excites all birds, groom your pet in a quiet, well-lit place. Make sure you have a good light to work under; this will make your job easier. Be sure to watch your bird for signs of stress (see chapter 2, "Your New Bird," for a description of these signs) and stop the procedure if your bird becomes stressed. Also, review the section entitled "Home-Care Suggestions for a Bleeding Feather" in chapter 14, "Medical Emergencies," before proceeding.

Your grooming tools will include:
* an assistant who will hold the bird in a safe, secure manner while you groom it
* a well-worn washcloth or small towel in which to wrap your bird
* small, sharp scissors to do the actual trimming
* needle-nosed pliers to pull any blood feathers you may cut accidentally

Once you've assembled your supplies and found your work place, have your assistant drape the towel over his or her hand and catch your bird with the toweled hand. Grab the bird by the back of its head and neck, and wrap it in the towel. Have your assistant hold the sides of the bird's head securely with his or her thumb and index finger. Covering the bird's head with the towel will calm your bird and will give it something to chew on while you clip its wings. (See chapter 5, "Bird Restraint," for more information on proper restraint techniques.)

Lay the bird on its back, being careful not to constrict or compress its chest (birds have no diaphragms to help them breathe, so their chests must be able to expand and contract), and carefully spread its wings to look for blood feathers that are still growing in. These can be identified by their waxy, tight look and their resemblance to porcupine quills, which is caused by the blood supply to the new feather.

If your bird has a number of blood feathers, you may want to postpone trimming its wings for a few days--fully grown feathers cushion those just coming in from life's hard knocks. If your bird has only one or two blood feathers, leave a mature feather or two next to each to protect the incoming blood feather, then trim the rest accordingly.

To trim your bird's feathers, separate each one from its adjacent flight feathers and cut it individually (remember, the goal is to have a well-trimmed bird that's still able to glide down if it needs to). Use the primary coverts (the set of feathers above the primary flight feathers on top of your bird's wing) as a guideline on how short you can trim.

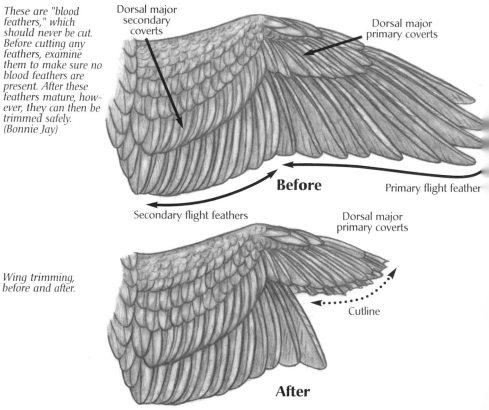

These are "blood feathers," which should never be cut. Before cutting any feathers, examine them to make sure no blood feathers are present. After these feathers mature, however, they can then be trimmed safely. (Bonnie Jay)

Dorsal major secondary coverts

Dorsal major primary coverts

Before

Primary flight feather

Secondary flight feathers

Dorsal major primary coverts

Wing trimming, before and after.

Cutline

After

Grooming

The number of flight feathers needing to be cut varies from species to species and even from bird to bird. The goal is to cut the minimum number of feathers necessary to prevent flight and ensure safe landings. A basic rule-of-thumb is to cut the outer six flight feathers from each wing. However some species such as Amazons and African Greys may only require four or less to reach this goal. On the other hand, cockatiels and macaws may require 8 to 10 feathers to accomplish the same thing.

If you do happen to cut or break a blood feather, remain calm. You must remove it and stop the bleeding. Panicking will not do you or your bird much good. You may want to pack the blood feather with styptic powder and take the bird to your veterinarian's office to have the blood feather removed. To remove a blood feather, have your assistant hold the bird's wing steady. Then you need to take a pair of needle-nosed pliers and grasp the broken feather's shaft as close to the skin of your bird's wing as you can. With one steady motion, pull the feather out completely while your assistant pulls from the opposite side using equal amounts of pressure to keep the wing stationary. After you've removed the feather, put a pinch of styptic powder on the feather follicle (the spot you pulled the feather from) and apply direct pressure for a few minutes until the bleeding stops. If the bleeding doesn't stop after a few minutes of direct pressure, or if you can't remove the feather shaft, contact your avian veterinarian for further instructions.

Although it may seem like you're hurting your bird by removing the broken blood feather, consider this: a broken blood feather could bleed a lot. If the feather stays in, the bird continues to bleed. Once removed, the bird's skin generally closes over the feather shaft and shuts off the faucet.

In order to be effective, *wing trimming must be done on a regular basis.* Many a "trimmed" bird has flown away because the owner forgot that new feathers grow in continually or because the feathers weren't trimmed correctly. There is no prescribed timetable for trimming wings. Every bird is different. Check your bird's wings about every three months and trim them as needed.

Nails

With birds, as with other animals, toenails grow continuously. Normal activity is often sufficient to maintain proper length. In a cage environment, however, toenails may grow too long,

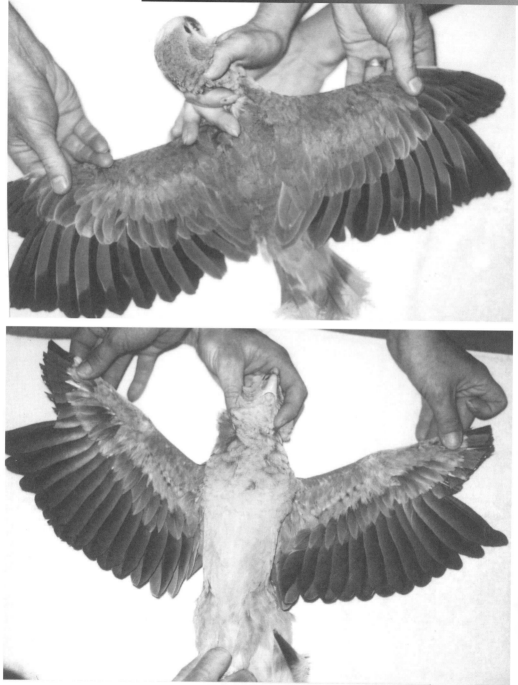

*This Amazon has
properly trimmed
wings.*

requiring periodic trimming. Overgrown nails can make perching difficult, and they can also catch on toys or carpeting, or cause foot problems.

The nails may also just be very sharp, but not overgrown. An owner may notice this when the bird perches on a hand or arm. Cutting the nail tips off, or "blunting" them, is all that is necessary.

Many cockatiels end up at bird rescue facilities because they flew away from home and later caught. Because cockatiels are such aerodynamic fliers, they need to have their wings trimmed regularly to prevent them from flying away unexpectedly. (Parrot Education and Adoption Center)

Nail Trimming

To check for overgrown nails, a good rule of thumb is that the toes should not be elevated off the ground when the feet are placed on a flat surface. A normal claw will curve down and form a right angle to the end of the toe. The "quick" is the living portion of the nail that contains the nerve and blood supply. It extends two-thirds to three-quarters of the way down the length of the nail. In light-colored nails, the quick can be seen as a pink coloration inside the claw. In dark-colored nails, the quick is not visible.

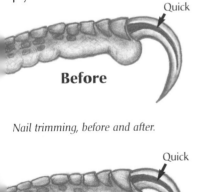

Before

Nail trimming, before and after.

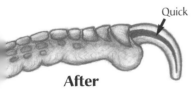

After

If the nails need to be shortened, you have to be prepared for bleeding. *Before* attempting to trim nails, read Home Care Suggestions for Bleeding Nails or Beak in chapter 14. Make sure to have styptic powder handy before starting.

When trimming bird nails, two people are usually needed: one to safely restrain the bird and one to do the actual trimming. Human nail clippers work very well on small birds. For larger birds, dog nail clippers are preferred.

Since bird nails often bleed when being trimmed, start by clipping off only a tiny amount. Continue to trim off tiny amounts until the proper length is achieved or the first sign of bleeding is observed. If bleeding occurs, use styptic powder as directed. Make sure the bleeding has stopped before continuing with the remaining nails. Cut off less on subsequent nails to avoid additional bleeding.

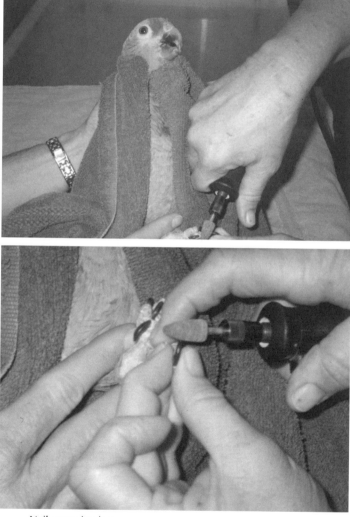

Nail grooming is a two-person procedure. One person holds the bird safely and securely while the other trims the bird's nails.

Nail-Trimming Tips

• If the nails bleed and are still too long, wait about two weeks and trim them again. The quick recedes a little each time the nails are cut.

• Nail trimming is more difficult than it appears. Consider watching a professional trim nails the first few times.

• After trimming, the bird may hold one of its feet up off the perch. The toes may be sore. Don't worry--this should last only for a day or so. If the bird continues to favor one of its feet, contact your avian veterinarian.

• Nails can be smoothed after trimming by using a Dremel tool with a grinding wheel to remove rough edges.

• Some birds can learn to tolerate having their nails filed. To see if your bird is a good candidate for this, try filing its nails gently with an emery board. Some birds will love the extra attention, while others won't.

140

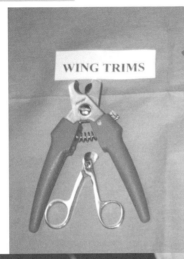

WING TRIMS

BEAK AND
NAIL TRIMS

Tools for nail grooming include a hand-held electric grinder with attachments, human fingernail or toenail clippers, a standard dog nail trimmer, and styptic powder (a syringe with the tip cut off can be filled with styptic powder and used to pack the powder onto a bleeding nail).

These are overgrown toenails.

Concrete perches may help keep a pet bird's nails trimmed. If you offer this type of perch to your bird, monitor the condition of its feet regularly, and remove the perch if you notice signs of irritation on your pet's feet.

• Some owners find that terra cotta or concrete perches help keep their birds' nails trimmed. If you place a concrete perch in your bird's cage, check to make sure that your bird's feet aren't reddened or inflamed from perching on the concrete. Offer different types of perches in the cage to give your bird's feet a break from the abrasiveness of the concrete.

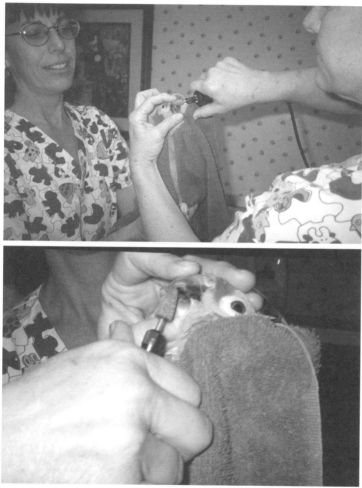

Beak

The beak is a marvelous, versatile tool which birds use to grip, grab, grind, groom, pry, crack, crush, attack, defend, feed their young, and make noise, as well as to give affection. It is important for a bird's survival that the beak functions effectively.

The beak is composed of hollow bone, with sinuses on the inside; the outer covering is composed of a thin layer of keratin. A nerve and blood supply is present. The upper beak grows from the top (where it connects to the head) and out from the center line, not from the tip, as is usually thought.

Beak grooming is a two-person job. One person holds the bird safely and securely while the other trims the beak. Because of the number of blood vessels in a bird's beak and the skill required to perform the task successfully, beak grooming is best left to professionals.

Average growth for a budgie's beak is said to be 1/4 inch per month, or three inches per year. The lower beak grows more slowly than the upper.

As the beak grows, the outermost layer of keratin begins to flake and peel. This is a normal process of shedding the oldest layers and does not indicate a health problem. For appearances, a light sanding with an emery board will help

142

remove these flaking layers. This requires good handling skills and should not be attempted by novices.

Chewing is an activity that most birds enjoy. It not only helps to keep the beak worn down, but it is also important in keeping birds mentally fit. Branches, knuckle bones (cow's, not yours!), mineral blocks, cuttlebones, and lava rocks are all good for conditioning the beak.

Normally, the hingelike action of the upper and lower beak will maintain proper length. If for some reason the hinge is not perfectly aligned, the beak will become overgrown and misshapen. Affected birds must have their beaks trimmed periodically to maintain proper function.

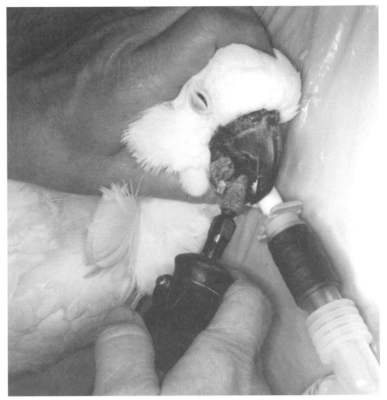

This cockatoo is having its beak shaped and smoothed with a grinding tool. It has been anesthetized to make the procedure easier and to reduce the possible risk of injury to the bird.

Normal, healthy birds do not need to have their beaks trimmed. If your bird develops a misshapen beak, contact your avian veterinarian's office for an evaluation. Overgrown or suddenly misshapen beaks often indicate an underlying disease process that needs treatment.

Note: Trimming beaks is difficult, and practice is required to do a good job without injuring the bird or getting bitten. If trimming is done incorrectly, it could interfere with the bird's ability to eat, it could injure the bird, or the owner could become injured. Beak trimming is an art. It is strongly recommended that a professional do the trimming, especially on larger birds.

Chapter 7

Creating a Happy, Healthy Environment

Home Safety, Microchipping, and Travel Tips

Creating a safe environment involves providing a place your bird can call home--a place where it has all the basic necessities of life. Foremost of these necessities is that your pet enjoys a sense of security. Food, water, and entertainment are very high on the list, as well. You will have to give considerable thought and engage in systematic planning to successfully provide the "home sweet home" that your bird requires. We've already looked at cages, food, and water in previous chapters. This chapter will focus on issues that impact the larger home environment, such as household safety, introducing your bird to other pets and children, and identification methods for your bird. Information on how to travel safely with your pet will also be provided.

Birds and children can share wonderful friendships. Before introducing them, consider both the temperament of the bird and the maturity of the children.

Introducing Your Bird to Other Pets and Children

The moment of bringing a new bird into your home is a very exciting event for the entire family. However, this is also the most dangerous time for all involved. For instance, you may have yet to birdproof your home. Precautions must be taken to ensure injury will not occur to your new pet or other family members during this getting-acquainted period.

Children

Safety and intelligent guidance are the keys to allowing children to interact with pet birds. Not only can beaks and claws cause injuries, but loud squawks can frighten youngsters. On the other hand, children can also pose a danger to the well-being and happiness of our pet birds.

The age of a child is not so much an issue as is the child's ability both to understand living things and to accord them respect to which they are entitled. Children must be taught to not put fingers, hands, or faces into or up against the cage. Teasing must be avoided. Children don't always know what constitutes teasing; the concept must be taught. They must learn to not feed anything to the bird without permission. Older children must be cautioned on the use of cleaning products, chemicals, and aerosols around birds. Above all, supervision is the key. Keep your eyes and ears attuned to potential problems. Also, remember that kids are constantly going outside, opening and closing doors. Make sure the bird is secure in its cage and that you have eliminated the possibility of escape.

Birds and children together are a wonderful sight to behold. The opportunity for your child to grow up with a bird as a companion is a treasured gift that must be treated accordingly. The future of aviculture is in the hands of our children. Encourage their interest and teach them well.

Bird Care Rules for Kids
Parents need to remind their children of the following when they're around birds:
1. Approach the cage quietly. Birds don't like to be surprised.
2. Talk softly to the bird. Don't scream or yell at it.
3. Don't shake or hit the cage.
4. Don't poke at the bird or its cage with your fingers, sticks, pencils, or other items.
5. If you're allowed to take the bird out of its cage, handle it gently.
6. Don't take the bird outside. In unfamiliar surroundings (such as the outdoors), birds can become confused and fly away from their owners. Most are never recovered.
7. Respect the bird's need for quiet time.

Other Pets

Contrary to popular belief, birds, cats, and dogs can mix well in the same household, but it takes planning and extra thought. Remember that cats and dogs are hunters by nature, and a bird's quick movements are attractive to them. The damage dogs and cats can cause to pet birds is often serious and may even be fatal. It is paramount to understand the possible dangers involved when different species are kept together under the same roof. Small birds, such as budgies, canaries, and lovebirds, move about very quickly in their cages, and this stimulates a cat's attention. Cats are very attracted to brightly colored objects that move quickly. Therefore, you must protect your smaller birds from a curious and agile cat. Remember that cats can jump, climb, and reach many places you might not think possible. Not all cats will be interested in birds, but for those that are, constant vigilance is imperative.

Larger species, such as amazons and macaws, are intimidating to cats and are, therefore, in less danger. Dogs pose the greatest threat to larger birds. Birds on the floor or outside their cages are most susceptible. Even the most mellow dog may snap if bitten or teased by a bird. Always stay close by when birds and dogs are in the same room. Prevent a tragedy before it happens.

Other pets, such as small exotic mammals and reptiles, are rather new companion animals, and little reliable information is available on how these animals fare with birds. Ferrets, for example, have a highly developed hunting instinct that may make them unsuitable companions for a pet bird. Many reptiles will leave birds alone, but interactions between pet birds and medium to large snakes should be monitored carefully.

Finally, if your bird tangles with another pet in your home, contact your avian veterinarian immediately. Such encounters can lead to bacterial infection (from a puncture wound), shock, or a broken bone (from being stepped on), and emergency care may be required to save your feathered friend's life.

Other Birds

Once the bird bug has struck, acquiring more birds is the next step. When introducing a new bird to a home with other birds, you'll need to consider some important points. First, keep the new bird completely separated from your existing birds for at least 30 days. This will help minimize the potential for disease spread.

Begin by only keeping the same species together--budgies with budgies, cockatiels with cockatiels, and so on. Larger birds generally do not mix well with other birds of different species. When trying to get birds acquainted with each other, first keep them in their own cages, in the same room, at a safe distance. Next, gradually move the cages closer. Try leaving the cage doors open with the cages facing each other and let the birds meet when they are ready. The first actual meeting should be outside of either cage, on neutral ground if possible. This is especially important with the larger birds. Make sure they are well supervised. You need to have an emergency plan at the ready to enable you to separate the birds in a hurry should they not get along.

Emergency plans should include the following: have two people who are knowledgeable about handling birds present in the room, along with readily available, big, thick bath towels and a spray bottle to wet down the birds. You may also find that turning off the lights helps settle down the birds and makes them easier to separate. Never leave the area until you are convinced the birds will be completely compatible. Many serious injuries can result when strange birds are left together unsupervised. The adage "an ounce of prevention is

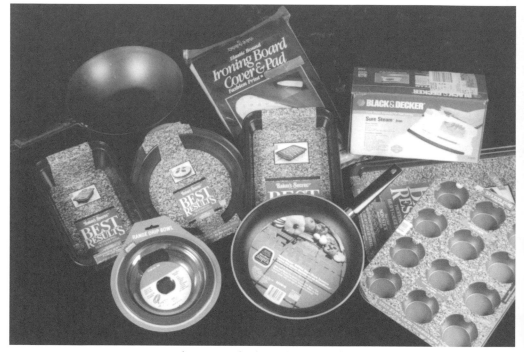

These are some of the common household products that may be coated with polytetra-fluoroethylene, a non-stick surface that can emit dangerous fumes when overheated. (Bonnie Jay)

worth a pound of cure" cannot be over emphasized. After the fact, many bird owners have sadly admitted, "I never thought this would happen." But it could! Don't let it happen to you and your pets. Use common sense and proceed with caution when first introducing your beloved pet bird to other animals.

Safety Around the Home

Birds are naturally curious creatures, and their natural curiosity is part of what makes them such appealing pets. This same natural curiosity can get a pet bird into trouble in a hurry, which is why pet bird owners must be extremely vigilant when their birds are out of their cages.

Part of this vigilance should include birdproofing your home. Some of the larger parrots have an intellectual level similar to that of a toddler. You wouldn't let a toddler have free run of your house without taking a few precautions to safeguard the child from harm, and you should extend the same concern to your pet birds.

Taking a few simple precautions—clipping your bird's wings and nails regularly, housing it in a safe and secure cage in a safe and secure spot in your home, paying attention to your pet's whereabouts whenever it is out of its cage (especially if you have cats or dogs in the home), feeding it a proper diet (including plenty of fresh water), using common sense when using chemicals in your home, and providing safe and entertaining toys to your pet—will help reduce the chance of accident or injury befalling your bird.

The "Bird's Eye" View

Look at your home from your bird's point of view, and you may see a great variety of temptations and potential dangers lurking for your feathered friend. Some household hazards outside your bird's cage you need to be aware of include:

- *unscreened windows and doors*
- *mirrors*
- *exposed electrical cords*
- *toxic houseplants*
- *unattended ashtrays*
- *Venetian blind cords*
- *sliding glass doors*
- *ceiling fans*
- *open washing machines, dryers, refrigerators, freezers, ovens, or dishwashers*
- *open toilet bowls*
- *uncovered fish tanks*
- *leaded stained glass items or inlaid jewelry*
- *uncovered cooking pots on the stove*
- *crayons and permanent markers*
- *pesticides, rodent killers, and snail bait*
- *untended stove burners*
- *candles*
- *open trash cans*

Creating a happy environment means keeping your bird safe from the dangers found in today's modern homes. Because of their small size and delicate respiratory systems, birds are especially susceptible to household hazards. Common household items you would never consider dangerous to humans, dogs, or cats can quickly become life threatening to birds. Becoming aware of these potential perils will help prevent some common disasters from befalling your bird.

Wings and Toenails

Although it may surprise most people, the easiest way to prevent a host of emergencies is to keep your bird's wings and nails trimmed (see chapter 6, "Grooming"). Some of the most common tragedies involve birds flying into ceiling fans or other objects. Also, they can mistakenly land in boiling water, hot oil, or even a bowl of soup. By keeping the wings trimmed, you can prevent these accidents from happening. Also, long toenails can easily become snagged in carpet, cages, and toys, increasing the chance of injury to your bird.

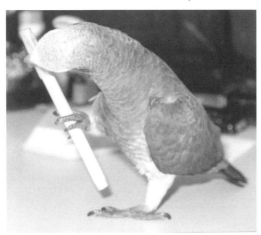

Birds are curious creatures. When given the opportunity, they will often chew on many potentially harmful objects, as this African grey is doing. Birds should not be left unsupervised in the home.

Open Windows and Doors

Birds can escape through open windows and doors. Some birds like perching on top of doors and have been injured when the door is closed. A bird can also be caught in a closing door while following an owner out of a room. Birds have also been known to fly into sliding glass doors, windows, and mirrors, perhaps not realizing they are solid objects.

Kitchen Hazards

Kitchens are the most dangerous room in the home for your bird. Hot stoves, boiling water and oil, cooking fumes, dishwater, and a battery of small kitchen appliances could all prove deadly to your bird. A bird's natural curiosity can get it into trouble from which it might not be able to get out. Therefore, birds should stay out of the kitchen. However, many bird owners continue to allow their pets into the kitchen. If you choose to allow your bird into the kitchen, become aware of these dangers and use good common sense.

Caution! The fumes from overheated nonstick cooking surfaces can be deadly to birds (see chapter 14, "Medical Emergencies"). These kinds of cooking surfaces should not be used in a home with birds. Be sure to read labels before buying and examine those items already in the home. If any products have nonstick surfaces, consider giving them to a birdless friend. Replace them with other types of cookware, such as aluminum, cast iron, stainless steel, or glass, that are not dangerous to birds.

150

The following items might have nonstick surfaces:

* *Pots and pans*
* *Cookie sheets*
* *Waffle irons and other appliances*
* *Drip pans for your stove*
* *Irons and ironing board covers*

Fumes

Because of the nature of the avian respiratory tract, birds are extremely sensitive to chemical fumes, smoke, and environmental toxins. After common kitchen odors, paint fumes, pesticides, and smoke are the most common problem areas.

Birds should be removed for at least 24 to 48 hours after any odor-producing chemicals are used in the home, or until all detectable smells have disappeared. For everyday household odors, air filters can be helpful.

Common Household Poisons

acetone	garden sprays	perfume
ammonia	gasoline	permanent wave solutions
antifreeze	gun cleaner	pesticides
ant syrup or paste	gunpowder	photographic solutions
arsenic	hair dyes	pine oil
aspirin	herbicides	plants
bathroom bowl cleaner	hexachlorophene *(in some soaps)*	prescription and non-
bleach	indelible markers	prescription drugs
boric acid	insecticides	rodenticides
camphophenique	iodine	rubbing alcohol
carbon tetrachloride	kerosene	shaving lotion
charcoal lighter	lighter fluid	shoe polish
clinitest tablets	linoleum *(contains lead salts)*	silver polish
copper and brass cleaners	lye	snail bait
corn and wart removers	matches	spot remover
crayons	model glue	spray starch
deodorants	mothballs	strychnine
detergents	muriatic acid	sulfuric acid
dishwasher detergents	mushrooms	suntan lotion
disinfectants	nail polish	super glue
drain cleaners	nail polish remover	turpentine
epoxy glue	nonstick cookware *(overheated	wax *(floor or furniture)*
fabric softeners	items emit toxic fumes)*	weed killers
firecrackers	oven cleaner	window cleaners
floor cleaners	paint, lead-based	wood preservatives
furniture polish	paint remover	
garbage toxins	paint thinner	

Drowning

Toilets, partially empty beverage glasses, and dishwater are all potential dangers to a curious bird. Some birds may try to drink from a toilet and fall in. Birds might also try to drink from a partially empty glass and fall in. They can actually drown in as little as half an inch of fluid. Take the necessary precautions.

Lead and zinc

Lead and zinc poisoning are real threats to birds. A bird's natural curiosity and strong beak make peeling and swallowing these soft metals very easy. Unfortunately, sources of lead and zinc can still be found in our homes today. See "Lead and Zinc Poisoning" in chapter 14 for more information on this subject.

Poisonous Plants

Many people do not realize that some of their favorite plants could be poisonous to their favorite pets. Once again, the natural curiosity of birds, their ability to fly and their need to chew makes any plant a potential target. Plants serve a very special function in our homes. They are pleasing to the eye. Spider plants in particular also do double duty as air cleaners, particularly in absorbing formaldehyde and other fumes (please don't let your birds chew on any plants that you've been using as air cleaners). Also make certain that you don't treat any of these bird-safe plants with insecticides or chemical fertilizers, as they won't be as safe as you'd like them to be.

In selecting plants for your home, make sure they are nonpoisonous. If needed, a nursery can identify plants already in your home. The following lists can help you select bird-safe plants for your home:

Plants Considered Harmful to Birds

Common name	Scientific name	Poisonous parts
Aconite	Aconitum sp.	all parts
Agapanthus	Agapanthus sp.	sap
Amaryllis	Amaryllidaceae	bulbs
American yew	Taxus canadensis	needles, seeds
Apple		seeds
Apricot		pits
Arrowhead vine	Syngonium podophyllum	leaves
Arum Lily	Arum sp.	all parts
Autumn crocus	Colchicum autumnale	all parts

Plants Considered Harmful to Birds (cont'd)

Avocado		pits, skin, flesh near pit
Azalea	*Rhododendron occidentale*	leaves
Balsam pear	*Memordica charantia*	seeds, outer fruit rind
Baneberry	*Actaia sp.*	berries, roots
Beans		all types if uncooked
Belladonna	*Atropa belladonna*	all parts
Bird of paradise	*Caesalpina gilliesii*	seeds
Bittersweet nightshade	*Solanum dulcamara*	immature fruit
Black locust	*Robinia pseudoacacia*	bark, sprouts, foliage
Blue-green algae	*Schizophycaea sp.*	some forms toxic
Boxwood	*Buxus sempervirens*	leaves, stems
Buckthorn	*Rhamnus sp.*	fruit, bark
Buttercup	*Ranunculus sp.*	sap, bulbs
Caladium	*Caladium sp.*	leaves
Calla lily	*Zantedeschia aethiopica*	leaves
Candelabra cactus	*Euphorbia lactea*	sap
Castor bean	*Ricinus communis*	beans, leaves
Chalice vine	*Solandra sp.*	all parts
Cherry		bark, twigs, leaves, pits
Chinese evergreen	*Aglaonema modestum*	all parts
Christmas candle	*Pedilanthus tithymaloides*	sap
Chrysanthemum	*Chrysanthemum sp.*	leaves, stems, flowers
Clematis	*Clematis sp.*	all parts
Coral plant	*Jatropha multifida*	seeds
Cowslip	*Caltha polustris*	all parts
Croton	*Codiaeum sp.*	sap
Crown of thorns	*Euphorbia milii*	sap
Daffodil	*Narcissus sp.*	bulbs
Daphne	*Daphne sp.*	berries
Datura	*Datura sp.*	berries
Deadly amanita	*Amanita muscaria*	all parts
Death camas	*Zygadenis elegans*	all parts
Delphinium	*Delphinium sp.*	all parts
Devil's ivy	*Epipremnum aureum*	all parts
Dieffenbachia	*Dieffenbachia picta*	leaves
Eggplant	*Solanaceae sp.*	all parts but fruit
Elephant's ear	*Colocasis sp.*	leaves, stem
English ivy	*Ilex aquafolium*	berries, leaves
English yew	*Taxus baccata*	needles, seeds
Euonymus	*Euonymus sp.*	all parts
False henbane	*Veratrum woodii*	all parts

153

Plants Considered Harmful to Birds (cont'd)

Flamingo flower	*Anthurium sp.*	leaves, stems
Foxglove	*Digitalis purpurea*	leaves, seeds
Golden chain	*Laburnum anagyroides*	all parts, esp. (laburnum) seeds
Hemlock, poison	*Conium sp.*	all parts, esp. roots and seeds
Hemlock, water	*Conium sp.*	all parts, esp. roots and seeds
Henbane	*Hyocyanamus niger*	seeds
Holly	*Ilex sp.*	berries
Horse chestnut	*Aesculus sp.*	nuts, twigs
Hyacinth	*Hyancinthinus orientalis*	bulbs
Hydrangea	*Hydrangea sp.*	flower bud
Iris (blue flag)	*Iris sp.*	bulbs
Ivy	*Hedera sp.*	leaves, berries
Jack-in-the-pulpit	*Arisaema triphyllum*	all parts
Japanese yew	*Taxus cuspidata*	needles, seeds
Java bean (lima bean)	*Phaseolus lunatus*	uncooked beans
Jerusalem cherry	*Solanum pseudocapsicum*	berries
Jimsonweed	*Datura sp.*	leaves, seeds
Juniper	*Juniperus virginiana*	needles, stems, berries
Lantana	*Lantana sp.*	immature berries
Larkspur	*Delphinium sp.*	all parts
Laurel	*Kalmia, Ledum, Rhododendron sp.*	all parts
Lily	*Lilium sp.*	bulbs
Lily of the valley	*Convallaria majalis*	all parts, inc. water in which flowers have been kept
Lobelia	*Lobelia sp.*	all parts
Locoweed	*Astragalus mollissimus*	all parts
Lords and ladies	*Arum sp.*	all parts
Marijuana	*Cannabis sativa*	leaves
Mayapple	*Podophyllum sp.*	all parts except fruit
Mescal bean	*Sophora sp.*	seeds
Mistletoe	*Santalales sp.*	berries
Mock orange	*Poncirus sp.*	fruit
Monkshood	*Aconitum sp.*	all parts
Morning glory	*Ipomoea sp.*	all parts
Narcissus	*Narcissus sp.*	bulbs
Nightshades	*Solanum sp.*	berries, leaves

Plants Considered Harmful to Birds (cont'd)

Oleander	*Nerium oleander*	leaves, nectar, branches
Parlor ivy	*Senecio sp.*	all parts
Peach		pits
Pencil tree	*Euphorbia tirucalli*	sap
Philodendron	*Philodendron sp.*	leaves, stems
Poinsettia	*Euphorbia pulcherrima*	leaves, flowers
Poison ivy	*Toxicodendron radicans*	sap
Poison oak	*Toxicodendron quercifolium*	sap
Poison sumac	*Toxicodendron vernix*	sap
Pokeweed	*Phytolacca americans*	leaves, roots, unripe berries
Potato	*Solanum tuberosum*	eyes, new shoots
Pothos	*Epipremnum aureum*	all parts
Privet	*Ligustrum volgare*	all parts, inc. berries
Ranunculus	*Ranunculus sp.*	sap
Rhododendron	*Rhododendron sp.*	all parts
Rhubarb	*Rheum rhaponticum*	leaves
Rosary pea	*Abrus precatorius*	seeds (seeds imported illegally to make necklaces and rosaries)
Skunk cabbage	*Symplocarpus foetidus*	all parts
Snowdrop	*Orinthogalum unbellatum*	all parts, esp. buds
Snow on the mountain (ghostweed)	*Euphorbia marginata*	all parts
Spindle tree	*Euonymus japonica*	all parts
Split leaf philodendron	*Monstera deliciosa*	all parts
Sweet pea	*Lathyrus latifolius*	seeds and fruit
Tobacco	*Nicotinia sp.*	leaves
Umbrella plant	*Cyperus alternifolius*	leaves
Virginia creeper	*Pathenocissus quinquefolia*	sap
Western yew	*Taxus breviflora*	needles, seeds
Wisteria	*Wisteria sp.*	all parts
Xanthosoma	*Xanthosoma sp.*	leaves
Yam bean	*Pachyrhizus erosis*	roots, immature pods
Yellow jessamine	*Gelsemium sempervirens*	flowers

Safe Plants for the Home

Acacia
African violet
Almond
Aloe
Aluminum plant
Arbutus
Ash
Aspen
Autumn olive
Baby's tears
Bamboo
Barberry
Bayberry
Beech
Begonia
Birch
Bladdernut
Bloodleaf
Blueberry
Bougainvillea
Bromeliads
Burro's tail
Cactus: Mostly nontoxic except for pencil cactus, peyote/mescaline, candelabra cactus
Camellia
Chickweed
Cissus (kangaroo vine)
Citrus (any)
Clematis
Coleus
Comfrey
Cotoneaster
Cottonwood
Crab apple
Creeping charlie
Creeping jenny
Dandelion
Dogwood
Dracaena varieties: corn plant, dragon tree, gold dust, red-margined

Elm
Emerald ripple peperomia
Eucalyptus
False aralia
Ferns: ball, bird's nest, Boston, brake, button, deer's foot, dish, elk's horn, Fiji, lomaria, maidenhair, mother, polypody, ribbon, squirrel's foot, staghorn, sword
Figs: creeping, rubber, fiddle leaf, laurel leaf, weeping
Fir: balsam, douglas, sub-alpine, white
Forsythia
Fuchsia
Giant white inch plant
Goldfish plant
Grape ivy
Grape mountain
Grape vine
Guava
Hawthorne
Hens & chickens
Hibiscus
Huckleberry
Jade plant
Kalanchoe
Larch
Lipstick plant
Madagascar dragon
Madagascar jasmine
Madagascar lace plant
Madrona
Magnolia
Mango
Manzanita
Marigold
Maternity plant
Monkey plant
Moon magic
Mother of pearls
Mountain ash

Safe Plants for the Home

Nasturtium
Nectarine
Nerve plant
Norfolk island pine
Oregano
Painted needle
Palms: areca, bamboo fern,
butterfly cane, date, European
fan, fishtail, golden feather,
howeia, kentia, lady,
Madagascar, miniature fan,
parlor, Phoenix, pygmy date,
robelein lady, sago, sentry,
wine
Papaya
Peacock plant
Pear
Pepperomia
Petunia
Piggyback begonia
Piggyback plant
Pilea
Pine
Pink polka dot plant
Pittosporum
Plectranthus
Plum
Polygonum baldschuanicum
Poplar
Prune
Purple passion
Purple tiger
Raspberry
Rose
Rosemary
Rubus odoratus
Russian vine
Sassafras
Sedum
Sensitive plant
Snowberry
Spider plant
Spruce
(black, Norway, red, white)

Swedish ivy
Tahitian bridal veil
Thistle
Thurlow
Thyme
Ti plant
Velvet plant
Wandering jew
Warneckei
Wax plant
White clover
White poplar
Willow
Yucca
Zebra plant

Temperature and Humidity

Most birds are from tropical environments where the temperature is always warm and the humidity is high. Few areas in the Northern Hemisphere can duplicate these conditions. Fortunately for us, most birds will still thrive in conditions different from their natural habitats.

Many birds are kept in outdoor aviaries year-round without any noticeable problems. Most pet birds are kept indoors with relatively little temperature variation. Birds should be kept warm--68 to 75 degrees Fahrenheit is ideal. However, most will do fine in the 60- to 90-degree range. Temperatures above 90 degrees may be dangerous, especially if birds are kept in direct sunlight. It is very important that any temperature changes in your bird's environment be made *gradually*. Rapid temperature change can cause problems for birds maintained in a controlled environment.

Heating a bird's environment is a necessity in many areas of the country, and doing so safely is as important for the humans involved as it is for the birds. If any type of heating is going to be used, be aware of potential fire hazards.

The sun's rays can be used for heating. Be careful, though, of the magnifying effects a window can have. On a hot day, birds can become overheated in a cage kept too close to a window. You can use an electric space heater, but be careful of the fire hazard. Use them only in areas that are free from clutter. Even falling bird dust and feathers over a long period of time could build up on the heater and cause a potential fire hazard. Also make sure to protect the power cord from a curious bird's beak to prevent your bird from being injured.

Infrared heat lamps are commonly used to provide accessory heat for birds. Use the 250-watt amber bulbs. This color is more relaxing than others and allows the bird to sleep at night. Beware, these lamps get very hot, so the light fixture must be properly rated to accept these high-wattage bulbs. Place the fixture two to six feet away from your bird's cage. Do not allow anything to come in contact with the bulb or the fixture. Also, make sure the fixture is secure and won't fall over.

Use heating pads with extreme caution. Birds can chew on them or be burned by them. They are not designed to be used with birds, so take precautions against both injury to your bird and a fire hazard to your home. Make sure the bird's beak cannot reach the pad. Place the pad on the side of the cage, not the bottom, to allow room in the cage for the bird to move away from the pad if it becomes too warm. Heating pads work best with smaller species, such as budgies. Wood-burning stoves and kerosene heaters require oxygen to burn. Therefore, for the safety of you and your bird, always keep a window open slightly when using this type of heating. Smoke and fumes can also pose a risk.

You can place a thermometer near the cage to accurately monitor the temperature. Also, during the winter, when windows are usually kept closed, you can use an air filter. In areas with extended periods of darkness, a special ultraviolet light available at pet stores can provide some benefits similar to sunlight. Follow the manufacturer's instructions regarding bulb replacement and remember these lights are not designed to replace sunlight for pet birds.

Humidity is very important for your bird--the higher the better. In a dry environment, spraying and bathing your bird frequently is highly recommended.

Fire/Disaster Preparedness

No one likes to think about calamities. However, birds are more susceptible to smoke from a fire than any other animal. Quick response is essential in an emergency if birds are to be saved. So, in addition to the emergency fire plan you have for your family, create one for your birds as well. Keep the following in mind when making you bird-emergency fire plan:

- *Can the cage be picked up and carried to safety?*
- *Does it have wheels that work?*
- *Is there a clear exit path from the house for a large cage?*
- *Can the bird be removed from its cage if disaster strikes?*
- *If so, where would it be put for safekeeping?*

Have an emergency kit for your bird. It will be different from a standard first-aid kit because the emergency kit would contain supplies for coping with a natural disaster. Imagine a situation in which you would be unable to visit your favorite pet store for a week to ten days and pack your emergency kit accordingly. Include items such as nonperishable food and water, extra food and water dishes, and a towel. These can be stored in a small carrier that can house your bird and be used for emergency transport.

Quick response is necessary during a disaster. Practice your family's plan on a regular basis. Everyone in the family should know what to do with your feathered friend and other pets in the event of a fire, earthquake, hurricane, tornado, or other natural disaster.

Stolen and Lost Birds

With a little luck and careful planning, you will never experience the heartache of losing a bird. Never forget, it can happen to even the most conscientious owner.

To keep from losing your feathered friend, its wings should always be properly trimmed (see chapter 6, "Grooming"). Your bird also should be microchipped for identification purposes. This procedure will be discussed later in this chapter in the section, "Bird Identification."

However, if your bird does manage to escape, keep calm and use its personality to your full advantage. First, always try to keep your bird in sight, or at least note the direction in which it's traveling. Use a favorite food, toy, companion bird, whistle, song, or anything you can think of to attract your bird's attention. If your escaped bird is in a tree, slowly and calmly try coaxing it down. If that's not possible, sometimes wetting its feathers with a hose will prevent it from being able to fly. Be careful, however; this effort could also cause the bird to become frightened and fly away.

Put your bird's cage outside where the bird might see it. If you have another bird in the home, put it outside, too. (Make sure the second bird's cage is secure before putting it outside or you'll have two escapees on your hands.) The sight and sound of another familiar bird might entice your bird home. Immediately notify neighbors of the loss. Post signs and place a lost bird ad in your local newspaper. Alert veterinary hospitals and animal shelters in your neighborhood in case someone brings your bird to one of them. Finally, don't give up. Theft of a bird is more of a problem for bird breeders than for owners of single pet birds. It is also most likely to occur with more expensive birds, such as macaws or cockatoos. If starting a breeding program or amassing a large collection of birds is in your plans, keep these safeguards in mind:

• Never brag about your birds to strangers. Make sure the background noise on your answering machine doesn't advertise your birds.
• When purchasing bird supplies from strangers, consider paying cash. Checks have your name and address on them.
• Never leave your bird unattended. It only takes seconds for a thief to strike.
• Take pictures or make a video recording of your bird; record its voice and any words or sayings it knows. Also, have all your birds microchipped to make identification easier.

Bird Identification

Bird owners can use two methods to positively iden- tify a bird that is lost or stolen. First, you can have a small microchip implanted under the bird's skin. This microchip, which contains an identification number, remains with your bird for life. If the bird is ever lost

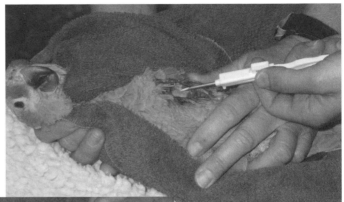

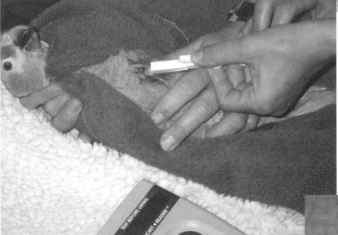

For permanent identi- fication, a tiny microchip will be implanted beneath the skin of this Amazon parrot. The microchip is in the lumen of the needle.

The needle has been inserted beneath the skin and the injecting device will implant the tiny microchip into the muscle.

or stolen, positive identification can be made easily and quickly. Microchips are highly recommended for larger birds.

Another method to help with identification involves chromosome "mapping" of a bird's blood. This process is most commonly used for sex iden- tification. However, your bird's unique map can be stored in a registry. If your bird becomes lost, and a question of ownership arises, a drop of blood can be collected, from which a new map can be made and compared to the one on file. No two birds will ever have the same map. Therefore, iden- tical maps can prove ownership. This is a foolproof identification method.

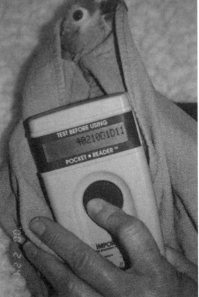

A close-up of the reading device dis- plays this bird's per- sonal ID number.

Travel Tips

Having pet birds is such a wonderful experience that many owners have not stopped to consider what to do with their birds when a trip out of town becomes necessary. This section will discuss the options available when traveling, with or without your bird.

The Decision:
To Travel with or without Your Bird

While many people would not consider leaving their pet in someone else's care, others would not consider taking their birds out into the real world. Many factors enter into the decision-making process. Below are many of the points to consider:

• Is your bird in good health? Do not travel with a sick bird.
• Is your bird acclimated to travel? If not, start with short trips in the car to help with confinement and motion problems.
• Do you have a travel cage or carrier for your bird? Airlines have special requirements. Call them for details.
• Does your destination allow birds? Some resorts and foreign countries do not allow pet birds to be brought in.
• Are the changes in travel and destination temperatures safe?
• Is a health certificate required? When leaving the state or country or traveling by air, an exam by a veterinarian is required to certify your bird's health. These exams are usually required within seven to ten days prior to departure. Check with airlines, embassies, or other governmental agencies. This is very important because laws change frequently.
•   Check with your destination's agricultural laws. Some types of birds are actually legally banned from some areas because of possible agricultural damage in the event of escape.

As can readily be inferred from the above, traveling with a bird can be very complicated. Unfortunately, most owners are not even aware that travel restrictions apply. Frequently, these details are never addressed until the last minute or a personal emergency arises. Remember, everyone who owns birds will have to leave home at some time or another. Will your bird stay at home or travel with you? Regardless of your decision, advance planning is essential!

Leaving "Birdie" Home

Many owners feel very comfortable leaving their birds in the hands of someone competent while they are away. They can choose to have someone come into the home to care for the bird, or they can take the bird to a boarding facility while they are away.

In-Home Care

In-home care can be provided by friends, relatives, neighbors, or a professional pet-sitting service. Most importantly, the bird-sitter must be responsible and trustworthy--any knowledge of birds they possess is an added bonus. When your bird stays at home while you travel, it retains the security of being in familiar surroundings. Everything basically stays the same; i.e., the cage, room, sights, and smells. However, the bird's routine will change a little since a different person will be feeding, cleaning up after, and entertaining your feathered friend. Your bird will also not be exposed to other birds. Another advantage of bird-sitters is that you do not have to leave your home vacant while you travel. Bird-sitters can live full-time in your home or stop by once or twice a day to feed, clean up after, and play with your bird.

Here are a few tips on leaving your bird with a sitter:
1. Make sure to leave explicit written instructions:
   •Feeding, cleaning, and entertainment guidelines
   •The bird's special likes and dislikes
   •Phone numbers of your avian veterinarian, bird store, and trusted, knowledgeable bird person
   •Phone number, if possible, where you can be reached
2. Stock up on all necessary supplies.
3. Consider leaving the cage locked, but be sure to leave the key and maybe a spare one, too!
4. Introduce the "bird-sitter" to your bird, home, and general routines *before* leaving.

Bird Boarding

Boarding your bird can be a way of receiving expert care. Most importantly, people who are knowledgeable about birds should be on the facility's staff. Boarding options include boarding kennels, veterinary hospitals, bird specialty stores, and specialized bird boarding and training facilities.

Many birds are stimulated by seeing other birds in the same environment. Listening to other birds may help with their talking ability. Many owners think their birds are happier getting out of the house once or twice a year.

Here are some things to keep in mind if you are thinking about boarding your bird:

- A veterinary checkup and a few diagnostic tests may be required *prior* to boarding.
- Ask about caging availability--do you need to bring a cage, or will one be provided?
- Make sure to leave explicit written directions regarding the needs of your bird.
- Ask about the foods the establishment uses and, if needed, bring your bird's regular food preferences.
- Ask about accessories, such as toys and cage covers. Do you need to bring these from home, or will they be pro vided?

Remember, it is a major responsibility for someone to care for your bird. Choose carefully.

Traveling with "Birdie"

In general, birds travel very well. However, some advance planning and preparation are necessary. For flying or driving across state lines or international borders with your bird, a veterinary-signed health certificate issued within seven to 10 days of departure is usually required.

By Car

This is certainly the least complicated way to travel. It's safest to keep the bird caged during the drive--either in its regular cage, if it fits in your vehicle, or in a travel carrier. The bird should be able to stand up, turn around and ideally extend its wings. Remove any hanging toys or swings that could injure the bird. Strap the cage to the seat with the seat belt. Bring along adequate food and a container of water for the journey. Fruit is also a good water source when traveling.

Be prepared for weather changes. A squirt bottle filled with water can help cool off a bird on a hot day. Hotel reservations should be made in advance, and be sure to ask if birds are welcome. Please be courteous and clean so other pets will be welcome in the future. Try to avoid leaving birds unattended in cars. Remember they are easy to steal. Birds left in closed cars may be more prone to heatstroke on hot days, and they could suffer from temperature extremes on cold days.

Some birds may experience signs of car sickness, such as regurgitation of food. While medications to prevent this problem are not recommended, withholding food before a short trip may help. Also, try covering the carrier or cage.
Remember, too, that birds will travel better in a smooth-riding motor home.

Do not place cages on the floor of the car. Toxic fumes and increased heat from the engine will be more concentrated in this confined area. In addition, smoking in the close confines of a car should be avoided.

Transport carriers are needed if the bird's cage is too large to be moved easily. Many different types of carriers can be used, as demonstrated here. Remember, cardboard and soft woods may not be practical for larger parrots.

By Train or Bus

As of this writing, pets are not allowed on major U.S. train and bus lines. While this may be the easiest way for people to travel, it is, unfortunately, the most complicated for pets. Advance planning is absolutely essential, especially in these days of heightened airline security. You must contact airlines ahead of time to find out their policy on transporting birds. Believe it or not, airline policies can even vary depending upon the person providing the information. Therefore, keep a record of the employee you spoke with and the date and time of your call.

Limitations and restrictions vary with each airline. Some allow under-the-seat carriers, while others allow only baggage compartment travel for pets. Specific requirements are in place regarding the size of the carrier. In addition, expect an extra charge for pets. Airlines also have different requirements for written health certificates.

165

One major obstacle in transporting birds by air is the temperature requirements. Some airlines will not accept pets in the baggage compartment if the outside temperature at any stopover or final destination is lower than 40 degrees Fahrenheit or higher than 80 degrees Fahrenheit. Unless pets can travel in the passenger cabin, this weather policy can be a problem. Remember, however, these policies are for the pet's benefit.

The carrier should contain food and little, if any, water. Oranges, apples, or other fruit can help provide needed fluids during flight. Consider lining the carrier with indoor/outdoor carpeting for insulation and padding. A perch should be positioned close to the floor and prevented from moving. Screws placed into the perch through the outside walls will hold it in place.

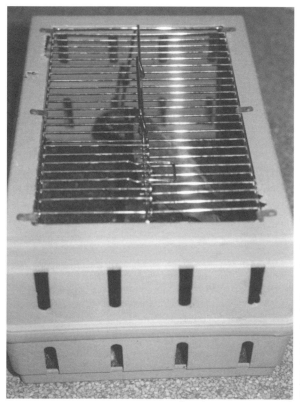

This type of transport carrier has been designed for "under-the-seat" airline travel.

Foreign Travel

If at all possible, avoid foreign travel with your bird. The obstacles to overcome can be overwhelming! First of all, each country has its own specific requirements. To make matters worse, this information can be very difficult to obtain. Considerable paperwork, government involvement and a number of different fees are just some of the problems associated with overseas travel. If traveling to a foreign country with a bird is essential, start planning up to seven months in advance so you can make all the arrangements.

First, contact the foreign embassy of the country or countries of your destination. Ask how to obtain the information on the requirements for bringing pet birds into the country. This will often require numerous phone calls or letters. As with flying, the information can be difficult to obtain and often varies from one person to another, so keep track of the names of the people to whom you speak. Because of the frequently changing rules around the world, the U.S. Department of Agriculture (USDA) cannot even provide much current information. They will, however, try to help when requested.

Once you are familiar with the country's regulations, you must contact the airline you are using for their specific requirements. Arrangements must also be made with a veterinarian specially licensed to issue foreign health certificates. The certificate must be sent to a district office of the USDA for an official U.S. government seal of approval. Another difficulty arises because airlines require health certificates to be issued only up to seven to ten days in advance. So, your receipt of all paperwork must go smoothly and quickly or problems could arise.

Immediately before returning to the United States, contact the USDA to obtain all the current requirements for bringing your bird back into this country. You will need to obtain another health certificate. Pet birds are only allowed into the United States through certain ports of entry (see list later in this chapter), and all birds entering the country will need to be quarantined.

General Advice For Traveling

- Plan ahead!
- Travel with a health certificate.
- Get wings and nails trimmed prior to leaving.
- Remove toys and swings from the cage to prevent injury.
- Use a seat belt to secure the cage when traveling by car.
- Never leave your bird unattended.
- Play the bird's favorite music if possible.
- Carry a spray bottle of water during hot weather.
- Keep fresh foods in a cooler with ice.
- Carry a container of water.
- Start preparing months in advance for international travel!
- Obtain a recommendation for an avian veterinarian in your destination area.

Bird Owner's Travel Checklist
The following recommendations will help make traveling easier and more enjoyable for you and your bird:

- Compile a list of avian veterinarians and/or bird club contacts along your route.
- Assemble or buy a prepackaged bird first-aid kit and take it with you.
- Take along some waterless antibacterial hand cleaner so you can wash when you're away from a water source.
- Have styptic powder along for broken nails, blood feathers, or beaks.
- Keep a spray bottle of water handy to cool down your bird during the day.
- Carry a cooler of your bird's favorite fresh foods.
- Bring ample water from home so your bird doesn't experience any digestive upsets during the trip.
- Provide your bird with a water bottle while traveling so it can drink while you're on the road.
- Bring along a supply of cage paper to make cleanup quick and easy.
- Bring along some of your bird's favorite toys to make the trip more enjoyable.
- Have a light-colored sheet or other cage cover available to cover your bird's travel carrier or cage.

Addresses and Phone Numbers
You May Find Helpful

Pet birds must enter the United States through one of the following ports of entry:

(Please Note: These locations, addresses and phone numbers are subject to change)

Honolulu, HI: Port Veterinarian,

3375 Koapaka St., Suite H420, Honolulu, HI
96819; (808) 861-8560, fax (808) 861-8570

Los Angeles, CA: Port Veterinarian,

9680 S. La Cienega Blvd., Inglewood, CA 90301;
(310) 215-2352; fax (310) 215-1314
(All California reservations are made in Los Angeles.)

McAllen, TX: Port Veterinarian,

320 N. Main St., Room 135, McAllen, TX 78501;
(210) 687-8314; fax (210) 687-1267

Miami, FL: Port Veterinarian,

P.O. Box 660657, Miami Springs, FL 33266;
(305) 526-2926; fax (305) 526-2929

New York, NY: Port Veterinarian,
JFK International Airport,

Cargo Building 77, Room 116, Jamaica, NY 11430; (718) 553-
1727; fax (718) 553-7543

San Ysidro, CA: Port Veterinarian,

P.O. Box 126, San Ysidro, CA 92073;
(310) 215-2352; fax (310) 215-1314
(All California reservations are made in Los Angeles.)

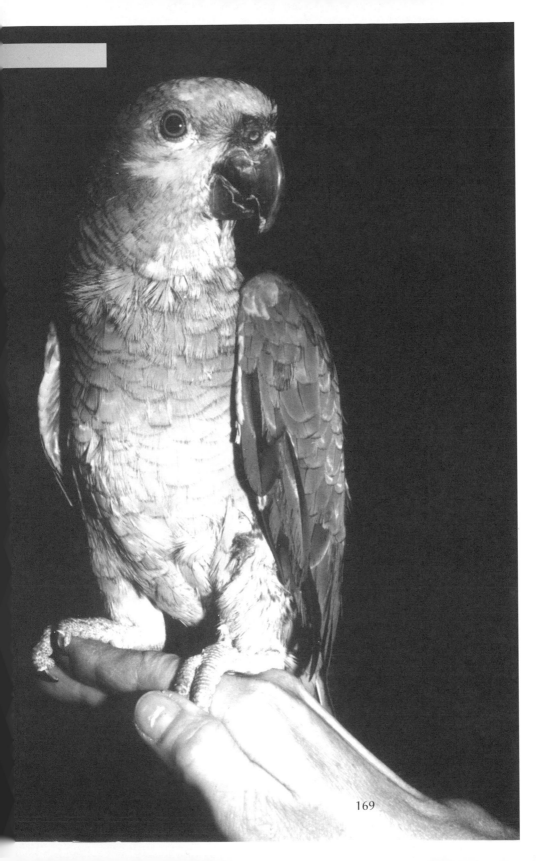

169

Chapter 8

The Well-Behaved Parrot

Helping to Create a Happy, Loving Pet

Pet bird behavior is a growing field of interest for both bird owners and avian professionals. During the past 20 years, the emphasis in pet bird care has shifted from basic maintenance to a desire to provide the best life possible for our feathered friends. To do this, we need to understand why pet birds behave in the manner they do. *This section isn't meant to be the definitive work on avian behavior; rather it is a summary of the work of experts and an overview of basic information. For more detailed information on avian behavior, consult with your avian veterinarian or a behavior consultant.*
The study and understanding of bird behavior is a constantly evolving process. It involves looking at the world from the bird's point of view. New books and videos on bird behavior are constantly appearing on the market. Loving bird owners need to evaluate the worth of these products by asking the following questions:
*   Does it make sense?
*   Is it *harmful* to the bird?
It is always a good idea to consult with an avian veterinarian for avian behavior issues about which you are not sure or have concerns.

Why Develop a Relationship with a Bird?

As a bird owner, you may wonder why it's important to spend the time and energy to develop a loving, trusting relationship with your bird. The answer is if you don't your bird will develop undesirable behaviors. When that occurs, owners frequently tire of their pet and start seeking a new home for it.

Unlike most cats and dogs, the average pet parrot will live in several homes over the course of its lifetime. If bird owners understand their birds' behavior and learn how to teach their birds to be well-behaved members of the family, there would be no need to get rid of them, and birds wouldn't be rehomed as often as they are.

Reasons People Give Up Pet Birds
*   New spouse/significant other
*   New baby
*   New job
*   Have to move
*   Aging/poor health
*   Screaming
*   Biting

How do we achieve this ideal of well-behaved parrots? By learning what are realistic expectations for a pet bird and by learning to establish boundaries and guidelines for a companion bird. Just as parents teach their children how to behave, bird owners must teach their pets to do the same. By doing this, a life-long loving, trusting relationship will develop between bird and owner.

Some birds lose their homes when their owners lose interest in them. Tiki the cockatoo was placed with a bird rescue group shortly after her owners brought their first child home from the hospital. (Parrot Education and Adoption Center/Viewpoint Photography)

Normal Parrot Behavior

Pet bird behavior is a term broad enough to encompass a wide range of species and corresponding personality types. We're going to focus on parrot behavior because parrots are the most commonly kept pet birds. Owners of canaries, finches, and softbills can find behavior information on their pets in the box, "Normal Canary, Finch and Softbill Behavior" in this chapter.

Let's look at what normal parrots do all day. Normal healthy birds will be bright-eyed and alert. They will perch upright. Healthy parrots roam their cages and hang upside down from the top. They swing and climb. They are inquisitive and notice everything about their environment, and they frequently investigate their surroundings. Even subtle changes in the environment do not escape their attention.

Healthy parrots love to vocalize and to play. Normal, healthy parrots are very messy. They will throw their food, dunk their food, and hide their food.

They love to chew and tear things up.

Healthy parrots will stretch out their necks and wings and make themselves appear larger than they are. They love to flap their wings in a flying motion. They use their feet for a lot of activities, including scratching their heads, picking up and holding food while they eat, playing with toys, climbing and hanging upside down, playing games, and waving goodbye. Some birds use their feet to pick a lock on a cage!

Parrots shake and ruffle their feathers occasionally. They shower and take baths. Most birds love to play in their water. Since most parrots are from tropical regions, humidity and water play a vital role in their well-being. They are taught to bathe by their parents at a very early age. Parents also teach their offspring how to properly preen their feathers. Under normal conditions, minimal time and energy are spent on this activity, and no damage is done to the feathers, feather shafts, or skin. They use the secretions from their uropygial gland (the preening gland) at the base of the tail to assist in conditioning their feathers.

In addition to eating, a healthy pet parrot uses its beak for balance, to hang from a branch, to make a nest, to preen feathers (or their owners' eyelashes), and to explore their world. Frequently, a parrot will reach for a branch or a finger with its beak to test its stability as a perch. An uninformed owner will jerk his or her hand back after misinterpreting this action as aggression or an attempt to bite. This leaves the bird feeling insecure, and the next time, it may hold on tighter to keep the finger from moving away until the bird is on board.

Preening is an important part of a bird's daily routine. This African grey is grooming its tail feathers. (Animal Environments)

Healthy parrots are naturally noisy. The jungle is a very noisy place. The only time the jungle is quiet is when predators are around. Birds coo, talk, chirp, sing, and scream. They are usually more vocal in the early morning and at dusk. Don't expect a bird to sit quietly around the house all day. It won't. If it does, it could be a sick bird.

Abnormal Behaviors

Most truly abnormal behaviors indicate illness. They include sitting at the bottom of the cage (not just exploring the cage bottom or chewing on papers), being extremely quiet, perching hunched over, excessive fluffing, dull eyes, sleeping all the time, loss of appetite, limping, droopy wings, and weakness. Weakness may be displayed by an inability to grasp its perch.

(Please read chapter 14, "Medical Emergencies," and chapter 15, "Medical Problems," for more details.)

Other abnormal behaviors may or may not be signs of an illness. Some of these behaviors involve the feathers. Abnormal behaviors involving the feathers include:

Excessive preening: The bird spends a very large percentage of its time preening its feathers.

Feather picking: The bird actually pulls out its feathers rather than preening them. These can be down feathers, contour feathers, flight feathers, or any other feathers it can

This blue-and-gold macaw is quite ill. Notice its fluffed-up appearance and its small droppings. Small droppings with minimal or no stool suggest that the bird is not eating.

Some birds that pick their feathers are placed in collars to give their feathers a chance to regrow. This cockatoo's collar shows signs of the bird chewing on it, which is preferable to the bird chewing on its feathers.

reach with its beak. Head and upper neck feathers will always be spared since the bird cannot reach these areas. If its head is bald, another bird is doing the picking or there is a medical problem.

Feather chewing: The bird doesn't pull the feathers out but chews on them. The feathers will appear shredded and tattered. The wing feathers are frequently the sites of attention in this scenario.

Other abnormal behaviors that may or may not be a sign of illness include:

Notice this cockatoo's aggressive stance, raised crest, and slightly fluffed feathers. He is defending his cage against his owner's daughter, whom he perceives as a momentary threat.

Extreme cage territoriality: All birds are territorial to some extent about their cages. However, a bird that absolutely will not let anyone near its cage or put a hand in its cage is displaying abnormal behavior.

Constant screaming: All birds are noisy and scream at some time or another. However, a normal bird does not scream constantly at anything and everything.

Sudden and overt aggression: Any sudden personality change is a cause for concern, especially aggression.

Phobias: A phobia is a deep-seated, unreasonable fear of something.

Biting: Birds are not biters by nature. They are taught to bite. Biting may be indicative of mistrust, fear, invasion of privacy, raging hormones or simply to see and hear the reaction of the person being bitten.

All the behaviors listed above may be signs of illness. They may also indicate a behavior problem. Since birds are wild, non-domesticated creatures, they are genetically programmed to show no sign of weakness. By the time they start acting sick, they are usually very sick. At the first sign of these or any abnormal behaviors, a bird owner should take his or her bird to an avian veterinarian for a complete examination.

Once a physical condition is ruled out, then a bird owner can seek the help of a behavior consultant. The problem may be an indication of the onset of sexual maturity, the result of past history, environment, or any number of reasons.

Weaning and Fledging Baby Birds

Many bird behavior problems begin as a result of the bird not being appropriately weaned or fledged. In the wild, a baby bird

Avian behaviorists teach classes in bird behavior and offer one-on-one consultations with pet bird owners. Some behaviorists have a background in avian veterinary medicine, while others are long-time bird owners.

These birds and owners have graduated from an avian behavior class. Avian veterinary clinics and bird specialty stores are beginning to offer behavior seminars and classes for their clients so the owners can better understand their pets' behavior.

is not weaned by its parents until it is fully fledged (has all its feathers), can fly well, and is capable of gathering its own food. Yet in captivity, some breeders, pet stores, and bird marts wean and sell babies that not only can't fly, they don't even have all their feathers. Birds acquired after being fully weaned are not only happier and more well-adjusted, they make better pets in the end.

As for weaning, there are many methods from which to choose. One highly regarded method is Phoebe Greene Linden's "Abundance Weaning[a]." Abundance weaning emphasizes feeding the bird when it is hungry, rather than on a human schedule. Linden also recommends feeding warm, wet food chunks, rather than just liquid formula because parent birds don't feed formula to their chicks. Some species, especially African greys, require hand feeding of warm, wet food for a long time past normal recommended weaning schedules. Any bird that is shy or insecure may require a lengthier weaning period. Even as an adult, many birds benefit from occasional hand feedings of warm, wet food. This is especially necessary during times of high stress or illness.

As consumers, we not only have a right, but a responsibility to demand birds that have been appropriately weaned and fledged. Until we make this demand and follow through with our pocketbooks, some breeders, pet stores, and bird marts will continue to sell insecure, wary, emotionally immature birds to unsuspecting buyers.

Juvenile Behaviors

Young birds exhibit many endearing behaviors. They beg for food, they explore everything with their beaks, and they are clumsy. Most owners adore their birds at this stage and spend a lot of time cuddling them and fussing over them. Some particularly clever birds learn how to exploit their situations using these behaviors, so owners have to learn to determine when the behaviors are genuine and when a bird is trying to work a situation to its advantage.

Many first-time owners with good intentions create behavioral problems in their baby parrots by spoiling them. Because the chicks are so cute and cuddly and helpless, owners often rush to their baby parrot each time the chick screams. In other cases, the owners hold their bird all the time and

The Importance of Flight
While clipping birds' wings is recommended, don't do it until they have learned to fly!

Learning to fly is a critical aspect of a normal, healthy, well-adjusted companion parrot. When a bird learns to fly, it learns to think. While flying, a bird has to evaluate its surroundings, distinguish appropriate landing sites, and learn how to bank (turn around or turn a corner while in flight). These necessary components of healthy development increase a bird's confidence. Just as children gain confidence when they learn to walk, so a bird gains confidence when it learns to fly. Only after a bird can confidently land, avoid obstacles in flight, and turn a corner in flight should its wings be clipped.

When it is time to clip the wings, you should begin doing so gradually, a few feathers at a time. Don't let the bird go from full flight to no flight all at once. If this happens, the bird may injure itself crash landing off a perch.

Allowing a bird to learn to fly requires a tremendous amount of diligence to prevent injuries! Prior to a flight lesson, drapes should be closed, mirrors covered, doors closed securely and ceiling fans turned off. Ideally, flight lessons should be in a large room with little or no furniture. All flight lessons must be *directly supervised.*

never encourage the bird to spend time by itself. These owners also do not teach the baby parrot to entertain itself, so the bird doesn't learn how to play. Finally, some owners spend every waking hour with their young bird. Then, the bird grows up and seems to resent its owner for trying to live a life in which the bird is not the center of attention. In all of these situations, the potential exists for creating spoiled, uncontrollable feathered monsters that will have behavioral problems.

To prevent this from happening, an owner should offer a baby parrot a balance of cuddling, attention, and care, as well as lessons in being independent, from the time the bird comes home. Provide it with a safe, secure home, plenty of interesting, nourishing food, and lots of clean water. Make sure it has the chance to take naps and get enough sleep. Take it to the veterinarian regularly to ensure its good health, and keep its nails and wings trimmed for its safety.

Check on a young parrot when it screams to make sure it isn't cold, hungry, or in danger, but don't rush to pick it up every time. Instead, occasionally pet the bird on the back and tell it it's a good, brave bird, or reward the bird by playing with it, feeding it a special treat by hand, showing it a new toy or by introducing it to its playgym. Be sure the parrot has adequate perching skills before it is allowed to sit on a playgym for any length of time.

As the bird grows up, its owner can reassure it when it is vocalizing with a simple, "I'm here. Are you being a good bird?" or some other comment that indicates that, although the owner has heard the bird's call, he or she isn't going to rush to its side after each vocalization. If the bird continues to vocalize, the owner should check on it because it could have tipped over its food or water bowl; it could have gotten its wing feathers stuck in its cage bars; or it could be in some other uncomfortable or potentially dangerous situation.

The Terrible Twos

You may have heard the phrase "the terrible twos" used in conjunction with the behavior of young children. Pet bird behaviorists also use the phrase to describe young parrots when they are around a year old. These behavioral changes can occur any time between the ages of six and 30 months, depending on the size of the parrot. Keep in mind that smaller birds mature more quickly than larger ones.

During this period, the parrot will vocalize and explore its territory more than ever before, and it may bite its owner and other humans deliberately. It will also challenge its position in the family, and it may frequently change its loyalties to the people in its family. The person who used to be the parrot's one and only best friend in the whole world may be shunned or chased away in the morning, only to be wooed back by nightfall. This is a very confusing time for the parrot, and it can make owners crazy, too, as the formerly well-behaved little bird seems to turn into a monster before their eyes.

It doesn't have to be this way. Yes, the young parrot is changing, but it doesn't have to become completely unmanageable. As a bird owner, you should start your bird on the road to self-sufficiency when it is young by teaching it the "up" and "down" commands and by encouraging the bird to play by itself. The young bird's adjustment to these behavioral changes will be less stressful than for birds who have had free rein and who have been spoiled rotten in the process. Still, there will be a period of adjustment as the parrot tries to figure out where it fits in the family flock.

In the wild, this is the time when a young parrot learns about its environment and its flock by exploring its world and testing its independence. It spends time away from its parents, but the young bird also wants to know where they are as it explores. In the home, a young bird will need attention and guidance from its owners as it explores its new home.

In the home "flock," a young parrot can test the limits of its environment and find its place in the family's pecking order by climbing, destroying toys, and flapping its clipped wings on a playgym or cage top. All these activities help a growing young parrot expend energy and work off its frustrations at growing up.

This period is a perfect time to start teaching the parrot to talk. In fact, the bird might surprise its owner one morning by saying "Hi!" or "How ya doin'?"

This is also the time to offer a wide variety of toys. Be sure to introduce each one carefully because young birds are a bit skittish about new things. By giving the bird several toys at a time, an owner allows it some control over its life by letting it choose the toy it wants to play with.

This is also the time to be sure the home is birdproofed because the bird will try to explore every inch of it. Take a few minutes to view things from the bird's point of view and put tempting items out of reach. By offering a safe environment and an appropriate selection of things to chew, owners can help ease the bird's transition through the terrible twos while, at the same time, reducing their own level of stress.

As a young bird enters this transitional period, owners need to be aware that some serious behavior problems--biting, screaming, feather picking--can take root if the parrot discovers that its owner will give it more attention (yelling at it, shaking a finger or fist at the bird, or paying attention to it when it's acting up) if it misbehaves than if it behaves. Owners must be careful not to fall into this trap because the bird will take every opportunity to test its owner's patience during this time. If an owner has laid the groundwork with the bird by teaching it the up and down commands and by encouraging it to entertain itself from time to time, he or she will survive this test.

If the bird will be spending long periods of time on its own during the day, an owner must be sure to pay attention to the bird when he or she is home. The owner must also provide entertaining and interesting things for the bird to do while its owner is away.

Everything Scares Me!

If a young bird suddenly displays a fear of absolutely everything, it is having an episode of phobic behavior. Although an owner may perceive no change in the household routine, the bird is reacting to changes within its maturing body. It is beginning to feel independent, but if it hasn't been taught how to explore its world safely, it will become phobic, preferring to stay in its cage all the time because the cage feels safe and secure.

If a bird displays an episode of phobic behavior, all is not lost. An owner can still help his or her pet learn how to explore its world safely. Take it to different rooms in the house and talk to it in a positive, upbeat tone. Tell your bird about its environment and reassure it that everything will be okay. Make sure the bird has time out of its cage so that it doesn't become either overly territorial about its cage or cagebound, both of which can cause additional problems later on. Most truly phobic birds, when let out of their cages, run under sofas or refrigerators where they pant in panic. If you believe that your bird has become chronically phobic, you should consult your avian veterinarian or an avian behaviorist as soon as possible to try and correct the problem.

Breeding Behaviors

All parrot owners eventually learn this lesson: Pet birds are influenced by their hormones. Some birds get through breeding season without harming themselves or their owners too badly, while other parrots bite, scream, or pick their feathers until their hormones subside.

When parrots reach sexual maturity and breeding season rolls around, many of them are motivated to mate. However, most birds are not set up to mate with other birds, so they try to mate with their owners, perches, toys, or other objects. If a bird mounts an object and rubs its vent against it, it's demonstrating mating behavior. Some birds cluck or honk while mating.

If a bird feels like mating, its owner is providing it with optimal care. Mating is an activity that birds do only when all conditions are right. There must be a sufficient, steady supply of food and water, the bird must be in good health, and it must feel comfortable and secure in its environment. Only healthy birds mate--sick birds don't have the strength or the energy for it.

Most birds, such as this umbrella cockatoo, prefer to step forward and slightly upward when perching on a hand or arm. (Bonnie Jay)

Developing and Fostering Life-Long Desirable Behaviors

While the causes of undesirable behavior are numerous, they usually share some common denominators. The following recommendations may help solve some avian behavior problems, or they can be used to prevent problems from occurring in the first instance.

Nurturing Guidance Training

Make sure your bird understands the up and down commands. To teach the up command, an owner should offer his or her finger and say, "up" or "step up." The bird should understand what is being asked right away, but if it doesn't, the owner can gently press a finger against its belly.

Teaching the down command is just as easy. The owner should say, "down" as he or she places the bird on its perch or in its cage. These two commands offer an owner control over his or her pet and should be used consistently. Use a firm, but loving, voice when practicing these commands. An owner is telling the bird to step up, *not asking* it to. This should be a fun exercise, not a discipline. Keep the exercise brief, but repeat it several times a day. Everyone in the household should work with the bird in this manner.

This African grey may be trying to perch on his owner's shoulder. To discourage dominant behavior, do not allow your bird to perch on your shoulder.

Make sure to practice the up and down commands in a "neutral room," which is any room other than the one your bird's cage is in. Have the bird step up and down onto a T-stand or the back of a chair. Once the bird is stepping up each and every time immediately, gradually move the perch out of the neutral room into the hallway. Continue moving the perch closer and closer to the cage. The object is for the bird to step up immediately, whenever and wherever the command is given, including in its cage.

This helps to establish or re-establish a pecking order and a sense of flock hierarchy. Even after the bird is well trained, it is always a good idea for all family members to practice this exercise regularly. It is also an excellent method of bonding with the bird.

Maintain Control of the Situation

As many avian behavioral consultants recommend, keep the bird off your shoulder. When a person puts a bird on his or her shoulder, that person relinquishes control and puts the pet in a position of power. Birds are very "tuned" into their human's faces. They respond to the slightest changes in facial expressions. Having a bird on your shoulder, so close to your face, gives the bird a feeling of being an equal or superior in flock hierarchy to it's owner. It also increases the likelihood the bird will perceive the human as its mate. Besides leading to a variety of behavior problems for the bird, it can also lead to facial injuries for the person. Birds will frequently bite their owners' faces to get them to move from some perceived danger. It is best to keep a bird on the hand (not the arm) and close to the chest at heart level. In this position, the person is in control but, more importantly, the bird feels secure, protected, and loved. Hearing a heart beat can be very soothing for the bird.

Also, don't allow a bird to play or perch on top of its cage. Height is power. Ideally when a person walks up to a bird's cage, the perches should be at the level of the person's heart or lower. If this is not the case, place a footstool near the cage and use it when interacting with the parrot in its cage. This way, you will step up before you ask the bird to step up. Playgyms, waist high, around the house are much more beneficial than the playgyms on top of the cages.

Clip a Bird's Wings

The need to clip a bird's wings is both a safety issue and a behavior issue. Trying to teach, train and work with a bird that flies away from you every time you approach it is a frustrating, often futile experience. Why should it listen to its owner when it can fly wherever it wants to go? More importantly however fully flighted birds get injured: they fly into windows, ceiling fans, hot water, hot grease, hot burners, soapy water, etc. The list of injuries veterinarians treat as a result of free flight is endless.

This Tres Marias Amazon may be trying to climb up its owner's arm to perch on a shoulder. Birds should be carried on the hand to maintain control over them and to prevent potential aggression problems that can develop if they are allowed to sit on their owner's shoulder.

Fully flighted birds also fly away. The newspapers and Internet always have lists of lost birds that flew away unexpectedly. In each case, the owners believed their birds would never leave them.

Many argue against wing clipping, claiming that "it's unnatural for a bird not to fly." True. However, it is also unnatural for a parrot to be in a house rather than in the rain forest! Owners who have accepted ownership of these wonderful creatures have a responsibility to keep them safe. That means clipping wings!

Give Your Bird Supervised Freedom

A bird should not spend all its time in a cage. Birds definitely need time out of their cages, but only under direct supervision.

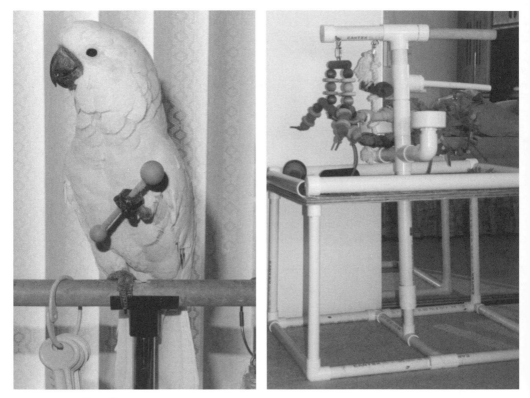

A mentally well-adjusted bird such as this cockatoo will enjoy human companionship and also will be able to play by itself on a perch or in a cage. (Bonnie Jay)

Portable playstands give birds a chance to be with their owners no matter what room of the house the owner is in. This stand was constructed from PVC pipe and plywood.

Place several waist-high or chest-high playgyms around the house, or have one portable playgym that can be moved from room to room. Birds like to be with the rest of the family, which they consider their "flock." If a playgym is available, they can interact and be with the "flock" without having to be held. Playgyms should not just be perches, but play areas with swings or ladders, toys, food, and water bowls.

However, don't allow a companion parrot to roam unsupervised. Lack of supervision always results in destruction or damage to the home, furniture, or clothing. However, the main reason this behavior should never be allowed is the potential danger to the bird. Electrical wires, cords, and outlets

184

can cause severe electrical burns or electrocution of the bird. Several common household items may be toxic. Carpet and material fibers can cause intestinal impactions. Household cleaners may be fatal if ingested.

Make Sure Your Bird Is Getting Enough Sleep

*Sleep deprivation is a common problem in most birds. Behaviorists recommend that birds receive approximately 12 hours of quiet, uninterrupted sleep in a dark room each night. A good rule of thumb is sundown to sunup. Unfortunately, most pet birds are lucky to get eight hours of sleep. If the bird's cage is in the middle of the living room, simply covering it at bedtime will not help the bird sleep unless the whole household is going to bed. Since birds are prey animals, they are very aware of their environment. Any light, noise, or activity (the television, radio, kids, dogs or cats milling round) is going to prevent them from sleeping soundly.

Having a bedtime cage is one solution to this problem. Rather than buying an actual cage, airline carrier kennels work well for this purpose. Turn the kennel upside down, slide a perch through the ventilation slats, attach a food/water container to the wire door, and you have a bedtime cage that you can place in a room that is quiet and dark.

A special sleeping cage can sometimes help otherwise restless sleepers settle down for the night. This Amazon's sleeping cage is a converted pet carrier that has been equipped with a perch and some bedtime snacks.

For cockatiels, parakeets, conures, and other small birds, the hard, clear plastic storage boxes work well. Drill air holes in the sides and put in small but heavy food and water bowls, along with a perch. Secure a wooden dowel to the "cage" itself by drilling holes in the side then insert wood screws into the dowel from the outside. With cockatiels that are prone to night frights, line the container with towels. This helps decrease the severity of injuries if the bird "freaks out."

• However, if you keep multiple birds in your home, consider creating a bird room. In this way the temperature, humidity, noise and light levels for all the birds can be controlled without disrupting the rest of the house. At bedtime, the lights go out and the door is closed.

Appropriately Situate Your Bird's Cage

•   Give a lot of thought to where you place the bird's cage. Birds need some privacy. Placing the cage in the middle of the room is not recommended. At least one side of the cage should be against a wall. Freestanding area screens can also be used to provide privacy.

Place some areas of privacy inside the cage. Large branches work well for this purpose. Also, you can put piece of wood in the corner of the cage to create some privacy. Cardboard boxes can provide privacy for small birds. When placing your cage, you should consider standing where the cage is and looking at the room from the bird's perspective. If anything looks frightening or otherwise unacceptable, either move the cage or change the environment. Thus, beware of skylights and open beam ceilings when placing the cage. You should also consider the effect of drafts from heating and air conditioning vents. Finally, wallpaper and pictures of anything that might be deemed frightening to the bird should be avoided.

Make Sure Your Bird Gets Physical Exercise

In the wild, birds are very athletic and active. In captivity, they tend to become "perch potatoes." This inactivity leads to obesity, fatty livers, decreased respiratory capacity as well as a host of behavior problems. Be inventive in getting your pet to exercise.

•   One exercise birds and owners can enjoy together is "flying," which your bird should do on a daily basis. Be sure your bird's wings are properly clipped before doing this exercise. The object is to invigorate your bird, not to have it fly away. Start slowly. This is especially important if the bird is overweight and out of shape.

Put the bird on your hand, hold the feet securely, raise the hand, then drop the hand gently but quickly. The bird will flap its wings. Do this until the bird starts to breathe heavy. This will indicate what shape your bird is in. Some very fat birds will only be able to fly one time. Repeat this exercise daily, gradually increasing the number of flights. Progress from this stationary flying to flying down the hall, around the house, or around the yard. Climbing and swinging are also excellent exercises. Ladders and swings are great toys. Place a ladder from the bottom of the cage to the floor. Put the bird on the floor and have it climb back into its cage. Any exercise birds and owners can enjoy together not only improves the bird's health but also strengthens the bond between bird and owner.

Make Sure Your Bird Gets Exercise for the Brain, Too!

• Providing mental stimulation is vital to raising a well-adjusted companion bird. Carefully select toys that make the bird think. Several puzzle-type toys are available. Foot toys are also great for developing mental stimulation.

• Hiding food in containers, such as toilet paper rolls with the ends twisted shut, is great. Stuff whole carrots, greens and other fresh raw food items into the top and sides of the cage. This gives the effect of a rain forest canopy. Making your bird forage for food can keep your bird occupied for hours, stimulating its brain and providing it with a healthy diet.

• You also might try making flash cards to play mind games with your bird. Cut various shapes out of different colored construction paper, hold them up, and announce what each is (blue circle, red square, etc.) Dr. Irene Pepperberg of the University of Arizona developed this method of using props with her African gray parrots to teach them how to identify many objects, colors, shapes, and materials. The game can also increase the bird's vocabulary. This is an especially good exercise for your bird if it tends to be introverted and needs to be drawn out. The game can also be played with objects such as keys, oranges, apples, shoes, or just about anything else in the bird's environment.

A word of caution about toys: Don't give a bird more than four or five toys in its cage at one time. Too many toys can be mentally overwhelming. They can also represent a physical danger. Cages crammed with toys have caused many wing, leg, and foot injuries. Too many toys seem to be more of a problem in small birdcages. In some parakeet cages, it is often difficult to even see the bird through all of the toys if there are too many.

Make sure you have several toys of each type, but only keep one of each type in the cage at a time and rotate them in and out once a week. Also rotate them into different positions within the cage weekly. Sometimes just moving a toy from one location to another within the cage will create a new level of interest for a bird.

Feed Your Bird a Healthy Diet

• Last but certainly not least, make sure you feed your bird a healthy diet. A bird eating a nutritionally complete and balanced diet is less likely to develop behavior problems that are based on metabolic deficiencies. Chapter 4, "Nutrition," deals with this subject in detail.

Discipline

The most important thing to remember when disciplining a pet bird is to *never hit a bird!* This will do more to destroy any trust the bird has in its owner than anything else the owner could ever do.

If you follow the guidelines for establishing control and a loving trusting relationship with your bird, most behavior problems will probably disappear. If, however, an area or two still needs adjustment, here are some suggestions:

• When the bird misbehaves, give it "the evil eye" look for a second or two, or ignore it completely for a few minutes. Remember the look your mother used to give you when you misbehaved in front of company? Use this same look to discipline a pet bird.

• When a bird bites, immediately "ladder" it. This takes the initial up command one step further. Have the bird step up from one hand to the other hand several times. Use a firm, unhappy voice, but don't be mean or nasty. When laddering is used as part of training, your tone of voice should not be as firm as when you are disciplining your bird. As the bird responds to the commands, praise it for obeying. If biting is a new behavior, revert back to the up and down training commands on a regular basis.

• Sometimes a timeout in the bird's cage is called for. This is especially helpful if the bird has been out of its cage for a long time and is getting fractious. In fact, your bird may just need some quiet time and a nap like any small child would. One positive aspect of a timeout is that it also gives the owners a timeout, a chance to cool off.

• Read the bird's body language. An Amazon with a fanned tail, eyes flashing, head down, and wings out is trying to tell its owner to stay out of its face! Leave it alone! Set your bird up for success, not failure. Avoid situations or circumstances that the bird will not be up for. Don't ask the bird to do something it's not ready for. Keep training sessions brief, positive, and progressive.

• Don't yell at a bird--they are creatures of drama! They love noise! They love yelling! A person who gets into a

188

screaming match with a bird always loses. Once a bird learns how to push its owner's buttons, it will.

Positive Reinforcement
When birds are being quiet, good little beings, owners tend to ignore them. Being the extremely intelligent creatures they are, they soon learn that noise and misbehaving gets our attention. Therefore, learn to lavishly praise a parrot when it behaves.
•   Stop work every few minutes to tell your bird how much you love it and how much you appreciate it when the bird is quiet.
•   When the bird is talking or chattering, chatter back. If the bird whistles, whistle back.
•   Stop by the cage or playgym several times for a pet, a head rub, and just to tell the bird what a special creature it is and how much you love it.
•   Interact with the bird as much as possible, playing, talking, or just involving it in family activities.
•   By using a playgym, keep the bird part of the family as much as possible.

Undesirable Behaviors and How to Curb Them
Parrots can be wonderful pets, but they do have some behaviors owners find puzzling, troubling, or downright dangerous. These behaviors include biting, chewing, screaming, feather pulling, self-mutilation, excessive egg laying, and dominance. In many cases, the behaviors make perfect sense to the parrot, but they can frustrate even the most patient and understanding parrot owner. The good news is many of them can be managed effectively or even prevented completely.

Whose Fault Is It?
In some cases, owners become upset when they cause their birds to behave in inappropriate ways. For instance, an Amazon owner who is roughhousing with his parrot shouldn't be surprised when the bird gets excited and bites him. An African grey owner who is playing with her bird's beak can expect to stimulate the bird to begin regurgitating its last meal to her. Finally, an owner who cuddles in the evening with a male cockatoo will cause him to initiate breeding behaviors, including displays and masturbation.

    In all these cases, the birds are reacting normally and naturally to the stimuli presented by their owners. It's the owners'

189

perceptions of how their birds should behave that are the problems here, and certainly the owners' behavior needs to be modified to prevent these situations from occurring again. When a parrot misbehaves, rather than getting angry at it, take a moment to see what caused the bird to misbehave. Parrots are not dumb animals that misbehave for no reason, and often the behavior is motivated by something we owners have done or by an environmental factor. Did the bird bite because it was frightened? Did the bird scream because it saw a squirrel on the balcony that needed to be chased away or did the bird feel abandoned by its owner?

By taking a moment to see what a bird's motivation for misbehavior is, an owner can often prevent the problem from recurring.

In many cases of apparent parrot misbehavior, the owners are the problem. Their expectations are too high or they want their parrot to be something it cannot be. Bonnie Munro Doane and Thomas Qualkinbush put it very well in their book, My Parrot, My Friend, when they said:

"To live happily with a parrot requires patience and tolerance for behavior that is normal to the bird. Acceptance of a certain amount of mess, noise, and destruction of property will go a long way in preventing the development of relationship difficulties between person and parrot. If the parrot has been properly socialized, its natural tendencies to boisterousness and self expression should not be unpleasant for the owner. Occasionally 'accidents' will happen, as they do with small children. But they should be the exception, not the rule. As long as the owner understands that there is no such thing as perfection with a parrot, the parrot/owner relationship should be mutually pleasant and satisfying."

In other cases, pet birds misbehave because they suddenly find themselves in control, and they have no clue whatsoever as to how to act. By offering a pet bird appropriate guidance and by setting limits and boundaries in its world, an owner will significantly reduce a bird's chance to misbehave. Let's look now at some problem behaviors in detail.

Biting

Let's start with biting. Getting bitten by a pet parrot hurts, and if the bird happens to be large, such as a macaw or a cockatoo, the potential exists for serious injury.

Biting is not a natural behavior in the wild. If a wild parrot wants to *intimidate* an opponent, it will scream, strut, or posture, rather than resorting to biting. Captive parrots, on the other hand, learn to bite for survival or to *intimidate* their owners. Survival biting often occurs when a bird is terribly frightened or it is injured. Intimidation biting means that a parrot is given some kind of reward that encourages it to bite again.

If your parrot bites while perched on your hand or if it begins chewing on clothing or jewelry, you can gently rotate your wrist about a quarter-turn. The bird will quickly associate the rocking of its perch with its misbehavior and will stop biting or chewing. Don't do this if the bird is young, however. Young birds are unsteady enough on their feet on their own, and a rocking arm could shake their confidence greatly. Some behaviorists recommend ignoring initial nips from baby birds because in many cases the birds are just trying to maintain their balance the only way they know how.

If a bird bites you, do not thump its beak as punishment. It's easy to react to the bird's behavior with a quick thump on the beak. In the past, it was a gesture encouraged by some bird tamers who worked with wild-caught parrots. However, parrot behaviorists have since discovered birds do not understand this kind of punishment, and such a gesture will encourage the bird to bite that much harder the next time it gets a chance.

Along the same lines, don't grab a bird's beak to discipline it. Grabbing a bird's beak can say several things to a bird: It can be a greeting, it can indicate sexual behavior, or it can be perceived as a challenge to fight. If a bird enjoys having its beak touched and gently wrestled with, reward it with these gestures, but don't use them to discipline a bird.

To prevent a bird from biting, make sure it has access to plenty of acceptable chew toys, an interesting variety of foods, and opportunities to exercise outside its cage.

Bird bites tend to hurt more than your finger or hand: They can also hurt your feelings. Many owners take bites from their birds personally. Recently bitten owners often say things such as "My bird must not like me any more because he bit me" or "Why did my bird turn on me? I hand-raised her." Although birds are intelligent creatures capable of a wide range of emotions, they don't equate liking or not liking a person with their ability to bite this person.

In many cases, the bird really does like the person it has bitten and is showing its affection in this way. If your bird bites you on the face, the bird may have been trying to encourage you to flee from some perceived danger (remember, birds relate most closely to our faces--they don't seem to know quite what to do with the rest of us). In other cases, the bird is expressing its hormonal surges or feelings of frustration at being unable to breed.

Don't take a bird bite personally. This is a normal part of bird ownership that's to be expected. To minimize the chances of being bitten, exercise caution when you handle a sexually mature parrot during breeding season, for instance. Please note it is unrealistic to believe you can train a parrot not to bite.

Whatever you do, don't stop handling your bird if it has bitten you--this can create additional problems that will result in a relationship neither bird nor owner enjoys very much. In this arrangement, the parrot is in control, but it never gets handled or played with. It may become overly attached to its cage, or cagebound, which makes it even more prone to bite because it feels compelled to defend its territory. In addition, the parrot will feel neglected and may develop other behavioral problems, such as feather picking or screaming, while the owner feels hurt and unloved by the bird.

Avoid this problem by offering a bird consistent discipline and guidance from the time it first comes home. Also pay attention to the bird's body language and the signals it sends out. Often, a bird gives plenty of warning before it bites--as long as a person knows how to interpret its body language. Another potential problem owners can avoid with their pets is in thinking that a parrot loves you like humans love each other. Yes, parrots demonstrate emotion, and yes, they do become attached to their owners, but love may be too human an emotion to credit to a pet bird. If an owner stops thinking in terms of his pet loving him, he will have an easier time accepting occasional episodes of misbehaving, some of which are caused by hormonal surges over which the pet bird has no control.

Chewing

Chewing is a normal behavior in which parrots engage to keep their beaks in condition. It becomes a problem behavior when the pet bird owner does not provide enough acceptable chew toys for his or her pet. The bird then chews unacceptable items, such as furniture, wallpaper, or paneling.

Bird owners can prevent chewing problems by anticipating a

bird's need to chew and providing acceptable chew items. These can include wooden or leather toys, cardboard rolls from paper towels or toilet paper, or nuts in the shell. Some birds are wild about chewing on seemingly indestructible things, such as manzanita perches or Plexiglas toys, for a change of pace. You can save some of the bird's favorite kinds of chew toys to use as a special treat and distraction when it seems determined to chew on anything it can get its beak on.

Although it may seem incredibly simple, a parrot's chewing tendencies can be controlled by limiting its access to chewable items in the home. This should fall under the general category of supervising the bird when it's out of its cage, but some people seem to make exceptions for chewing. If the bird can't get its beak on its owner's prized possessions, it can't chew on any of these items.

Screaming

Screaming is another behavior that makes perfect sense to a parrot but may cause owners to wonder why, in order to fulfill their pet-owning needs, they didn't adopt a nice quiet hamster or set up a fish tank with a bubbling filter.

Cody the Amazon was placed with a bird rescue group after she became too noisy for her owners. Her overgrown beak was caused by a poor diet. (Parrot Education and Adoption Center)

All parrots will make noise during the day. They often greet the dawn and say goodnight to the sun by being especially vocal early in the morning or late in the day. This is normal psittacine (parrot-like) behavior that can be curbed somewhat but not completely eliminated.

Sometimes, screaming parrots just need reassurance, so they scream to see where their people are. In these cases, simply call back to the bird, "I'm here. Are you okay?" or another reassuring phrase. In many cases, the bird will quiet down quickly after hearing its owner's voice.

At other times, birds may scream because something in the environment frightens them. In these cases, the owner will have to work with the bird over time to desensitize it to whatever is scary. For example, if your bird screams when you wear a particular hat, for example, set the hat on a table far away from the bird's cage and gradually (over a period of a few days or a week) bring the hat closer to the bird's cage.

Tell the bird how brave it is as the hat gets closer to the cage and cuddle it and pet it to further reward its bravery.

Still other birds scream because they think they have to protect their home and families. This hearkens back to the wild, when parrots alert each other to danger in the area by screaming or calling to one another. In these cases, before disciplining your helpful watch-parrot, it's a good idea to check to see if the bird has a legitimate reason for raising an alarm.

Other birds will scream when they are tired. In these cases, covering the cage for a few minutes does the trick. If the bird seems to be consistently tired and cranky, adjust its bedtime. Remember birds need about 12 hours of sleep a night, and the bird may be disturbed by evening activities. A sleep cage in a dark, quiet part of the house should do the trick in these cases. But remember not to banish the bird to some seldom-used part of the house because a bird who feels neglected and forgotten may also begin screaming.

Some screaming birds learn how to scream from other parrots in the home. If you have one screaming bird, you shouldn't be surprised if other birds pick up on the behavior, especially if you have mistakenly rewarded the screaming bird by yelling at it or engaging in other dramatic outbursts of emotion every time the bird screams.

Remember to give a bird consistent attention; allow it ample opportunities to exercise outside its cage by flapping or climbing; provide it with an interesting environment, complete with a variety of toys and a well-balanced diet; and leave a radio or television on when it's alone to provide background noise. If you do these things, the bird shouldn't become a screamer.

Birds sometimes lose their homes when they develop behavior problems that their owners are unable or unwilling to resolve. Kiwi the Eclectus was placed with an adoption group after he became sexually mature and began picking his feathers. (Parrot Education and Adoption Center/Viewpoint Photography)

If the bird likes to scream, you may be able to train it to whistle or say "hello" instead of screaming. To do this, when the bird screams, respond by whistling or by saying whatever you want the bird to say instead of the screaming. Reward the parrot with attention when it whistles back or repeats the phrase and ignore it when it screams. The bird should quickly catch on, and the screaming problem hopefully will be resolved!

Other Problem Behaviors

Feather picking, self mutilation, egg laying, or dominance can cause problems for parrots and their owners. Many things can cause a bird to pull its feathers or mutilate itself, including illness, boredom, stress, and the desire to breed. The desire to breed may also cause a female bird to lay eggs, and some species may be prone to laying large number of eggs during breeding season.

Some birds have been set up by their owners to be dominant because the birds have unlimited access to their owners' shoulders or to high places in the home, or they live in tall cages allowing them to frequently have their heads higher than their owners'.

When setting up your bird's home, you need to remember that height is "power" in the parrot world. Flock leaders perch higher in the treetops than other flock members. Remember, you are suppose to be the flock leader in your home. If a bird's cage allows it to be taller than most family members when it is atop the cage, lower the cage height slightly or provide steps or other means for shorter family members to gain height when dealing with the bird. Make sure to hold and carry the parrot at mid-chest height to allow some control over the parrot and its behavior.

If you want to teach your bird to talk, speak slowly and distinctly to it. Make sure you have the bird's full attention and keep your training sessions short. Although Eclectus parrots are not known for their talking ability, Rosebud has a small, but growing, vocabulary she uses regularly.

No Quick Fixes

Although as an owner, you will want to solve bird behavior problems promptly, don't settle for quick-fix solutions, such as putting the bird in a dark closet or spraying it in the face with water. Remember birds don't think in cause and effect terms, so they won't understand why they are being punished. These seemingly quick fixes will actually do more damage to the long-term relationship between owner and pet, which could lead to even more behavior problems in the future. A bird's problem behaviors can't be resolved without taking the time to see why the bird is behaving in a particular way. Also, the bird's misbehavior probably didn't start overnight, so why should you expect an instant solution to the problem?

Will My Bird Talk?

The bird's ability to talk has been one of the most appealing parts of pet bird ownership since the days of the ancient Romans. A description of parrots written by the Greek historian and physician Ctesias tells of the talking ability of a parrot he called Bittacus, which experts now believe was a plum-headed parakeet. This bird could speak both Greek and an Indian language.

Some species are more adept at talking than others. African greys, Amazons, budgerigars, and mynahs are considered among the best talking birds, but none of them are guaranteed to talk. With persistence and patience on your part, a bird from a species not noted for talking may learn a few words or even a few phrases.

Three parrots have amassed particularly noteworthy vocabularies. Puck, a budgie in northern California, holds the Guinness World Record for largest vocabulary by an animal. Puck's owner estimates her bird has a 1,728-word vocabulary! Another parrot, an African grey named Prudle, reportedly had a 1,000-word vocabulary when he retired from public life in 1977.

Sparkie, a budgie that lived in Great Britain from 1954 to 1962, held the record for a talking bird in his time. He won the BBC's Cage Word Contest in 1958 by reciting eight four-line nursery rhymes without stopping. At the time of his death, Sparkie had a vocabulary of 531 words and 383 sentences.

The suggestions offered below are a compilation of the opinions and insights of many noted avian behaviorists. They may help an owner teach a pet bird to talk, but please don't be disappointed if your pet never utters a word.

• Owners may notice their parrots are more vocal early in the morning or at dusk. A bird may be more receptive to speech lessons at these times of day.

• You need to remember that language, whether it's bird or human, helps members of a species or group communicate. Most baby birds learn the language of their parents because it helps them communicate within their family and their flock. A pet bird raised with people may learn to imitate the sounds it hears its human family make, but if there is more than one bird in the home, the birds may find communicating with each other easier and seemingly more enjoyable than trying to learn human language.

• An owner will be more successful in training a bird to talk if a single pet bird, rather than a pair, is kept. Birds kept in pairs or groups are more likely to bond with other birds. By the same token, don't give the bird any toys with mirrors on them because the bird will think that the bird in the mirror is a potential cagemate with whom it can bond.

Start with a young bird because the younger the bird is, the more likely it is to want to mimic human speech.

Pick one phrase to start with. Keep it short and simple, such as the bird's name. Say the phrase slowly so the bird learns it clearly. Some people teach their birds to talk by rattling off words and phrases quickly, only to be disappointed when the bird repeats them in a blurred jumble that cannot be understood.

• Be sure to say the chosen phrase with emphasis and enthusiasm. Birds like a "drama reward" and seem to learn words that are said emphatically, which may be why some of them pick up bad language so quickly!

• Try to have phrases make sense. For instance, say, "Good morning" or "Hello" when the bird's cage is uncovered each day. Ask, "Want a treat?" when the bird's meals are offered. (Phrases that make sense are also more likely to be used by family members when conversing with the bird. The more your bird hears an interesting word or phrase, the more likely it is to say that phrase some day.)

• Don't change the phrase around. If the bird is learning to say, "Hello," for example, don't say, "Hello" one day, then, "Hi" the next, followed by, "Hi Petey! (or whatever the bird's name is) another day.

• Keep training sessions short. Ten to 15 minutes seems to be the ideal time frame.

• Train the bird in a quiet area, but be sure to keep the bird involved in the household routine because isolating it completely won't help it feel either comfortable or that it is a part of the family. Remember a bird needs to feel comfortable in its environment before it will draw attention to itself by talking. Be patient with the bird. Owners should stop the training sessions if they become frustrated. The bird will sense something is wrong and will react by becoming bothered itself. This is not an ideal learning situation. Try to keep the mood upbeat. Smile a lot and praise the bird when it does well!

• Graduate to more difficult phrases as the bird masters simple words and phrases. Consider keeping a log of the words the bird knows (this is especially helpful if more than one person will be teaching the bird to talk).

• Some owners may wonder if the talking tapes and compact discs sold in pet stores and through advertisements in bird magazines work. The most realistic answer is sometimes. Some birds learn from the repetition of the tapes and CDs. Fortunately, these recordings have gotten livelier and more

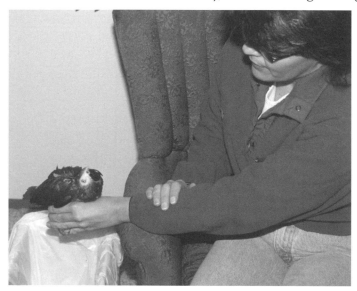

interesting to listen to in recent years. Other birds benefit from having their owners make tapes of the phrases the bird is currently learning and hearing those tapes play when their owners aren't around. Don't barrage a bird with a continuous loop of taped phrases during the day because the bird is likely to get bored hearing the same thing for hours on end. If it's bored, the bird will be more likely to tune out the tape and tune out the

Although many people don't believe it, pet birds like this African Grey can be trained to eliminate on command. Owners need to be attentive to their birds' body language and be prepared to move their pet to an approved spot, such as over the trash can, before the bird eliminates.

training in the process.

• Finally, if patient, consistent training seems to be going nowhere, an owner may have to accept the fact his or her bird isn't going to talk. If this is the case, continue to love it for the unique creature that it is.

Potty Training Your Parrot

Although some people don't believe it, parrots can be toilet trained so they don't eliminate on their owners. To toilet train a bird, choose a word that will indicate the act of eliminating to the bird, such as "go poop" or "go potty." While the bird learns to associate the chosen phrase with the eliminating, an owner will have to study his or her pet's body language and actions that indicate it is about to eliminate, such as shifting around or squatting slightly.

Once the bird seems to associate "go potty" with eliminating, pick it up and hold it until it starts to shift or squat. Tell the bird to "go potty" while placing it on its cage, where it can eliminate. Once it's done, pick it up again and praise it for being such a smart bird! A few accidents are to be expected as birds and owners master this trick, but soon the bird will be toilet trained so it can be put on its cage about every 20 minutes or so, hear the command, and eliminate on command.

There is a down side to "potty training." Once potty trained, some birds tend to "hold it" until they are taken out of their cages and given the command. If an owner isn't around to do this, the bird can be subject to discomfort and possible physical problems. If you and your bird are separated for a prolonged period of time, such as a vacation or a hospital stay at your avian veterinarian's office, be sure to alert your bird's caretakers that it is potty trained and needs to be taken out of its cage regularly to eliminate.

Macaws are good candidates to learn tricks. Here, Mikey the blue-and-gold macaw bows following a performance.

Trick Training Parrots

If you have established a good rapport with your parrot, the bird may be able to learn some tricks. Some parrots can learn to wave or to roll over, while others can learn to hang upside down from their owner's hand or climb a rope.

Only birds that are completely comfortable with their owners will allow themselves to be held in this manner.

To trick train your parrot, avian behaviorist Christine Davis suggests the following:

• Respect the bird's likes and dislikes--If a bird is interested in playing with balls or lying on its back, it's more likely to be a good candidate for learning tricks than one that just likes to sit on its owner's hand and have its head scratched.

• Keep training sessions short-- Parrots have the attention spans of toddlers and, like toddlers, can become cranky if forced to do one thing too long. Try to limit training sessions to about ten minutes in length, end on a high note when-

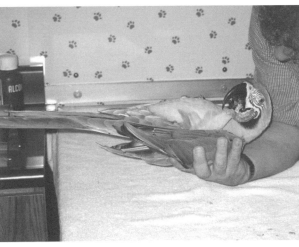

Mikey the blue-and-gold macaw has learned to play basketball.

Waving is a trick many pet birds learn easily.

ever possible, and repeat them several times a day.

• Keep sessions fun for both bird and owner--Make sure both parties are enjoying the training sessions. If this isn't the case, stop them. Also, don't starve a bird in order to get it to perform. Reward good behavior with favored treats, such as sunflower seeds or walnut pieces, but parrots also love to be praised and tickled, so use these rewards for performing a trick correctly.

• Love your bird for what it is, not what you expect it to be. If your bird just doesn't seem to grasp the concept of the trick it's being taught, you shouldn't force the issue. Instead, you should appreciate the bird for its good points and love it for being your bird buddy.

• Before trick training sessions begin, find a quiet place to hold your sessions. In this quiet place, set up a T-stand for the bird and some special treats to reward its behavior. Be ready to use a "bridge" or sound cue to let the bird know that it has performed a trick correctly (this can be a hand-held clicker or the word "Good!" said in a bright, positive voice), and verbal cues or hand signals to go with the behaviors being taught.

To teach a bird to ride in a wagon, first get the bird accustomed to the wagon. Roll the wagon in front of the bird to show it what the wagon will do. After a few days of short sessions watching the wagon roll by, put the bird in the wagon. Praise it and pet it as it sits in the wagon. Let it practice sitting in the wagon for brief periods of time for a few days.

200

The Well-Behaved Parrot

When the bird seems comfortable sitting in the wagon, pull the wagon a short distance. Praise the bird for its good behavior if it sits calmly; comfort and reassure it that everything is okay if it seems panicked by the wagon's movement. Put the bird in the wagon for short rides several times a day and gradually increase the length of those rides.

To teach a parrot to wave, put a hand out as if the bird will step up onto it. When the bird puts out its foot, pet it and praise it lavishly.

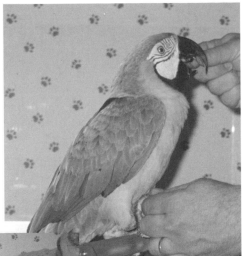

Sunflower seeds can be used as training rewards. Mikey the blue-and-gold Macaw receives a treat after successfully performing a trick.

Mikey's owner has taught him to enjoy the towelling process. To help your pet tolerate being towelled, try to make it a game for both of you.

Some birds can learn to drop coins into a bank as part of their repertoire of tricks.

After a few sessions of simply having the bird lift its foot, continue the training by stepping far enough away from the bird so it cannot get on the hand, but offer the hand just the same. If you praise and pet the parrot for raising its foot, the bird will soon get the idea that it is supposed to raise its foot. When the bird understands the concept of raising its foot, raise your hand, then wave at the parrot. Chances are it will mimic the action. Praise and pet it for its ability to follow the lead, and pretty soon the bird will wave!

Normal Canary, Finch and Softbill Behaviors

Parrots are not the only birds commonly kept as pets, although they are among the most popular. If you are a bird fancier who does not keep parrots, the following descriptions of behaviors common to canaries, finches and softbills may provide some insight into these feathered friends! Aggression: Finches show aggression in several ways: threatening, pecking fights, and ousting fights. When a finch threatens another finch, it extends its neck with an open or closed bill. Cut-throat finches make a threatening sound with this gesture.

In pecking fights, two birds go after each other with their bills, trying to grab the opponent's head or chest feathers. Some finches also spread or flatten feathers as they peck at their opponents. In ousting fights, one finch chases another and tries to keep it from perching. These fights are commonly seen during mating season as finches battle for territories. Bathing: Zebra finches especially enjoy their baths. They also consume large quantities of water during warm weather and during breeding season, so be sure to keep drinking water receptacles full and to provide ample bathing opportunities. Finches may bathe in wet lettuce leaves if owners provide them with damp greens. Other finches enjoy bathing throughout the day, flying through sprinklers or splashing in shallow water dishes. Let canaries bathe daily. They are more enthusiastic about bathing in the spring and summer, but provide them with a small, flat dish of lukewarm water each day to encourage them to bathe and keep their feathers in condition. Be sure to provide the bath water in the morning so the bird has adequate time for its feathers to dry before bedtime.

Mynahs enjoy daily water baths, and some like to take baths in warm, dry sand, as well.

Colony breeding:

Some species of finches, such as mannikins and munias, breed more successfully if they are kept in large colonies of a single species, rather than keeping a mixed collection that may be prone to territorial disputes and other hindrances to breeding success. Many finch breeders recommend keeping finches in colony breeding setups, as opposed to setting up individual pairs in breeding cages.

Contact sitting: Exotic finch species practice contact sitting to varying degrees. In some cases, such as munias, chestnut-breasted finches, masked grassfinches, and some African waxbills, the birds sit huddled together in long rows. Other species, such as long-tailed grassfinches, parson finches, and zebra finches, pair up when they contact sit, and still other species--crimson finches and star finches--contact sit only during the breeding season. Painted, Gouldian, and parrot finches practice contact sitting as young birds, but they do not sit close together once they are mature.

Drinking: Some finches--the diamond finch, the zebra finch, the owl finch, the Gouldian finch, and the parson finch--drink their water in a continuous sucking motion, rather than the scooping motion seen in parrots and other birds. This ability allows these birds to spend less time at watering holes and lets them fly farther in arid regions in their homelands. Long-tailed grassfinches, parson finches, and masked grassfinches can drink from deep water, such as cattle troughs, as opposed to shallow puddles as other Australian finches do. These finches also only drink in the morning and evening, which allows them to fly far from their watering holes during the day in the wild. Other Australian finches have to find water every hour in the wild.

Eating: Zebra finches have a tendency to drop seed hulls back in their seed dishes, which can make the dishes appear fuller than they are. When feeding finches, check their seed dish daily to make sure it has seeds and refill when necessary. Egg eating: Finches may pick at or eat their own eggs. Some pairs may also kill and eat their chicks. Causes of this behavior include vitamin and mineral deficiency, boredom, or an uneasy feeling about the environment. Take appropriate measures to remedy any problems in a finch collection.

Fear: A frightened finch will sit straight up and try to make itself as thin as possible. Frightened finches will also hide in cage corners and lay their feathers down as flat as they can.

Feather picking: Finches sometimes pick their cagemates' feathers because of boredom, stress, vitamin or mineral deficiencies, or overcrowding. If a finch suddenly turns up with bald spots on its body, suspect it is being picked. Improve your finches' diet, thin out the collection if the aviary is overcrowded, and add some ropes or interesting foodstuffs to the cage to alleviate boredom.

Live food eating: During breeding season, many finch species seek out live food; you will need to provide this for them to ensure breeding success.

Male feeds chicks while hens incubate next clutch: Male canaries take over the feeding duties for the family while the females begin work on the next clutch of eggs. The male will do this until the chicks have weaned and are completely independent. The male will also feed the hen while she is on the nest if he stays in the cage while she is incubating the eggs. In some finch species, the male birds continue to feed the chicks for a few weeks after they leave the nest.

Mating dance: Male finches dance to attract the attention of females during breeding season. They often sing songs and hold a blade of grass or twig in their beaks. The males may dance around the females or they may chase their potential mates around the aviary. After the dance is done, the pair will inspect nesting sites around the aviary. The female looks at sites the male chooses, and she often rejects his choices and forces him to find another site for the nest.

Mutual grooming: Exotic finches that practice contact sitting also practice mutual grooming. This means the birds groom the necks, heads, and throats of the birds sitting next to them. One bird raises its head or neck feathers and turns its head or neck to its neighbor to be groomed. If the groomer tries to touch other parts of the "groomee's" body, that bird pecks at the groomer bird or flies away.

Nest building: Zebra finches will build nests until they run out of material, even if it means building a nest on top of already laid eggs. Finchkeepers should limit the amount of nesting materials given to zebras to ensure they don't over-build their nests. Zebra finches kept in aviaries are less likely to build these "sandwich nests," as some experts describe them, because the larger flying space in aviaries makes the birds less likely to overbuild their nests.

Finches demonstrate a wide variety of nest-building behaviors. Weaver species weave a few blades of grass around a twig, then form a ring-shaped side wall, and finally a roof. After the male weavers have built several nests, they turn to the all-important task of attracting females (weavers are polygamous birds) to these nests. Estrildid finches like waxbills, on the other hand, build nests in the fork of a tree branch, to which they add sides and a roof.

Nest desertion: If a finch or canary is unsure of her surroundings or uneasy in them, she may not set on her eggs properly and may even desert the nest. If birds desert their nest, check the surroundings for potential stressors, such as high levels of activity in the area, rodents, or other disturbances.

Nuptial plumage: Some species of finches, especially whydahs and weavers, molt into special, brightly colored plumage just before breeding season to attract mates. These special feathers are described as nuptial plumage or breeding plumage, as opposed to the eclipse plumage the males sport the rest of the year.

Parasitic brooding: Weavers and whydahs are prone to being parasitic brooders, which means that the hens lay their eggs in the nest of another bird and leave the other bird to do the work of incubating the egg and raising the chicks. Unlike another famous brood parasite, the cuckoo, the young weaver and whydah chicks do not displace other chicks in the nest, but instead are raised alongside them. Not all species of weavers and whydahs perform this behavior.

Polygamous breeding: Some species of weavers are polygamous, which means one male bird defends a nesting territory in which he keeps several nests, each under the care of a different female. The males take no part in the incubation or chick-raising chores.

Preening: Finches preen their feathers daily using their beaks and feet. They clean their wing and tail feathers with their bills and use their feet to arrange the feathers on their necks, cheeks, and heads. During the course of preening, finches often fluff their feathers, which allows them all to fall into place. Preening often follows bathing.

Canaries preen for much of the day. They use their bills to preen most of their feathers and scratch at their cheeks, necks, and heads with their feet to put the feathers in order. After a canary is finished preening, it will shake all its feathers once to set them in their proper places. Like finches, canaries often preen following a bath.

Singing: Canaries sometimes start singing when they hear water. Owners of nonsinging birds may want to try running water for their pets. Also, covering the cage at night to delineate night from day sometimes helps stimulate a bird to sing.

Male finches sing to attract mates. These songs are soft and difficult to hear from far away. In certain species, such as the Gouldian, star, and cut throat, several males will gather to listen to another male sing. These listeners will gather around the singing bird as if they are trying to catch every note and inflection.

Sleeping: Finches sleep by pulling their heads in between their shoulders or by tucking their bills into their wing feathers. They puff their feathers slightly and pull one foot into their belly feathers to rest it. Most finches do not nap during the day, but they sleep soundly at night. Some finches sleep on perches, while others sleep in nests.

When mynahs sleep, they hunker their heads down between their shoulders, rather than tucking their heads into their back feathers as parrots often do.

Canaries sleep only at night because they are instinctively designed to stay awake and keep watch during the day. They tuck their bills into their wing feathers or hunch their heads down toward their shoulders.

Territoriality: During breeding season, some male finches will select and defend territories. They will also start to sing to attract mates to these newly established territories.

Shaking hands is a simple extension of the waving gestures. Hold out a hand as you would to have the bird step onto it and let it take hold of a finger with its foot. Begin shaking the parrot's foot gently. Repeat this series of gestures several times and soon, the parrot will shake hands!
A parrot that likes to be petted and can be turned over by its owner is a good candidate to play dead. First, get the bird accustomed to the feel of a hand on its back while it is perching on its cage or playgym. When the bird seems comfortable with a hand on its back, hold it on its side between the hands.

When the bird is comfortable being held in this way, move on to holding it between the hands on its back. When it seems comfortable with being held on its back in a hand, remove the hand on its feet or belly, and the bird is playing dead in the hand!

A bird will have to have an inordinate amount of trust in you before it will allow being flipped over onto its back. This is not a common parrot behavior, although conures are more likely to lie on their backs than other species, and some birds may never be comfortable in this position. If the bird seems distressed when it is flipped over on its back, it may have to be taught some other trick.

Birds are beautiful, loving, intelligent beings. We have removed them from their natural environment and brought them into our houses. They turn a house into a home. They add more joy to our lives then we ever imagined possible. They become members of the family and a vital part of their owners' lives. To be able to watch these magnificent creatures grow and develop their own unique personalities is a thrill and a privilege.

As with all privileges, this comes with tremendous responsibilities. Since some of these species are very near extinction in the wild, those responsibilities are increased beyond imagination.

We have a responsibility to provide and care for their every need: physical, mental, and emotional. We also have a responsibility to do what we can to preserve them from extinction in the wild.

If we do this, they will reward us beyond our wildest dreams with a love and devotion that surpasses all understanding. Is it worth it? You bet!

The Well-Behaved Parrot

Author's Note: I would like to thank the following avian behavior consultants, in addition to those cited in the text, for their invaluable contributions to this chapter. Their ideas, theories, and insights into bird behavior have truly allowed me to call this edition of the book "complete:"

Sally Blanchard, whose "Nurturing Guidance Techniques" have stressed the importance of training birds early and then staying the course to correct misbehavior when it occurs;

Christine Davis for her thoughts on positive reinforcement;

Jennifer Hubbard, author of *The New Parrot Handbook*, for her knowledge of trick-training;

Phoebe Greene Linden of the Santa Barbara (CA) Bird Farm for her contributions on young bird behavior and particularly for her theory of "abundance weaning;"

Liz Wilson, for recognizing that a bird's home is its castle.

Chapter 9

Bird Clubs and Bird Shows

And the Winner Is...

You've really come to enjoy your pet bird and other bird owners you've met through visits to your favorite bird supply store and your avian veterinarian's office. You want to take the next step—showing your bird—but you're unsure of how to go about it.

First, you need to join a bird club. A list of national bird clubs is included in Appendix B of this book. Attend meetings of your local bird club to see if they have exhibitors who are willing to help people, like you, who are new to showing birds. Go to bird shows as an observer and see which birds win. Talk to the breeders of those birds after the show to see if they have chicks available for purchase. Ask the breeder of your birds, as well as other breeders in the club, to help you start training your birds for the show season, which kicks into high gear in the fall. (We'll discuss conditioning birds for the show circuit shortly, too.)

Once you have some promising show birds, you'll need to know when the show is scheduled to take place. Bird magazines, club newsletters, and even bulletin boards in pet stores and veterinary offices can be good places to locate this information. Along with the date and location of the event, the contact person's name, address, and phone number are usually listed. Call or write this person to obtain a show catalog, which is your guide to the particulars of the show you've chosen to enter. When you make your catalog request, ask again for the date and location of the show, along with the name of the hotel most of the exhibitors will be staying in (this is especially important if you will be traveling to the show, since you'll probably want to make some new friends along the way).

As you read over the show catalog, note the check-in time for your birds (late birds don't have to be accepted for judging) and any entry fees. You will also learn who will be judging your category and what time judging is set to begin, along with what awards will be given out.

The show catalog will also contain information on the divisions, subdivisions, sections, and classes that will be judged in this show. Study this information carefully, because you will need to know what information to write down on your show tags and entry forms. Birds that are entered in the wrong classification may be disqualified, so make sure the information you put on your forms is correct.

As you fill out the forms, you will have to decide at what level of competition you want to start: novice, intermediate, or champion. You can enter at either novice or intermediate, but you cannot drop back to novice if you choose intermediate. A novice or an intermediate becomes a champion when the exhibitor places a bird on the top bench in its division and/or places a bird in the top 10 of the show.

The show catalog will also contain the judging standard for the birds that will be shown. This standard of perfection describes an ideal specimen of the species being judged. So far, this ideal bird does not yet exist, but breeders keep trying.

Looking Good

Now that you have an idea of what the judges are looking for, how do you get your bird to live up to its own standard of perfection? You train it and groom it and show it off in a proper show cage.

Show birds must demonstrate grace under pressure during judging. They must appear calm, but alert, and comfortable in their show cages (which may or may not be their regular cages). They must also be able to accept and adjust to a stranger looking closely at them and tapping on their cages. Finally, they must be in perfect feather and tiptop overall condition. Sounds like a tall order? It is, but it can be done! To train your bird for the show circuit, get it used to its show cage well before show season starts. Several months before its first show, put your bird's show cage where your bird can see it. Gradually move the show cage closer to your bird's home. When your bird appears curious about, but not frightened of, the show cage, put your bird in the show cage with the cage door open. Allow your pet to explore the new cage, but encourage it to stay on its perch.

After your bird has learned to stay on the perch, invite some friends over to simulate a show. Reinforce your pet's good behavior (such as staying on its perch and not showing signs of panic) with praise and a small treat after the "show." Next, ask a friend to "judge" your bird. Have this person get close to the cage and give your bird a thorough visual inspection. Ask the judge to tap lightly on the show cage with a pointer or pencil and to poke gently at the bird with this object. Praise your bird for its good behavior. (If, however, your bird seems uncomfortable with this added attention, you may want to reconsider the show circuit for this bird.)

After you have your bird trained, you'll need to work on its grooming. It will need to be fully feathered, have its wings and nails trimmed, and its feet clean to show well. If your bird suddenly breaks out in pinfeathers, you may want to reconsider showing it at that time or you may want to still enter the show as practice.

Finally, there's the matter of the show cage. To show your bird in the best light, you will need to have a clean cage and one in good condition. Some species are shown in special show cages, which you can either build yourself or purchase; others are allowed to be shown in a small parrot cage. Again, an experienced exhibitor can help you with this important aspect of showing your bird.

At the Show

Plan to arrive early during the registration period. Fill out your tags carefully. (You may want to consult the show catalog frequently while writing out the tags to make sure you're entering the right information about divisions, subdivisions, sections, and classes.) Turn in your tags, bird, and fees promptly and pleasantly, then move on to the show hall or commercial exhibits. Walk around and look at the other birds in the show until it's time for your bird to be judged.

During the show, keep these tips in mind:

- Follow all rules, signs, and notices at the show.
- Maintain a positive attitude throughout the show.
- Show consideration for show staff members and fellow exhibitors.
- Remain in designated areas during judging.
- Be a good loser and an even better winner.

Remember, all judging decisions are final.

Most importantly, have fun while you're at the show. Whether your bird wins or not, shows are good opportunities to see the best of different species and to meet some new people who share your passion for birds.

Chapter 10

Bird Breeding Basics

Matchmaker, Matchmaker...

Quick profits and a minimal time commitment--these are two of the most common misconceptions many people have about breeding birds. If this was as easy as breeding cats and dogs, birds would be considerably less expensive and more people would be in the bird-breeding business. Successful breeding requires hard work year-round. There is much to learn, a lot of time required, and many obstacles to overcome before successes begin to outweigh failures. If you are going to breed your birds, you should think of it as a labor of love rather than a money-making operation.

Before jumping in and spending a lot of money, take the time to learn about birds and how to breed them. Most importantly, remember that simply placing a male and female bird together does not mean that they will produce offspring. The more knowledge a breeder has about the breeding requirements of a particular species, the more likely chicks will be produced.

Make the acquaintance of bird breeders in your area and begin learning from them. Ask to tour their facilities. Find out what some of their early setbacks were and what they learned from the experience. Join bird clubs on the local and national level. Travel to conferences and conventions, if possible, to learn about aviculture and avian medical developments. Before you set up your breeding birds, calculate about how much money it will cost. Consider the cost of at least one pair of breeding birds, a suitable flight cage, nest boxes, an incubator, a brooder, hand-feeding formula and supplies, food for the parent birds, and veterinary care for both breeding birds and offspring.

The History of Aviculture

Before we discuss the day-to-day aspects of bird breeding, let's look at how bird breeding developed as a vocation. From the start, the pet trade depended heavily upon trapping parrots in the wild to turn them into pets. Between 1974 and 1992, between 300,000 and 900,000 birds were imported into the United States each year, and 75 percent of these were wild-caught exotic birds. Until the late 1970s, importing wild-caught birds was accepted as the normal way of doing things. About this time, some forward-thinking parrot keepers began to set up pairs of commonly imported species to produce parrots specifically for the pet trade.

By the 1980s, some species, such as the sun and jenday conures, were bred with regularity in captivity. These domestically bred birds had all the exotic appeal of their wild-caught cousins. The pet-owning public began to respond to these domestically bred birds, which were less prone to fear biting and other behavior problems seen in wild-caught birds, and breeders turned their attention to other species. Wild-caught parrots still dominated the market, however.

Between 1980 and 1992, breeders began to produce more and more domestically raised birds for the pet trade. Although fewer species of birds are available now, the birds themselves are healthier and better adjusted to life as a pet. Since 1992, when the Wild Bird Conservation Act essentially outlawed importation of birds into the United States, the pet bird industry has depended upon breeders of domestically raised birds to supply the pet industry's demand for birds.

What to Consider

Before you begin a breeding program, you will need to consider a number of factors. The following is only a short overview of some of the more important elements.

- Popularity of species
- Feeding requirements
- Cost of birds
- Personality
- Breeding tendencies
- Housing requirements
- Time and attention required

In addition, you will incur monthly maintenance expenses, such as food, utilities, repairs, maintenance, and possible veterinary bills.

Choice of Species

Finches, budgerigars, and canaries are recommended for beginning breeders. These species breed readily in captivity, they are often sexually dimorphic (males and females have different coloration), and they have minimal feeding and housing needs. Most importantly, they can be a good gauge of whether or not you will enjoy bird breeding without having to invest large sums of money immediately.

Bird Breeding Basics

Although the larger birds are more eye-catching and are a greater status symbol, they are considerably more difficult to breed. Breeders who raise these species must be more experienced and more dedicated to achieve success. With larger birds come larger investments of money, as well.

Site Selection and Housing

Considerations here include:

- Neighbors and noise
- Zoning restrictions on your property
- Ability to expand
- Security and safety of birds
- Hobby vs. occupation
- Indoor vs. outdoor aviary
- Weather
- Space availability
- Number and species of birds

Management

Regardless of the size of your operation, bird breeding means plenty of chores. Many of them must be performed daily, so being organized and sticking to a routine are essential. Good management of the birds is the best hope for success in the future.

Many of these responsibilities are listed below:

Social contact: Breeding birds need to be familiar with their caretaker so they will not become stressed while sitting on eggs or feeding chicks. Changes in the routine can cause some birds to destroy eggs or kill chicks.

Inspection and observation: Each bird needs to be observed each day (see the "hands-off" physical examination section for details). Report any problems to your avian veterinarian promptly.

Recordkeeping: Like any business, good records are essential to a bird breeder. Each bird should have its own record, consisting of age, weight, sex, band number, health history, and breeding successes. Newly hatched chicks require a record, too. This will include hatch date, daily weight, parent-fed or hand-fed, food requirements, general observations, and weaning date. This important information will help a breeder determine what's working and what needs to be changed within the aviary. It will also help a breeder detect problems

215

early, and it provides a record that can be referred to and shared with other breeders. Good recordkeeping also helps a bird-breeding business look more professional at tax time.

Feeding and watering: This routine should be done at about the same time each day. Uneaten fresh foods from the previous meal should be discarded during the feeding routine.

Environmental temperature: Be concerned about extreme weather changes. Healthy birds can generally adapt well to cold, but dampness and cold together may cause illness.

Seasonal management: Enclose outdoor flights in cold climates. Consider feeding warm foods during cold weather, and be sure the water supply doesn't freeze. Cover the outside walls with removable polyethylene sheeting. During hot weather, protect the birds from sun with shadecloth or awnings, and provide good ventilation. Consider installing a sprinkler system to mist the birds.

Cleaning cages and flights: Clean cages and concrete floors daily. Flights should be cleaned every few days. Disinfect the entire aviary periodically. Replace wooden nest boxes after each clutch.

Vermin control: Rodents and insects can carry disease, eat bird food, and disturb nesting birds, so take appropriate measures to keep the aviary pest-free.

Nest box inspection: During the breeding season, carefully inspect nest boxes twice a day. Look for eggs as well as problems, such as an egg-bound hen or cracked eggs. During the rest of the year, check the boxes for pests.

Sick birds: Isolate all sick birds from the rest of the aviary residents. Provide treatment as needed.

Vacations: Birds cannot be left alone for even short periods of time. A bird breeder's ability to pack up and go is limited severely. You must find a qualified caretaker to tend the birds during any absence.

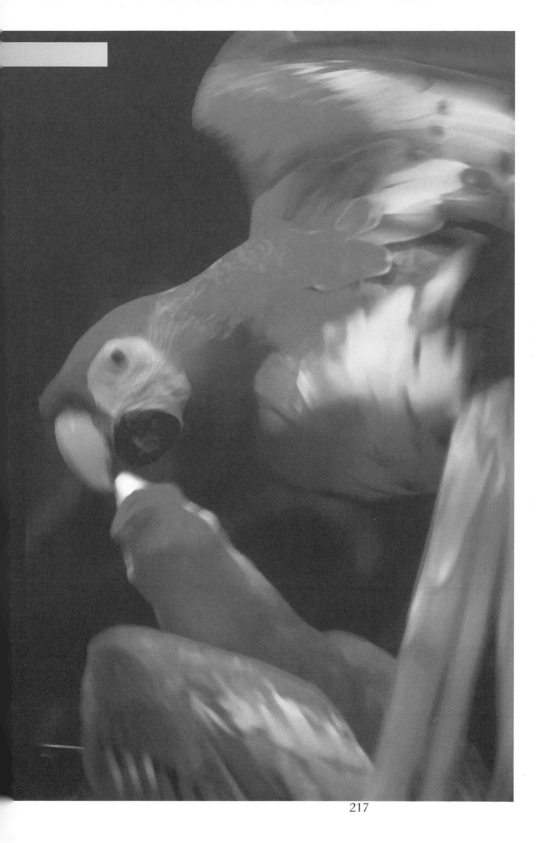

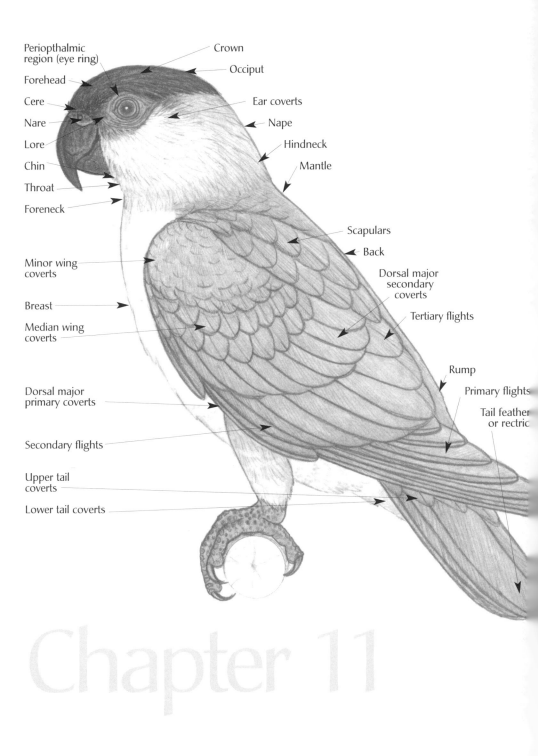

Periopthalmic region (eye ring)

Crown

Forehead

Occiput

Cere

Ear coverts

Nare

Nape

Lore

Hindneck

Chin

Mantle

Throat

Foreneck

Scapulars

Back

Minor wing coverts

Dorsal major secondary coverts

Breast

Tertiary flights

Median wing coverts

Rump

Dorsal major primary coverts

Primary flights

Tail feather or rectric

Secondary flights

Upper tail coverts

Lower tail coverts

Chapter 11

Avian Anatomy and Physiology

Only the Basics, Really...

"It's only through understanding the normal, that you can better understand the abnormal." I heard this statement repeatedly throughout my years in veterinary school, and it is with this statement in mind that I have written this chapter, which is a very brief introduction to the body of information explaining the structure and function of the various parts of our fine feathered friends. Specifically, each of the major organ systems will be discussed, along with how birds differ from mammals.

First of all, remember a bird's body, in its most basic form, is very similar to that of a mammal. Obviously, birds are unique when compared to other animals. Their ability to fly and other remarkable characteristics have helped make birds the most successfully adapted creatures on earth!

To begin with, the body in its smallest unit is composed of millions and millions of cells, all invisible to the naked eye. Cells are the workhorses of the body, performing all the various functions necessary to sustain life. Tissues and organs are groups of cells with specific functions. An organ system is a set of interconnected organs working together for a common purpose. The heart is an organ. It is also a part of the cardio-vascular system, which includes other organs and tissues such as the blood and blood vessels. The systems--respiratory, digestive, cardiovascular, and reproductive, to name a few-- are all interconnected, each with their own responsibilities, but working together to sustain life.

Anatomical Differences in Birds as Compared to Mammals

Skin:	Very thin and nearly transparent
	No sweat glands
	Feathers
Musculoskeletal:	Lightweight and air-filled bones
	Large, keeled sternum
	Massive pectoral muscles
	Numerous fused bones in wings and legs
	"Wishbone" is formed by fusion of clavicles
Reproductive:	Egg laying
	No mammary glands
	No penis, internal testicles
	Functional ovary and oviduct on left side only
	Female determines sex
Respiratory:	No vocal cords
	Syrinx for talking and noise production
	Small, compact, and nonexpandable lung
	No diaphragm
	Air sacs
Cardiovascular:	Large heart
	Very fast heart rate
Urinary:	No urinary bladder
	Urine is semisolid
Digestive:	No teeth
	Crop
	Two-part stomach
Lymphatic:	No lymph nodes

Nervous System

Birds and mammals have similar nervous systems. To coordinate the multitude of cellular functions and chemical reactions occurring throughout the body, good communication is essential. The brain is the body's central computer. It integrates and coordinates all these activities. The nerves are the messengers relaying information from every part of the body to and from the brain. These messages are transmitted, interpreted, and answered in minute fractions of a second!

Endocrine System

The endocrine system, like the nervous system, communicates with and controls many of the organs in the body. Hormones, secreted from glands, travel through the bloodstream and have specific effects on the activity of a certain organ or organs. Hormones exert very powerful influences on the body. When they are secreted in abnormal amounts, the results can be some of the most dramatic seen in the body.

The pituitary gland is thought of as the master gland because it stimulates secretions of hormones from other glands. The thyroid glands exert powerful control over body growth, metabolic rate, and molting. The parathyroids and ultimo-brachial glands control calcium metabolism. The adrenal glands play important roles in electrolyte balance and carbo-hydrate and fat metabolism. The pineal gland responds to changes in amount of light (changing seasons) and exerts influence over the reproductive cycle.

The pancreas, testes, ovaries, liver, small intestine, kidneys, uterus, and a few other organs also secrete hormones, in addition to performing their other functions.

The Senses
Vision

The basic structure of the avian eye is similar to that of mammals. Some of the more important differences will be discussed.

The eyes of birds are relatively large and well developed. Their ability to see detail (i.e., sharpness of vision) is better than mammals. Birds can distinguish colors.

Each eye operates independently of the other. However, the eyeball's range of motion (the ability to move in different directions) is very limited. This is compensated for, however, by

Cross-section of an eyeball.

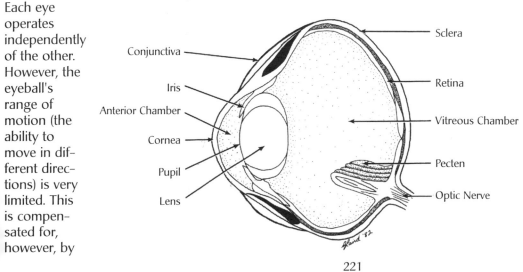

Conjunctiva
Iris
Anterior Chamber
Cornea
Pupil
Lens

Sclera
Retina
Vitreous Chamber
Pecten
Optic Nerve

221

the tremendous mobility of the head and neck. The eyelashes have been replaced with tiny bristle-like feathers called semi-plumes.

The iris regulates the amount of light entering the eye. It gives the eye its characteristic color. The iris is brilliantly colored in some species of birds. In many parrots, the iris is darker in the young birds, but lighter and more pigmented in the mature bird. In cockatoos, iris color most often indicates gender--in males, the iris is black or dark brown, and in females it's reddish or burnt orange. Gender determination by iris color is a characteristic unique to cockatoos.

Birds have three eyelids, similar to some mammals, such as dogs and cats. The upper and lower eyelids move up and down, while the third eyelid, or nictitating membrane, moves horizontally, sweeping across the eye from the inner corner. Birds do not blink like humans. When a bird blinks, its third eyelid flicks across the eyeball. This happens 30 to 35 times per minute.

Hearing

Ears are the organ of hearing and balance in all animals. In birds, they are hidden from view. To find the ears, look behind and below the eye. The feathers lie directly over or cover the ears have a slightly different texture and appearance. Part them, and the ears will be apparent. Notice there are no pinnae or ear flaps. What you see is the beginning of the external ear canal.

This photo shows the location of this baby macaw's ear. Notice there is no "flap" or pinna. (Bonnie Jay)

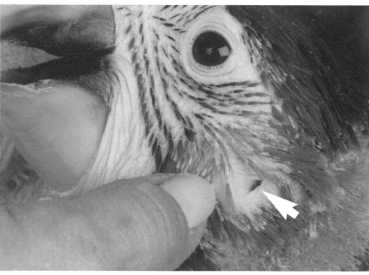

A bird's ability to discriminate among sound waves and to localize the direction of sound is well developed and similar to that of humans. However, birds appear less sensitive to higher and lower vocal tones as compared to humans. Their ability to differentiate various sounds is 10 times faster than humans. In other words, a canary's song would have to be

222

slowed down 10 times before the human ear could identify all the notes that are learned by a canary chick. Most birds, including parrots, do not hear ultrasonic vibrations.

Smell

Birds have a sense of smell, but it is poorly developed. Odors quickly fade above the ground where birds are flying.

Taste

Birds can taste, but compared to mammals, this sense is poorly developed. The number of taste buds in the mouth is much fewer than in humans or other animals. Taste buds in birds are found on the roof of the mouth, not on the tongue. In a study involving birds, but not specifically parrots, they were able to distinguish tastes. The birds disliked bitter and salt flavors and accepted sour flavors, but there was variation among the species. Sweet flavors were inconsistently accepted.

Integument (Skin)

A bird's skin is different from a mammal's in that it is very thin and delicate, and it appears nearly transparent. The red hue that you see when looking at the featherless areas is actually the underlying muscle being seen through the skin. The beak, cere (nasal area), claws, and scales on both the feet and legs are all modifications of the skin.

This close-up of a bird's skin shows numerous new, immature feathers wrapped in their keratin sheaths.

During nesting, the lower chest area loses its feathers, develops an enriched blood supply, and thickens to form a brood patch. This area provides extra warmth to the eggs during the incubation period.

The cheek patch is a featherless area on the face of some parrots, such as macaws. This patch will often blush or redden with excitement or stress. A few minutes after the stimulus is gone, the color returns to normal.

The uropygial gland (u-ro-PIJ-e-al), or preening gland, is located on the lower back, at the base of the tail. This gland is found on all parrots except Amazons. It produces an oil that is spread over the feathers by the beak during preening (grooming). The oil waterproofs and increases the durability of the feathers. It also appears to help prevent skin infections. Amazons, although lacking this gland, ordinarily maintain healthy and strong feathers in any case.

Unlike mammals, birds have no sweat glands. To cool themselves, overheated birds breathe rapidly (pant) and lift their wings away from their bodies. Birds that are cold will fluff their feathers and crouch to conserve heat.

Feathers

Feathers are part of the skin and similar to hair on mammals. A budgie has between 2,000 and 3,000 feathers on its body. Feathers primarily insulate and help maintain the normally high body temperature in birds. They are also used in courtship and aggressive displays, as nest material and, of course, for flight.

Feathers grow from feather follicles arranged in tracts or rows called pterylae (TER-i-la). In contrast, mammalian hairs grow randomly. The bare or unfeathered areas between the tracts are called apteria (AP-te-ree-ah).

Primary feather types are the contour, plume, and semiplume.

Contour feathers cover the contour, or outline, of the body, including the tail and wings. They are divided into flight feathers and body feathers. The primary flight feathers are the longest ones at the end of each wing. Next to these are the secondary flight feathers. There are about 10 primaries and 10 secondaries. The body feathers, or coverts, cover most of the body and base of the flight feathers.

Down feathers cover the newly hatched chick and are the fluffy feathers of adult birds. They form the undercoat and provide insulation. One type of feather unique to cockatoos, cockatiels, and African greys is powder down.

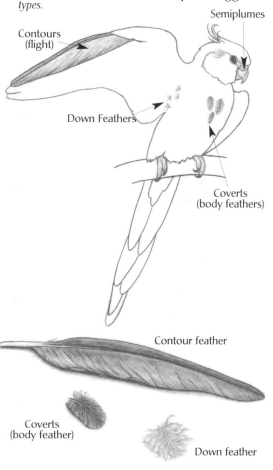

Common feather types.

Contours (flight)

Down Feathers

Semiplumes

Coverts (body feathers)

Contour feather

Coverts (body feather)

Down feather

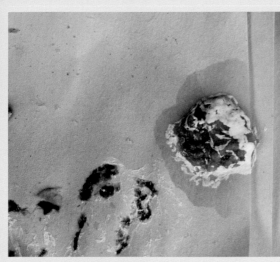

Normal parrot droppings.
(Bonnie Jay)

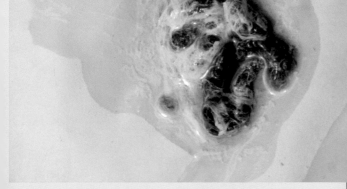

Increased urine is seen in this dropping.
This could be normal, such as when birds
consume a lot of fruits. It can also be
observed with stress, excitement, disease,
and poisoning.

Urates should always be nearly white in color. The lime-green urates in this photo usually indicate some type of liver disease.

Yellow urates also usually indicate liver disease.

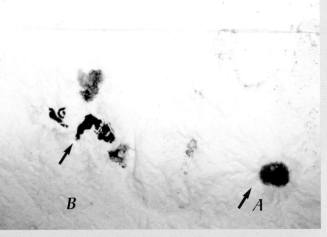

Blood covering the stool.

There is an obvious distinction between (A) regurgitation and (B) normal droppings.

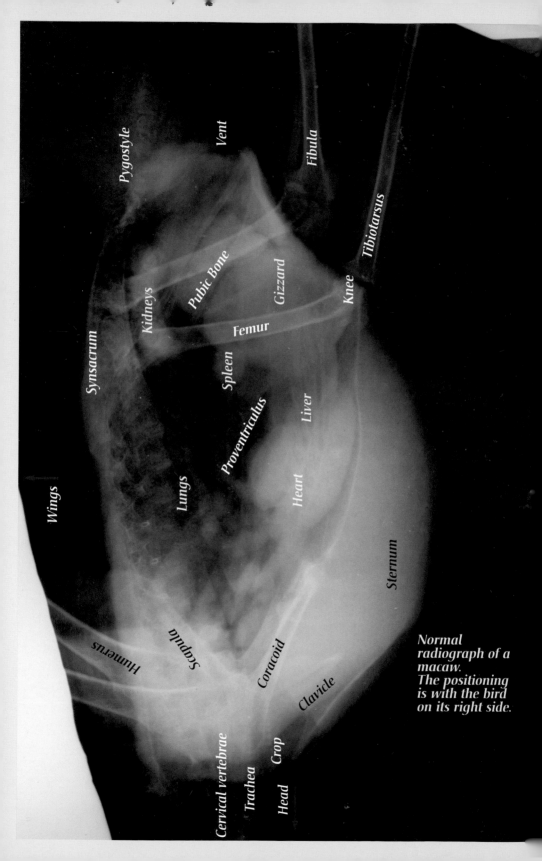

Normal radiograph of a macaw. The positioning is with the bird on its right side.

Wings

Pygostyle

Vent

Fibula

Tibiotarsus

Synsacrum

Kidneys

Pubic Bone

Gizzard

Knee

Femur

Spleen

Liver

Proventriculus

Lungs

Heart

Sternum

Humerus

Scapula

Coracoid

Clavicle

Cervical vertebrae

Trachea

Crop

Head

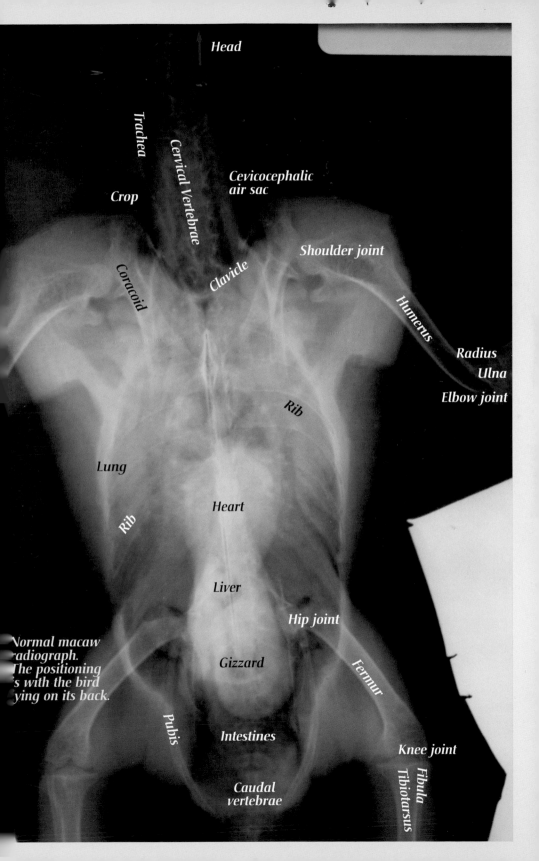

Head

Trachea

Cervical Vertebrae

Crop

Cevicocephalic
air sac

Shoulder joint

Clavicle

Coracoid

Humerus

Radius

Ulna

Elbow joint

Rib

Lung

Rib

Heart

Liver

Hip joint

Normal macaw
radiograph.
The positioning
is with the bird
lying on its back.

Gizzard

Femur

Pubis

Intestines

Knee joint

Fibula
Tibiotarsus

Caudal
vertebrae

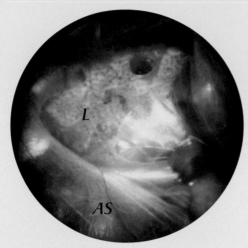

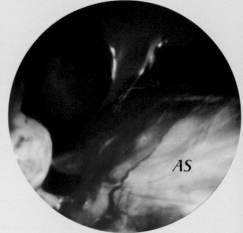

Endoscopic view shows the left caudal thoracic air sac (AS) and lung (L) of a red-tailed hawk. (Michael Taylor, D.V.M.)

Endoscopic view shows a chronic granulomatous inflammation in the left caudal thoracic air sac (AS). Compared with the photo of a normal air sac, note the increased blood supply and loss of transparency and clarity in this air sac. (Michael Taylor, D.V.M.)

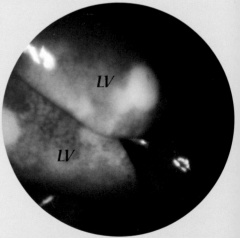

Endoscopic photo shows the view down and through the trachea. (Michael Taylor, D.V.M.)

Endoscopic view shows liver cancer (seen as white "spots") in an Amazon parrot. Liver tissue is indicated by LV. (Michael Taylor, D.V.M.)

F

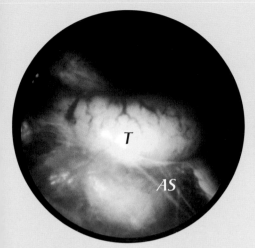

Endoscopic view shows the testicles (T) and air sac (AS) of a mature Amazon parrot. (Michael Taylor, D.V.M.)

Endoscopic view shows the ovary with numerous follicles (O) and air sac (AS) of a mature Amazon parrot. (Michael Taylor, D.V.M.)

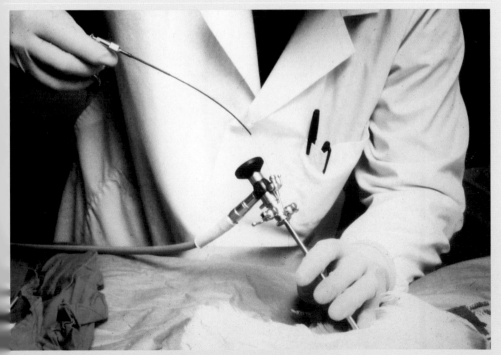

Biopsy forceps are being inserted down a channel alongside the endoscope. (Michael Taylor, D.V.M.)

G

These feathers grow in patches on both sides of the flank, just above the hips. The white powdery dust that emanates from these feathers appears to help with water repellency. The dust can often be found on the cage and on everything else around it. Excessive powder down could aggravate an owner's allergies.

Semiplume feathers are bristle-like and found along the edges of the feather tracts. This includes areas around the beak, nose, and eyelids. They help with insulation and may have a sensory function similar to whiskers in mammals.

This Amazon has numerous immature or pin feathers.

Feather Growth: For a new feather to begin growing, the old feather must first fall out. The earliest indication of a developing feather is a thickened, pointed projection of skin. Soon afterward, the emerging feather, called a pin or blood feather, appears, wrapped in its own protective keratin sheath. Each of these young growing feathers contains its own artery and vein. If a new feather is damaged or broken, bleeding will occur. When the feather grows in completely, its blood supply dries up. The sheath then falls off or is removed by the bird. The feather, now fully mature, is essentially a dead structure.

If a feather is pulled out or plucked, the follicle will be damaged slightly. However, a new feather will usually still begin to grow. If a mature feather is cut, as with wing trimming to prevent flight, the feather shaft remains and a new feather will not develop until the next molt.

Molting: Molting is simply the process of losing old feathers and replacing them with new ones. Factors influencing the frequency and extent of the molt are time of year, temperature, photoperiod (natural and artificial light cycles), nutrition, reproductive cycle, and species. After hatching, chicks pass through a series of molts, eventually producing adult plumage. Thereafter, wild birds usually molt once a year, after the breeding season. Pet birds rarely show this classic pattern of molting. They either continuously lose a few feathers at a time, or pass through a series of light molts two or three times a year. The reasons for this are the relatively constant temperatures and lighting cycles in our homes.

During a molt, birds do not lose all their feathers at one time. If this were so, they would be bald, cold, and flightless. Feathers are lost in an orderly pattern and the process takes about six weeks.

Molting is a stressful time. Nutritional requirements are greater and resistance to disease is lower. Follow the recommendations in chapter 2.

Feather Color: Feather color results from pigments within the feather and light reflecting off its surface. These colors can be altered by dirt, oil from hands, bleaching agents, age, disease, hormones, diet, physical damage, and temporarily by water.

Musculoskeletal System

Muscles and bones protect, support, and move the body. They also play critical roles in swallowing, blood circulation, respiration, elimination, egg laying, and much more. The marrow cavity, found within some of the bones, produces the red and white blood cells and platelets (involved in blood clotting).

The ability to fly has resulted in many changes in the structure and function of the bones and muscles. Here are a few of the more important and interesting adaptations:

- Certain bones, referred to as pneumatic bones, contain air sacs. In addition to being thought of as part of the musculoskeletal system, these bones also form an integral part of the respiratory system. The ribs, vertebrae, pelvis, sternum, humerus, and sometimes the femur are pneumatized.
- Bones are very light and thin-walled. Fractures (broken bones) can occur easily. Think of it as similar to the snapping of a toothpick.
- Bones of the skull have fused together, giving added strength and power to the beak. Spinal bones in the neck have formed in a unique manner, creating a long, extremely flexible neck. As a result, the head can actually rotate about 180 degrees. The sternum, or breastbone, is massive and along with the powerful pectoral muscles enables birds to develop the powerful forces needed for flight.
- In passerines (canaries, finches, and mynahs), three toes point forward and one backward. In parrots, two toes

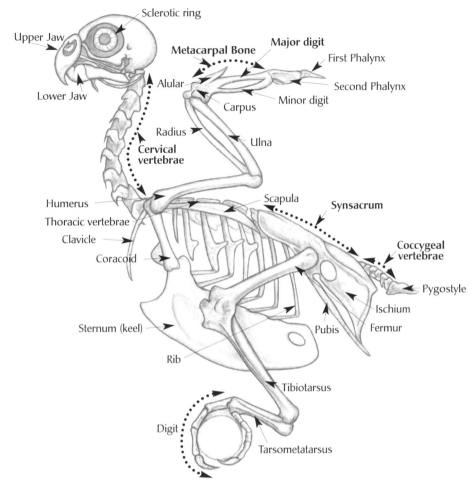

Parrot skeleton.

point forward and two point backward. These adaptations help birds catch and hold prey or other food sources, much like a hand.

- About 20 percent of a bird's body weight is due to its pectoral (breast) muscles.
- The basic structure of the muscles is similar to that of mammals. One interesting difference, however, is the existence of both red and white muscles. Red muscle fibers use fat rather than carbohydrates as their energy source. Since fat releases more energy than carbohydrates, red muscles are better adapted for sustained exercise. In strong fliers, such as parrots, the pectoral muscles contain mostly red fibers, accounting for its deep red color. In chickens, which are poor fliers, the predominant muscle

227

fiber is white and the color is very pale (this is why the breast is called "white meat").

Cardiovascular System

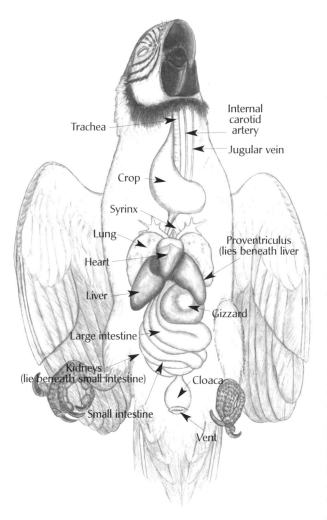

Trachea

Internal carotid artery

Jugular vein

Crop

Syrinx

Lung

Heart

Proventriculus (lies beneath liver

Liver

Gizzard

Large intestine

Kidneys (lie beneath small intestine)

Cloaca

Small intestine

Vent

Some of the major internal organs of a parrot.

The cardiovascular system's primary responsibility is the transportation of oxygen and nutrients to the cells. In addition, carbon dioxide and other waste products are carried away from the cells by the cardiovascular system. Water, electrolytes, hormones, enzymes, and antibodies are all transported throughout the body via the bloodstream.

The design of the heart, arteries, and veins is similar to that of mammals. The heart has four chambers, two atria and two ventricles. The heart is relatively large, and the heart rate is *much* faster than that of mammals. A human heart beats 60 to 80 times a minute. At rest, a canary's heart beats 500 to 1,000 times per minute, and a large parrot's heart beats 150 to 300 beats per minute! Cardiac output is the amount of blood pumped through the heart each minute. It has been estimated to be seven times greater in a flying budgie than in a person exercising at maximum capacity! Their circulatory systems working in unison with the other organ systems has enabled birds to utilize tremendous amounts of energy very efficiently.

Blood is composed of three different types of cells that are suspended in a liquid called plasma. Red blood cells carry oxygen to the body's cells. White blood cells combat the invasion of foreign organisms, and they produce and transport antibodies. Platelets are responsible for normal blood clotting.

Respiratory System

Respiration is simply the exchange of two gases, oxygen and carbon dioxide, in the lungs. Oxygen provides fuel for cells to produce energy. Carbon dioxide is the waste product of this exchange. Birds have a very high requirement for oxygen, especially during flight.

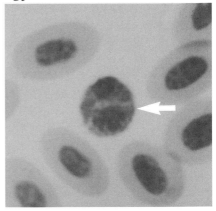

This is a photo of avian blood cells. One white blood cell is seen among the red cells (arrow).

Air enters the nares, which are the paired openings in the cere. These structures are located just above and behind the beak. Air passes through cavities, called sinuses, located inside the upper beak and skull. It then flows into the pharynx (throat).

Above the pharynx, and easily seen along the roof of the mouth, is a slit-like opening called the choana (ko-A-nah). This is part of the *nasal cavity*. Acting like a mini-filter, humidifier and heater, the nasal cavity cleans, moisturizes, and warms the incoming air.

Once in the mouth, air passes through the larynx and into the trachea (windpipe). Birds do not have vocal cords. The syrinx is the bird's voice box and is located at the base of the trachea in the neck area. Unfortunately, veterinarians are sometimes asked to surgically curtail a parrot's ability to make sounds, especially with an unusually noisy bird, but you can't "debark" a bird as you can a noisy dog. The location and structure of the syrinx is such that a safe and effective procedure has *not* been developed.

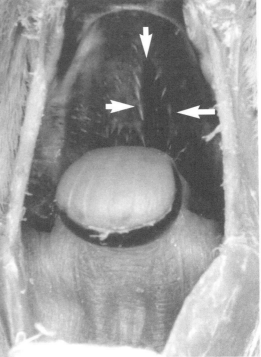

Airways called bronchi split off from the trachea and continue to channel air into the lungs. In birds, unlike mammals, the lungs do not expand and contract with each breath. Assisting the lungs are unique structures called air sacs. These are hollow spaces located in the body cavity and, as mentioned, also in some of the bones.

The arrows outline the passageway known as the choana slit, which lies between the oral cavity and sinus cavity.

A bird's lungs exchange oxygen and carbon dioxide more efficiently than those of any other animal. The actual mechanics of breathing, compared to mammals, is strikingly different.

Birds have no diaphragm separating the chest cavity from the abdomen. The chest and abdominal cavities unite into a single large space called the coelom (SE-lom).

Respiration works similar to a bellows system, with the body wall expanding and contracting on each breath. When a bird breathes and its body wall expands, air is filling the air sacs, not the lungs. The bellows action is pulling and pushing air in and out of the lungs.

In mammals, one complete breath is required to circulate air through the entire respiratory tract. In birds, two complete breaths, two inspirations and two expirations, are required! Humans breathe at a rate of 12 to 16 breaths per minute. Compare this with a canary that takes 60 to 100 breaths per minute at rest and a large parrot at 25 to 40 breaths per minute.

Birds are magnificent athletes. However, because their respiratory system is more complex, they are more susceptible to respiratory disease. Even a simple respiratory infection can quickly become serious or even life-threatening.

Lymphatic System

The lymphatic system is actually part of the circulatory system and consists of lymphatic vessels and lymphatic tissues. Lymphatic fluid transports water, electrolytes, hormones, and proteins from the tissues and returns them to the general circulation.

Parrots do not have lymph nodes. Lymphatic tissues include the thymus, cloaca bursa (often called the Bursa of Fabricus) and spleen. Lymphocytes produced by these tissues manufacture the antibodies necessary for immunity (resistance to disease). The spleen removes old red blood cells from the circulation. It does not appear to be a reservoir for blood, as it is in mammals.

Digestive System

Digestion is the process whereby food is converted into simpler compounds so it can be absorbed into the bloodstream and used for fuel by the cells.

The energy requirements of birds are incredibly high, and conversion of food into energy must be very rapid. A small bird will eat upward of 20 percent of its own body weight daily. This would be similar to a 150-pound person devouring 30 pounds of food in a single day! The by-product of all this food being turned into energy is heat: The body temperature of birds is very high compared with mammals (104 to 112 degrees Fahrenheit for birds vs. 98.6 degrees Fahrenheit for humans).

A bird's digestive tract functions similar to a mammal's. However, there are some important differences. Birds lack teeth, but they use the beak and tongue to prepare food for swallowing by crushing, hulling, and tearing. Hard, ridge-like structures on the base of the upper beak and inside the mouth aid in crushing hard food. Parrots can also use a foot to grasp food and raise it up to the beak.

Parrots have relatively dry mouths, since only a small amount of saliva is produced. The esophagus, which connects the mouth to the stomach, contains glands that moisten and lubricate food. The crop is a sac-like, esophageal enlargement, located at the base of the neck. It continues the process of food softening and also functions to slowly supply a continuous amount of food to the stomach.

Birds have one stomach divided into two distinct portions. The proventriculus, or true stomach, adds digestive juices to the food as it passes through. The gizzard, a muscular stomach, then pulverizes the food as it moves along. In the small intestine, the digestive process continues, and the food is finally absorbed into the bloodstream. It is transported throughout the body to provide fuel for the cells. The solid wastes, unusable portions of the food, pass on to the large intestine, then through the cloaca (klo-A-kah). The cloaca is the common chamber through which fecal, urinary, and reproductive elements pass before expulsion from the body. It opens to the outside through what is called the vent.

The pancreas, located alongside the small intestine, supplies the enzymes necessary to digest protein, carbohydrates, and fats. The liver has many various functions, and it works very closely with many other organs. Some of its more important jobs include blood filtration, producing and storing energy in the form of carbohydrates, and numerous other metabolic functions.

In birds, droppings are frequent because they can only store small amounts of feces in their cloacas. It only takes a few hours for food to pass through the entire digestive tract.

Urinary System

The urinary system of birds consists of paired kidneys and ureters. There is *no* bladder or urethra. Urine is produced in the kidneys, transported via the ureters into the cloaca and subsequently eliminated.

The kidneys are the filtering system for blood, removing poisonous waste materials. They play a role in regulating the balance of water and electrolytes (sodium, chloride and potassium).

Urine is only partially liquid. The primary portion is the white, semipasty material known as uric acid or "urates" mixed in with the feces. Uric acid is the end product of protein metabolism. It is manufactured in the liver, transported by blood and eliminated through the kidneys. Since no bladder is present, storage is limited and birds must urinate frequently.

Birds and reptiles have evolved a unique pattern of blood flow, different from that of mammals. Blood returning from the legs, reproductive system and lower intestines passes through the kidneys *before* entering the general circulation. This is important to understand because an infection in one of these organs could also cause a kidney infection. Also, injected drugs should *not* be given in the legs or lower abdomen. The kidneys could inactivate the drug *before* it has a chance to circulate throughout the body.

Female Reproductive System

In birds and mammals, the female reproductive tract consists of the ovary, oviduct, and vagina. In mammals, both the left and right ovaries and oviducts are fully functional. In birds, the left ovary and oviduct develop normally. However, the right ovary and oviduct remain underdeveloped. Interestingly, female birds determine the sex of offspring, whereas in mammals, males have this distinction.

Depending on the stage of the breeding cycle, the reproductive system varies considerably in size and shape. Stimulation of reproductive activity is influenced by environmental factors, with increasing periods of daylight being most important. Hormones similar to those found in mammals control ovulation.

The oviduct is actually divided into *five* distinct regions. It is here that both fertilization and growth of the egg occur. The uterus produces the calcified shell around the egg. The vagina pushes the egg through the cloaca and on to the outside. This entire process, from ovulation to egg laying, requires about 25 hours.

Eggs can be laid spontaneously, without fertilization and without another bird being in the cage. Cockatiels, especially, can be prolific and lay multiple clear, or infertile, eggs throughout the year.

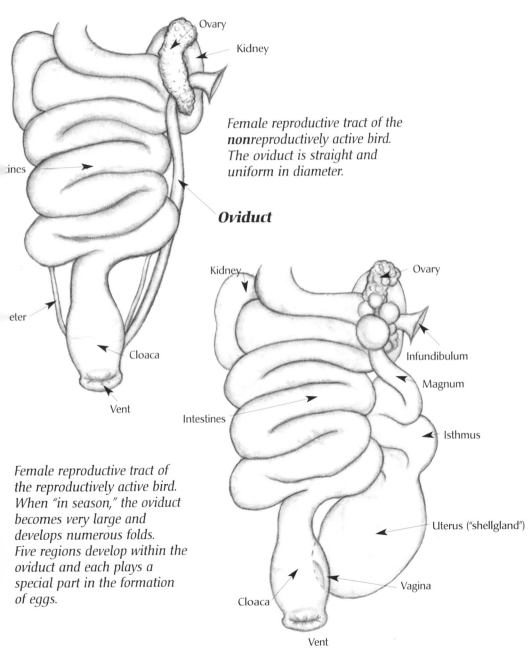

Ovary

Kidney

*Female reproductive tract of the **non**reproductively active bird. The oviduct is straight and uniform in diameter.*

Oviduct

:ines

eter

Cloaca

Vent

Kidney

Ovary

Intestines

Infundibulum

Magnum

Isthmus

Uterus ("shellgland")

Vagina

Cloaca

Female reproductive tract of the reproductively active bird. When "in season," the oviduct becomes very large and develops numerous folds. Five regions develop within the oviduct and each plays a special part in the formation of eggs.

Vent

233

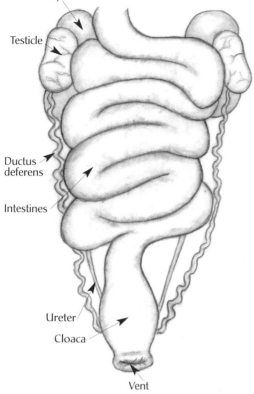

Kidney

Testicle

Ductus deferens

Intestines

Ureter

Cloaca

Vent

Male Reproductive System

The male bird's reproductive tract consists of paired testes, epididymis, and the ductus deferens. There is no prostate gland. The testes are located within the abdominal cavity next to the kidneys. The increased temperature in the abdomen does not affect sperm production and development in birds, as it would in mammals. Testosterone is the primary hormone in male birds.

A true penis–like structure does not exist in parrots. Mating still occurs through joining of the cloacas. Ejaculated semen is deposited on the everted cloaca of the female. The volume of semen is only one or two drops. It can retain its fertilizing powers for many days and sometimes even weeks.

235

Chapter 12

Home Physicals

Learn the Early Warning Signs

Birds are generally very healthy and resistant to disease. However, like all living beings, pet birds are going to become ill. It may not happen tomorrow, next month, or even next year, but unfortunately it will happen. Even pet birds that are never exposed to another bird or never venture outdoors will become sick. With good loving care, common sense, and a little luck, hopefully the effects of any disease can be minimized. Bird owners today have two advantages over bird owners of the past when it comes to keeping their pets healthy: Today's pet birds are predominantly captive bred, and they eat healthier diets than their predecessors.

This chapter is designed to assist in the recognition of diseases in their *early* stages. The survival instinct in birds is very strong. Even when they are sick, birds in the wild will continue to act normally for as long as possible. This act continues even in pet birds. In most instances, birds that just got sick yesterday have in fact been ill for some time.

<u>Read and then reread this chapter. It is perhaps the most important chapter in this book for pet bird owners to understand.</u> *<u>The sooner diseases are recognized and treatment started, the better the odds for a speedy recovery!</u>*

Author's Note: Throughout the text only the word sign is used to describe a particular appearance in a sick bird. Signs are the objective evidence observed by a person about his or her pet, as opposed to symptoms, which are a subjective feeling described by the patient. Since birds cannot communicate with us, they always show signs, never symptoms. Alas, there have been so many times in my career when I yearned for my patient to simply tell me where it hurts.

Sick Birds: The Signs of Illness

Many signs of illness will not be obvious to the casual bird owner. As you become more familiar with the normal appearance of your bird, these signs will be easier to detect. You should always be on the alert for the following basic changes in your bird:

This Amazon parrot is seriously ill. Notice how it leans to one side, how its wings droop and how its feathers are fluffed. Also, the bird has its eyes closed, and a nasal discharge is evident.

Changes in Activity
(Personality or Behavior): Less active, less talking and/or singing, more sleeping, decreased responsiveness to various stimuli.

Changes in Appearance:
Ruffled feathers, weakness, not perching/remaining on cage floor, bleeding, injuries, convulsions, distended abdomen. Changes in appearance related to specific health problems include the following:

Breathing Problems
Noisy breathing: wheezing, constant panting, or "clicking" sounds
Heavy breathing: shortness of breath, open-mouth breathing, tail-bobbing (pronounced up-and-down motion of the tail)
Nasal discharge and/or area surrounding eye swollen
Loss of voice

Digestive Problems
Vomiting/regurgitation
Diarrhea (specifically, loose stool), may contain blood, mucus, or undigested seeds
Straining to eliminate

Musculoskeletal Problems
Lameness
"Droopy" wing
Change in posture

Eye Problems
Eyelids swollen or "pasted" closed
Increased blinking
Discharge, including excessive tearing
Cloudiness of eyeball
Squinting

Rubbing eye or side of face

Skin Problems
Any lumps or bumps
Excessive flaking of skin or beak
Overgrown beak or nails

Feather Problems
Prolonged molt
Picking at or chewing feathers
Broken, twisted, crushed or deformed feathers

Change in Food or Water
Intake: Most sick birds will eat and drink less; weight loss and dehydration are common. Some diseases, such as diabetes, are exceptions and cause an increase in food and water consumed.

Changes in Droppings: Any variation in the number, consistency, or color (see the discussion of droppings later in this chapter).

The "Hands-Off" Examination
Learning the daily routine and nor-

Monitoring a bird's weight is one of the best ways to ensure its health. Avian veterinarians use special scales that weigh in grams and can be outfitted with perches to make it easier to weigh their avian patients.

mal behaviors of your bird is essential. The longer your bird is in your home, the easier this will become. Any change or variation from these usual routines could suggest a problem.

Every day, you or another family member will, at the very least, walk by your bird's cage. Someone will probably feed the bird, clean its cage, and, hopefully, include some playtime. During these times, observe your bird and its surroundings. Take a moment to really *look* and *listen*. A few seconds is all it takes.

A "oneness", or sixth sense will soon develop between you and your bird. When that inner voice is talking, or even whispering, that something is wrong, listen to it! Your instincts are probably correct. You may detect something vaguely wrong, which some bird owners describe as the "ADR" or "ain't doing right" syndrome. Contact your avian veterinarian's office for an evaluation as soon as you notice something out of the ordinary in your bird's daily routine to help ensure its good health.

239

This very brief daily routine should include asking yourself a few questions.

Look at the bird:

- Is there *anything* out of the ordinary?
- Has any daily routine or ritual changed? For example, first thing in the morning, is your bird greeting you the same as always?
- Eating habits normal?
- Vocalizing pattern, if any, about the same? If there is any variation, a problem *could* be developing. Birds are creatures of habit and generally follow established routines.

Look at the cage. In just a moment's glance:

- Food eaten?
- Water consumed?
- Are any items missing or chewed upon?
- Is anything present that doesn't normally belong in the cage?

Look at the cage floor:

- Are the droppings normal? Check the location of the droppings. An active bird will leave droppings all around the cage. If the droppings are piled up in one or two places, it could indicate an inactive and depressed bird.
- Are there any feathers or blood on the floor?

Look at the food dishes:

- Are the cups full of uneaten food?
- Is the water clean? If it becomes dirty with droppings regularly, move the water dish to a different location in the cage.

Nervous System

The signs to watch for with a nervous system problem are varied. They will depend on the underlying cause, the part of the nervous system affected and other organ systems that may be involved.

Signs To Watch For

- Changes in behavior, responsiveness, or coordination (loss of balance or clumsiness)
- Abnormal head positions
- Postural changes
- Unusual eye movements
- Blindness
- Paralysis (loss of movement or sensation)
- Seizures
- Lameness

A lameness or paralysis in one or both legs could suggest a tumor or egg in the abdomen. In budgies, tumors in the abdomen can put pressure on the sciatic nerve and result in lameness. A concussion (violent shock or jarring of the brain) can occur when birds collide with a window or mirror.

Endocrine System

There are many glands and organs, each producing specific hormones. Therefore, the signs to watch for are variable.

Signs To Watch For
- Increased appetite or thirst
- Abnormal growth
- Bone and reproductive problems

There are more signs than those listed, but they are too numerous and nonspecific to mention here. For instance, hypothyroidism can present in many different ways, including obesity and feather problems. Diabetes, another endocrine disease, also has many presenting signs, but classically, dramatic increases in appetite and thirst are seen.

Healthy adult birds rarely fall from their perches. If this occurs, consider that your bird could have an underlying problem.

The Senses

Vision: Both eyes should *always* appear similar in color, size and shape. Compare one with the other; if you see a difference, it suggests a problem. A complete eye exam requires special instruments and testing procedures.

241

Note: Eye problems are potentially serious; consult your veterinarian immediately.

Signs To Watch For

- The eyelids should be open wide and appear smooth and clean. They should not be crusted or pasted closed. The feathers surrounding the eyes should be clean, lie in neat rows and not be caked together.
- The conjunctiva (delicate membrane lining the eyelids) should be pink and glistening. It should not be red and swollen.
- The cornea (transparent outer covering of eyeball) should appear clear and radiant. If injured, it becomes cloudy and loses various degrees of its transparency.
- The pupils should both be the same size and shape. The size of the openings should adjust with the amount of light. Stimulation or excitement causes dilation of the pupils.
- The lens is located immediately behind the iris and on the back side of the pupil. It is transparent and normally can not be seen. A white spot in the center of the pupil suggests a cataract. (See chapter 15 for more information on cataracts.)

Hearing: Ear diseases are uncommon.

Signs To Watch For

- The *internal ear canal* controls balance. Watch for the head held in a constantly tilted or in an awkward position, or problems with balance.
- The *external ear canal* should be clean and dry, and there should be no sign of swelling. Watch for discharge and rubbing or scratching the area around the affected ear. This could be suggested by the feathers over the ear being wet, ruffled, or stuck together.

Smell: Signs to watch for are general and nonspecific. Plugged nares (stuffy nose) would probably affect the sense of smell and could affect appetite.

Taste: Signs to watch for are general and nonspecific. An upper respiratory infection could affect the sense of taste. Appetite could be decreased.

Home Physicals

Integument

The skin is very thin and nearly transparent. Don't be fooled by its normal reddish–purple appearance. This is normal because the muscles can be seen through the skin. There are few blood vessels in the skin and therefore, bleeding is usually very minimal.

Signs To Watch For

- Examine the skin for any wounds, cuts, or bruises. An area of wet or matted feathers could suggest a skin problem.
- Any swellings, lumps, or bumps on the skin are abnormal.
- A thickening of the skin or a soft, smoothly rounded mass felt beneath the skin could suggest fat. It usually builds up in the upper chest and abdominal areas. Budgies, cockatiels, rose-breasted cockatoos, and Amazons are particularly prone to developing obesity.
- A whitish honeycomb-like crusting at the corners of the mouth, around the beak and sometimes the legs could suggest mites (see chapter 15, "Medical Problems"). This is most commonly seen in budgies.
- Watch for overgrown toenails or beak (see chapter 6, "Grooming").

Feathers: The appearance of the feathers are another good indicator of a bird's overall health. Sick birds usually develop a ruffled, unkempt appearance.

Signs To Watch For

- The feathers should be arranged in neat rows. They should all appear in good condition and have a nice, shiny glow.
- Watch for signs of feather picking (see chapter 8, "The Well-Behaved Parrot" and chapter 15, "Medical Problems"). Areas on the chest, back, wings, and legs are the sites affected. The feathers on the head and upper neck remain undisturbed and should appear normal.
- If blood is found on the feathers, it usually suggests a damaged immature feather or a skin injury.

Musculoskeletal

Palpation (examining with the fingers) of the pectoral muscles provides an excellent indication of weight. The muscle should be full, rounded slightly, and about even with the leading edge of the sternum (keel bone). When you look at the bird's chest, it should resemble a letter "**U**." In an underweight bird, the pectoral muscle begins to take on the shape of an arrowhead and the keel feels sharp and more prominent. These birds' chests will resemble a letter "**V**." In extremely underweight birds, the sides of the "**V**" will be drawn in. In an overweight bird, the muscle becomes rounded and extends slightly above the keel. If you look at an overweight bird, its chest will resemble a letter "**W**" with slightly rounded "points" on the "**W**."

Signs To Watch For
• The joints should flex easily, and there should be no evidence of pain or swelling.
• The wings should be at equal height and lie adjacent to the body. An injured wing will droop and be held slightly away from the body.
• Both legs should bear weight equally when the bird is standing.

Coelom
The coelom is the body cavity. The major organs, including the heart, lungs, liver, gizzard, and kidneys, are all contained within this space. Although it is hidden from view, there are still signs to watch for that would suggest a problem within the body cavity.

Become familiar with your bird's normal abdominal shape. Simply move your index finger gently around the area just above the vent. It should feel flat or even slightly drawn-in.

Signs To Watch For
• Labored breathing, suggested by forceful and pronounced expansions of the body wall or tail-bobbing (pronounced up-and-down movements of the tail)
• An enlarged or distended abdomen, a potbellied appearance

These are serious problems; consult your veterinarian.

Cardiovascular
Signs To Watch For
• Tiring easily, coughing, and abdominal swelling. These could suggest a heart problem.
• Bleeding. This is a medical emergency; Refer to chapter 14, "Medical Emergencies" and *contact your veterinarian immediately.*

Estimating heart rate is very difficult. The heart beats very fast, and this, combined with relatively tiny blood vessels, makes it nearly impossible to locate a pulse on most birds. The heart can be heard using a stethoscope placed on the lateral chest wall (the area beneath the bird's wings). However, since the heart rate is incredibly fast, murmurs are very difficult to hear.

Respiratory

Signs To Watch For

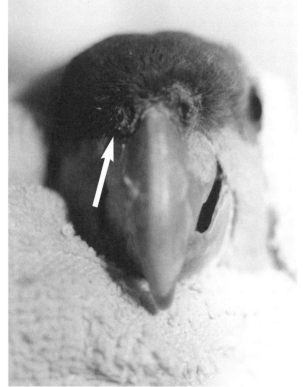

Notice that this bird's right nare is "plugged" and has a discharge around it.

- Stand a few feet from the cage and observe the pattern of your bird's breathing. It should be easy, smooth and rhythmic. Watch for rapid breathing, gasping for breath, holding wings out and away from the body, open-mouth breathing, and panting at rest.
- The nares should be clear of debris, and the area around them clean. There should be no swelling, redness, or discharge.
- Listen for unusual sounds. Sneezing can be pronounced as an "achoo" or as subtle as a soft click. Wheezing sounds similar to a wet whistling noise. A cough is softer but similar to a human's. A change in pitch or tone of the voice could suggest a syrinx or lower tracheal problem.
- Swelling below one or both eyes could suggest sinusitis (infection of the sinuses).

    Diseases of the lung and air sacs are nearly impossible to diagnose without radiographs and other diagnostic tests.

Author's Note: Be very careful when handling birds with respiratory disease. If capture and restraint are necessary, keep the time to an absolute minimum. If giving medicine, have the proper dosage drawn up and ready to go before handling the bird.

Lymphatic System
Signs of lymphatic system disease are vague and nonspecific. Diagnosis is difficult and requires specialized testing.

Digestive System
Signs To Watch For
- The normal shape and length of the beak varies with each species. Compare your bird's beak with other birds of the same species.
- Swallowing of food should be effortless. Birds having difficulty swallowing will stretch their necks and hold their heads back. If a swallowing problem is suspected, the back of the mouth needs to be inspected.
- The mucous membranes lining the mouth and throat should appear pink. There can also be various amounts of black pigmentation normally seen. Look for problems such as white, creamy patches covering the roof of the mouth. Bleeding is always abnormal. Any mouth odor suggests a problem.
- Vomiting or regurgitation is usually not normal. Regurgitation can also be a sign of courtship behavior.
- Become familiar with the appearance and number of your bird's droppings (see discussion later in this chapter).
- In young, hand-fed birds, watch for a crop that empties very slowly or not at all (see chapter 14, "Medical Emergencies").

Cloaca and Vent
Signs To Watch For
- The area around the vent should be clean and dry. There should be no matted feathers or accumulation of droppings.
- The vent sphincter should be closed tightly.
- There should not be any tissue or growth protruding from the vent.

Urinary System
Urine and urates should be normal color and consistency (see discussion later in this chapter).

Female Reproductive System
Signs To Watch For
- Acute swelling of the abdomen. Excessive straining, squatting, or walking penguin-like. This could suggest an

egg-laying problem. A history of recent egg laying or breeding along with these signs would be very suspicious.

• Excessive straining could result in a cloacal prolapse.

Note: These problems are a medical emergency. Refer to chapter 14, "Medical Emergencies" and contact your veterinarian immediately.

Male Reproductive System

There are no specific signs that suggest a problem with the male reproductive system.

The "Hands-On" Examination

The last part of the examination involves actually capturing the bird and performing a complete physical examination. This last step of a complete exam is best left to a veterinarian. It takes years of study and practice to understand the technique, which includes developing a systematic approach, differentiating normal from abnormal, interpreting the findings, and making recommendations for the best course of action. Also, proper restraint, for everyone's safety, requires a great deal of training and experience.

Droppings: A Reflection of Your Bird's Health

Bird droppings are a mess, and they're unsightly. However, they also reveal a great deal of information about the overall state of a bird's health. A change in the appearance, color, or quantity of the droppings is one of the earliest signs recognized in sick birds. Unfortunately, owners frequently overlook this important clue. In birds, unlike dogs with a digestive problem, there are no foul odors, no messes to clean up, no mistakes in the house. A similar problem in birds could go unnoticed for a long period of time.

Pet bird owners should get in the habit of taking a moment to look over their pet's droppings each day.

Normal Droppings

It is important to become familiar with the appearance of your bird's normal droppings. Within any given period of time, the droppings will vary slightly. Factors such as diet and stress can quickly change their appearance. Learn to recognize these normal variations.

Unlike mammals, birds urinate and defecate at the same time. In fact, the digestive, urinary, and reproductive tracts all empty into the same receptacle, the cloaca.

The droppings consist of three distinct portions:

1. Feces are the solid waste material from food. The feces should be tubular in shape and formed into a coil. Their color and consistency is affected by diet. A diet consisting mostly of seeds produces a dark green to near black-colored feces. Formulated diets (pellets) produce a more brownish stool.

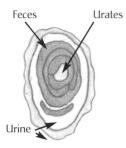

Feces   Urates

Urine

Normal dropping

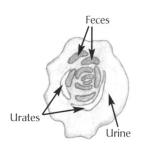

Feces

Urates

Urine

Increased urine output
("wet droppings")

This "wet" dropping has too much urine. The feces are formed; therefore, this is not diarrhea. "Wet" droppings can be seen with stress, many diseases, and diets high in fruit.

2. Urine is the liquid portion. It is normally clear. Diets high in fruits and vegetables will produce more urine.

3. Urates, also called uric acid, is the creamy-white or chalk-like substance on top of and around the feces.

Abnormal Droppings: Interpretation

Once the appearance of the normal droppings are known, recognizing abnormal ones will be much easier.

Feces: Abnormal changes in appearance

DIARRHEA (soft or liquid feces): Diarrhea is uncommon. An increase in urine, which produces wet droppings, is frequently mistaken for diarrhea. Remember, if the feces are solid and formed, it is not diarrhea. Increased urine can cause the feces to become wet and slightly loose. Diarrhea is not a disease. It is only an indication that a problem is involving the digestive tract.

Causes Of Diarrhea

- Diet (sudden change in diet, addition of new food, spoiled food), intestinal infection, ingestion of foreign object or poison
- Diseases of other organs
- Egg ready to be laid or egg binding
- Abdominal hernia
- Overtreatment with antibiotics
- Stress
- Parasites
- Cancer

BLOODY (red, reddish-black, or tar-like):
Bleeding in digestive tract, severe intestinal infections, bleeding disorders, some poisons, cloaca papillomas, tumors, ingestion of foreign objects, parasites, egg laying.

UNDIGESTED FOOD
(whole seeds or pieces of pellets in feces): Poor digestion, parasites, intestinal infection (e.g., proventricular dilatation), pancreatic disease, oil ingestion.

INCREASED VOLUME (bulky feces):
Egg laying, poor digestion.

DECREASED VOLUME (small, scant and dark feces): Appetite loss or shortage of food, intestinal obstruction.
Urine: Changes in Volume

INCREASED URINE OUTPUT (wet droppings, polyuria): Normal with increased stress, diets high in fruits and vegetables; abnormal with infections, diseases (i.e., diabetes, kidney disease), poisons, drug reactions.

These droppings are typical of those produced by a dehydrated bird. Note the lack of urine around the stool.

DECREASED URINE OUTPUT:
Dehydration.
Urates: Change in Color
Remember, urates should always be white or whitish-beige in color. Color changes indicate a serious problem.

YELLOW OR YELLOW/GREEN DISCOLORATION:
Liver disease.

RED OR REDDISH/BROWN DISCOLORATION (bloody):
Poisoning, liver disease.

Color changes can also indicate an overindulgence in a favorite food, such as beets, pomegranates, or blueberries. Don't be fooled by the red dye in some newspaper ads when they are used as cage tray lining. When a wet dropping comes in contact with this red dye, the color can "bleed" through, and it has been mistaken for blood in the droppings.

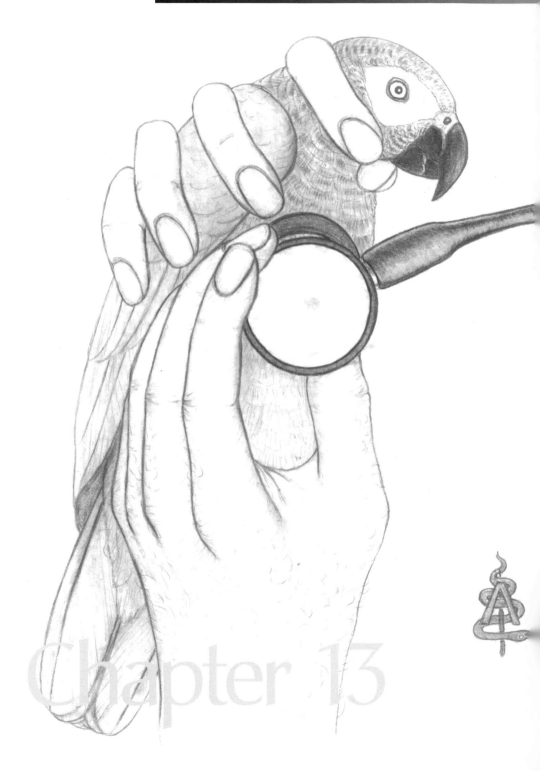

Chapter 13

Veterinary Care

Bird Doctors, Diagnostic Testing and Therapeutics

Today, a sick bird is a much luckier bird than ever before. Long gone are the days when a sick bird was a dead bird. The advances in avian medicine have enabled veterinarians to provide health care for birds in ways never imagined. Avian medicine is one of the fastest-growing disciplines in veterinary medicine. More and more veterinarians are developing the knowledge and skills necessary to provide good veterinary care for pet birds. The nation's veterinary colleges have recognized the dramatic increase in the number of households with pet birds and the need for well-trained veterinarians to treat them. The Association of Avian Veterinarians (AAV) now boasts more than 3,000 members throughout the world. These doctors all share a common interest--birds! They also fund research on avian diseases, reproduction, conservation, and education.

The need for veterinary services will arise sooner or later for every pet bird owner. With birds, this need often arises very quickly. Therefore, plan ahead and establish a relationship with a veterinarian knowledgeable in avian medicine.

This chapter includes a discussion on a wide range of veterinary-related topics, including how to find a qualified avian veterinarian, what to look for while visiting the clinic, and a discussion of the latest in diagnostic and therapeutic medicine.

Veterinarians: When to Seek Professional Help
New Bird Checkups

It is always best to have a newly acquired bird examined by a veterinarian. A thorough exam is a good insurance policy for the long-term health of a bird (see "The Medical Work-Up" in chapter 15, "Medical Problems"). If any problems are found, the buyer, seller, and veterinarian should discuss the available options.

New bird owners usually have many questions on nutrition, behavior, and preventive medicine. They have already heard many conflicting do's and don'ts on pet bird care. The veterinarian and clinic staff can help resolve any concerns and answer questions.

The Association of Avian Veterinarians

The Association of Avian Veterinarians (AAV) was founded in 1980 by a group of veterinarians who wanted to provide educational opportunities for veterinarians who worked with birds. Initially, 175 veterinarians from the United States and Canada joined the group, but the AAV now has more than 3,000 members in 43 countries around the world.

The AAV educates its members and the general public as to all aspects of avian medicine and surgery by offering conferences, practical labs, avicultural programs, client education brochures, and a professional magazine devoted to all aspects of avian medicine. The AAV also provides funding for a variety of topics of interest to aviculture and avian medicine.

In September 1993, the first avian medicine board certification test was offered. Veterinarians with a special interest in birds and who meet other requirements can choose to take this demanding test, which requires months or even years of preparation. Achieving board certification in avian medicine demonstrates a high level of proficiency in the field.

In Health...

The importance of prevention and early detection of medical problems is well known in all areas of medicine. Most dog and cat owners understand the value of yearly checkups and disease prevention through vaccinations. However, many bird owners still do not understand the importance of yearly exams for their birds.

Birds mask illness until problems are usually well advanced. They also can't communicate how they're feeling. As a result, many birds are unnecessarily presented to veterinarians in a serious or life-threatening condition. Birds often carry potential disease-causing organisms, and when the conditions are right, these bugs can cause problems. Annual physical exams will not only help prevent disease but also minimize the seriousness when disease occurs.

Yearly exams also provide a way for owners to stay current as new information on pet bird care becomes available. This includes information on nutrition, behavior, and preventive medicine. Vaccines are available to protect pet birds from certain diseases, but they are not routinely recommended for most pet birds. Ask your veterinarian if he or she recommends vaccinations for your bird. An annual examination by a qualified avian veterinarian is a valuable tool for the overall health and vitality of a pet bird.

...in Sickness

Time is critical in the treatment of sick birds, and the sooner the bird gets to a veterinarian, the better. Whenever your bird shows any signs of sickness, you should consult a veterinarian.

Unfortunately, many birds receive home remedies before a veterinarian is consulted, and this delay in treatment can complicate matters. Although home remedies may not harm your bird directly, the delay in beginning effective treatment saps your bird's energy and strength, which could make its recovery longer.

Obviously in an emergency, you should seek veterinary care immediately. In these instances, it's best to have previously established a relationship with a knowledgeable avian veterinarian.

Veterinarians: How to Find One Knowledgeable in Avian Medicine

The best time to start looking for a qualified veterinarian is before your bird needs one, and the best way to start looking would be to ask local veterinarians, the veterinary association in your community or state, local pet stores, and bird clubs. Usually, if you ask enough bird people, certain names will be mentioned consistently. Veterinarians with a bird interest become known and develop a reputation throughout the community. Virtually every large town and city should have a veterinarian with a special interest in birds.

Relying solely on yellow pages advertising is not recommended as a method of selecting a veterinarian. Unfortunately, many veterinarians who advertise that they treat birds have not taken the time to learn the necessary basics of avian medicine.

All veterinarians with a serious interest in birds should be members of the Association of Avian Veterinarians (AAV). This is well worth asking about. Being a member of AAV does not attest to a veterinarian's avian medical abilities, but it is a very good start.

This is an example of an examination checklist used by avian veterinarians. (Courtesy Association of Avian Veterinarians)

What to Look for When Visiting an Avian Veterinarian

A good bedside manner is important but does not necessarily indicate competence in medicine. Determining competence can be a quite difficult matter. Most pet owners are not really capable of evaluating the quality of medicine practiced. This is the reason an avian veterinarian's reputation is so important. As recommended in the previous section, spend the time, do your homework, and find a highly skilled avian veterinarian before you need one.

In addition to a good bird reputation, evaluate the doc-

ASSOCIATION OF AVIAN VETERINARIANS
CERTIFICATE OF VETERINARY EXAMINATION
Caged or Aviary Bird

Reference # _____

Owner: _____ Date: _____
Address: _____ Telephone: _____
Bird's Name: _____

IDENTIFICATION
Species _____ (Tattoo, Band, Microchip Number) _____
Age _____ Sex _____ Weight (in grams) _____

HISTORY
Origin of bird: ☐ Wild-caught ☐ Captive-bred (Name of Breeder _____) ☐ Hand-fed ☐ Unknown
Diet _____
Medical History _____

PHYSICAL EXAM	Normal	Abnormal	Not Examined	Notes
General appearance	☐	☐	☐	
Integument	☐	☐	☐	
Feather condition	☐	☐	☐	
Beak	☐	☐	☐	
Nares	☐	☐	☐	
Eyes	☐	☐	☐	
Feet	☐	☐	☐	
Pharynx/choana	☐	☐	☐	
Vent /cloaca	☐	☐	☐	
Musculoskeletal	☐	☐	☐	
Respiratory system	☐	☐	☐	
Cardiovascular	☐	☐	☐	
Neurological system	☐	☐	☐	
Urine/urates	☐	☐	☐	
Feces	☐	☐	☐	
Other				

RADIOGRAPHIC FINDINGS _____

LABORATORY TESTS AND DIAGNOSTICS

Test	Date run	Lab/method	Normal	Abnormal
			☐	☐
			☐	☐
			☐	☐
			☐	☐
			☐	☐

Clinic _____ Examined By _____
Address _____ Phone _____
City _____ State _____ Zip _____

This form is not a guarantee of good health. Rather, it is intended for clients to monitor the progress of their avian pets.

tor's hospital and staff. Here are a few suggestions to help you assess the overall quality of care provided:

- Is the hospital clean and inviting? Are bird-related items on display in the reception area or exam room?
- Does the hospital seem equipped to treat birds? Some of the standard equipment should include a gram scale, incubators, a radiograph ("X-ray") machine, laboratory facilities, isoflurane or seroflurane gas anesthesia, and a clean and organized surgery room. Ask for a hospital tour!
- Are the staff members friendly, professional, and knowledgeable? Many clinics employ Registered Veterinary Technicians (RVT) or Certified Veterinary Technicians (CVT), who are licensed veterinary nurses. These highly trained professionals are an asset to any veterinarian and will help ensure that the animals receive high-quality medical care.
- Does your veterinarian fulfill Dr. James Harris' "Three C's" for a successful veterinarian: competency, communication, and compassion? A veterinarian should take a complete history and perform a hands-on physical exam. Capture and restraint should be done gently, carefully, and with minimal effort. Your veterinarian should both thoroughly explain the suspected cause or causes of your bird's problem and discuss diagnostic and treatment options with you in simple and understandable terms. All your questions should be answered.
- Are fees discussed openly? Cost estimates, preferably in writing, should be given before any tests or treatments begin. Remember, medicine is not an exact science and estimates are just an approximation of costs. However, if the health status of your bird changes and the estimate is no longer valid, it is customary for the veterinarian to inform the owner. If necessary, ask about billing policies.

Small businesses may not be able to offer loans, but the use of credit cards, debit cards, CareCredit®, Pet Insurance and other options usually exist.

CareCredit® plans allow pet owners to establish a credit account for their pet's health care needs. These accounts offer low monthly payments and even interest-free payment plans. The accounts cover both routine and emergency medical care, and other pet supplies may also be eligible for the plan. CareCredit® plans are available in all 50 states, so ask your veterinarian's office for more information.

- Is follow-up care provided? Your veterinarian should be available to answer any questions on cases currently under their treatment.
- Does the hospital provide after-hours emergency coverage? Inquire about their policy concerning emergencies outside regular officehours. Find out which animal emergency centers in your area are qualified to treat birds, and get directions to these facilities before you need them.

What Veterinarians Look for in Clients

Health care is a team approach. Veterinarians are looking for clients who understand that health care for their birds is a two-way street. A good client is a partner in this relationship, willing to do what it takes to achieve success. This requires good communication.

For example, the veterinarian is responsible for providing clear and exact home-care instructions for the owner to follow. Veterinarians depend on clients to follow through with the home treatments properly. No matter how competent the veterinarian is, if an owner gives home treatments incorrectly, the animal may not recover. The veterinarian would be under the mistaken impression the medication failed, when in fact this was not the case. As a client, you need to comply with instructions the veterinarian gives you. Always ask if you need your veterinarian or a member of the hospital staff to clarify instructions if you don't understand them.

In addition to following directions, you should keep the following in mind:

- Do not expect a veterinarian to make a diagnosis over the phone. Even the best veterinarian cannot see or feel a bird over the phone. Remember, many different diseases and injuries appear very similar.
- Clients must have confidence in their veterinarians. If this is not the case, you should find another doctor for your bird's health needs.
- A client must understand that a veterinarian can never guarantee a pet will recover, only that the very best effort will be made. Veterinarians care greatly for the welfare of their patients, but they cannot save them all. A good client tries to understand this despite difficult circumstances.

255

• Excessive waiting time to see the doctor can frustrate clients. In any hospital, unexpected emergencies occur frequently. These cases must receive first priority. Clients need to remember that most doctors really do try to do everything possible to minimize the wait.

• Clients should arrive on time, if not a little early, for their scheduled appointments. This is especially important if paperwork needs to be filled out prior to a pet seeing the veterinarian, as in the case of a new client's first visit or an established client bringing in a new pet.

• Clients should expect their veterinarian to offer alternatives for the treatment of their pet birds. This might include sending medication home vs. performing diagnostic tests, or home treatment as opposed to hospitalization. The veterinarian's responsibility is to offer these options. However, if circumstances dictate that the ideal and most complete approach is not possible, clients need to understand the odds for recovery will be lessened and the veterinarian should not be held responsible.

Going to the Veterinarian: Things to Remember

• Call ahead and make an appointment. If this is a first-time visit, arrive 15 minutes early to fill out the necessary paperwork. For an emergency, still call ahead. Make sure the doctor is in and allow the staff time to prepare for your arrival.

• Birds should be carried into the hospital in some type of cage or carrier. It's best to bring the bird's own cage (do not clean it, so the veterinarian can see the actual environment, including the droppings). If the cage is too large to move, use a cardboard box, pet carrier, or travel cage. The cage or carrier should have ventilation holes. Be sure to bring along the cage paper and a sample of food the bird is currently eating.

• Just before leaving home, consider emptying water cups so they don't spill. Also, lower or remove perches if the bird is unsteady or excessively weak, also remove swings or toys that could injure the bird during the ride to the clinic. Covering the cage for the trip can help some birds relax more.

• Bring any medications or other supplements the bird has been given recently.

Bird Insurance?

A new development aimed toward helping pet bird owners is pet bird health insurance. The pet bird health insurance plan was designed by avian veterinarians to help owners pay for medical expenses when a bird becomes ill or injured. Policyholders can visit any licensed veterinarian, worldwide. Office calls, diagnostic tests, treatments, hospitalization, prescriptions, and even surgery are covered. Pet Buddy discounts are available for bird owners with more than one feathered friend. The plan is currently available only in the United States and is provided by Veterinary Pet Insurance Company. For more information, ask your avian veterinarian, call (800) USA-PETS or visit the company's Web site at http://petinsurance.com.

256

• Write down a list of questions. In the exam room, clients frequently forget questions they wanted to ask.

The Examination

The cornerstones of any examination are a thorough history and a physical examination. When visiting the veterinarian, be prepared to answer these questions:

• Age and sex of bird, if known
• Length of ownership and where purchased (private breeder, pet shop, adopted from friend or family)
• Why is the bird here? What are the signs and when did they first appear?
• Has the bird been exposed to other birds? Are any other birds sick? Are any newly acquired birds in the home? Are any family members ill?
• Does the bird have previous medical problems? (If your bird has been treated by another veterinarian, have its records forwarded to the new doctor.)
• Reproductive history, if any?

A cardboard box makes a good transport cage for a sick bird. Notice the low perch and the easy access to food and water that this cockatiel has.

Your avian veterinarian's staff can provide you with the latest information on bird care. Take-home handouts are often available that help you refresh your memory after the visit.

• What has the bird been eating? Has its appetite changed?
• Has the activity level remained normal? Is the bird sleeping more? Talking less? Are there new or strange behaviors?
• Any regurgitation or vomiting? Coughing or sneezing? Change in droppings?

257

- Have changes been noticed in the feathers?
- Have there been recent changes in the bird's home environment?
- Is the bird allowed to fly free in the home?
- What type of cage does the bird live in?
- Has the bird chewed on any strange objects in its cage or around the house?
- What home treatments have been tried and for how long?

In chapter 12, "Home Physical Exams," the basics of the "hands-off" physical examination were discussed. In addition, there is the "hands-on" physical examination. While it may be easy to teach someone the steps involved in conducting these exams, it is another thing to have acquired the knowledge and practical experience to determine what is normal and what is abnormal. Also, differentiating one problem from another, similar-appearing one requires a great deal of skill. It takes years of study and practice to interpret the findings and make recommendations as to the best course of action. This is the job of the avian veterinarian.

Birds that cannot perch are weighed at an avian veterinarian's office in this metal container, which is placed on the scale.

In cases of severe respiratory distress or shock, a veterinarian might choose to delay the physical exam until the bird can be stabilized. Good medical judgment is important to avoid further compromising an already distressed patient.

Diagnostics

Veterinarians perform laboratory tests to help them arrive at an accurate diagnosis. This is the key to effective treatment and a rapid recovery. Numerous tests are available. No one test alone will consistently yield a diagnosis. Frequently, a few different tests must be performed in order to piece the puzzle together accurately.

Diagnostic testing does not guarantee a successful outcome for a pet bird, but it does greatly increase the chance for one. The more information that a veterinarian can learn about the problem and its severity, the more aggressive and specific the treatment can be.

The various diagnostic tests, including how they are collected and how they are interpreted, are described briefly.

Blood Tests

Recent advances in laboratory medicine now allow a battery of tests to be performed on minute amounts of blood. The sample is usually collected directly from a vein in the neck, wing, or leg.

Blood tests often can detect disease before any outward signs become apparent. They assist in establishing a diagno-

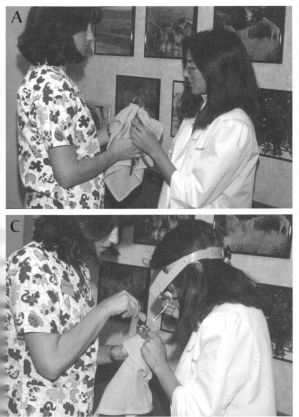

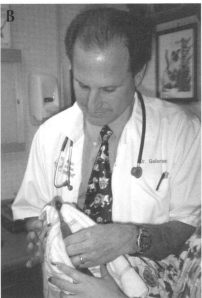

A thorough avian examination should include a) listening to the bird's heart with a stethoscope; (b) hands-on monitoring of the bird's muscle mass and feather condition; and (c) a close-up examination of the bird's mouth and throat.

sis, a future outcome (prognosis), and allow a veterinarian to monitor a patient's progression more closely than by depending solely upon visible appearances.

Complete Blood Count and Differential: An excellent initial screening for the presence of infection, inflammation, anemia, blood parasites, and protein levels. Includes: packed cell volume (PCV, hematacrit), plasma protein concentration, total white blood cell (WBC) count, and a microscopic evaluation for the blood cells' appearance and platelet estimate, and to count the various numbers of different types of cells.

Blood Chemistries: Evaluation of chemical components in the blood provides important information that helps to formulate an accurate diagnosis, prescribe appropriate therapy, and monitor response to treatment. These assays look for imbalances in certain biochemical functions that, when present, could point to the possibility of organ dysfunction.

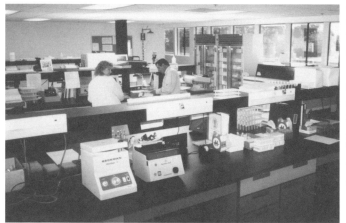

Some specific diseases that can also be diagnosed through blood tests include chlamydiosis, psittacine beak and feather disease syndrome, polyomavirus, aspergillosis, and lead and zinc poisoning.

Protein Electrophoresis: This test is another valuable tool used to uncover hidden disease. The basic principle involves applying plasma on

A modern avian diagnostic laboratory. (Avian and Exotic Clinical Pathology Laboratory)

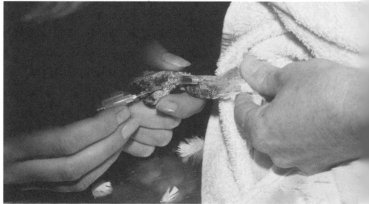

Getting ready to collect blood from the neck vein of an anesthetized budgerigar.

Blood sample is being collected from a leg vein.

Exotic CBC	Results	Reference Range
WBC Count	51.3 (H)	10.3-22.6
HCT	34.0 (L)	45-53
Heterophils	68	43-75
Heterophil Bands	9	
Lymphocytes	22	20-58
Absolute Heterophil	34884 (H)	2919-13400
Absolute Neutrophil Band	4617	
Absolute Lymphocyte	11286 (H)	4500-10300
Thrombocytes	Adequate	
Polychromasia	Slight	
Blood Parasites		
No Parasites Seen		
Remarks		
Heterophils appear moderately toxic		
Moderate reactive lymphs present		
Reticulocyte Estimate	1+	
Avian Chemistries		
SGOT (AST)	1212 (H)	91-300
CPK	10734 (H)	39-550
Amylase	6582 (H)	276-594
Albumin	0.7 (L)	1.2-1.6
Total Protein	3.0	2.5-4.4
Globulin	2.3 (H)	0.9-1.9
Glucose	196 (L)	200-350
Calcium	6.8 (L)	9.0-13.0
Uric Acid	11.8 (H)	2.5-11.0

Acacia Animal Hospital

a gel substrate to an electrical field. The various blood proteins (albumins and globulins) migrate to different locations depending on their charge and are subsequently measured. Changes in the levels of these proteins can be another good indicator of an acute or chronic inflammation or infection.

These are laboratory results of a complete blood panel from a bird. The actual results are in one column and the reference ranges, or normal values, for that particular species of bird is listed in the other column.

Radiology ("X-ray")

Taking "X-rays" of birds requires using a few tricks of the trade. These include specially designed restraint boards that enhance safety by lessening the stress to the bird when being handled. For highly stressed or large birds, many times anesthesia is the best and safest method of restraint.

Radiographs 'X-rays': The ability to see inside the body is one of the most valuable diagnostic tools available for birds. Bone abnormalities, size and relative relationship of internal organs, presence of foreign bodies, tumors, the condition of the lungs, air sacs and heart, and much more can all be evaluated with radiographs.

Bacteriologic Exams

A sterile cotton swab is used to collect samples. The samples can be taken from any site on the body, but the most common are the mouth, cloaca, eyes, nares, skin, and feather folli-

261

cles.

Since infections are the most common problem in pet birds, these are very useful tests. They can confirm the existence of an infection, identify the actual organisms present and help in selecting the most effective medication.

Gram stain: The gram stain is a simple screening test for the presence of bacteria and yeast. A cotton-tipped applicator

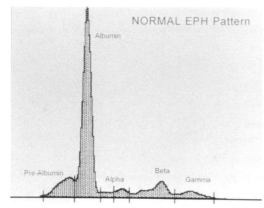

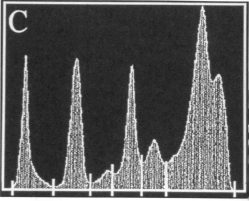

Normal protein electrophoresis (left) and abnormal protein electrophoresis of a bird with acute chlamydiosis (right).

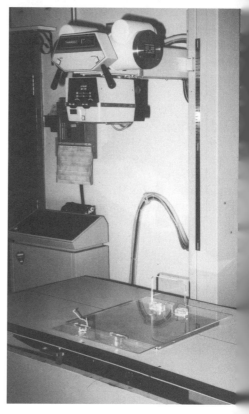

Here is a radiography machine with a plexiglass avian restraint board sitting on top of the radiographic film cassette.

(cotton swab) is used to collect samples from the mouth, vent, feather follicle, or almost anywhere else on the body where an infection may be present. The sample collected is rolled onto a microscope slide, color-stained and examined microscopically. It determines the presence and approximate quantity, and it classifies bacteria into gram-positive and gram-negative categories. This ratio of gram-positive to gram-negative bacteria is

262

important and is used to determine if a significant infection is present.

Bacteria Culture & Sensitivity and/or Fungal/Yeast Culture: Bacterial culture & sensitivity and/or fungal/yeast culture tests provide more in-depth and detailed answers than the gram stain. Samples are collected in a similar fashion but are instead rolled onto a special growth-enhancing culture medium. The numbers and types of organisms are specifically identified. The bacteria sensitivity portion then selects the antibiotics most effective for treating the infection.

This cockatoo is safely restrained for a radiograph.

Fecal Analysis

Feces are collected from cage paper. Samples can also be collected directly from the cloaca using a cotton swab.

The fecal analysis is a microscopic exam of the stool to detect intestinal parasites (worms) and abnormal amounts of yeast and bacteria.

Urine Analysis

Urine is collected directly from the droppings. Wax paper lining the cage floor will help to separate the urine portion from the feces.

Urine analysis is not commonly performed on birds. It can, however, be helpful when problems, such as urinary tract infections, kidney disease, or diabetes, is suspected.

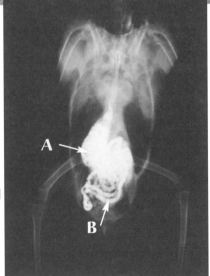

Biopsy

Veterinarians use two types of biopsies—core and fine-needle aspirate—to examine tissue. In a core biopsy, a small piece of tissue is removed surgically from an affected organ. In a fine-needle aspirate biopsy, a needle attached to a syringe is inserted into an organ or tumor and a sample is withdrawn with little discomfort to the patient.

The tissue collected is examined microscopically by a specialist in avian pathology. Biopsy is primarily a means of diag-

This is an upper gastrointestinal radiographic contrast study. Barium is tube-fed to the bird, and the result is a very clear visualization of the digestive tract. Arrows point to the proventriculus (A) and intestinal loops (B).

nosing cancer, but it can also identify infections, inflammations, and parasites within tissues.

Endoscopy

An endoscope is very precise optical instrument. Equipped with magnification and a light source, an endoscope can provide the veterinarian with a very detailed and clear image of various internal organs.

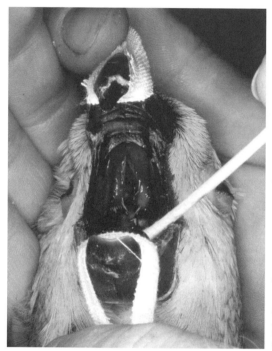

Endoscopic examination is one of the most accurate methods used to diagnose disease. The shape, size, and color of a bird's internal organs can change when disease is present. The endoscope allows the avian veterinarian to visualize the internal organs as well as the sinuses and trachea. Furthermore, biopsies (small samples of tissue) can be collected safely during the endoscopic examination. These samples can then be analyzed by an avian pathologist.

In birds, endoscopy is most commonly used to view the internal organs. Under anesthesia, the veterinarian will make a tiny skin incision on the side of the abdomen and insert the endoscope. Endoscopy provides a first-hand look at the shape and size of organs. In larger birds, endoscopy can also be used to view the inside of a portion of the sinus cavity and the trachea.

Throat cultures can help an avian veterinarian diagnose disease. A sterile swab is used to collect a sample from the bird's throat for analysis.

The coelomic cavity is open and a liver biopsy is being collected on this anesthetized bird. Magnification and specialized instruments are necessary when performing surgery on birds.

Electrocardiogram (ECG)

An ECG is a recording of the electrical activity of the heart that is printed on a moving strip of paper. It is a safe and simple procedure, and although not commonly performed on birds, an ECG is helpful in the diagnosis of heart disease. In general, heart problems are not common in pet birds.

264

Ultrasound

Ultrasound uses very high frequency sound waves, similar to sonar, to create an image of internal organs. Ultrasound allows a veterinarian to see the internal structure of organs. Although it is not yet commonly used in avian medicine, ultrasound can help in identifying diseases of the heart, liver and reproductive tract of birds.

Necropsy (Postmortem)

Necropsies are conducted after death and requires the dissection and examination of a body to determine the cause of death. If a necropsy is going to be done, the body needs to be refrigerated, not frozen, and transported to the veterinarian as soon as possible. Wrap the body in newspaper and then place it in a small sealable plastic bag.

Postmortems are routine in most avian practices. For the owner's benefit, determining the cause of death may help ease the pain of loss. Also, if the owner keeps other birds, preventive measures could be suggested to help control a potential disease outbreak. For the veterinarian's benefit, the knowledge gained will also improve the care of future patients.

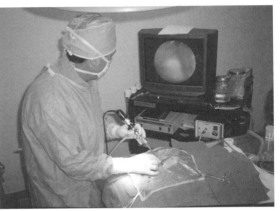

Endoscopy is being used to view the organs and tissues of the coelomic cavity. The magnified image is being viewed on the monitor. Biopsies and some surgeries can be performed using special endoscopic surgical instruments.

Sex Determination, or "Gee, He Laid an Egg!"

Many pet birds do not show any external sexual characteristics. (Exceptions to this rule include budgies, Eclectus parrots and some color mutations of cockatiels.) In other words, the boys and the girls look very similar--they have the same size, color, shape, and behaviors. Special testing methods are required to differentiate a male from a female bird.

For aviculture, having the correct sexes paired is obviously essential for a successful breeding program. For pet birds, on the other hand, the bird knows its sex and that's all that usually matters. However, for medical problems related to the reproductive tract, determining the proper gender is critical in establishing a correct diagnosis. Also, for those owners who just have to know, simple and safe methods are now available for sex determination.

Observation: Unless an egg is laid, this method is not reliable for pet birds. Do not attempt to identify sexes based on observed behaviors. No actions, attitudes, habits, or tendencies are consistent with one sex or the other. Females can spontaneously lay infertile eggs even with no contact with a male bird.

DNA Sexing: This technique involves analyzing the red blood cells to determine the presence of male or female chromosomes. It is a reliable, convenient, and reasonably priced test that can be performed on any age bird. Only one drop of blood or a few plucked feathers are required. Samples are mailed to a lab, and the results will be known within two to three weeks. DNA fingerprinting for positive individual bird identification is also available.

Surgical Sexing: Of all the methods, this is the oldest and quickest way to determine gender. The veterinarian passes an endoscope into the body cavity of an anesthetized bird and then looks for an ovary or testicle. Although this technique involves both anesthesia and minor surgery, an experienced avian veterinarian can perform it with very minimal risk. Surgical sexing also provides an opportunity to perform a visual internal examination of the bird.

Sometimes healthy pet birds surprise their owners by laying eggs. This African grey had been a pet for 14 years before she laid an egg. Other, less surprising methods of determining sex are discussed in this chapter.

For the method best suited to your specific needs, consult an avian veterinarian. Each of these methods has advantages and disadvantages.

It's worth mentioning here that a German study discussed at the 1999 Association of Avian Veterinarians conference may help veterinarians and bird owners better understand how birds determine the gender of their fellow birds. Some birds are equipped with the ability not only to see light in the visible spectrum as people do, but they can also see ultraviolet light. This ability to see ultraviolet light may play a role in gender determination because birds' feathers appear to look different to the birds than they do to us.

Vaccinations

Vaccines are used to immunize or protect the body from specific diseases. They stimulate the body's immune system to produce antibodies against disease-causing organisms. These vaccines have been modified in such a way to ensure only protection. They cannot cause the disease.

The vaccines currently available for pet birds include Pacheco's disease, polyomavirus, and pox virus. For individually kept pet birds, the risk of contracting either of these diseases is low. Some vaccine reactions have been reported, and therefore the question of whether to vaccinate should be discussed with an avian veterinarian.

A vaccine for psittacine beak and feather disease syndrome is being developed. Hopefully, this is just the beginning. Vaccines were one of the true medical wonders discovered in the 20th century, and they will continue to benefit patients in the future.

Therapeutics: The Art and Science of Healing

Primum non nocere (First, do no harm). This ancient physician's oath is one of the guiding principles in all branches of medicine. However, nowhere does it take on more importance than in the field of therapeutics. The science, and especially the art, of medicine helps decide which "weapons" from the vast arsenal of therapies will be safest and most effective. Veterinarians spend many years in school and in practice learning, developing, and polishing their skills in this area. Many options are available for the treatment of sick birds. No single approach will always be effective. Veterinarians must weigh many factors when they select the best treatment regimen. These include:

- Age and species
- History and physical examination findings
- Unique anatomy and physiological characteristics
- Unique nutritional and environmental requirements
- General health
- Diagnostic test results
- Severity of disease or injury
- In-hospital or home care
- Owner's ability to restrain and handle bird
- Combined effects of all drugs and other therapies given
- Finances

This section will briefly discuss many of the treatment options available in avian medicine. This list continues to expand as research and technology evolves.

Hospital vs. Home Care

Sometimes the decision as to whether or not to hospitalize a sick bird is very easy and sometimes it's not. A severely ill bird that requires special treatments such as surgery, oxygen, therapy, supplemental fluids, "force" feeding, and close monitoring (i.e., for shock, seizuring, poisoning, severe breathing difficulties) will need to be hospitalized. Also, especially with the larger birds, owners are simply unable to handle and medicate their birds. In these instances, the bird will have to be hospitalized or will require daily visits to the hospital.

The vast majority of birds, on the other hand, will not

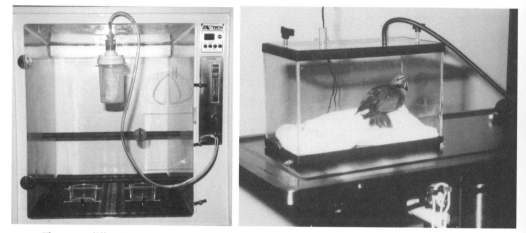

These are different types of hospital incubators used for sick birds.

require hospitalization. These birds can be treated adequately and effectively at home. Home care has the distinct advantage of providing a familiar and stress-free environment. It is also considerably less expensive.

The ultimate decision should be made in the partnership between owner and veterinarian. Many factors need to be considered, and each case must be handled individually.

Hospitalized birds should be kept in an incubator, which is an enclosed container with settings that allow for maintaining proper temperature and humidity. It also has see-through sides for easy viewing and monitoring of the patient. An oxygen-enriched environment can be set up when breathing difficulties are a problem.

Medications/Drugs

Drugs are any substances used to aid in the diagnosis, treatment or prevention of diseases, and other problems. They can relieve pain and promote healing. When administered correctly, drugs are an aid to the ultimate healer--Mother Nature.

Selecting the most effective drugs and using them correctly are essential. Birds can react unfavorably to any medication. Drugs that are safe for humans, dogs, cats, and other animals may not be safe for birds. Also, since birds are relatively tiny creatures, drugs must be used at their correct dosage. The choice of drugs must be based on the above list of factors. Only veterinarians, and specifically avian veterinarians, have the specialized knowledge necessary to make these decisions.

This Amazon is being properly restrained to receive oral medication. A needle-free syringe allows for accurate dosing.

Once the choice to use a drug is made, still more decisions are necessary. These include:

* Dosage (amount of drug to be given; many drug dosages vary within specified limits)
* Frequency (How many times daily? Once, twice, three times, or more?)
* Duration of therapy (How many days is medication to be given?)
* Route (oral, injection--i.e., intramuscular, subcutaneous, intravenous--and topically are the most common methods)
* Form (liquid, injectable, powder, "crushed-up" pills, capsule--many drugs come in a variety of forms)
* Possible side effects
* Cost

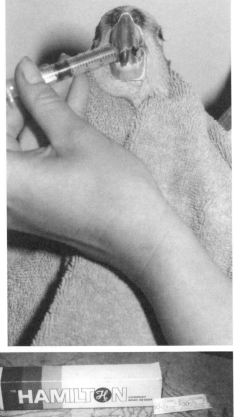

Method of Administration
Oral
Directly into the Mouth: This is a very good method for small birds and birds that are easily handled. For larger birds, medication given by mouth may be difficult. Towel restraint is necessary; the head has to be held steady and accurate dosing can be a problem. Do not use a glass eyedropper to administer medication. Some drugs are not available in an oral form.

Medicating the Water: This is the least effective method. Sick birds usually drink less water; therefore accurate dosing is not possible. Many medications do not dissolve evenly in water or will give it an unpleasant taste. Medicating the water is best used in healthier birds, when medications are given long term or when treating a large group of birds.

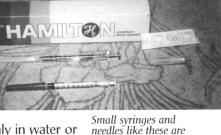

Small syringes and needles like these are typically used to inject medication into pet birds.

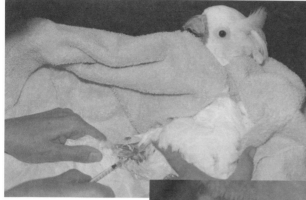

Medicating the Food: There are commercially formulated diets that contain antibiotics. These generally work well, especially when long-term treatment is necessary or with difficult-to-handle birds. Problems can arise because birds must be converted to these diets as their only source of food.

Another method is to bury medication in soft foods. This method may be the easiest one to use with larger birds. When using this option, be sure the bird eats all the medicated food.

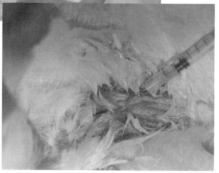

This cockatoo is receiving an intravenous injection into the wing vein. Also shown is a close-up of the injection site.

This Amazon is receiving an intramuscular injection into its pectoral muscles.

Injectable

This is the most accurate method of administering medications. Once owners have been properly instructed in the technique, it can safely be done at home. It is rapid, painless, very low risk, and is also less stressful on the bird than giving medications directly into the mouth. Predictably, owners are very fearful at first, but quickly learn the method is really quite easy. The most difficult part is the restraint.

Intravenous (into a vein): These are used by veterinarians to gain rapid effects of life-saving drugs.

Intramuscular (into a muscle): This is the preferred route for most injectable drugs. It is also the most common route used by owners for administering antibiotics at home.

Subcutaneous (beneath the skin): Used most frequently by veterinarians for giving fluids to dehydrated birds.

Intraosseous (within the bone): Veterinary-administered medications, usually fluids, given through a needle placed directly into the marrow cavity. This method is generally reserved for very sick birds.

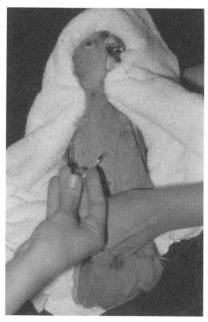

Topical (Applied Directly To Area Being Treated)

Dermatological (for skin and feathers): Topical

skin and feather medications have limited use. Avoid oil or greasy compounds unless you are directed to use them by your veterinarian because they will damage feathers.

Intraocular (into eye): Commonly used for eye infections or other eye problems. Use only medications specifically labeled for eye use. Be extremely careful when using eye medications on your pet bird because certain eye medications can potentially do more harm than good. It's always best to use only those eye medications prescribed specifically by your veterinarian for your bird's condition.

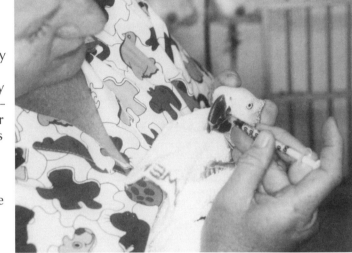

Intranasal (into nares): Medications can be flushed or instilled into the nose for sinus infections.

Intrasinus (into sinuses): Used by veterinarians for sinus infections. Helps to clean and treat infected sinuses.

Some recuperating birds, such as this African grey parrot, that are too weak to drink on their own are given water by syringe to help keep them hydrated.

Fluid Therapy

Many sick birds will not drink enough water and, as a result, become dehydrated and weak. Providing additional fluids can sometimes be the most important part of the treatment. Fluids are usually given by injection or, sometimes, orally with tube feeding.

Birds who are in shock are usually given fluids directly into a vein or a bone. Subcutaneous fluids are used in birds that are stable and only slightly dehydrated. For long-term fluid administration, fluids can be given through a catheter and dripped into a vein or into the bone marrow.

Inhalation Therapy
(Breathing Medication Into Lungs)

Vaporization or Nebulization: Medication is suspended in a very fine liquid mist. These microscopic droplets are inhaled deep into the respiratory tract. They soothe and moisturize inflamed linings. It is an especially beneficial method for birds with air sac infections or obvious breathing difficulty.

Nutritional Support

Tube Feeding: If sick birds are not eating well, they will often require force feeding. Tube feeding can sustain a bird nutritionally until it is well enough to eat on its own. Tube feeding is done with a tube attached to a syringe and using specially prepared food. The tube is inserted through the mouth directly into the crop, where an appropriate amount of food is given. Fluids and medications can also be given through the tube and with the food. In inexperienced hands, tube feeding could severely injure a bird or even cause asphyxiation. Therefore, it is not recommended as a home treatment.

Types of Medications

Analgesics: Analgesics help relieve a patient's pain. Recent studies have shown that animals who receive analgesics actually heal more quickly than those that do not.

Antibiotics: These drugs have saved many lives that otherwise would have been lost. Antibiotics kill or inhibit bacteria. They are not effective against viruses. They can be used in a viral infection to prevent bacteria from causing more problems. Many different antibiotics are in use. This is because all antibiotics are not effective against all the various types of bacteria. Selection is based on many of the factors already discussed and, in addition, on the results of a culture and sensitivity test when available.

Antiyeast/Antifungal: Just as their name states, these drugs kill or inhibit the growth of yeast and fungi. These organisms commonly cause infections in pet birds.

Antiinflammatory: These medications suppress inflammation. They can help control pain and are used in birds to treat shock, some cancers, joint problems, allergies, and sometimes skin problems.

(A) This macaw is receiving intravenous fluids.
(B) This close-up view shows the intravenous catheter that allows for the easy administration of intravenous medications. A syringe containing medication can be easily inserted through a rubber cap which allows easy access to the vein.

272

Anthelmentic (ANT-hel-MIN-tik): This is the medical name for drugs used to eliminate parasites.

In addition to this very brief overview of drug therapies, a wide assortment of other medications are used in avian medicine. These include anticancer medications, antidotes for poisons, antivomiting and antidiarrheal drugs, blood modifying agents, hormones, antiseizure, antiviral, vitamins, minerals, sedatives, anesthetics, respiratory and heart drugs, behavior modifiers, appetite stimulants, and still more! They must be used correctly and under the supervision of a veterinarian. If used incorrectly, drugs can do much harm.

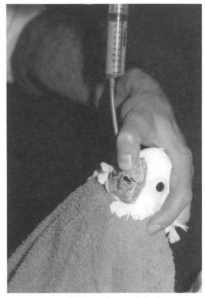

Surgery

New anesthetic protocols and surgical techniques are constantly evolving. They allow the avian veterinary surgeon to successfully perform more and safer surgeries on birds than ever before.

In addition to the age-old scalpel blade, avian veterinary surgeons can now use electrocautery, cryosurgery, and laser surgery to treat patients.

In recent years, avian surgery has become more highly developed, and the most important advancement has been in the field of anesthesia. General anesthesia renders the patient totally unconscious, thereby eliminating the patient's feeling of pain.

This cockatoo is being fed via a tube that has been passed into its crop. To keep the bird's mouth open and to keep the tube from being chewed on, the bird's upper beak has been placed carefully inside its lower beak.

Isoflurane and the newer seroflurane are the safest gas anesthetics available for birds. Nowadays, complicated and more prolonged surgeries can be performed with little anesthetic risk to the avian patient.

Surgery may be necessary for tumors, broken bones, abscesses, lacerations, retrieval of foreign bodies, obstructions, prolapses, and sometimes for egg binding. The actual surgical preparations and procedures are very similar to those used in other animals:

- Prior to anesthesia, radiographs and blood tests may be needed, not only to gain more information about the problem, but also to check for other factors that could increase the risk of anesthesia and surgery.
- The patient should be as relaxed as possible before surgery. Therefore, the bird should be in the hospital a few hours prior to, or even the night before, the surgery.
- Isoflurane or seroflurane should be used for anesthesia.
- Once the bird has been anesthetized, the feathers around the surgical site will be gently removed and the skin surgically prepped.

273

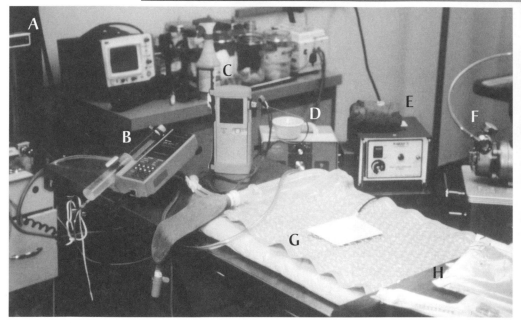

This photo shows anesthetic and surgical equipment used with birds:
a) anesthetic machine,
b) auto-syringe fluid pump,
c) pulse oximeter,
d) electrocautery machine,
e) light source for endoscopy,
f) suction,
g) hot water heating pad,
h) sterile instruments.

• The patient's heart rate, breathing rate, and other vital signs will be monitored closely to evaluate the depth of anesthesia and for unexpected problems that could occur.

• The surgery should be performed under generally accepted sterile conditions. Surgical instruments designed for human eye surgery are often used because of their small size, and suture material of very small diameter is used to close incisions and wounds both inside the body and on the skin. Blood loss must be kept to an absolute minimum.

• Recovery from anesthesia usually takes only minutes, sometimes even less. Ask to be called immediately after your bird recovers from anesthesia.

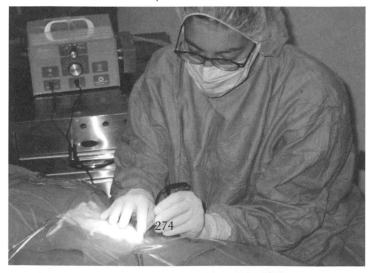

Electrocautery is being used to make the initial skin incision for surgery in this anesthetized bird. In birds, this technique is usually preferred over the use of a scalpel blade because it results in less blood loss. The blue electrocautery unit is seen in the background and the surgeon is holding a pair of cutting bipolar forceps.

274

Veterinary Care

Bandages, Splints, and Collars

The application of bandages, splints, and collars is frequently necessary. Properly applied, they support and protect a muscle, ligament, or tendon injury, or broken bone.

They also protect cuts and bruises and will keep a bird from picking at the area. It requires considerable skill and experience to apply one of these devices properly.

If they are applied improperly, they can cause serious injury to a bird. It is recommended that only veterinarians apply a bandage, splint, or collar to a bird.

Restraint collars used to be applied routinely for feather-picking birds. They are still used, but usually only in severe cases. Collars are usually made of plastic or leather. They encircle the bird's neck and prevent the beak from reaching the bird's skin and feathers.

When a collar is used, a bird can become very stressed, initially fighting the collar, and may stop eating. You must watch a bird closely for the first several hours after the collar has been applied. Within a short time, most birds will accept the collar. Depending on the problem, collars can be left on for days, weeks, and sometimes even months.

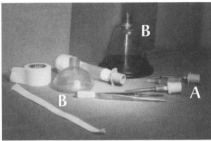

Anesthetic equipment used to administer the anesthesia directly to the bird: a) endotracheal tubes that are placed in the bird's mouth and trachea, b) these masks can be placed over a bird's face. Tape strips are used to hold the equipment in place.

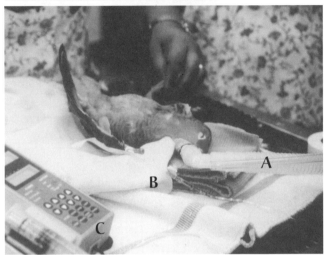

This Amazon has been anesthetized and prepared for surgery on its right leg. a) Anesthetic tubing is attached to the endotracheal tube, which is in the bird's mouth and trachea. b) An interosseous catheter has been inserted into the humerus bone of the wing. Fluids for hydration are administered through this catheter. c) A microliter fluid pump is used to measure accurately the small amount of fluids administered to this bird.

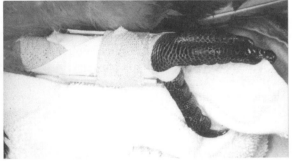

Splints help immobilize a broken bone so it can heal properly. The top layer of tape has been left off this leg cast to show the wood splints in place.

275

Important Points to Remember with Bandages and Splints

- Keep it dry! A wet splint or bandage can cause infection and delay healing.
- Watch for picking. Light "preening" of or a little playing with the bandage is normal, but digging and tearing at it are not.
  - If part of the bandage comes off or slips down, the entire bandage will probably need to be changed.
  - If toes or a wing tip are exposed below the bandage, check them daily for swelling. If swelling is noted, the bandage could be too tight and will need to be changed. If any of these problems develop, call your veterinarian immediately.

This Amazon has its foot and lower leg bandaged.

Complementary Avian Veterinary Medicine
By Stacy Stephens D.V.M.

Alternatives to conventional veterinary medicine are an evolving science, and their popularity continues to increase. Alternative medicine includes a vast array of treatments that are not included in mainstream Western medicine. Most veterinarians who are trained in alternative medicine actually practice complementary medicine, which means they apply both Western therapies and holistic approaches to best meet the needs of the individual patient.

Even if you are considering alternative treatments, it is still important to have a complete medical workup to formulate a diagnosis. As with Western medicine, the success of any treatment is greatly increased when the underlying medical problem is known. Nutrition is also very important because the best medicine cannot overcome a poor diet. Remember, just because a product is natural does not mean that it is completely safe. Many herbs contain potent, even toxic, chemicals, and an owner should never give such products to any animal without the advice of a veterinarian who can scale a dosage to the size and type of animal. This is especially important when treating birds because of their small size.

While many types of alternative medicine exist, this section will discuss the three most common disciplines: traditional Chinese medicine (which includes acupuncture and Eastern herbal therapies), Western herbal medicine, and homeopathy. Traditional Chinese medicine (TCM) involves an ancient and complex philosophy which, simply put, is based on the principle of balancing the energy, or Qi (pronounced chee), in the body. It also involves harmonizing a being with nature and the environment, thus allowing the body to return to a healthy state. TCM uses two methods of treatment to accomplish this goal: acupuncture and Eastern herbal remedies.

This leg splint for a budgie was fashioned out of a paper clip. Avian veterinarians often have to be creative and use objects or tools designed for other purposes.

Acupuncture is the art of inserting fine needles through the skin, treating illness by stimulating specific, defined areas called "points." Acupuncture points correspond to specific organs or energy pathways (meridians). Stimulation of these points, alone or in combination, may either increase or decrease Qi to achieve the desired result.

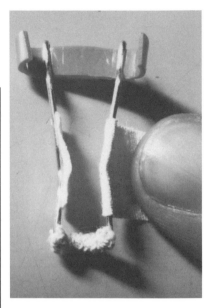

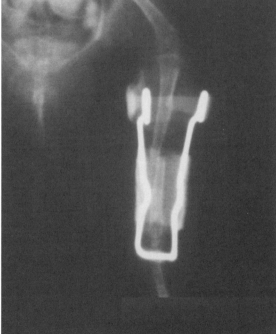

Here, the paper-clip splint is applied to a budgie's leg.

This radiograph shows the budgie's fractured leg and the splint in place.

When using acupuncture in birds, we must contend with their inquisitive nature. While some birds will allow needles to be inserted and remain in place, many birds are too active or will remove the needles before the desired time. As an alternative, many avian veterinarians will use aquapuncture. This is a specific method of stimulating acupuncture points by injecting small amounts of sterile fluid at the point. The fluid may be a common electrolyte solution, saline, or a dilute vitamin solution. Most birds tolerate this well, thus enabling us to stimulate a point for an adequate amount of time.

TCM also includes Eastern herbal medicine, which utilizes plants, minerals, insects, and other substances to help the body heal itself and return to harmony. Herbal medicines may be formulated in liquid teas, extract granules, or tablets. Due to the small size of birds, liquids or extract granules are typically used to achieve a dose small enough to prevent toxic side effects.

Western herbal medicine uses plants found on the continents of North America and Europe. Throughout history, many people have used various plant parts for their medicinal properties. Research has shown that many of these traditional remedies have therapeutic properties. In fact, many drugs are derived from plants. For example, digoxin, which is used to treat some heart conditions, is derived from the plant Digitalis. Many holistic practitioners prefer herbs in their natural state because the secondary chemicals help reduce undesirable side effects and may enhance the effectiveness of the primary therapeutic component.

Homeopathic medicine is based on the theory that illness can be treated with a substance that causes similar symptoms when ingested. Homeopathic medicines are substances that are prepared by a specific process of dilution and succession (mechanical shock). This process is called "potentization." The more potent the product, the more times it has been through the dilution and succession process. Homeopathic treatment requires a thorough history of both physical and mental (emotional) signs to select the appropriate remedy. The goal is to select a single remedy that best corresponds with the patient's signs. This can be challenging in animals because we must interpret behavior from the emotional signs that are seen. Special texts and references have also been developed to help veterinarians better understand and compensate for these limitations.

Veterinary Care

Finally, if you have an interest in alternative treatments for your bird, let your veterinarian know. He or she may practice complimentary medicine or may be able to refer you to another veterinarian with the appropriate training. When selecting a holistic veterinarian, it is important to find out what type of training the veterinarian has had in the specific areas he or she utilizes. Many veterinarians take special courses, after which they may be tested and given a certificate of completion upon passing. However, many times there are no specific courses, and veterinarians simply attend many continuing education classes in these areas and belong to organizations promoting alternative medicine education and research.

This Amazon is undergoing acupuncture treatments for chronic sinusitis.

Chapter 14

Medical Emergencies

Spills, Thrills 'n' Oops...

Table 1
Common Avian Emergencies

Three STARS ✪✪✪

indicates a life-threatening situation requiring immediate veterinary attention.

Two STARS ✪✪

suggests a situation in which an avian veterinarian should evaluate the bird sometime during the same day.

One STAR ✪

is suggestive of a situation where it may be O.K. to wait up to 24 hours for a veterinary examination.

This chapter is intended to serve as reference to help bird owners learn and apply basic first aid for many of the most common medical emergencies they will see in their pet birds. The chapter also serves as a preventive guide in regards to these emergencies. The best way to use this chapter is to become familiar with its contents so that when a problem arises, you will already have a basic idea about how to deal with it. The simple act of being aware of and knowledgeable about potential dangers will help to prevent them.

This chapter emphasizes medical emergencies, but the reader should use it in conjunction with the section entitled "Diagnosing Disease" on p. 326 of chapter 15, "Medical Problems." In many emergency situations, you will not immediately know the underlying cause. When you need to make a diagnosis, that section will explain the best method to reach an appropriate diagnosis. Why is this so important? A proper diagnosis is essential for selecting the best treatment, which not only resolves the problem in the shortest possible time, but significantly increases the probability of a successful outcome and allows for a more realistic prognosis.

Medical Emergencies

A medical emergency is a serious and/or potentially life-threatening injury or disease that requires immediate care. This chapter reviews many of the emergency medical situations encountered in pet birds. Each section of the chapter discusses a specific problem. In addition, each situation is ranked in terms of severity based on a rating scale of from one to three stars. Three stars ✪✪✪ indicates a life-threatening situation requiring immediate veterinary attention. Two stars ✪✪ suggests a situation in which an avian veterinarian should evaluate the bird sometime during the same day. One star ✪ is suggestive of a situation where it may be O.K. to wait up to 24 hours for a veterinary examination.

Please be aware that these are only general guidelines. Regardless of the star ranking, if you feel your bird is unstable and doing poorly, contact an avian veterinarian immediately! In many cases, it's difficult for bird owners to know if a problem is truly an emergency. When in doubt, follow your instincts and use common sense. If there's any doubt in your mind, it's an emergency!

Emergency, Emergency! What to Do First
Keep Calm and Think Clearly!

Remember, the injured or sick bird is already stressed and excited, and someone needs to be thinking in a clear and orderly fashion.

1. If the bird is stuck or trapped in something, figure out a way to free it safely. Be careful when doing this. Even friendly, loving birds may bite when excited.

282

2.   Try to determine the seriousness of the problem. Is it really life threatening? (refer to Table 1)

3.   Will some type of home treatment help to stabilize the bird or will home treatment simply delay the professional medical care only a veterinarian is able to provide?

If *home treatment* is indicated, refer to the section in this chapter and in chapter 16, "Home Care for the Sick Bird," that discusses the problem.

If *immediate veterinary care* is indicated, phone your avian veterinarian office right away. Inform them as to the nature of the problem and follow their instructions. The next few sections of this chapter will discuss how to safely transport the bird to the veterinarian and what to expect upon arrival at the clinic or hospital.

Before Leaving Home...
Phone Ahead, Alert Your Veterinarian

Before leaving home, call your veterinarian. Very few animal hospitals are open seven days a week and 24 hours a day! Most facilities have limited hours. Some clinics may even close for lunch. Hospital hours are frequently different from the veterinarian's hours. A veterinarian may be in the hospital, but could be involved in a major surgical procedure and simply not be immediately available.

When you first acquire a pet bird, you should visit a veterinarian to get a new bird check-up. At that time, ask the veterinary staff about the hospital's policy for handling medical emergencies, especially after-hours policies, when they are closed.

The staff will most likely ask that, during normal business hours, you call before bringing your pet. When you do call, immediately tell them your name, pet's name, and the nature of the problem. They will help decide if immediate veterinary care is required. Listen carefully to their instructions. Your advance call allows the hospital to be better prepared for your arrival; when they know what to expect, they can have the appropriate personnel available, along with medical supplies and equipment.

Veterinary hospital policies differ in the way they handle avian medical emergencies that arise after office hours. The after-hours phone system at most animal hospitals is connected to some type of message machine and/or answering service. Most veterinarians use a pager, cellular phone, or both. Some veterinarians will respond to an after-hours emergency phone call, while others will refer you directly to another veterinarian or an emergency animal hospital. In most metropolitan areas, there are small animal emergency clinics. These facilities specialize in animal emergencies and are open nights and weekends when most daytime veterinary facilities are closed.

Transporting the Sick or Injured Bird

Sick or injured birds must be handled as little as possible. These birds really need to be kept quiet and allowed to rest. However, the benefits of professional veterinary care outweigh the risk associated with the stress of transportation.

Ideally, the bird should be transported in its own cage. This will help reduce stress on the bird and also allow the avian veterinarian the opportunity to thoroughly evaluate the cage environment and the bird's droppings. Follow these suggestions:

Food and water should be within easy reach of the bird. However, to avoid spilling water, pour some of it out or remove the water bowl.

Consider removing perches and toys from the cage. This will help reduce the possibility of the bird being injured during transport.

Cover the cage with a blanket or towel. This provides added warmth and will help reduce stress.

Do not clean the cage. Veterinarians prefer to inspect the cage as is.

If moving the cage is not possible, use a cardboard box or other similar container. Many bird owners actually keep a spare transport cage around the house for this kind of situation. Follow these suggestions:

- Follow the recommendations in chapter 5, "Bird Restraint," to learn how to safely move a bird from one enclosure to another.
- Use a towel to pad the floor of the enclosure.
- If you have a small bird and it's cold outside, place a hot water bottle under the towel.
- Be sure there is plenty of fresh air. Punch holes in the box if necessary.
- Fold up the cage paper from the bird's regular cage and bring it along.
- If you have given the bird any medications, bring them along. Also, if you have even a slight suspicion the bird has come in contact with or ingested a poisonous sub

stance, be sure to bring the manufacturer's container along too.

- Consider enlisting the assistance of another person to drive to the animal hospital. This would allow you quiet time to watch and comfort the bird while you're in the car. Birds are also safest riding in a rear seat of the car.

Author's Note: A word of caution. Fear, pain, and sickness can cause unexpected changes in behavior. When a bird--even a loving, tame pet bird--is sick or injured, it may be more apt to bite. Therefore, be careful! Be prepared, don't rush, and think clearly before reaching out to catch and restrain a sick or injured bird.

Author's Notes

General Signs of a Sick Bird:

Throughout this chapter, where the "Signs to Watch for" are discussed, you will notice the term "General Signs of a Sick Bird." In order to avoid repetition, this term will be used to encompass the range of signs a sick bird may show. These signs include: appetite loss, unkempt feathers ("fluffed" or "fluffed up"), decreased activity (listlessness), increased sleeping, decreased vocalizations, change in behavior, and abnormal droppings. Also refer to the section entitled, "Sick Birds: Signs of Illness," on page 237 of chapter 12, "Home Physicals."

General Supportive Care:

In general, sick birds usually experience weight loss resulting from both a decreased appetite and decreased water intake. In these instances, the patient will benefit from "General Supportive Care." Once again, in order to avoid repetition, this term will refer to basic treatments administered by an avian veterinarian that would benefit any sick bird. This would include any or all of the following: extra warmth, fluid administration for hydration, supplemental feeding for extra nutrition, a quiet and relaxed environment, and other general forms of basic supportive care. (see page xx in this chapter for a more detailed discussion). Also refer to the section entitled, "Therapeutics: The Art and Science of Healing," on page 267 of chapter 13, "Veterinary Care."

Treatment Suggestions:

The medical information included in the Home Care Suggestions and in chapter 16, "Home Care for the Sick Bird," is not meant as a substitute for veterinary care. These suggestions are generally safe and simple methods of treatment. However, they are not going to work in every case. It is strongly encouraged that you consult an avian veterinarian prior to initiating treatment of any kind. Remember, your fine feathered friend is fragile, and even the act of restraint and administering medications can be dangerous. Above all, when it comes to health problems, my hope is that you'll be able to detect the early warning signs of both disease and emergency before either becomes life-threatening.

General Signs Usually Associated with Emergencies

Shock: What Does This Really Mean?

Any serious medical emergency or disease can result in "shock." Shock is a critical situation that results when the cardiovascular system fails to supply adequate blood to the organs of the body. As a result, low blood pressure develops, and the cells in the body do not receive adequate amounts of nutrients and oxygen. Shock can result from any serious insult to the body, and it usually leads to death if not treated aggressively.

In mammals, the signs of shock are well-defined and relatively easy to identify. They include: severe weakness and/or unconsciousness, weak or rapid pulse, pale or muddy-colored gums, and low body temperature (i.e., cold hands and feet).

SIGNS TO WATCH FOR: The general signs of a sick bird in shock are a weak appearance, depression, rapid breathing, and a fluffed-up appearance. If your bird displays these signs, shock should be suspected.

HOME-CARE SUGGESTIONS: None! There is no effective home treatment for shock. If shock is suspected, keep your bird warm, cover its cage, and transport it to your veterinarian's office immediately. As previously discussed, be sure to call the avian veterinarian's office first, before leaving home.

AVIAN VETERINARY CARE: Birds in shock constitute a true emergency and require immediate care. When you take a bird in shock to your veterinarian, a brief, but thorough, history will be taken and a physical examination will be conducted, after which the underlying problem, if it can be identified, will be treated first. For example, if the bird is bleeding, this must be controlled. After this, the general treatment for shock could include fluids for rehydration, oxygen to ease difficult breathing, extra warmth, shock-specific, medications, and close monitoring of the patient.

Once the bird is stable, diagnostic tests will likely be recommended. These can be very important in that they allow a better assessment of the extent of the injuries; they also enhance the veterinarian's ability to offer a realistic prognosis and to monitor the response to treatment.

Breathing Problems✪✪✪

Anytime an animal is having difficulty breathing, it should be considered an emergency. If respiratory distress is apparent, a bird's condition can rapidly deteriorate. Refer to page 335 of chapter 15, "Medical Problems," for a discussion of the various respiratory disorders that can affect pet birds.

SIGNS TO WATCH FOR: Obvious signs of breathing problems with your bird can be wheezing, rapid breathing, open-mouth breathing, or nasal discharge. Less obvious signs could include tail bobbing (pronounced up-and-down motion of the tail), frequent stretching of the neck, swelling around the eye, loss of voice, and sometimes a clicking sound when breathing.

Birds usually breathe through their nares. Prolonged open-mouth breathing, such as seen in this conure, usually indicates a respiratory problem.

HOME-CARE SUGGESTIONS: Keep the bird warm, keep the environment calm and relaxed, and consider placing a towel over the cage to further help reduce the stress. Also, turning on a vaporizer near the cage for short periods of time or placing your caged bird in a steamy bathroom may help to ease the breathing a little. Call your veterinarian's office and, if the breathing difficulty is severe, ask to be seen immediately.

AVIAN VETERINARY CARE: Following the examination, General Supportive Care will be provided as needed. An oxygen-enriched environment and nebulization will help make breathing easier. Once the bird is stabilized, diagnostic tests will likely be recommended to determine the underlying cause of the breathing problem. More specific treatment can then be administered.

Nebulization (see also page 271) is a treatment that can combine medication in a solution of sterile saline. This solution is heated in a nebulizer and a very fine mist is sprayed into the air. As the bird inhales this mist, it passes directly into the lungs and air sacs. Nebulization is the most effective method of delivering drugs to the air sacs.

Bleeding ❍❍❍

The presence of blood, whether you see it on the bird or in its cage or surroundings, is always a cause for concern. It's an emergency and requires immediate attention.

SIGNS TO WATCH FOR: Blood anywhere on the bird, its cage, playpen, toys, or other areas it has recently been.

HOME-CARE SUGGESTIONS: First, try and stop the bleeding. Also, examine the bird closely to try and determine the source of the blood.

Bleeding, Where Could It Be Originating?

EXTERNALLY: Beak, nail, feather or skin

INTERNALLY: Nares, mouth, vent, or in the droppings
Blood Volume and Blood Loss (hemorrhage): How much blood can a bird can lose and still survive? First, blood volume is the total amount of blood in the body. It accounts for 6.5 to 10 percent of a bird's total body weight. In other words, 6.5 to 10 milliliters (5 milliliters equals 1 teaspoon) for each 100 grams (28 grams equals one ounce, 454 grams equals 1 pound) of body weight. A healthy bird can easily lose 10 percent of its total blood volume without danger and, if it is in otherwise good health, possibly up to 50 percent! The following chart compares blood loss as a percentage of body weight for three popular species of pet birds:

Species	Weight	Total blood volume	10% loss	30% loss
Budgie	30 g. *(1 oz.)*	3/5 tsp. *(60 drops)*	6 drops	18 drops
Amazon	450 g. *(1 lb.)*	9 tsp. *(900 drops)*	1 tsp. *(90 drops)*	2.7 tsp. *(270 drops)*
Macaw	1,000 g. *(2.2 lb.)*	20 tsp. *(2,000 drops)*	2 tsp. *(200 drops)*	6 tsp. *(600 drops)*

External Bleeding ❍❍❍

External bleeding is usually the result of injury. This includes: broken blood feather, broken nail, or a cracked/fractured beak.

HOME-CARE SUGGESTIONS FOR BLEEDING NAIL OR BEAK:

1. If the bleeding appears minimal, do nothing and see if it stops on its own.
2. If the bleeding continues, catch and restrain the bird (see chapter 5, "Bird Restraint").
3. Apply direct pressure. Use a towel, paper towel, or finger.
4. If direct pressure is not enough, apply styptic powder, which acts as a coagulant. All birds owners should have this readily available. Firmly pack it onto the bleeding area. If applying it to the beak, keep it out of the mouth. In an emergency, baking powder, cornstarch, or even flour can be used.
5. Once the bleeding has stopped, observe the bird for at least one hour because the bleeding can restart.
6. Refer to chapter 16, "Home Care for Sick Birds," and follow suggestions for general support.
7. If blood loss seems excessive or if the bird appears weak, call your avian veterinarian immediately.

HOME-CARE SUGGESTIONS FOR BLEEDING FEATHER: In the case of a broken, immature blood feather, the entire feather needs to be removed. If this is not done, the broken feather could continue to bleed. Two people are required for this procedure--one to restrain the bird and one to remove the feather:

1. Act immediately: catch and restrain the bird (see chapter 5, "Bird Restraint").
2. Using firm pressure and sturdy tweezers or needle-nose pliers, pull the feather out. To do this, grasp the feather as close to the skin margin as possible. Be gentle and apply smooth, even pressure. If you are dealing with a broken wing feather, have an assistant firmly hold and support the wing as the feather is pulled out. The assistant will also need to very carefully apply equal and opposite traction on the front edge of the wing as the feather is being pulled out.

    Bird bones are fragile and there is a risk of fracturing the bone. Therefore, consider having an avian veterinarian remove the damaged feather.
3. After the feather is removed, bleeding from the empty follicle is a common occurrence. If this happens, apply direct pressure for one or two minutes using a cotton ball, towel, or fingers. Large feathers, such as primary wing

feathers, may require up to 10 minutes of direct pressure in order to stop the bleeding. While you are administer ing pressure, you should not see any bleeding. If there is bleeding during this time, check and make sure pressure is being applied directly over the bleeding follicle. Be patient. Once 10 minutes has passed, release pressure and make sure the bleeding has stopped.

Styptic powder should not be used on or in the feather follicle. It can permanently damage the follicle and, as a control for bleeding, it does not work as well as direct pressure.

4. Once the bleeding is controlled, observe the bird for at least an hour because the bleeding can recur.
5. Provide supportive care.
6. If bleeding cannot be stopped, or if blood loss seems excessive or the bird appears weak and listless, call your avian veterinarian immediately.

HOME-CARE SUGGESTIONS FOR SKIN WOUND (bleeding or not): Blood loss from minor skin wounds is usually mini- mal unless a blood vessel has been damaged.

1. Act immediately, catch and restrain your bird (see chapter 5, "Bird Restraint").
2. Apply direct pressure to the bleeding area using a towel or paper towel. If the bleeding doesn't stop with direct pressure, apply styptic powder or, in an emergency, baking powder, cornstarch, or even flour.
3. Clean the wound. Flood the area with an antiseptic solution such as 3 percent hydrogen peroxide, betadyne solution, or chlorhexidine solution. A moistened cotton- tipped applicator (such as a Q-tip) can be used to help clean and remove debris. Be gentle and keep the surrounding area clean and dry.
4. Apply a topical antibiotic spray or powder. *Do not apply any greasy or oily medication.*
5. Observe the bird for several hours. *Be aware, birds some times will pick at their wounds and, as a result, the bleed ing could start again.*
6. An avian veterinarian should be consulted. See below.

AVIAN VETERINARY CARE FOR EXTERNAL WOUNDS:
Bleeding will need to be stopped first. This can be accom- plished with such things as cauterization (the sealing of blood vessels with electric current or chemicals), bandages, direct

pressure, and sometimes even surgery. General Supportive Care as needed. A complete exam is essential, and this may be followed by a blood test to determine the amount of blood actually lost. Excessive blood loss may necessitate fluid replacement to maintain blood pressure; the veterinarian may also prescribe treatment with antibiotics, to control infection, and other medications, as indicated. Surgery may be necessary to repair an extensive skin wound. A broken or cracked beak or nail may require simple trimming, or if severe, surgery. Blood transfusions are available, but not commonly used.

Internal Bleeding ✪✪✪

Internal bleeding should always be considered life threatening. Blood coming from the mouth, nose, vent, or observed in the droppings is serious and could be caused by trauma, foreign body, disease, cancer, poison, infection, or a bleeding disorder (blood fails to clot normally).

Even if the bleeding appears intermittent rather than continuous, it should be considered very serious. Any amount observed, even small specks of dried blood, could indicate something life-threatening. When you look for blood in the droppings you may observe it as fresh red blood or the feces could appear black, almost tar-like.

HOME-CARE SUGGESTIONS: No home treatment should be attempted. Call your avian veterinarian and ask to be seen immediately.

AVIAN VETERINARY CARE: The source of the bleeding, amount of blood loss, and general health of the patient must first be determined. Internal bleeding is difficult to stop unless the actual source is identified. General Supportive Care will be provided first. Once the patient is stable, diagnostic testing is usually necessary to try and determine the source of the blood. Once this is known, specific treatment can be started.

Convulsions *(Seizures)* ✪✪✪

A seizure is a series of violent and involuntary muscle con-tractions. It is not a diagnosis; rather, it indicates a very seri-ous, underlying medical problem.

Seizures are the result of any number of problems including: head trauma, infection, lead or zinc poisoning, some nutri-tional deficiencies, low blood sugar, low blood calcium, heat-stroke, neurological disease, and epilepsy (a brain malfunction causing periodic or recurring seizures).

SIGNS TO WATCH FOR: In the minutes before a convulsion, a bird may appear apprehensive and restless. A convulsion may only affect a single wing or leg, or it could involve the entire body. Specific signs include uncontrolled shaking, trembling, or twitching of the entire body or affected limb. The bird may also lose its balance and fall to the floor or even lose consciousness.

Convulsions usually last only a few seconds, but can last up to a minute or two. The time interval between them can vary from only a few minutes or could be up to days or even months apart. In rare instances they can continue non-stop and seemingly never end.

HOME-CARE SUGGESTIONS: There is no effective home treatment for convulsions. The underlying cause must be determined and treated to prevent convulsions. However, during a convulsion, protect the bird from further injury by removing objects in its cage, such as perches, toys, or food dishes. Cover the cage with a towel if it could help to calm the bird. This is an emergency and an avian veterinarian will want to examine the bird immediately.

AVIAN VETERINARY CARE: If the bird is actually having a convulsion upon presentation, medication is available to calm the bird and stop the violent muscle contractions. General Supportive Care, as needed. Since there are many causes, diagnostic testing will likely be recommended to try and identify the cause of the seizures. There is specific and effective treatment for many of the causes of convulsions.

Falling Off Perch ✪✪

Adult birds are normally sure-footed and rarely slip or fall off a perch. If they do, it could suggest of a serious underlying problem. Young birds, on the other hand, may show clumsiness, but this can be very normal for them as they are just learning to perch and also learning their way around their new environments.

When adult birds become unsteady on their perch, problems to consider include: exposure to toxins, foot and/or leg problems, weakness and listlessness from internal disease, or a seizure. Regardless of the cause, the problem should be investigated with an avian veterinarian.

Medical Emergencies

SIGNS TO WATCH FOR: Sudden onset of unsteadiness or clumsiness, and General Signs of a Sick Bird.

HOME-CARE SUGGESTIONS: Lower the bird's perches and remove any objects in the cage that could injure the bird should it fall. Check to make sure all perches are securely attached to the cage walls. Add an energy supplement, such as Gatorade, Karo syrup, or even simple sugar to its water source. Call your avian veterinarian and schedule an appointment.

AVIAN VETERINARY CARE: As always a complete history and physical exam are essential. General Supportive Care, as needed. Diagnostic tests are usually necessary to help in identifying the underlying cause. Specific treatment cannot be started until a diagnosis is obtained.

PREVENTION: Keep your birds in optimal health. Pay close attention and be observant for early signs of disease. Remember, young birds naturally tend to be a little clumsy when they are first getting around in their new cage.

Appetite Loss ✪

Birds usually lose their appetite when they are sick. In an emergency, birds are likely to show an abrupt loss of appetite. This is not a diagnosis; rather, it is simply the result of some medical problem. Remember, healthy birds have healthy appetites!

When birds suddenly lose their appetite, an observant owner should notice right away. However when a bird gradually loses its appetite over time, it is much more difficult to notice. It is even more difficult when there is only a 10 to 20 percent decrease in food consumption.

If you suspect that your bird is not eating as much as it normally does, weigh it. It is a good practice for bird owners to regularly weigh their pets and keep the results in a written record. Weight loss can be a good, early indicator of a medical problem. Concerns should arise when weight loss approaches 10 percent of the normal weight. It is essential to purchase a reliable scale that weighs in grams, not ounces. Grams scales are much more accurate at detecting small but significant changes in weight.

Birds have rapid metabolic rates. To maintain their optimum body weight they require a lot of calories in relation to

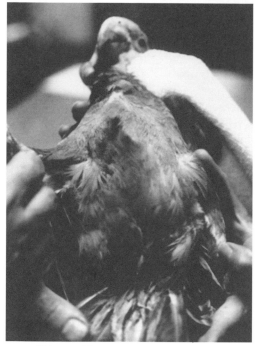

This parrot is very thin. Notice the severe muscle loss, which results in a prominent keel bone (arrow).

their size. Therefore, if small parrots, such as budgies and cockatiels, go for more than 12 hours without food, or if larger parrots go longer than 24 hours without food, an emergency situation may be developing.

HOME CARE SUGGESTIONS: Try to tempt the bird with a variety of favorite foods. Also, try warming the food in an effort to make it more appealing. Hand-feeding or spoon-feeding can also be attempted. If, after a short period of time (about 12 to 24 hours), there is no improvement in appetite, call your veterinarian.

AVIAN VETERINARY CARE: Tube feeding can easily be administered by gently passing a feeding tube into the crop and instilling high-quality, calorically dense, liquefied food. Once the bird is stabilized with needed food, fluids, and possibly medications, it will be important to try and determine the underlying cause for the loss of appetite. Once this is done, more specific therapy can be administered. In addition, there are specific medications that can be used to stimulate appetite.

Diarrhea ✪

Diarrhea is not a diagnosis. Rather, it is simply the result of some intestinal disorder. Dehydration and loss of nutrients will result.

Diarrhea is actually uncommon in pet birds. Excessive urine is much more common and frequently mistaken for diarrhea (page 248 of chapter 12, "Home Physicals").

Remember, if the stool is solid and formed, it is not diarrhea. Increased urine, will however, cause the stool to become wet and slightly loose.

Causes of diarrhea can include: diet (sudden change in type of food or spoiled food), intestinal infection, poisoning, ingestion of a foreign object, parasites, disease, and simply stress. (Refer to page 344 of chapter 15, "Medical Problems," for a more detailed discussion on digestive tract disorders.)

SIGNS TO WATCH FOR: Loose, watery or unformed stool. Droppings stuck or pasted around the vent.

HOME-CARE SUGGESTIONS: Remove any non-food items the bird is chewing on. Feed a bland diet of soft fresh foods, such as pasta, rice, beans, and cooked oatmeal. Pepto–Bismol or Kaopectate, though minimally effective, could be tried in the following dosages:

Finches/canaries	4 drops every 4 hours
Budgies	6 drops every 4 hours
Cockatiels	10 drops every 4 hours
Amazons	20 drops (1cc) every 4 hours
Cockatoos and macaws	30 drops (1.5cc) every 4 hours

Any treatment offered at home will delay more specific treatment by an avian veterinarian. This time delay may be very significant if the bird has a serious health problem. If diarrhea continues for more than 24 hours, contact your veterinarian.

AVIAN VETERINARY CARE: Since diarrhea is the result of a problem and not a diagnosis of the problem itself, the underlying cause needs to be identified to more quickly resolve the diarrhea. As always, a thorough history and physical exam will be performed, followed by General Supportive Care, as needed. Diagnostic tests such as stool analysis and or culture, radiographs, and blood tests may be recommended. Specific treatment as indicated.

Regurgitation and Vomiting ✪✪✪
A Sign of Disease or Simply Affection?

Regurgitation is the expulsion of undigested material from the mouth, esophagus, or crop. Vomiting is the expulsion of partially digested material from the proventriculus, ventriculus and/or intestines. Although for diagnostic reasons it is ideal to differentiate between regurgitation and vomiting, in practice this is not always possible.

CAUSES: Juvenile birds: infection (bacterial, fungal, viral), foreign object, overfilling of crop, improper formula or temperature, crop stasis, or sometimes just stress or excitement (see also "Crop Disorders" on page 345, in chapter 15, "Medical Problems").

Adult birds: diet (spoiled food), ingestion foreign object, poison, infection, food allergy, parasites, digestive tract obstruction, generalized disease, medications, stress, and excitement (see also "Digestive Disorders" on page 345 of chapter 15, "Medical Problems").

In adult birds, regurgitation can also be a normal sign of affection and courtship that birds show to a favorite toy or beloved owner. This natural behavior reflects a mother feeding her young. Removing the object of affection will often stop the regurgitation. It can sometimes be challenging to determine if the regurgitation is a sign of illness or simply a unique way of showing affection.

SIGNS TO WATCH FOR: Expulsion of food, whole or digested. In many instances, regurgitation may not be observable. However, since birds may shake their heads back and forth after regurgitating, look for the feathers and facial areas to be "plastered" with specks of food. The feathers in this area may also be sticky and stuck together.

HOME-CARE SUGGESTIONS: It is difficult to make general recommendations for home treatment since there are many different causes for regurgitation in a sick adult bird. *In young birds, absolutely no home treatment is recommended.*

Conditions causing regurgitation in young birds can be rapidly life threatening. In these instances, call your avian veterinarian immediately.

Although not particularly effective for this problem, Kaopectate or Pepto-Bismol could be given with a plastic medicine dropper to help soothe an inflamed lining of the digestive tract in adult birds. (See above section on diarrhea for recommended dosages.)

Call your avian veterinarian's office for an appointment if your adult bird doesn't improve in 24 hours. Remember, home treatment also delays the bird from receiving more specialized veterinary care.

AVIAN VETERINARY CARE: A thorough history with questions including when the regurgitation began, how often the regurgitation is occurring, and what, if anything, may be stimulating it. A physical examination and diagnostic tests including radiographs and microscopic analysis of the crop contents may be recommended in an attempt to determine the cause. Specific treatment as indicated.

Crop--Slow Emptying ○○

Slow crop emptying is usually a sign of serious disease. As a result, there is a lack of nutrients and energy being supplied to the body.

This is a problem most frequently encountered in young birds or very seriously ill adult birds. Some of the problems causing a delayed emptying of the crop are bacterial, fungal or viral infections, some poisons, impactions of food or foreign body, enlarged thyroid glands, lower digestive tract diseases, and any other serious illness. Improperly prepared formula in young pre-weaned birds can also cause this problem (see "Crop Disorders" on page 345 of chapter 15, "Medical Problems").

SIGNS TO WATCH FOR: The crop is situated along the base of the neck. If it is not emptying properly, you will see a bulge in this area that does not decrease in size within a few hours. Be careful and do not push or squeeze on the full crop. There is a risk of food being forced back up into the mouth and aspirated into the respiratory tract.

In young birds, a large pendulous crop that fails to empty after a few hours suggests a problem. Adult birds have much smaller crops, even when full, relative to their larger size. Adults with delayed crop emptying may be lethargic, have a decreased appetite, and may regurgitate.

HOME-CARE SUGGESTIONS: Home treatment is not recommended. There are too many causes to advise any safe and effective treatment. Call your avian veterinarian for an appointment.

AVIAN VETERINARIAN CARE: After the history and examination, the crop will likely be emptied, lavaged (irrigated or washed out), and its contents microscopically analyzed and cultured. Radiographs may also be suggested to rule out foreign objects or obstructions. General Supportive Care will be provided as needed. For crop infections, antibiotics and/or antifungals are frequently used. Occasionally, surgery is necessary to remove a foreign object or an obstruction.

Animal Bites ✪✪✪

Animal bite wounds are life-threatening emergencies. Not only do they cause the obvious puncture wounds, but they can also result in internal injuries and fractures resulting from the crush of the animal's jaws.

Serious infections can develop from animal bites as well as from an animal's claws. Once bacteria gain entry into the body from even a very small puncture wound, infection can spread via the bloodstream and develop rapidly into a life-threatening situation. The first 48 hours after a bite is a critical time period. Even if the bird appears bright and alert immediately following an attack, within this window of time serious infection could develop.

SIGNS TO WATCH FOR: Sometimes bite marks can be seen, but often they are hidden by the feathers. Look for general signs of trauma, which could include: blood, matted feathers, lameness, droopy wing, unsteadiness on the perch, or an unusual increase of feathers around the bird's living environment.

HOME-CARE SUGGESTIONS: There is no effective home treatment. Call your avian veterinarian's office first and then transport the bird there immediately.

AVIAN VETERINARY CARE: The traumatized bird will first be checked for stability and if it appears severely injured and/or in shock, General Supportive Care and treatment for shock will begin immediately. On the other hand, if the bird appears stable, a complete physical exam will be given first and this will be followed by appropriate treatment. Antibiotics are essential. Diagnostic tests may include radiographs to examine for internal injuries and a blood test.

PREVENTION: Be careful and use common sense when keeping birds with other pets, especially dogs and cats. If a bird is out of its cage when other pets are around, supervise them closely.

Beak Injuries ✪✪

Beak injuries constitute emergency situations because a bird needs both its upper and lower beak to eat and preen properly. Infections in the beak can also occur if it is fractured or punctured (see "Beak Disorders" on page 362 of chapter 15, "Medical Problems").

Beak injuries can result from an attack by another bird, flying into a windowpane or mirror, a collision with an operating ceiling fan, or all sorts of other types of trauma.

SIGNS TO WATCH FOR: The beak may be cracked, punctured, or part of it may be missing. Blood may also be noted coming from the beak or from the skin adjacent to it.

Medical Emergencies

HOME-CARE SUGGESTIONS: Control bleeding (refer to "Home Care Suggestions for Bleeding Nail or Beak," page 289). Specific beak injuries should be examined and treated by an avian veterinarian.

AVIAN VETERINARY CARE: Following an examination, General Supportive Care will be provided if the bird is weak or stressed. Minor injuries can be cleaned, medicated, and trimmed away if needed. More serious injuries could require surgery. Antibiotics and topical antiseptics will probably be administered.

In any event, a reluctance to eat is common after a beak injury. This could last for just a few days or up to a week or longer. Try offering softer foods, food cut into very small pieces, warmed food, and in some instances some form of force feeding may be required.

PREVENTION: Keep the bird's wings properly trimmed to prevent it from flying into walls or windows. Turn off fans when the bird is out of its cage. Birds have been known to occasionally attack one another, so be careful when birds, especially larger parrots, are kept together. Also, always exercise caution when other household pets, especially dogs and cats, come in contact with birds.

This budgie suffered a broken beak. With a combination of immediate veterinary care and follow-up home care, these birds can often live normal, healthy lives.

Burns ✪✪✪

Burns can be very serious and painful to pet birds. They can be caused by exposure to high temperatures (a flame, hot liquids, steam, or hot object), electricity, or chemicals.

SIGNS TO WATCH FOR: The obvious--seeing a bird come in direct contact with one of the items mentioned above. In addition, burns should be suspected if an area of the skin has an inflamed, irritated appearance or if the feathers are greasy or burnt.

HOME-CARE SUGGESTIONS: First, try to determine the cause of the burn. This is important.
•   HOT WATER/STEAM BURNS: Mist the burned area with cool water. If it is a leg or foot burn, try immersing the area in a bowl of cool water. A non-greasy antibiotic, with or without an anti-inflammatory medication, can be applied topically. To

299

avoid further damage to the feathers, this medication should be a water–soluble liquid, spray, or powder. Do not apply any oily or greasy substances (these include butter) because they can permanently damage the feathers.

• HOT GREASE BURNS: Lightly coat the burned area with flour or cornstarch to help absorb the grease. See "Oiled Bird" section, page 315.

• ACID BURNS: Contact with toilet bowl or drain cleaners are examples of chemicals that could cause an acid burn. Gently flood the area with cool water to dilute the chemical, then lightly coat the burned area with a paste of baking soda and water.

• ALKALI BURNS: Contact with ammonia or lye could cause alkali burns. Gently flood the burned area with cool water, then coat the affected area with vinegar.

• ELECTRICAL BURNS: If the bird has been chewing on a power cord, be sure to turn off the power and disconnect the cord. No home care is recommended.

The above recommendations are only meant to serve as the initial first-aid care. It is critical to consult your veterinarian for further advice and care.

AVIAN VETERINARY CARE: Treatment for shock and General Supportive Care, as needed. Following a thorough history and physical examination, the type of burn and its severity will be determined. More specific treatment could include antibiotics, special dressings, bandages, and sometimes a collar to pre-vent the bird from irritating the wound while it is healing.
PREVENTION: Keep birds out of the kitchen, especially when you are cooking. They can easily be burned by hot liquids or landing on a hot stove. Keep all cleaning supplies and other chemicals in closed cabinets. Birds should be watched closely when they are near power cords and lit candles.

Cloaca Prolapse ❂❂❂

A cloaca prolapse is the protrusion of tissue through the vent. It is never normal to have anything protruding from the vent. A prolapse is always considered an emergency.

There could be various tissues--lower intestines, uterus, or cloaca--prolapsed through the vent. In addition, a tumor (see cloaca papilloma, page 352), egg (see egg binding, page 303) or foreign object could also be found protruding from vent. To complicate matters, birds sometimes pick on these exposed tissues and can rapidly make the condition a lot worse.

SIGNS TO WATCH FOR: Tissue that is pink, red, brown, or even black in color protruding from the vent. If you ever see blood on the beak, perch, or cage it is a good idea to examine the vent area. Also, you may note droppings stuck or pasted around the vent.

HOME-CARE SUGGESTIONS: Apply 'lubricating jellly' (i.e. KY® jelly) or other water–soluble lubricant to prolapsed tissue to help keep it moist. No other home care is recommended. Contact your avian vet-erinarian's office for immediate care. Time is critical. The longer this tissue is allowed to remain outside the body, the more serious the situation becomes.

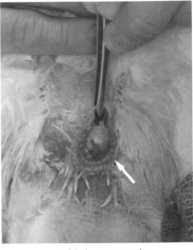

AVIAN VETERINARY CARE: An examination must be performed first to determine the type and severity of the prolapse. As always, General Supportive Care, as needed. If the prolapse is a very recent one and the tissue is moist and healthy, it can usually be reduced (gently pushed back inside), with lubrication, and minor surgery can be performed to keep it inside the body. In selective cases, major surgery may be required to permanently keep the protruding tissue inside the body.

This is an example of a minor cloaca prolapse (arrow) in a cockatoo.

Constricted Toe Syndrome ✪✪

Constricted toe syndrome is an emergency because a bird can lose a toe as a result, and/or a potentially serious infection could develop. It is most common in young birds. A string or other material may be seen wrapped around a bird's toe. In other instances, a narrow band of tissue may simply constrict on its own. The actual cause for this is not known, but it may be related to low brooder humidity or toe injuries.

SIGNS TO WATCH FOR: Toe appears swollen or inflamed.

HOME-CARE SUGGESTIONS: Use magnification to deter-mine if there is a small piece of thread wrapped around the affected toe. Think carefully about trying to remove a tightly wound thread from around a toe. It is a very delicate procedure. In mild cases, soaking the affected toe in warm water and gentle massage therapy might help. Topical antibiotics and antiinflammatory medication may help to soothe the painful toe. Remember, these treatments could also make the injury worse and delay the bird from getting the veterinary treatment it needs. Contact your avian veterinarian's office for further instructions.

AVIAN VETERINARY CARE: A complete examination is necessary; magnification will often be used to closely evaluate the affected toe. Treatment may include careful removal of strings or fibers around the toe, removal of infected tissue, warm water soaks, massage, and appropriate dressings. In the worst cases, surgery could be necessary.

Crop Burn ✪✪

Crop burns most frequently occur in baby birds during the time they are being hand-fed. After hand-feeding, the formula sits in the crop and, if it is too hot, it can actually burn its way through the crop and the skin. To prevent this emergency, avoid hand-feeding a formula that is more than 105 degrees Fahrenheit and make sure that you thoroughly stir microwaved formula to eliminate hot spots.

SIGNS TO WATCH FOR: Minor burns will result in inflammation of the crop lining. This will not be visible. However, in severe cases, a hole will actually be burned through the crop and overlying skin. Formula will leak from this hole, and the surrounding feathers at the base of the neck will be moist and matted. Over time, a scab will usually form over the hole. You may notice a foul odor. In either of these instances, there is often slow weight gain, prolonged weaning time, and crop infection.

HOME-CARE SUGGESTIONS: Minor cases will heal spontaneously and do not require any treatment. Severe cases, such as those causing an obvious hole in the skin, will need to be treated by an avian veterinarian.

AVIAN VETERINARY CARE: Holes in the crop require surgery to close them properly. In addition, medication such as antibiotics, antifungals, and/or anti-inflammatories, will be usually be required.

PREVENTION: Crop burns can be prevented by paying close attention to the proper temperature of the formula, stirring it thoroughly, and being very careful when heating it in a microwave. Microwave heating can create hot spots within the formula that can easily burn the crop. In general, you should avoid hand-feeding a formula that is more than 105 degrees Fahrenheit.

Egg Binding ✪✪

Birds generally lay eggs without difficulty. However, on occasion, an egg may get stuck inside and not be laid on schedule. This can rapidly lead to serious medical problems. Factors such as reproductive disorders, excessive egg laying, disease, and poor nutrition can all lead to egg binding, as can a lack of exercise and obesity.

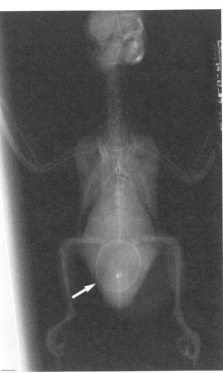

SIGNS TO WATCH FOR: Birds with a history of difficulty laying eggs; plus General Signs of a Sick Bird; straining; squatting in a penguin-like position; sitting on the cage floor rather than perching; panting or shortness of breath; specific weakness or even paralysis of one or both legs. The bird may possibly have a swollen abdomen. An egg may or may not be visible from the vent.

　　Please remember these signs are NOT diagnostic for egg binding. Many other problems can appear similar. Usually, gentle abdominal palpation performed by an avian veterinarian and a radiograph is necessary to confirm this diagnosis!

This radiograph shows an egg-bound cockatiel. The egg is fully calcified and should have been passed before this bird came to the veterinarian with a complaint of "not doing well."

HOME-CARE SUGGESTIONS: Home care can be attempted. However, if no egg is passed, precious time will be lost and the bird's condition could continue to deteriorate. Therefore, it is recommended that you contact your avian veterinarian immediately.

Caution: If you observe any portion of an egg protruding from the vent and that egg is not laid within 10 minutes, DO NOT attempt home care.

If no veterinarian is available or if home care is the only option, follow these suggestions:

Notice the egg as it is gently being pushed out. The bird is anesthetized.

1. Place hen in small cage, box, or aquarium.

2. Increase environmental temperature to 85 to 90 degrees Fahrenheit.

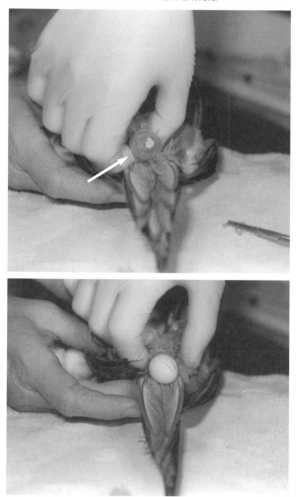

3. Increase the humidity. Try placing her in a steamy bathroom, create a small tent over the cage using plastic sheeting, and turn on a vaporizer for about an hour at a time or place a wet warm towel on the cage floor. Regardless of method used, be careful and don't "overcook" the bird!

4. Provide energy supplements in her drinking water. Gatorade, Karo syrup, or even a little sugar can be mixed in the water.

5. Refer to chapter 16, "Home Care for the Sick Bird," for additional supportive care suggestions.

6. If an egg is not laid within four hours, veterinary care is recommended.

AVIAN VETERINARY CARE:
Following the examination, a radiograph will usually be recommended to confirm the diagnosis and determine the size, shape and calcium content of the retained egg. General Supportive Care will be provided as needed. Specific medication is usually given first in an attempt to stimulate contractions to help the hen push

The "stuck" egg has been removed successfully. If the egg could not have been removed manually, other methods, including collapsing the egg by removing its contents or surgery, would have been recommended.

the egg out. If medication alone doesn't work, the hen may need to be anesthetized for egg removal. Anesthesia relaxes the bird and, with gentle manipulation, usually allows the egg to be removed. Occasionally even this does not work and surgery becomes necessary to remove the retained egg.

PREVENTION: To prevent egg binding, keep laying hens healthy and provide a good diet. Also, refer to "Excessive or

Chronic Egg Laying," page 360, for suggestions on how to reduce egg laying.

Eye Injury ✪✪

Eye problems, although usually not life threatening, should be considered an emergency. Even a minor eye injury can rapidly progress to irreversible damage, infection, or blindness. Refer to the section entitled "Eye Disorders" page 315 for a more detailed discussion of specific eye problems.

This sun conure was egg-bound. Medication was administered that stimulated her to lay the abnormal soft-shelled egg (arrow) seen at the left of the photo.

SIGNS TO WATCH FOR: Eyelid(s) swollen and/or pasted closed, increased blinking or squinting, fluid leaking from the eye, and/or rubbing of the eye. In addition, the surface of the eyeball could lose its normal transparency and appear cloudy or hazy.

HOME-CARE SUGGESTIONS: As mentioned, any eye problem should be considered serious. Home treatment will delay proper veterinary care that could mean the difference between saving or losing an eye.

However, home treatment could include examining the eye carefully for any tiny foreign objects. Magnification usually helps. If a toxin or chemical has gotten into an eye, the eye should be rinsed for 10 minutes with an over-the-counter human eye wash, such as a saline solution, contact lens wetting solution, or even plain tap water. Call your veterinarian immediately after rinsing the eye. No other safe home treatments can be suggested.

This cockatiel has a severe infection involving its eye.

AVIAN VETERINARY CARE: After the history and general exam, the eye will be closely examined. A special eye stain will usually be applied to determine if a scratch or abrasion exists on the surface of the eyeball. An ophthalmoscope may be used to examine the interior structures of the eye. Treatment usually consists of eye medications that will need to be instilled into the affected eye several times a day until it heals. Surgery is sometimes necessary to repair an injury or to temporarily cover the eye to protect it.

Foot Injuries ⊙⊙

Foot injuries can be painful, can bleed, or can result in infection. If left untreated, birds may chew the affected area and create a much more serious problem. Foot injuries can result from fractures, toe problems, broken or cracked nails, trauma, frostbite, and even from some internal diseases. (Refer to "Leg and Foot Disorders," page 366, for a discussion of some specific foot problems).

SIGNS TO WATCH FOR: Toes or foot could appear swollen, misshapen, or bleeding. You may notice lameness or even a reluctance by the bird to place weight on the affected foot.

HOME-CARE SUGGESTIONS: Stop any bleeding (page 289), lower all perches and keep food and water within easy reach. Contact your avian veterinarian's office for further instructions.

AVIAN VETERINARY CARE: History and a thorough examination, which will include not only the foot, but also the entire leg. Diagnostic tests such as radiographs are helpful to identify a fracture, joint involvement, or a bone infection. Treatment could include both topical and systemic medications, bandage for support, and/or protection, and if severe, possibly surgery.

Foreign Object Ingested ⊙❖

On occasion, birds do swallow foreign objects. (See "Foreign Object in Digestive Tract," page 351).

Foreign Object Inhaled ⊙⊙⊙

Inhaled foreign objects are considered emergencies because they can obstruct major airways. As a result, movement of air through the respiratory tract can be partially or completely blocked.

SIGNS TO WATCH FOR: The primary signs of a foreign object becoming lodged in the nares or sinuses may include open-mouth breathing, panting, tiring easily and nasal discharge. If a foreign object, such as small piece of food or small object, is aspirated into the trachea, then very serious breathing problems will develop immediately. Watch the bird to see if it is gasping for air or experiencing an inability to vocalize. Even loud and high-pitched breathing can be a clue.

HOME-CARE SUGGESTIONS: None. Call your avian veterinarian because the bird will need to be seen immediately.

AVIAN VETERINARY CARE: Brief history and physical exam. If breathing difficulties are noted, the bird will probably be placed in an oxygen-enriched environment and given drugs to aid in breathing. If breathing is severely compromised, a special breathing tube placed into the lower portion of the body cavity can help to significantly improve breathing. Foreign objects in the nares can usually be easily and carefully removed. Endoscopy is ideal for visualization and removal of sinus foreign objects. Foreign objects in the trachea present more of a challenge. Endoscopy is ideal for identifying foreign objects in the trachea. In many instances, especially in larger parrots, endoscopy and special grasping forceps can be used to remove the foreign object. In smaller parrots, sometimes the foreign object can be aspirated or suctioned out of the trachea. If this does not work, surgery may be necessary.

Fractures ❖❖

Fractures are obviously painful, preventing normal movement and function of affected limb, but beyond the injury itself, they are an indication that the bird could have sustained even more serious internal injuries. Bird bones are brittle and can easily be broken. Pet birds fracture legs more commonly than wings. Skull and spinal fractures are very serious and, fortunately, uncommon.

Fractures are usually caused by accidental injuries. However, poor nutrition and certain diseases can actually weaken bones and make them more susceptible to fractures.

SIGNS TO WATCH FOR:
Fractured leg bone: non-weight bearing (holding leg up), leg hanging in awkward position. Severe bruising and/or swelling.
Fractured wing bone: injured wing hanging lower than normal wing, inability to move wing, severe bruising and/or swelling.

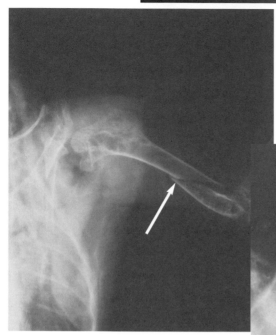

LEFT: Radiographs of "Jake", an Amazon parrot with a spiral fracture of his humerus (arrow). Repair of this fracture required surgery. Simple external support using bandages, splints, or slings would probably not have been sufficient for proper healing to occur.

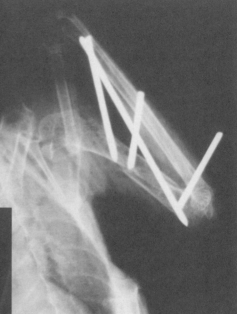

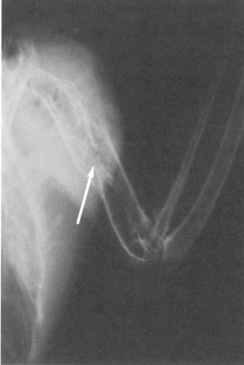

ABOVE: This radiograph was taken immediately after surgery. Four pins were placed into the humerus, two above and two below the fracture site. Although not visible, a moldable, fiberglass-like connecting material secured the pins together outside the body and along the length of the fractured bone. External skeletal fixation is the name of this type of repair.

LEFT: This radiograph was taken months after the surgery. Although there is some overlapping of the prior two humerus bone fragments, the fracture has healed well (arrow).

Here's "Jake" a few months after surgery. The wing is now fully healed.

Fractured skull or spinal cord: depends on severity and location but can range in severity from loss of consciousness to and including total paralysis.

Other problems, such as arthritis, dislocation (joint tearing and displacement of bone), foot problems, muscle, ligament, or tendon injuries, and abdominal tumors, can present with nearly identical signs.

HOME-CARE SUGGESTIONS: Confine the bird to its cage or a small carrier. Pad the cage or carrier with a small towel. Don't handle your pet unnecessarily. Keep it warm and contact your avian veterinarian.

AVIAN VETERINARY CARE: Fractures of the legs and wings are usually not life threatening. However, if the bird presents in shock or is very weak, General Supportive Care will be pro-

309

vided first. Once the bird is stabilized and following a complete examination, radiographs will be taken. Radiographs can rule out the other problems listed above that can mimic a fracture. In addition, once the severity and location of the fracture is known, the treatment options can be discussed. Bandages and splints can be used to repair many fractures. However, sometimes surgery to repair the broken bone is necessary. With proper care, fractures require about four to six weeks to heal.

Frostbite (hypothermia) ○○

Frostbite is painful and life threatening. Feet and toes are most commonly affected.

SIGNS TO WATCH FOR: The frostbitten area is very painful, cold, and hard to the touch. After several days, the affected area may become very hard, dry, and black in color.

HOME-CARE SUGGESTIONS: Place the bird in a warm environment (85 to 90 degrees Fahrenheit). Warm the damaged tissue very gradually in a warm, circulating water bath. Food and water should be easily accessible. Your avian veterinarian will want to examine the bird.

AVIAN VETERINARY CARE: Complete examination followed by General Supportive Care as needed. The bird will be warmed gradually by placing it in an incubator and administering warm fluids. Warm-water soaks and gentle massage for affected toes may also be performed. If after several days the affected area does not appear to be healing well, surgery may be necessary.

PREVENTION: Keep birds indoors during extremely cold weather. Most pet birds can tolerate outdoor temperatures that dip down to 30 degrees Fahrenheit. However, you should acclimate birds to a colder air temperature gradually, by reducing the air temperature over time. Cold temperatures combined with dampness and/or wind create an ideal environment for frostbite to develop. Birds housed outdoors in cold weather should not be kept on metal perches.

Head Trauma ✪✪✪

Head trauma is an emergency because, as a result, a bird may sustain a serious concussion (bruising of the brain). A concussion is caused by a blow to the head and can lead to a loss of consciousness. This is most often the result of a bird flying into a window or wall.

SIGNS TO WATCH FOR: At first, the bird may act depressed, lose its balance, show weakness in its wings or legs, make unusual movements of its eyes or entire head, have seizures, or even lose consciousness.

HOME-CARE SUGGESTIONS: Home treatment is not recommended. Protect the bird from further injury and contact your avian veterinarian's office--ask to be seen immediately.

AVIAN VETERINARY CARE: Shock, if present, will be treated first. A history and physical exam will be needed to better assess the extent of the injury. General Supportive Care and other appropriate medications will be used as needed. Diagnostic testing may be useful to further determine the seriousness of the injury.

PREVENTION: Keep bird's wings trimmed to prevent it from flying free in the home. Proper wing trims are essential (see page 134). Place decals on large windows so birds will not mistake a window for open space. Supervise birds when they are out of their cage. Watch young birds carefully because they are more clumsy than adults and are more likely to hurt themselves.

Heatstroke (hyperthermia) ✪✪✪

Heatstroke is an emergency because overheated birds can go into shock quickly. Permanent brain damage or even death can result.

SIGNS TO WATCH FOR: A bird that is panting, holding its wings down and away from its body, particularly in an environment that is very warm. The bird will also be extremely weak and could go into shock or a coma. Young, old, or overweight birds are more susceptible.

HOME-CARE SUGGESTIONS: First, remove the bird from its hot environment and place it in a cool area. Start to reduce its body temperature by placing it in an air–conditioned room, in front of a fan, or spraying it with cool water from a mister bottle. Make sure the feathers are wet to the skin. If the bird is strong enough, offer it cool water to drink, or even try squirting drops directly into the mouth (see page xxx). Contact your avian veterinarian's office for further instructions.

AVIAN VETERINARY CARE: Complete examination followed by General Supportive Care. The patient will be placed in a cool, well-oxygenated, and moist environment. Fluids will be administered to treat dehydration. The bird should be closely monitored for at least 24 hours.

PREVENTION: A bird's chances of suffering heatstroke can be reduced by keeping it out of direct sun, providing it with ample supplies of clean, fresh water, and avoid keeping birds, and all other pets, in a car on a hot day. Interior temperatures in a car can rise quickly during hot weather.

Infections ✪✪
Infections are an emergency because if they are not treated, potentially serious and life–threatening problems can result. Bacteria, fungi, and viruses are the microscopic organisms that cause infections. Refer to chapter 15, "Medical Problems," for a discussion of infections and the diseases caused in pet birds.

SIGNS TO WATCH FOR: Signs are variable depending on the location of the infection within the body. General Signs of a Sick Bird accompany most infections.

HOME-CARE SUGGESTIONS: Home treatment is not recommended. Call your avian veterinarian for an appointment.

AVIAN VETERINARY CARE: History and physical exam will help determine seriousness. General Supportive Care is usually necessary. Antibiotics, antifungals, and sometimes antiviral drugs are available to fight the infection. A bacterial or fungal culture and sensitivity identifies the organism causing the infection and helps the veterinarian determine the best medications to use. Blood tests are useful to diagnose the presence of infection and monitor response to treatment.

Joint Swelling ✪✪

Joint swelling can be caused by an infection, arthritis, trauma, dislocation (a displacement of bone out of the joint), or gout (see page 367) in or around the joint.

SIGNS TO WATCH FOR: Pain, swelling, or stiffness (decreased range of motion) in the affected joint. You may notice lameness if a leg joint is involved. If a wing joint is impaired, you may observe the bird holding the affected wing lower than the normal wing.

HOME-CARE SUGGESTIONS: Too many different causes and treatments exist for any type of safe and effective home care. Keep the bird quiet and comfortable and call your avian veterinarian for further instructions.

AVIAN VETERINARY CARE: A thorough history and physical examination should enable the veterinarian to identify the joint(s) involved. Diagnostic tests may be necessary to identify the actual cause of the joint problem. Radiographs and, if infection is suspected, a joint tap may be recommended to analyze the joint fluid. Treatment will be prescribed once the underlying cause is determined.

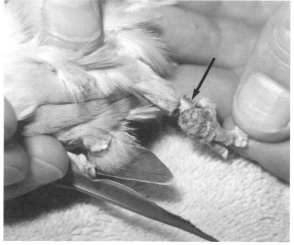

When leg bands are left on, they should be loose-fitting. This bird suffered a leg injury, and with a snug-fitting band, the damage became worse.

Leg Band Problems ✪✪

If a banded leg gets injured and becomes swollen, the leg band could cause additional damage because a tight band can interfere with normal blood flow in the leg. Leg bands can also get caught on various objects in a pet bird's environment and if this happens, the leg is susceptible to injury. (See page 28 for a discussion of leg bands.)

SIGNS TO WATCH FOR: The skin around the leg band is swollen or puffy, or the band is no longer "free-floating" on the leg. Leg bands should fit loosely around a bird's leg.

HOME-CARE SUGGESTIONS: Do not attempt to remove leg bands, especially when they are too tight on the leg. Removing these bands is a very delicate procedure and

313

should only be performed by an experienced person, preferably an avian veterinarian. The reason for this is that even in experienced hands, leg injuries can occur.

However, if the bird's leg band becomes caught on a toy, its cage, or something else, try to carefully and gently undo the entanglement and free the bird. If necessary, carefully use wire cutters to cut wire or try and take apart whatever the leg band is caught on. Wrap the bird's leg and apply pressure if it is bleeding. Call your avian veterinarian.

Cockatiels can be prone to night frights. This bird injured itself because it panicked after a small earthquake and threw itself into its cage bars.

AVIAN VETERINARY CARE: A close examination of the affected leg is obviously very important. If the leg is swollen and the band tight, anesthesia of the bird may be necessary. This allows a more quiet and relaxed patient and a safer removal of the band. If the leg is obviously injured, a radiograph may be recommended to rule out any bone or joint problems. Bandaging of the leg is usually required.

PREVENTION: If the bird has an open leg band, ask your veterinarian to remove the band to protect your pet from injury. If your bird is a domestically bred parrot with a closed leg band, discuss the possibility of removing it with your veterinarian. Some veterinarians recommend leaving closed bands on birds because they can help you trace a bird's genealogy. However, any band can cause injury, and birds can be microchipped as a safe alternative for permanent identification.

Night Frights
[aka "Cockatiel Thrashing Syndrome" or "Earthquake Syndrome"] ✪✪

A bird that experiences thrashing episodes will be startled from its sleep by any loud noises or vibrations, leading it to awaken and to try and take flight. During one of these thrashing episodes, a bird will become highly stressed and could injure itself.

SIGNS TO WATCH FOR: In the case of caged pet birds, the thrasher may injure its wing tips, feet, chest, or abdomen on toys or cage bars when it tries to flee from the perceived danger. Cockatiels, particularly lutinos, seem more prone to this behavior.

314

HOME-CARE SUGGESTIONS: Assess the bird for bruises, cuts, broken feathers, or other injuries. Calm and comfort the bird. Call your avian veterinarian's office for a checkup.

AVIAN VETERINARY CARE: A history and complete physical examination should be able to determine the extent of the injuries in most cases. General Supportive Care and treatment for minor injuries is usually sufficient.

PREVENTION: Bird owners can help protect their pets from harm in the following ways: install a small night light near the bird's cage to help the bird see where it is during a thrashing episode; place an air cleaner in the bird's room to provide "white noise" to drown out some potentially frightening background noises; or place the bird in a small sleeping cage that is free of toys and other items that could harm it if it becomes frightened.

Oiled Feathers ✪✪
When a bird's feathers become coated with oil, the bird loses its ability to regulate its body temperature. If a bird falls into oil and swallows some, it can suffer from breathing problems, eye problems, and poisoning. If the bird has fallen into hot oil, also see the section on burns (page 299) and call your veterinarian.

This cockatiel fell into a pot of cool cooking oil. For reasons mentioned in the text, this can quickly become a life-threatening condition. Veterinary care is essential.

SIGNS TO WATCH FOR: Oily, greasy, and slicked-down feathers.

HOME-CARE SUGGESTIONS: Contact your avian veterinarian's office for immediate assistance. Cleaning an oil-soaked bird requires multiple steps and, for maximum safety, should be done by an experienced and knowledgeable individual. However, if there is not an avian veterinarian available, follow these guidelines to remove oil from a bird's feathers:

1. Dust oiled feathers with cornstarch or flour. This helps soak up excess oil. Keep the powder away from the bird's eyes and nose. A good method is to place some cornstarch or flour in a small pillowcase or bag, then place the bird inside the bag with its head exposed. Hold the bag around the bird's neck and gently shake the bag to dust the feathers. Allow the powder to stay on for about 30 minutes. Brush off excess.

2. Wrap the bird in a towel, which reduces heat loss and prevents the bird from ingesting the oil.

3. Remove oil from the bird's nostrils, mouth, and around its eyes with a moistened cotton swab.

4. Fill a sink with warm water and add a very small amount of dishwashing liquid. Protect the bird's eyes. Immerse the bird in the water. Wet all affected feathers by handling them gently and following their natural contour. Dip the bird slowly in and out of the water for one to two minutes. Rinse the feathers well with fresh warm water. Repeat as needed.

5. Blot the feathers dry with towels. Do not rub. A hair dryer set on low is also very useful.
6. Wrap the bird loosely in a towel and place it in a warm cage, aquarium, or box. Increase the environmental temperature to 85 to 90 degrees Fahrenheit for a short time until the bird is dry. Avoid drafts.

7. Follow the guidelines in chapter 16, "Home Care for the Sick Bird," if your bird is weak and not eating.

8. If oiling is severe, do not try to remove it all at once. The above steps may need to be repeated over several hours or perhaps even days.

9. Observe the bird closely over the next several hours. Shock and dehydration could develop and are serious concerns.

10. Call your avian veterinarian.

AVIAN VETERINARY CARE: A physical exam is necessary to assess the severity and stability of the bird.

General Supportive Care and treatment for shock may be necessary. Once stable, a procedure similar to the one listed above will be followed for a thorough cleaning of the damaged feathers. Hospitalization and close monitoring may also be part of the treatment for the first 24 to 48 hours.

PREVENTION: Limit your bird's access to sources of oil, especially beware of the kitchen and garage areas.

Poisoning ✪✪✪

All substances are poisons. The right dose differentiates
a poison and a remedy.
  Paracelsus (1493-1541)

By nature, birds are curious creatures. Mouthing, chewing, tasting, and even swallowing dangerous liquids or objects are all possible. Any product labeled poisonous for humans will be poisonous to birds. Some poisons can kill a bird quickly. Others can cause clinical signs ranging from a mild digestive tract upset to a violent illness.

SIGNS TO WATCH FOR: Sudden regurgitation, diarrhea, bloody droppings, breathing difficulties, redness or burns around their mouth, convulsions, paralysis, or shock. Sometimes, only General Signs of a Sick Bird.

Remember, many diseases and other medical problems can also present with the same type of signs. Many are discussed in this book. Therefore, unless it's obvious, poisoning should be considered only a possibility and not a definite diagnosis.

HOME-CARE SUGGESTIONS: First, try to determine what may have caused the poisoning. Birds can be poisoned by inhaling fumes, by ingesting a poisonous plant or chemical, or by having a poisonous substance come in contact with their skin.

1. Remove poison and put it out of reach of all animals and family members.

2. For eye, respiratory, or skin involvement, do the following:
• *Eye involvement:* flush affected eye with lukewarm water.
• *Fume intoxication:* ventilate the room immediately--open
    windows, use a fan.
• *Skin involvement:* flush the area with water or ideally move bird to a safe area.

3. Call your avian veterinarian and ask to be seen immediately. Be sure to bring the poison and its original container.

If no avian veterinary care is available or you just want some immediate answers to questions conderning poisoning of your bird, or other family pet, call the ASPCA Animal Poison Control Center at the University of Illinois-College of Veterinary Medicine (APCC). This is an emergency hotline providing 24 hours a day, 7 days a week, telephone assistance to veterinarians and animal owners. the APCC's veterinarians can quickly answer questions about toxic substances found in our everyday surroundings that can be dangerous to birds and other animals.

There is a flat-fee consulting charge to the calling party. However, if your bird ingested a particular brand of product, the fee might be waived if the manufacturer is a sponsor of the poison control center. Regardless, this call could mean the difference between life and death of your feathered friend. the APCC's phone numbers are: **888/426-4435** (credit card payment) or **900/443-0000** (billed to long distance carrier account). List these numbers near your telephone with other numbers you might need in an emergency! For more information, visit their website: **www.aspca.org** and find the link to their Animal Poison Control Center.

When you call the APPC hotline or your veterinarian, be ready to provide:
• Your name, address and telephone number
• Information concerning the exposure (specific agent, amount ingested or exposed to, time of exposure, etc.)
• The species, age, sex, weight (if known)
• The problem(s) your pet is experiencing

AVIAN VETERINARY CARE: Stabilizing the bird is most important, especially if it is in shock, convulsing, or having breathing problems. A complete physical evaluation is essential. General Supportive Care will be provided as needed. If an antidote to the poison is available, it will be administered. If the poison was ingested, medication can be given to reduce the absorption of the poison into the bloodstream.

PREVENTION: The risk of poisoning can be reduced by following these steps:
•   Make sure food and water is always fresh.
•   Wash all fruits and vegetables before serving them

- Keep potentially poisonous household products out of reach.
- Do not let birds fly free in the kitchen or bathroom.
- Do not use products with strong fumes, such as cleaning products, around birds.
- Do not use fungicides, herbicides, insecticides, or rodenticides around birds without consulting your avian veterinarian.
- Do not let birds near houseplants.
- Do not leave cigarettes or other tobacco products where birds can reach them. Do not smoke around birds.
- Do not use nonstick cookware around birds because overheated nonstick items can emit fatal fumes (see page 322).
- Immediately consult your avian veterinarian if there is any suspicion of potential poisoning problems.

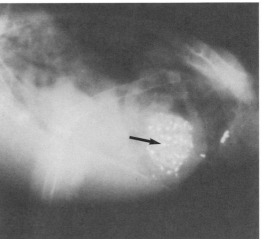

This radiograph shows metal flakes in a bird's gizzard (arrow). The brighter fragments are metal, and the small round objects in the background are grit. Radiographs can help veterinarians diagnose metal poisoning in pet birds.

Lead and Zinc Poisoning ⊙⊙⊗
(Heavy Metal Poisoning)

Lead and zinc poisoning cause serious and life-threatening problems in pet birds. These two substances, which are poisonous if ingested, are grouped together because their signs and treatment are very similar. They are one of the most common toxins found in pet birds.

SIGNS TO WATCH FOR: A bird with lead or zinc poisoning generally shows signs involving the digestive and neurological systems. General Signs of a Sick Bird are common, especially depression, weakness, and appetite loss. Digestive tract signs may include vomiting, regurgitation, delayed crop-emptying times, abnormal colored urates (yellow, green, pink or red colored), abnormal stool (loose, black or blood-tinged), increased thirst and increased urination. Neurological signs may include feather picking, falling off the perch, unbalanced when walking, twitching, abnormal head movements, convulsions, paralysis and blindness.

HOME-CARE SUGGESTIONS: There is absolutely no home treatment recommended. Lead and zinc poisoning require an early and aggressive start to treatment. Make an appointment to see your avian veterinarian.

AVIAN VETERINARY CARE: Diagnosis can be challenging. In most instances pet bird owners do not realize that their bird could have been chewing on any suspicious metal objects and therefore deny the possibility when asked.

A history and physical exam are essential, but they alone cannot diagnose these problems. Radiographs are essential in helping to establish an early diagnosis because metal particles are often, but not always, seen in the digestive tract. Blood tests to assay for lead and zinc levels in birds are now available to confirm the diagnosis. However, these blood tests require a few days to get the results. Since an antidote is available and effective, a dramatic improvement in the patient's signs are very suggestive and help make a tentative or early diagnosis of heavy metal poisoning.

Treatment is aimed at stabilizing the patient and removing the metal from both the digestive tract and body tissues. General Supportive Care will help stabilize the sick bird. As mentioned above, a specific antidote is administered to bind and remove metal from the body tissues. In addition, for small metal fragments, lubricating and/or bulking agents can be given orally to help speed the passage of the metal through the digestive tract. Large metal pieces can sometimes be removed with the aid of endoscopy or, if indicated, surgery. In addition, other medications including antibiotics are given as needed. Duration of treatment varies and may require several days, weeks, and occasionally months to complete.

PREVENTION: Simply being aware of and avoiding some of the most common sources of lead and zinc in the bird's environment can frequently prevent this type of poisoning.

COMMON SOURCES OF ZINC:

Galvanized cages
Powder coated cages
Metal toys
Metal toy hangers
Galvanized metal dishes
Washers, nuts, snap fasteners
Cage "chrome" (actually polished galvanized metal)
Pennies, minted after 1982
Paint

Potential Pet Bird Poisons in the Home

Following are categories of items that can cause poisoning in a pet bird. The list is by no means complete, but it is provided to give pet bird owners "food for thought". Take steps to protect birds from being poisoned by preventing their access to these items.

Home remodeling--Fumes from new carpeting, paint, paneling and particle board, or fumigation chemicals can poison pet birds.

Household chemicals--Fumes from cleaners, disinfectants, bleaches, detergents, or insecticides can make pet birds ill.

Personal care products--Fumes from hairspray, cologne, deodorant or cosmetics can harm pet birds. Birds can also become ill if they ingest any of these items or if they eat human medications, either over-the-counter or prescription varieties.

Space heaters, fireplaces, and wood stoves--Fumes from these can poison birds.

Kitchen items--Fumes from overheated nonstick cookware and accessories, or from self-cleaning ovens.

Craft items--Birds can become ill from the fumes from glue guns, marking pens or paints, or by ingesting these items.

Varnish
Adhesives (including duct tape)
Twist ties

Caution: *Any metal object, including bird cages, toys, and food dishes, will likely contain some zinc, unless it is made of stainless steel or are certified zinc-free. If a bird likes to bite, chew, and gnaw on these items, it is at risk for developing zinc poisoning. Zinc builds up very slowly in a bird's body. Therefore, many birds that are suffering from zinc toxicosis may show only subtle signs of poisoning, such as increased thirst or feather picking.*

COMMON SOURCES OF LEAD:
air rifle pellets
antiques
bases of light bulbs
batteries
bird toys with weights
bullets and buckshot
costume jewelry
curtain weights
dolomite
fishing weights
hardware cloth
foil from wine and champagne bottle seals
mirror backing
lead-framed doors and windows
old paint
old plaster
putty
sheet rock
solder
stained glass ornaments and lampshades
unglazed ceramics
zippers (some types)

A little-known source of lead are the wicks in some long-lasting candles. A consumer interest group in Houston, Texas, tested candles to see if they created any air pollution problems. In the course of their testing, the group discovered some long-lasting candles with lead in their wicks emit lead levels that are high enough to harm children. If long-lasting candles in a bird owner's home have silver threads visible in the wick, they may contain lead and should not be burned around a pet bird.

321

"Teflon Toxicity" "Polymer Fume Fever" ☻☻☻

Polytetrafluoroethylene (PTFE) is a synthetic polymer used as a nonstick surface in cookware. The brand names Teflon, Silverstone, and T-Fal are the best known, but PTFE-coated products are also manufactured under other trade names. These products can also be found on such surfaces as drip pans, heat lamp covers, and irons.

Dr. Peter Sakas has succinctly explained the dangers of PTFE:

"Under normal cooking conditions, PTFE-coated cookware is stable and safe. When PTFE is heated above 530 degrees Fahrenheit, however, it undergoes breakdown and emits caustic (acid) fumes. Most foods cook at lower temperatures: Water boils at 212 degrees, eggs fry at 350 degrees, and deep frying occurs at 410 degrees. But when empty PTFE-coated cookware is left on a burner set on the high setting, it can reach temperatures of 750 degrees or greater. Thus, if a pan is being preheated on a burner and forgotten, or if water boils out of a pot, breakdown of the PTFE can occur. In other words, PTFE-coated cookware has to be 'abused' to emit toxic fumes, but this is not as rare as it might seem; many people fall asleep after they put pots or pans on the stove to heat."

SIGNS TO WATCH FOR: Birds kept in areas close to the kitchen will usually die very shortly after breathing the fumes. Even birds kept in another room are at great risk. Severe breathing difficulties especially gasping for breath, loss of balance, and depression may be seen just prior to death.

HOME-CARE SUGGESTIONS: Remove the bird(s) immediately from the home and supply ample fresh air. Call your veterinarian immediately.

AVIAN VETERINARY CARE: If a bird is presented with severe breathing difficulties, it will be placed in an oxygen-enriched environment, treated for shock, provided General Supportive Care and other medications, as indicated. During this time, a history and physical examination will be performed.

Plant Poisoning ✪✪✪

Indoor plants can be poisonous to birds. In reality however, plant poisoning in pet birds is actually rare. Birds do like to chew on plants; however, birds generally tolerate the ingestion of potentially poisonous plants better than mammals.

SIGNS TO WATCH FOR: Variable depending on type of plant eaten and its principal toxin. Most commonly, irritation in the mouth, depression, and/or mild digestive tract upset, which could include regurgitation and loose droppings. However, as with any poison, more serious problems, including death, could occur.

HOME-CARE SUGGESTIONS: No home treatment is recommended. Try and identify the type of plant ingested. Call your avian veterinarian immediately.

AVIAN VETERINARY CARE: Following the examination, General Supportive Care, as needed. Medications could be given to bind and inactivate the toxin and prevent further absorption. The specific treatment is dependent on an ingested plant's principal toxin.

Self-Mutilation ✪✪

Feathers, skin and toes can be severely damaged by a bird picking and gnawing at itself. Refer to "Self-Mutilation" section in chapter 15.

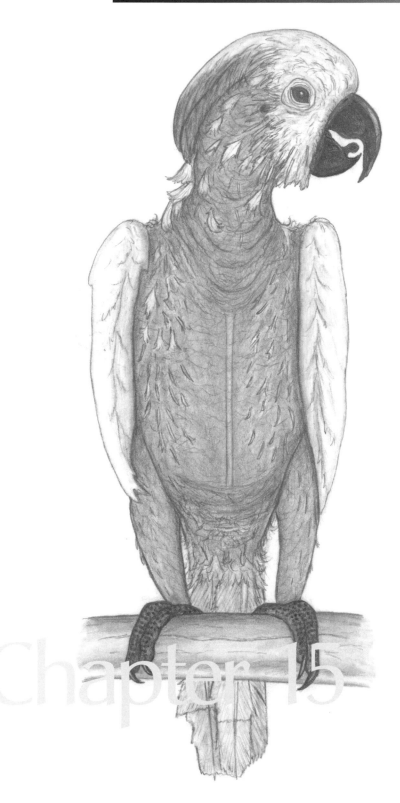

Chapter 15

Medical Problems

Aches, Pains 'n' Infectious Diseases

All birds (even indoor pet birds) will, if they live long enough, get sick sometime during their lives. The study of diseases and their effect on living things is very complex and continues to evolve. Veterinarians spend many years in school studying diseases and then continue this learning process even when they are in practice treating sick pets. Many medical researchers spend their entire careers studying a single disease.

Because of the complexity of disease, this chapter serves only as a simple overview to many of the common diseases affecting pet birds. The purpose is not to teach the pet bird enthusiast how to diagnose and treat disease, but rather to introduce bird owners to the diversity of illnesses affecting their beloved feathered friends. It is hoped this increased awareness will allow for earlier recognition of problems. This is very important. *The longer a disease is allowed to run its course, the more damage occurs, and the more difficult it will be to treat effectively.*

By definition, diseases have specific causes and recognizable signs and, to varying degrees, they prevent the body from functioning normally. A wide variety of diseases affect pet birds. The most challenging aspect of practicing medicine is recognizing them and diagnosing and treating them correctly. There is no such thing as a standard or "cookbook" approach to any disease. The art of "practice" has been so named because it involves combining the science of medicine, with the finely honed skills necessary to bring to light the correct diagnosis and treatment.

How Diseases Get Started

Even indoor birds in single-pet households are exposed to potential disease-producing organisms everyday. No pet lives in a sterile, non-contaminated environment. Such an environment does not exist. Then why are birds, and for that matter all living creatures, healthy most of the time? No simple answer exists to this question. There are, in fact, many reasons. One of the most significant is a strong, healthy functioning immune system. Birds get sick when the immune system is weakened. The body's ability to successfully fight off so many different organisms is therefore influenced by the health of the immune system.

The immune system must be kept strong and healthy to protect the body against disease. The strength of a bird's immune system is influenced by age, gender, species, diet, environment, and heredity. Many of these factors cannot be controlled. However, keeping a bird on a nutritious diet and in a healthy, stress-free environment will help keep the immune system working at peak efficiency.

Classification Of Diseases

There are actually many ways to classify diseases. For this section, diseases are grouped together based on their actual cause. Later in this chapter, when specific diseases are discussed, they are classified under primary organ system affected.

Infectious Disease

Infections are caused by microorganisms too small to be seen without the aid of magnification. Those of medical importance include bacteria, viruses, and fungi (including yeast). Whether or not a bird develops an infection actually depends on a number of complex factors working and interacting together. Some of the more important factors include the type and strain of organism, the number or concentration of organisms present, the length of time the organism has to invade the body, and, as previously discussed, the health of the immune system.

Transmission or spread of an infection can occur by many different routes, including contact with contaminated food and water, through the air, via contact with other animals, contamination of objects within the living environment, and even occasionally from the hands and clothing of a loving, conscientious owner.

Medications--antibiotics and antifungals--are available and used properly, can successfully treat many bacterial and fungal infections. Infections are much easier to treat early in the course of disease. On the other hand, viral infections are difficult and frequently impossible to treat. This is because viruses live within an animal's cells, and any drug used to kill viruses will usually also kill the cell in which the virus lives. The best defense against viral infections is prevention. Vaccines are used for this reason. They can prevent a disease from infecting an individual.

With birds, however, the most important step a bird owner can take is to prevent their bird from coming in contact with sick birds.

Metabolic Disease

Metabolism is defined as the process by which animals produce and utilize energy. Several internal organs that must be functioning normally are critical for this process to occur. The major organs involved are the liver, kidneys, pancreas, and thyroid glands. Metabolic diseases occur when these organs malfunction. When they do, various chemicals build up abnormally within the body, and the animal develops medical problems. Examples of diseases in this category include liver disease, such as fatty liver disease and iron storage disease; kidney disease, such as gout; pancreatic disease, such as diabetes; and thyroid disease, such as goiter and hypothyroidism.

Nutritional Disease

A balanced, nutritious diet is essential for achieving optimal health. Birds can become ill if they receive an excess or deficiency of a variety of essential nutrients. For example, seeds contain little or no vitamin A. Therefore, birds on predominantly seed diets can develop a vitamin A deficiency disease, which is actually a rather common problem. All nutrients need to be provided in proper amounts and often in balance with other nutrients. Birds require similar, but somewhat different, nutrient concentrations from other animals. Non-nutritional factors also can affect the nutritious status of an animal. For example, genetic diseases can prevent birds from properly utilizing the nutrients provided in their diet. In these instances, a specially formulated diet or a specific nutritional supplement as prescribed by a veterinarian could help control such a problem.

Parasitic Disease

Parasites are tiny living organisms that live on or in another living organism, obtaining some advantage at the expense of the host. Parasites usually benefit from acquiring food and/or shelter at the expense of their host. Mites, lice, and intestinal worms are examples of parasites.

Toxic Disease

A toxin is any poisonous substance that irritates, damages, or weakens the body's normal activities. Toxins are usually associated with a protein produced by certain plants, animals, or bacteria that is poisonous to other living creatures. Toxins can be eaten, inhaled, or absorbed through the skin. The home environment has many potential toxins that can harm a bird. Therefore it is important for bird owners to become familiar with and recognize these substances so as to prevent toxin exposure. Chapter 7, "Creating a Happy, Healthy Environment," and Chapter 14 "Medical Emergicies" contains information about many potential home toxins.

Cancer

A cancer is the abnormal and uncontrolled growth of cells. Such cells can form masses (tumors) that invade and destroy surrounding tissue. Cancer can also metastasize, or spread, via the bloodstream and lymphatic system and cause serious disease in other organs. Secondary problems such as bleeding, obstructions, and infections can result. The natural progression of cancer results in death.

Cancer produces neoplasms, or tumors, which are the direct result of the abnormal, uncontrolled growth of cells. Malignant tumors are more invasive and metastasize. Benign tumors grow only in a localized area, do not metastasize and have a much more favorable prognosis for recovery.

Developmental and Degenerative Disease

Developmental disease is associated with problems during the growth phase starting in the egg and extending into adulthood (e.g., birth defects). Degeneration is a process by which tissue deteriorates and loses its ability to function normally, such as in the aging process or in arthritis.

Diagnosing Disease

An accurate diagnosis is essential to selecting the proper treatment, resolving the problem in the shortest time, and significantly increasing the probability of a successful outcome. In other words, if you don't know what's broken, how can you fix it? Indeed, many challenges and roadblocks exist to correctly diagnosing a medical problem in pet birds. First, there are many diseases, but there are actually only a limited number of ways the body can respond or change. Different diseases will look alike and cause similar damage to the tissues, resulting in similar behavioral changes. Second, birds can't really communicate with us and tell us where it hurts.

Lastly, birds are very good at hiding or masking signs of disease. It is, therefore, difficult to differentiate one disease from another.

The essential steps a veterinarian takes to correctly make a diagnosis are a thorough history, physical exam, and frequently diagnostic tests. This process is collectively known informally as the work-up.

The Medical Work-Up

Many important clues concerning the actual underlying cause of a disease process will be discovered with a thorough history and physical examination. This is where it all starts, and it cannot be accomplished over the phone. These two essential steps, performed by a veterinarian, begin the process of establishing a correct diagnosis. Although a history and physical exam alone will often not provide all the necessary information to make an exact diagnosis, they will narrow down the list of possible causes.

History

This is the story of the bird's past, including a chronological record of events surrounding the disease. It begins the process, one step at a time, of identifying the problem. Since the patient cannot communicate with its veterinarian, the more aware and observant the owner, the more helpful the history.

ORIGIN: Where did the bird come from: Pet store? Wild-caught? Breeder? Was it hand-fed or parent-raised? Is the bird's age known?

OWNERSHIP: How long? Is the bird a pet or a breeder? Are there other birds in the household? If so: How many? What kind? Any sick birds?

LIFESTYLE: How much interaction (playtime) does the owner spend with the bird? Has the amount of time changed recently? If so, more or less? How much sleep does the bird normally get? Is the cage covered? Does the bird bathe regularly? Is the bird confined to the cage, or free to roam in the house? Regular grooming: beak, wings, and nails? How often? Egg laying? If so, how often? When?

CAGING: Type of cage? Size of cage? Type of metal or other materials used in construction? Painted? Cage location in house? Cleanliness of cage? Does the bird chew or gnaw on cage bars? Toys available? What kinds? Cage flooring, materials used?

DIET: Types of food offered? Types of food actually eaten? Food available all day long or part of each day? Appetite? Finicky eater?

ENVIRONMENTAL CHANGES: In other words, any recent changes in the bird's life? Birds are creatures of habit, and any change can be stressful. This can lead to disease as well as behavioral problems. Has there been any loss or addition of family members, either human or animal? A recent move, of home or cage location? Remodeling or workmen in the home? A recent vacation?

PRESENT PROBLEM: What does the owner think the cause of the problem is and why? How long has the problem been apparent? Any changes in appetite or activity levels? Any specific changes in behavior?

PRESENTING SIGNS (in medical jargon, CLINICAL SIGNS): Has the owner noticed coughing, sneezing, voice changes, regurgitation, diarrhea, feather picking, lumps or bumps on the skin, appetite loss, change in water intake, bleeding, etc.?

MEDICAL HISTORY: Has the bird had any previous medical problems or prior surgeries? Has the bird been tested for chlamydiosis or other avian diseases? Have any blood or diagnostic tests ever been performed? When? Results?

HOME TREATMENT (if any): What has been used? For how long? What was the response? If any medications have been used, bring them along, and show them to the veterinarian.

Physical Exam

This part of the work-up follows the history. A thorough, complete hands-on physical examination is essential. This involves the entire body, not just the affected area. An avian veterinarian will be able to detect and recognize subtle abnormalities in a bird's appearance and demeanor, and this helps lead to a correct diagnosis.

Every veterinarian develops his or her own routine and style for performing a physical exam. However, established guidelines exist for completeness and thoroughness. An avian physical exam should include:

- Observing the bird from a short distance
- Breathing pattern, feather appearance, posture, and attitude
- Examining the cage and the bird's droppings (remember, don't clean the cage)
- An accurate weight in grams (not ounces)

- A safe and knowledgeable catch and restraint of the bird

A head-to-toe examination includes the eyes, ears, nares, beak, and inside the mouth. Hydration may be tested with a small pinch of the eyelid. A healthy weight is determined by feeling for fullness of the pectoralis (breast) muscle. The body is examined for skin lesions or growths. The abdomen of the bird is gently felt to check for distension that could indicate organ enlargement, an egg, infection, or a tumor. The cloaca (vent) and the uropygial (preen) gland are examined. A stethoscope is used to auscultate (listen to) the heart and breathing pattern. The wings, legs, feet, toes, and foot pads are manipulated and felt for abnormalities. Last and certainly not least, the appearance and general health of the feathers are noted.

In addition certain problems require the use of specialized medical instrumentation. This could include magnification, focused light sources, special eye or ear equipment, speculums, and other unique "tools of the trade".

Diagnostic Testing

The patient's history is really only the owner's observations of their bird's behavior and environmental lifestyle. The patient's physical exam is the veterinarian's findings from evaluating primarily the superficial or "outside" structures on the bird's body. What about all the internal or "inside the body" organs that can't be seen or easily examined? For an accurate diagnosis, specific treatment protocols, and prognosis (forecasting probable outcome of disease), these internal structures must be evaluated.

The history and physical examination do not usually provide a definitive diagnosis, rather they generally help narrow down the range of possible causes. They help suggest the path to follow toward establishing an accurate diagnosis. This is important because a wide assortment of diagnostic tests can be performed on birds. Since most bird owners have financial limitations, the history and physical examination can greatly reduce the number of tests that will likely need to be recommended.

The following is a list of the most common avian diagnostic tests. Their significance and how they are interpreted is discussed in chapter 13, "Veterinary Care." Less commonly used tests will not be discussed.

- General Health Screen (CBC, chemistry panel, and radiographs)

- Blood tests for specific diseases: e.g., chlamydiosis, aspergillosis, psittacine beak and feather disease, lead and/or zinc poisoning.
- Bacteriologic and fungal/yeast exams: Gram stain or culture and sensitivity
- Endoscopy with or without biopsy
- Cytology and fluid analysis

Treatment Of Disease

Ideally, a veterinarian should arrive at a diagnosis before any treatment begins. However, hours and even days can pass before a veterinarian learns the results of diagnostic tests that hopefully will lead to an accurate diagnosis. As previously mentioned, however, the history and physical examination can suggest which organ system(s) are involved, or can at least narrow the list of possibilities. Therefore, when there is a delay in establishing a diagnosis, a veterinarian will weight the desire to withhold treatment until the diagnosis is made against the benefits of initiating some preliminary treatment based on the results of the history and physical. In most cases, sick birds benefit from beginning treatment sooner rather than later. As the results of the diagnostic tests become known, the veterinarian can begin to use more specific and effective treatments.

The aggressiveness of treatment is dictated by how sick the bird appears. Mild illness is usually treated on an outpatient basis. The patient often receives some type of initial treatment in the hospital/clinic, and the veterinarian will send the bird home with its owner, along with some medications to administer. More severely sick birds could require hospitalization. During their stay in the hospital, birds can be treated with a wider variety of treatments and be observed more closely.

Most importantly, remember that the earliest possible recognition of a medical problem, followed by prompt veterinary medical care, provides the greatest probability of a rapid recovery.

Avian Diseases

Eye Disorders

SIGNS TO WATCH FOR

• Eyelids swollen and/or pasted closed
• Increased blinking
• Eye discharge, including excessive tearing
• Cloudiness of the eyeball
• Squinting
• Rubbing the eye or side of the face

Conjunctivitis
("Pink-eye")

Conjunctivitis is an inflammation of the membrane covering the inside of the eyelids and outer surface of the eyeball. When only one eye is affected, an injury from a small seed, feather, piece of dirt, or other type of trauma might be the suspected cause. If both eyes are involved, an infection or allergy, from such things as dust or smoke, should be suspected. In some instances, conjunctivitis can result from a respiratory infection or even from a more serious problem affecting the entire body.

Author's Notes:
Within each of the various bird species, certain diseases are more common than others. In this book, with few exceptions, the identification of which species are most prone to certain diseases has been omitted. The reason for this is to encourage the pet bird owner to consider the range of disease possibilities with an open mind. Remember, any species and any individual bird could develop any of the diseases mentioned.

General Signs of a Sick Bird: Throughout this chapter, as in chapter 14, where the Signs to Watch for are discussed under diseases, mention will be made of the term General Signs of a Sick Bird. In order to avoid repetition, this term will be used to encompass the range of signs a bird may show when sick. These signs include: appetite loss, unkempt feathers (fluffed or fluffed up), decreased activity (listlessness), increased sleeping, decreased vocalizations, change in behavior, and abnormal droppings. Also refer to "Sick Birds: Signs of Illness" on page 237 of chapter 12, "Home Physicals."

General Supportive Care: Sick birds, in general, usually have weight loss resulting from a decreased appetite and water intake. In these instances, the patient will benefit from General Supportive Care. Once again, as in chapter 14, in order to avoid repetition, this term will be used to refer to basic treatments that would benefit any sick bird. This would include any or all of the following: extra warmth, fluid administration for hydration, supplemental force feeding for extra nutrition, a quiet and relaxed environment, and other general forms of basic supportive care. (See page 285 for a more detailed discussion.) Also refer to "Therapeutics: The Art and Science of Healing" on page 267 of chapter 13, "Veterinary Care."

SIGNS TO WATCH FOR: Normal pink color of tissue surrounding the eye becomes inflamed and deep red in color. There is often a discharge from the affected eye(s).

AVIAN VETERINARY CARE: Eye problems require immediate treatment. The eye will be thoroughly examined for the presence of foreign objects, growths, and corneal scratches (see below). Depending on the underlying cause and severity of the problem, an appropriate eye medication will be selected and sent home to be applied onto the eye several times daily.

Corneal Abrasion (Scratch on surface of eyeball)

Injuries to the cornea can be serious, as well as painful. Some of the causes include trauma, infection, irritating substances and self-inflicted injuries from excessive rubbing of the eye. *SIGNS TO WATCH FOR:* Squinting is common, and the cornea may appear cloudy or lose its normal transparency. *DIAGNOSIS:* Abrasions are usually not visible to the "naked eye". They are detected with the combination of a special stain, ultraviolet light, and magnification. *AVIAN VETERINARY CARE:* Immediate veterinary care is required; an antibiotic eye medication will be prescribed for use in the eye several times daily. Medications containing corticosteroids (anti-inflammatories) should never be used. They delay the healing process and can cause more serious problems. Surgery to repair a deep corneal ulcer is occasionally necessary.

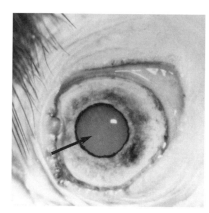

A cataract in the eye of this older macaw causes the lens to appear cloudy.

Cataract(s)

These most frequently develop in the eyes of older birds. They are usually hereditary, but they can also result from diabetes or trauma to the eye. *SIGNS TO WATCH FOR:* A whitening of the lens suggests a cataract. The lens is normally invisible because it is transparent. If a cataract is present, instead of the characteristic black hole appearance of the pupil, the lens will appear white. *AVIAN VETERINARY CARE:* An examination is needed and a blood test may be recommended to rule out diabetes. If diabetes is not the cause, treatment is usually not necessary.
HOME CARE: Cataracts are not painful, but over time, they can result in blindness. Birds that are blind usually do very well and quickly learn their way around their cages. In such cases, it is recommended that you be consistent in the placement of food, water, and perches so that the birds do not get confused.

Foreign Object in Eye

Occasionally, a bird will get something in its eye, such as a small feather, fragment from a toy, or a seed hull. *SIGNS TO WATCH FOR:* Excessive blinking, head shaking, watery eye, or rubbing of the eye
AVIAN VETERINARY CARE: The foreign object can usually be easily removed with good restraint and the proper instru-

ments. The eye should be stained to check for a corneal abrasion. Antibiotics will usually be prescribed to aid in healing and to help guard against infection.

Respiratory Disorders

Specific Signs To Watch For

- Noisy breathing: wheezing, frequent panting or clicking sounds
- Difficulty breathing: shortness of breath, open-mouth breathing, tail bobbing (pronounced up-and-down motion of tail), or frequent stretching of neck
- Nasal discharge or matting of feathers around the cere
- Swollen area around eye (may suggest eye problem or sinus infection)
- Loss or change of voice

As discussed in chapter 11, a bird's respiratory system is markedly different from that of a mammal. Therefore, a basic knowledge of a bird's respiratory anatomy and physiology is vital to understanding and treating problems affecting their respiratory system.

Respiratory infections in pet birds are common. A human's common cold should not be confused with similar problems in birds. Since birds have developed a highly specialized breathing apparatus, problems are, unfortunately, more involved and more difficult to treat. Even a simple runny nose or sneeze should be taken seriously. Problems can quickly become life threatening, and therefore, early recognition and treatment is very important.

This conure is suffering from an acute sinus infection. Note the dramatic swelling of the bird's face.

Rhinitis/Sinusitis

These are medical terms for inflammation of the membranes in the nose or sinuses. An infection in the nose actually extends into the sinuses. As many humans know, sinus infections are difficult to treat and can easily become a chronic problem.

SIGNS TO WATCH FOR: Plugged nares, runny nose, sneezing, head shaking, sinus infections may also show puffy cheeks or swelling around one or both eyes.

DIAGNOSIS: Radiographs can be helpful, as well as microscopic examination or culture and sensitivity of the membranes around the choanal slit and/or sinus cavity. Endoscopic exam with or without biopsy of the oral cavity and portions of sinus cavity can also be used to help identify the cause of these infections. Diagnostic testing is important because other diseases, such as allergies, foreign bodies or tumors of the nasal cavity, may show similar signs.

AVIAN VETERINARY CARE: Simple infections are treated with antibiotics. Depending on the severity, other options include decongestants, antifungals, sinus flushes, vaporization, and nebulization (for an explanation of nebulization, (refer to page 269). Sinus infections can frequently become a long-term problem, and aggressive treatment is recommended.

Hypovitaminosis A *(Vitamin A Deficiency)*

Vitamin A is essential for the maintenance of healthy skin, good vision, bone development, and even reproduction. Since a type of skin (epithelium) lines the inside of the respiratory and digestive tracts, a deficiency often causes problems in these areas. This results from the weakening of the skin's normal defenses against microorganisms. Poor nutrition, such as in an all-seed diet, is the most common cause. Seeds contain little or no vitamin A.

SIGNS TO WATCH FOR: As mentioned, refer to General Signs of a Respiratory Problem and General Signs of a Sick Bird, decreased appetite, poor vision, frequent yeast infections, poor fertility, and hatching problems. One of the more commonly recognized problems, especially in Amazon parrots, are infections in the mouth. These appear along the roof of the mouth and under the tongue. Look for white, "cheesy" patches, excessive redness, ulcers, or small tumor-like abscesses.

DIAGNOSIS: History suggesting poor diet, signs as mentioned above, microscopic examination of affected tissue, and a throat culture and sensitivity.

AVIAN VETERINARY CARE: Vitamin A supplementation is given, usually by injection. Secondary bacterial or yeast infections are also frequently present and must be treated. Many birds are not eating and drinking well because the oral sores are painful. In these cases, birds need to be provided General Supportive Care along with antibiotics and vitamin/mineral supplementation. Surgery is sometimes needed to lance abscesses, especially if eating or breathing becomes difficult.

PREVENTION: Improving the diet is essential. Cod liver oil is a good oral source of vitamin A, and it can be added to food.

However, it spoils rapidly, and treated foods should be dis-carded after about 12 hours. Animal sources of vitamin A include liver, fish oils, and egg yolk. Plant sources include deep green or dark orange vegetables, such as sweet pota-toes/yams, spinach, broccoli, carrots, squash, red peppers, endive, and parsley. Fruits that are high in vitamin A include papaya, cantaloupe, and apricots. Please note: vitamin A in excess can also cause problems. Consult an avian veterinarian for recommendations on the proper use of supplements.

Laryngitis, Tracheitis, Syringitis, Bronchitis, Pneumonia and Air Sacculitis

These medical terms are used to describe an inflammation of a specific area of the lower respiratory tract. In actuality, most lower respiratory infections involve two or more of these areas simultaneously. Bacterial and fungal infections are the most common organism identified as a cause, although aller-gies and occasionally foreign bodies can also cause problems in this area.

SIGNS TO WATCH FOR: General signs of a respiratory prob-lem and General Signs of a Sick Bird.

DIAGNOSIS: Diagnosis presents many challenges. Among them is listening to the lungs and heart with a stethoscope. In mammals, this simple instrument yields a tremendous amount of very useful information. However, in birds, a stethoscope is not as useful. Respiratory sounds are not as audible in birds because of their massive pectoral muscles, very rapid heart rate, nonexpanding/contracting lungs, and the small size of these tissues and organs.

Culture and sensitivity, and microscopic examination of tracheal secretions, blood counts, radiographs, and endoscopy with and without biopsy may be needed for an accurate diagnosis.

AVIAN VETERINARY CARE: Depending on the cause and severity this could include antibiotics, antifungals, deconges-tants, hospitalization, General Supportive Care, nebulization (for an explanation of nebulization, see page 271) and oxygen therapy.

Air Sac Infections

Air sac infections deserve special mention. Diagnosis and treatment are especially difficult. Air sacs are at the end of the line, so to speak, of the respiratory system and form a con-venient reservoir for contaminated air. Blood supply to the air sacs is scant, and therefore the accumulated debris escape most of the body's normal waste-removal and defense mechanisms. Treatment is difficult since oral and injectable drugs require a good blood flow to carry them to the site of the problem.

In the early stages of an air sac infection, birds usually do not appear sick. As a result, by the time the illness is recognized, the condition is well established. Infections can be bacterial but the fungus *Aspergillus* frequently infects the air sacs.

SIGNS TO WATCH FOR: General signs of respiratory problems as listed above, especially a tail bob, open-mouth breathing, and listlessness.

DIAGNOSIS: May require all or some of the following: Radiographs, tracheal cultures, blood tests (complete blood count and/or a blood test for Aspergillosis), and often endoscopy of the lungs, air sacs, and trachea.

AVIAN VETERINARY CARE: General Supportive Care is usually very beneficial. Aggressive antibiotic and/or antifungal therapy is necessary. Most birds also require several days of nebulization therapy in the hospital. Oxygen therapy may also be necessary. On occasion, surgery may be recommended to remove diseased air sac tissue. Air sac disease may require several months of treatment.

Aspergillosis

Aspergillosis is a fungal disease most commonly causing air sac and lung infections. Birds with weakened immune systems combined with stress are particularly susceptible. Those kept in crowded, moist, poorly ventilated, and unkempt areas are at greatest risk. The disease is transmitted by birds inhaling airborne fungal elements.

SIGNS TO WATCH FOR: General signs of respiratory disease and General Signs of a Sick Bird, especially rapid breathing, open-mouth breathing, voice changes, wheezing, and listlessness.

DIAGNOSIS: Fungal culture of the affected area, aspergillosis blood test, radiographs, and endoscopy with biopsy may all be necessary. Diagnosis can be challenging.

AVIAN VETERINARY CARE: Even with antifungal medications, this is a very difficult disease to treat. Hospitalization, General Supportive Care, and months of home treatment are often required. Medication given directly into the trachea or via nebulization can be beneficial.

Some Other Common Respiratory Problems
Allergies

Allergies do occur in birds. Birds are probably similar to mammals in that virtually anything could trigger an allergic reaction. However, some of the most likely causes would include certain types of perfumes, tobacco smoke, molds, pollens, incense, and feather dust.

SIGNS TO WATCH FOR: Sneezing, runny eyes and nose, coughing, and sometimes digestive tract problems.

DIAGNOSIS: A complete blood count, radiographs, and endoscopy with biopsy will help the veterinarian identify allergic causes in the respiratory tract. At present, actual allergy testing is not available for birds.

AVIAN VETERINARY CARE: Medications such as anti-inflammatories and antihistamines may be used and can sometimes relieve allergy signs. Identification followed by removal of the substance or item the bird is allergic to can potentially cure the problem. Positive identification of allergens is difficult and challenging.

PREVENTION: To help decrease the allergens that a bird is exposed to, HePA air filters can be used to help remove dust, mold, smoke, pollen and other particles from the air. A bird should never be exposed to tobacco smoke, incense, scented candles, or other aerosols with strong odors. Birds should be kept in well-ventilated environments.

Inhaled Foreign Objects

Small seeds can become lodged in a nare, in the roof of the mouth or even in the trachea. Small birds, especially cockatiels, are most susceptible. Severe breathing difficulties, such as gasping for air, are readily observed.

If you suspect your bird has inhaled a foreign object into its trachea, call your avian veterinarian immediately; this is an emergency!

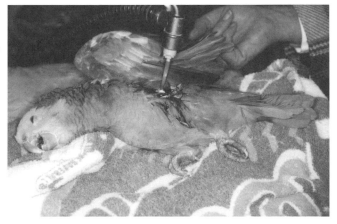

This Amazon is being anesthetized using an air sac tube. It had a foreign object in its trachea, so it could not be anesthetized with a mask over its face. Bird's unique respiratory anatomy allows them to actually be anesthetized with the anesthetic gases being delivered directly into the abdominal air sacs. From here, the gases pass into the lungs and the bird is safely kept anesthetized.

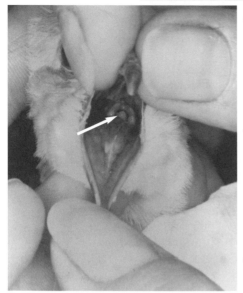

Look carefully to see the seed lodged in the trachea of this small bird. The photo was taken after the bird died.

Respiratory Mites

Respiratory mites are found primarily in finches and canaries. These parasites live in the trachea, lungs, and/or air sacs.

TRANSMISSION: Food or water, from one bird to another, including from parent to chick.

SIGNS TO WATCH FOR: Breathing difficulties with a characteristic clicking sound, voice changes, gasping for air.

DIAGNOSIS: Microscopic exam of throat secretions is helpful. Use of a highly illuminated and focused light source can also be used to actually visualize mites through the skin that are living in the trachea.

AVIAN VETERINARY CARE: The drug ivermectin is generally used and is very effective.

Chlamydiosis (klah-MID-e-O-sis) [also known as psittacosis (sit-ah-KO-sis), ornithosis, or parrot fever]

Chlamydiosis is a common and highly contagious disease of pet birds. It can be transmitted to humans. (See page 382 for information regarding human infection). *Chlamydophila psittaci* is the name of the organism causing this disease. Young, newly acquired birds are at a higher risk of developing the disease. However, it can occur in adult birds. Stress appears to increase the chance of a bird becoming ill.

TRANSMISSION: This disease can be spread in many ways, including contact with sick birds, shedding the organism in their respiratory secretions, droppings, feather dust, or through contaminated food and water supplies. In addition, parents can infect their nestlings while feeding them. Birds can also be carriers, showing no outward signs of disease, but able to infect other birds that come in contact with them.

SIGNS TO WATCH FOR: There are no distinctively characteristic signs for chlamydiosis. However, the following signs in a sick bird can be suggestive: General Signs of a Sick Bird, watery, yellow or lime-green urates (see page 249), sneezing, conjunctivitis, loss of appetite, weight loss, depression, listlessness, and nasal discharge. Any of these signs are suggestive, especially when seen in a young, newly acquired bird. There is a more chronic state of this disease, with affected birds developing signs of poor feathering, diarrhea, and weight loss. In more advanced cases, birds can even show neurological signs, including seizures, tremors, and paralysis.

DIAGNOSIS: As of this writing, no single test will detect this disease in all infected birds. Therefore, diagnosis can be challenging. In almost all instances, it is not financially possible to run all the available tests on every sick bird. Each of the tests work best when performed under specific circumstances, and an avian veterinarian must decide which test(s) to perform. In addition, a good history, physical exam, complete blood panel, radiographs, and a few other tests can also be very helpful in leading to the diagnosis.

AVIAN VETERINARY CARE: Whenever chlamydiosis is suspected or confirmed, treatment should begin immediately. The antibiotic tetracycline is used for treatment. It is available in different forms and has various routes of administration (oral, injectable, medicated pellets, or as a food additive). The type of tetracycline and its most effective route of administration will be determined by the avian veterinarian. Treatment must be continued for at least 45 days. Very sick birds will also require General Supportive Care. Recovered birds can become reinfected at a later time. Therefore, periodic testing of affected birds following treatment is advisable.

In addition to the treatment above, follow these other important recommendations: Isolate all sick birds, thoroughly clean and disinfect the cage and its surroundings (for disinfectants, see page 88), keep circulation of feathers and dust to a minimum. Human contact should be also kept to a minimum.

PREVENTION:
- All newly acquired birds should be examined by a veterinarian and tested for chlamydiosis.
- Buy birds only from reputable suppliers.
- Isolate all new birds from other birds for at least 30 days.
- Consider having your birds tested periodically for chlamydiosis, especially if they come in contact with other birds. Unfortunately, there is not a vaccine currently available for prevention.

Thyroid Gland Enlargement (Goiter)

The paired thyroid glands are located alongside the trachea at the base of the neck. These glands may become markedly enlarged if a bird's diet lacks sufficient iodine. The enlarged glands place pressure on the trachea and breathing problems can develop. Budgies seem to be affected most often.

SIGNS TO WATCH FOR: Breathing difficulties, swallowing difficulties, regurgitation, and slow crop emptying time.

DIAGNOSIS: Unless the thyroid glands are large enough that they can be felt (which is uncommon), this disease can be very difficult to diagnosis. Radiographs may be suggestive of enlargement of these glands. There are also no reliable blood tests. Therefore, if this disease is suspected, the veterinarian will usually treat and then monitor the response.

AVIAN VETERINARY CARE: Iodine supplementation with dosage determined by veterinarian. A balanced formulated diet should also be fed for both a treatment and a preventative.

Sarcocystosis (sar"ko-sis'do'sis)

Sarcocystis falcatula, a protozoan parasite, causes this disease. It has an unusual and quite interesting life cycle. The host of this parasite is the North American opossum. The parasite reproduces inside the opossum and the parasite's sporocysts (microscopic eggs) are released into the opossum's feces. Cockroaches then ingest the opossum's feces containing this parasite's eggs. The cockroach can then enter and contaminate a bird's cage and food supply. A pet bird can actually develop sarcocystosis by eating the parasite's eggs in opossum feces, eating a cockroach, or via contaminated food. Once ingested, the parasite spreads rapidly throughout the bird's internal organs. The lungs and spleen are particularly susceptible.

SIGNS TO WATCH FOR: This is usually a fatal disease. However, some birds can have chronic infections and show only mild but usually develop progressive signs. Infected birds may show General Signs of a Sick Bird, breathing difficulties including: open-mouth breathing, coughing up blood-tinged fluid, and increased respiratory rate. Other signs include generalized weakness, decreased appetite, diarrhea, or head tremors. In extreme cases, sudden death can occur.

DIAGNOSIS: Radiographs may show fluid build-up in the lungs and enlargement of the spleen and liver. White cysts in the breast muscle may also be seen during the physical examination. A blood test specific for sarcocystosis is also available.

AVIAN VETERINARY CARE: This disease is usually acutely fatal (birds die within 24 hours). However, birds can also present with only mild signs. If a diagnosis can be confirmed early enough, antiparasitic medications, along with General Supportive Care, can sometimes prove successful.

PREVENTION: Birds housed outdoors are at the highest risk. If birds are going to be kept outside, good pest control is most important in preventing infection. To prevent roach infestations, cages should be kept clean and sanitary.

Pesticides are toxic to birds, and their use is not recommended. Biological control methods, such as keeping insect-eating animals like chickens or geckos, can help control roach problems. Opossums could be kept away by installing an electrical fence or other barrier around the aviary. Keeping cages off the ground is also an important means to prevent birds from ingesting contaminated feces.

Nonrespiratory Causes of Breathing Difficulties

Diseases involving organs outside the respiratory system can also result in breathing difficulties. Examples would include heart and liver problems, abdominal tumors, malnutrition, and even certain poisons. For this important reason, diagnostic tests such as radiographs and blood tests are necessary to distinguish between the various causes of respiratory distress.

Heart Disease

Birds can be born with heart defects. They can also develop infections involving the heart muscle or develop heart problems with advancing age, such as heart-valve disease. They can even develop arteriosclerosis (thickening of the heart's blood vessels). With heart disease comes the difficulty of pumping blood throughout the body. In more advanced cases, fluid can build up in the abdominal area.

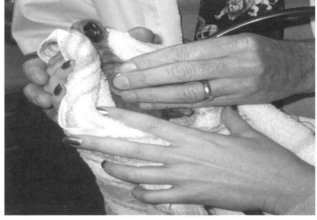

Auscultating a bird's heart is the first step in diagnosing heart disease. This should be part of a complete physical examination.

This is called ascites, and birds will often present with breathing difficulties, muscle wasting, and abdominal distention.

SIGNS TO WATCH FOR: General Signs of a Sick Bird, coughing, shortness of breath, swollen abdomen.

DIAGNOSIS: Radiographs may show an enlarged heart or be suggestive of ascites. A heart murmur may or may not be heard with a stethoscope. Electrocardiography (ECG) can be used to diagnose heart disease in birds. However, due to some difficulties specific to birds, it is not commonly used.

AVIAN VETERINARY CARE: Critical patients may need supplemental oxygen and General Supportive Care. If ascites is present, draining of some of this excess fluid often improves breathing. Medication is also available to help remove the excess fluid from the bird's abdomen. Specific heart medications to improve the strength and efficiency of heart contractions can also be used in birds. Dietary changes should also be a part of the long-term treatment plan.

PREVENTION: A nutritious diet that is low in fat may help prevent some forms of heart disease (sound familiar?).

Liver Disease

Enlargement of the liver can make it difficult for a bird to breathe. See page 354 for more information on liver disease.

Mimicking of Humans

When all else fails, remember a bird could always be "faking" a cough. Many birds can learn to copy a cough or sneeze. Consider the bird's talking ability, exposure to coughing noises, health status, and common sense to determine if this is possible. If this is suspected, it would still be highly recommended to have your avian veterinarian perform a complete physical examination.

Digestive Disorders

The anatomy and physiology of the digestive system of birds is significantly different from mammals. It is necessary to have a basic understanding of these areas to fully appreciate the following section. The reader is referred to page 230 of chapter 11, "Avian Anatomy and Physiology," for a discussion of the bird's digestive system.

SPECIFIC SIGNS TO WATCH FOR:
- Vomiting/regurgitation
- Diarrhea (specifically loose stool); may contain blood, mucous, or undigested seeds
- Straining to pass droppings
- Droppings contain urine and no stool (consider constipation, obstruction, and, of course, not eating)

Oral Cavity (Mouth) Problems

A thorough examination of a bird's mouth is not as easy as it might seem. "Open up and say 'ahh'" just doesn't work! To begin with, good restraint is essential (see chapter 5, "Bird Restraint"). The best time to examine the mouth is immediately after capture, when the bird is often vocalizing. Any method used to forcibly open a bird's mouth is not recommended, except in the experienced hands of an avian veterinarian. The normal membranes of the mouth are pink, shiny, slightly moist, and with near uniform coloration. Some species may also normally show various degrees of a black pigmentation on the tongue or roof of the mouth.

SIGNS TO WATCH FOR: Excessive wetness or inflammation, decreased number or *blunting* of the papilla lining the roof of the mouth. More advanced cases might also include: ulcerations, tumors, or abscesses that appear as white cheesy deposits. In addition, there may be appetite loss, voice changes, or nasal congestion.

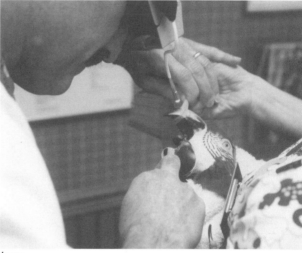

Vitamin A Deficiency
This can be a contributing factor in the development of oral infections (see page 336).

Trichomoniasis
Parasites such as trichomonas (tri-KOM-o-nas), a protozoan, occasionally cause problems in the mouths of pet birds. It is more common in pigeons and raptors.

Avian veterinarians often use gauze strips to hold a bird's beak open during an examination. The strips help prevent injury to the beak.

SIGNS TO WATCH FOR: White cheesy deposits or dry scabby lesions.
DIAGNOSIS: Microscopic examination cells lining oral cavity.
AVIAN VETERINARY CARE: Antiprotozoan drugs.

Oral Tumors
Cancerous and non-cancerous (e.g., benign papillomas) can be found along the roof of the mouth or the back of the throat.
SIGNS TO WATCH FOR: growths or masses in mouth.
DIAGNOSIS: Microscopic exam of tumor cells or biopsy of tumor.
AVIAN VETERINARY CARE: Surgical removal of tumors.

Crop Disorders
The crop can normally be felt in the area around the base of the neck. It must be examined gently. If it is full, there is a risk of food being pushed up into the mouth and/or aspirated into the airway. For this reason, only an avian veterinarian should perform this exam.

SIGNS TO WATCH FOR: General Signs of a Sick Bird, regurgitation, unusual head and neck movements, slow crop emptying time, swelling at the base of the neck, sour smell coming from the mouth.

You will often not see the regurgitation, but clues to suggest it has occurred can often be seen. Look for food debris sprayed or caked over the skin and feathers of the face and head. Closely examine the cage paper. Regurgitation appears as a blob of semi-digested food, which looks different from a dropping. Remember, regurgitation can also be a normal sign of affection or courtship (see page 295).

Conditions that could be mistaken for an enlarged crop include: fat deposits, especially in budgies, ruptured air sac, and tumors in the neck area.

Crop Infection

These are most commonly diagnosed in young birds. Bacteria and yeast (candida) are the most likely underlying causes.
SIGNS TO WATCH FOR: General Signs of a Sick Bird and, more specifically, a slow-emptying crop. Crops should normally empty within a few hours of feeding. An enlarged crop will appear as a large, pendulous swelling at the base of the neck that does not get smaller with time. These problems are an emergency--do not delay in contacting your avian veterinarian.
DIAGNOSIS: Microscopic analysis and/or culture of crop contents, radiographs are also helpful and could reveal a foreign body in the crop or a more serious problem involving the lower digestive tract.
AVIAN VETERINARY CARE: General Supportive Care as needed. Antibiotics, antifungals, crop-contracting stimulants as indicated; the crop may also need to be emptied manually and flushed (crop lavage) to remove stale food and instill medication to treat infection.

Crop Impaction

In this case, an impaction refers to the formation of a solid mass of food material preventing the crop from emptying normally. The causes for this include: infection, overeating of grit, dehydration, ingestion of a foreign object, or any serious, debilitating disease.
SIGNS TO WATCH FOR: General Signs of a Sick Bird, swelling at the base of the neck, slow crop-emptying time.
DIAGNOSIS: A hard or doughy mass can be felt during

examination. Radiographs are helpful to rule out a foreign object and problems involving the proventriculus (the true stomach). A crop culture will identify infectious organisms that may have caused the crop impaction.

AVIAN VETERINARY CARE: General Supportive Care as needed. The impaction will need to be removed from the crop. Manual removal is usually effective. This is accomplished by either "milking-out" the impaction, or flushing and then massaging the crop to loosen and break up the impaction. Occasionally surgery will be necessary to remove the impaction. Medications including antibiotics, antifungals, or crop-contracting stimulants may be needed.

It's also important to remember there are other possible causes of crop problems which include: enlarged thyroid glands, any type of digestive tract problem and even any serious debilitating disease.

Proventriculus Disorders

The proventriculus is the true stomach in birds. It secretes the juices necessary for digestion of food. No simple way exists to diagnose problems of this organ. The history, physical exam, and the Signs to Watch For with all digestive tract problems are not specific enough. Diagnosis is therefore difficult, and diagnostic tests will be necessary. Most problems are the result of an infection, foreign object, parasites, or occasionally, a tumor.

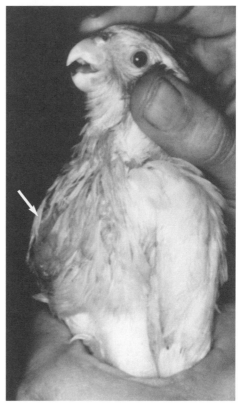

This cockatiel has an impaction of the crop. Notice the swelling over the crop area.

Proventricular Dilatation Disease (PDD)
(Formerly Macaw Wasting Disease, Neuropathic Gastric Dilatation)

PDD is a serious viral disease of the digestive tract. It was first discovered in macaws, but it has now also been found in numerous other species of parrots. Once infected with this disease, birds usually die. The disease is most often seen in young birds, but birds of any age may be affected.

PDD affects the nerves of the digestive tract. Specific nerves stimulate contractions throughout the digestive tract. These contractions are essential for both the movement and digestion of food. The virus attacks these nerves and, subse-

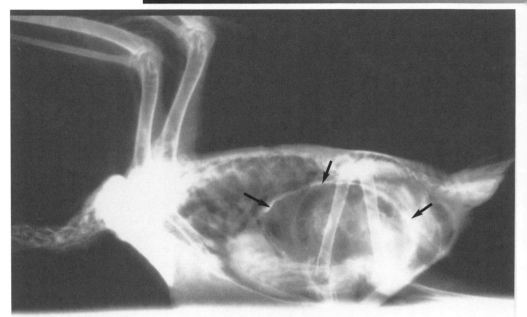

This is a radiograph of a bird with proventricular dilatation disease (PDD). The three arrows indicate the border of the dramatically enlarged proventriculus.

quently, food cannot be properly digested, causing the bird to begin losing weight. The PDD virus can be spread from one bird to another. As of this writing, how it is transmitted from one bird to another has not been determined.

SIGNS TO WATCH FOR: General Signs of a Sick Bird, regurgitation, undigested food in droppings, diarrhea, progressive weight loss, general weakness, and sometimes neurologic signs including loss of balance, tremors, and general weakness. Some birds may actually continue to have an excellent appetite but will still progressively lose weight.

DIAGNOSIS: As of this writing, no specific blood test exists to confirm this disease. Radiographs may reveal a distended, balloon-like proventriculus; however, other diseases may also cause this distention. If PDD is suspected, a biopsy of the crop or gizzard can confirm the diagnosis. However, even with proper collection of the biopsies the disease can sometimes still be missed. Avian researchers are hard at work developing a simple and reliable blood test for diagnosis of PDD.

AVIAN VETERINARY CARE: No cure is available. Treatment consists of General Supportive Care; a soft, easily digestible diet, and medicine to help stimulate digestive tract contractions. Certain anti-inflammatory medications can also be helpful in helping control some of the problems seen in this disease. They may also be beneficial in slowing down it's progression. Avian researchers are also trying to develop a vaccine that will prevent PDD.

Gizzard Disorders (Muscular Stomach)

The gizzard grinds up the food. As with proventricular disorders, there is no simple way to diagnose problems in this organ. Most problems are the result of an infection (e.g., PDD {see page 345}, bacterial, or fungus), a foreign body, or occasionally a tumor. Ingested foreign objects such as grit or metal will collect in the gizzard. Grit impactions in the gizzard sometimes occur.

DIAGNOSIS: Radiographs and sometimes an Upper Gastrointestinal Study (Upper GI) are necessary to help visualize the gizzard.

An Upper GI is a special radiographic procedure in which the bird is tube-fed a thick solution of barium. This contrast liquid appears white on radiographs and clearly outlines the inside walls of the digestive tract. This dye study is more helpful than "plain" or standard radiographs for identifying obstructions, ulcers, tumors, infections, digestive tract motility disorders, and swallowed foreign objects.

AVIAN VETERINARY CARE: Grit impactions will frequently resolve on their own but often require General Supportive Care, and antibiotics to prevent secondary infections. Surgery of the gizzard is difficult and should be attempted only if no other options exist.

Intestines

The intestines normally harbor good bacteria to aid in the digestion process. During an infection, the gut linings often become inflamed, allowing these bacteria to escape into the bloodstream (septicemia, blood poisoning). As a result, other organs can become secondarily infected. Diarrhea is common with intestinal problems. But with severe diarrhea comes a loss of fluid, electrolytes, enzymes, and nutrients. In extreme cases, shock can occur and a life-threatening problem develops. Therefore, immediate veterinary care is recommended.

Intestinal Infections

Intestinal infections are common in pet birds. They are caused primarily by bacteria, but yeast, fungi, and viruses can also cause problems.

SIGNS TO WATCH FOR: General Signs of a Sick Bird, diarrhea, and other signs as previously listed for digestive tract problems.

DIAGNOSIS: Specifically, cultures to identify bacteria, fungus, and yeast. Fecal analysis to rule out parasites. Radiographs for evaluation of appearance of intestines and to rule out foreign objects and obstructions. Blood panels to screen for infection and evaluate health of other organs.

AVIAN VETERINARY CARE: General Supportive Care. Specific treatment for intestinal infections is variable and depends on the cause and condition of the bird. Antibiotics are highly effective against most bacteria causing intestinal infections. Anti-yeast and anti-fungal medications can also be used as needed. A number of specific medications are available for such things as regurgitation, vomiting, and diarrhea.

Salmonella Infection

Salmonella infection deserves special mention because it is a bacteria that can be transmitted to humans (see page 382). Intestinal infections, as well as infections in virtually all other organ systems, can occur.

SIGNS TO WATCH FOR: General Signs of a Sick Bird. In addition, signs are variable depending on what organ system(s) is affected. Refer to Signs to Watch for throughout this chapter.

DIAGNOSIS: Culture of organism. It is very important to remember that almost any organism (and there are many) can present with virtually identical signs.

AVIAN VETERINARY CARE: General Supportive Care as needed. Specific treatment for salmonella-infected birds is controversial. Elimination of infection can be difficult and, even after treatment, birds could remain carriers and potentially transmit infection to other living creatures.

Intestinal Parasites

A variety of worms can cause intestinal disorders. Most people think of parasites as appearing worm-like. This is not always the case, however. In fact, many parasites are microscopic one-celled organisms. A fecal analysis is recommended for all newly acquired birds. Birds living in a typical home environment rarely have problems with intestinal parasites.

SIGNS TO WATCH FOR: Diarrhea, weight loss. Rarely are worms observed in the droppings.

DIAGNOSIS: Microscopic exam of feces

AVIAN VETERINARY CARE: There are a variety of intestinal parasites. No one dewormer can effectively eliminate all of them. Therefore, positive identification of parasites becomes important. Fecal analysis is usually sufficient. These results will guide proper selection of deworming medication.

Giardia: This is a relatively common intestinal parasite in pet birds and deserves special mention. Budgies and cockatiels seem to be most susceptible. This parasite can potentially be transmittable to humans (see page 384)

SIGNS TO WATCH FOR: Weight loss, diarrhea, dry flaky skin, itching, and feather picking.

DIAGNOSIS: Requires a very fresh stool specimen--ideally, a sample collected directly from the cloaca and immediately examined under a microscope. Special staining techniques may be required to identify giardia in the droppings. Diagnosis can be challenging because these parasites are usually only passed intermittently in the droppings. Therefore, to increase the probablility of finding these parasites, it is often recommended to collect samples of the stool over several days.

AVIAN VETERINARY CARE: Specific medications are available for treatment.

Other Causes of Intestinal Problems

Malnutrition, cancer, metabolic diseases, poisons. Foreign objects (e.g., metal) and disorders of other organs can result in diarrhea and other intestinal problems.

Constipation

Constipation is actually rare in birds. The causes for constipation include dehydration, intestinal obstruction and pressure on the outside of the intestines by an egg, tumor, or simply obesity. Remember, if a bird is not eating, little or no stool will be produced. This is frequently mistaken for constipation by concerned pet bird owners.

SIGNS TO WATCH FOR: Consistently, no stool being passed or only tiny amounts, straining to eliminate.

DIAGNOSIS: Thorough history, visual examination of droppings, radiographs

AVIAN VETERINARY CARE: Treatment depends on the underlying cause: fluids for rehydration; medical or surgical treatment for foreign object, removal of an egg, or surgical removal of an abdominal tumor. Laxatives as needed.

Foreign Object in the Digestive Tract

Birds do swallow foreign objects. However, most suspected cases presented to a veterinarian end up as false alarms. In other words, no object was ever ingested. For example, birds may frequently remove the back of an earring or play with a small object in their mouths, but they will not usually swallow it. If the plaything suddenly disappears, first thoroughly examine the entire area around the bird. If the object cannot be found, immediate veterinary attention is warranted.

DIAGNOSIS: The mouth will be opened and examined. If the object was recently swallowed the veterinarian may be able to feel the object in the crop. Radiographs can help confirm and locate a swallowed object. An Upper GI study (see photo page 263) is indicated if the standard radiographs do not show the object known to be swallowed and/or to rule out a digestive tract obstruction.

AVIAN VETERINARY CARE: If the object is lodged in the mouth or esophagus, it may be easily removed manually. Sometimes, a very small foreign object will simply pass through the digestive tract, and no special care is required. Other times, endoscopy and/or surgery will be necessary.

Cloaca Disorders

The cloaca is a sac-like chamber that serves as the common reservoir for stool, urine, and eggs. The vent is the outer muscular sphincter controlling the frequency of eliminations.

SPECIFIC SIGNS TO WATCH FOR: Any protrusion of tissue from the vent. Blood around vent, including actual picking or chewing of area

Cloaca Prolapse

A cloaca prolapse is the protrusion of tissue through the vent opening. The visible exposed tissue could be cloaca, lower intestines, or uterus.

Emergency veterinary care is required (see page 300 in chapter 14).

Cloaca Papilloma

Papillomas are benign growths of tissue. They can actually occur almost anywhere on the body, but the cloaca, mouth, and feet (see page xxx) are the most common sites. They can be confined to the inside of the cloaca or they can protrude through the vent and be confused with a prolapse. A virus is the suspected cause, but this has not been proven.

SIGNS TO WATCH FOR: Straining to eliminate, droppings frequently bloody and may be seen pasted around the vent; bleeding can sometimes occur. If the tissue is exposed, it will appear cauliflower-like, and the bird will frequently pick at it. In these cases, the bird's beak may be bloody.

DIAGNOSIS: Physical and endoscopic examination of the vent and cloaca. Biopsy is necessary to confirm diagnosis.

AVIAN VETERINARY CARE: Surgery is required to remove the growth. Papillomas sometimes recur.

PREVENTION: Since papillomas are probably caused by a virus, a bird that is known to have cloacal or oral papillomas should not be in contact with other birds. These should also not be used for breeding.

Chlamydiosis *[also known as psittacosis or "Parrot Fever"]*

See page 340 for information on the disease in birds and page 382 for its potential to be spread to humans.

Tuberculosis (TB)

In birds, TB primarily involves the digestive system. This is in contrast to humans, where the respiratory tract is usually primarily involved. The disease has a slow onset, and any signs will appear gradually over a prolonged period of time. There are various strains of this organism, but *Mycobacterium avium* is the most common one to infect birds. Avian TB may have the potential to infect humans; however, this is considered to be uncommon (refer to page xxx). Human TB can potentially infect birds as well.

TRANSMISSION: Sick birds spread the infection via their droppings. It is acquired through ingestion of contaminated food, water, or soil.

SIGNS TO WATCH FOR: General Signs of a Sick Bird. More specifically, the signs are extremely variable and depend on which organs are affected. No signs are distinctively characteristic for tuberculosis. Signs that could be suggestive include chronic diarrhea, masses beneath the skin, joint problems, respiratory difficulties, or simply a bird that has been sick for a long period of time.

DIAGNOSIS: TB is challenging to diagnose. A simple blood test for TB is not available. Usually, a combination of tests is needed to diagnose TB. These could include complete blood count, radiographs, microscopic examination of feces with a special staining technique, and biopsy of affected tissue(s).

AVIAN VETERINARY CARE: There are two distinct schools of thought on whether or not birds with confirmed cases of TB should even be treated. One opinion is that all TB-positive birds should be euthanized. The rationale is that the disease can potentially be transmitted to humans. Also, at the time of this writing, no drugs have been specifically tested for their effectiveness against avian TB.

The opposing view advocates treatment using medications proven effective for human TB, the rationale being that the disease is actually very rarely transmitted to humans and therefore, treatment is the reasonable thing to do. There has also been success in treating these birds.

Regardless of the approach taken, human risks are still associated with exposure to avian TB, and people with weakened immune systems are most susceptible. Even birds under treatment can be contagious. The treatment of all cases of TB should be thoroughly discussed with your avian veterinarian and personal physician.

Liver Disorders

Liver disease is common in pet birds. Problems can either begin in the liver itself or, since the liver plays a role in filtering blood, diseases in other organs can easily spread to the liver. The term hepatitis simply means inflammation of the liver. It is not specific for any one particular type of liver disease. Most liver diseases, with the exception of chlamydiosis, are not contagious to humans. They could, however, be spread to other birds.

CAUSES: Numerous microorganisms (i.e., bacteria, viruses, and fungi), chlamydiosis, metabolic diseases such as hypothyroidism, diabetes, gout and allergies, poisons, and drug reactions can all damage the liver. Heart failure, cancer, and parasites can also cause liver disorders.

SIGNS TO WATCH FOR: Mustard yellow or green urates, appetite and weight loss, regurgitation/diarrhea, feather and beak changes, distended abdomen, breathing difficulties, and General Signs of a Sick Bird. However, icterus/jaundice (classic yellow appearance of the skin in a mammal with liver disease) is very rare in birds.

DIAGNOSIS: Blood tests and radiographs are very helpful. These tests can determine if liver disease is present. However, they can neither identify the type of liver disease nor what caused it. A liver biopsy is necessary for an accurate diagnosis and prognosis and can be relatively easily collected using an endoscope.

AVIAN VETERINARY CARE: Since numerous causes of liver disease exist, a wide variety of treatments are available. The more specific the treatment, the more likely the underlying problem can be effectively eliminated or at least controlled. Birds may require temporary hospitalization with General Supportive Care.

Medical Problems

Pacheco's Disease

Pacheco's disease is a viral hepatitis affecting only psittacines. Passerines, such as canaries and finches, are not susceptible. Also, individually kept birds are generally not at risk. This is a disease associated with facilities, such as aviaries, pet shops, and quarantine stations that house multiple birds in the same area. Individual birds would be at risk only if they had just been acquired from one of these places. As is the case with many diseases, stress appears to play a major role. The stresses associated with large collections along with the introductions of new birds can trigger the disease. Some birds can be resistant to Pacheco's disease, but at the same time spread the disease to other birds.

SIGNS TO WATCH FOR: The most consistent sign is rapid death in one or more birds kept in close proximity to each other. Sometimes, all or nearly all, the bird's in a collection will die. It frequently takes only hours and sometimes up to a day or two after the first hint of disease for the birds to die. The only signs prior to death may be diarrhea followed by appetite loss and depression.

DIAGNOSIS: The history of multiple birds kept together, especially with new birds recently introduced, and Signs to Watch for as listed in the beginning of this section should make Pacheco's disease highly suspect. The definitive diagnosis is usually made on postmortem (also called necropsy).

AVIAN VETERINARY CARE: Pacheco's is generally considered an untreatable disease, in part, because it kills so quickly. However, some success in reducing death rates has been reported with a particular antiviral drug.

PREVENTION: A vaccine is available for prevention of Pacheco's disease, but it is usually not recommended for individual pet birds. Vaccination should be considered in those birds, noted above, that are at high risk.

Iron Storage Disease (Hemachromatosis)

Iron storage disease is the result of an excessive build-up of iron in the liver and, sometimes, in other tissues. A diet high in iron, genetic factors and altered intestinal absorption rates can predispose a bird to the onset of this disease. Toucans, toucanettes and mynah birds are the species most commonly affected.

SIGNS TO WATCH FOR: Sudden death in toucans that may not have shown any prior warning signs. Mynah birds usually develop breathing difficulties, weakness, and coughing.

DIAGNOSIS: Clinical signs and history, along with blood tests and radiographs, can identify liver enlargement and abnormal liver function. Liver biopsy is required for confirmation.

AVIAN VETERINARY TREATMENT: Critically ill birds must first be stabilized and supportive care administered. Abdominal fluid (ascites), if present, may be removed. Phlebotomies to periodically remove small amounts of blood are beneficial. Long-term therapy also includes feeding a low-iron diet. Periodic blood tests are needed to monitor disease progression.

PREVENTION: Feeding a diet that contains less than 100 ppm iron will help prevent iron storage disease in at-risk species.

Hepatic Lipidosis (Fatty Liver Syndrome)

Hepatic lipidosis, an abnormal accumulation of fat in the liver, is relatively common in some species of pet birds. High-fat diets, heredity and some toxins are suggested causes.

SIGNS TO WATCH FOR: Overweight to obese birds, appetite loss, lethargy, abnormal droppings, poor feathering, and abdominal enlargement. Some birds may also develop over-grown nails and beaks.

DIAGNOSIS: Physical exam, radiographs, and blood tests can be highly suggestive. Liver biopsy is required for confirmation.

AVIAN VETERINARY CARE: General Supportive Care as needed. Low-fat diet for long-term control. Medications as indicated.

PREVENTION: Feeding a healthy, low-fat diet and increasing a bird's activity level can help prevent this disease.

Kidney Disease

Kidney disease is a fairly common problem in pet birds. The kidneys filter the blood, remove poisonous waste products, and regulate the electrolyte balance in the body. As a result of these and other functions of the kidneys, they are susceptible to a variety of diseases.

Many of the poisons discussed in the previous chapter and many of the diseases discussed in this chapter can cause kidney disease. More specifically, infections, parasites, poisons, malnutrition, drug sensitivities, cancer, and gout to name a few, can all be associated with kidney problems.

SIGNS TO WATCH FOR: There are no specific signs for any of the types of kidney disease. General Signs of a Sick Bird. More specific signs could include increased thirst and increased uri-nation, dehydration, and occasional lameness.

DIAGNOSIS: In mammals, kidney disease can be diagnosed from routine blood tests and urine analysis. However, in birds, blood and urine tests for kidney disease are not consistently reliable. Therefore, diagnosis is challenging. Radiographs can indicate a change in kidney size and appearance, but still do not provide a clear diagnosis. Uric acid increases may be detected in the blood. Endoscopic visualization and biopsy of the kidneys is the best method of diagnosis.

AVIAN VETERINARY CARE: General Supportive Care, fluid therapy, dietary changes, and antibiotics. If a biopsy is performed and the exact cause for the kidney disease is known, treatment can be more specific and a better prognosis provided.

Pancreatic Disorders

The pancreas plays two important roles within the body. First, it supplies enzymes necessary to digest food. Secondly, it produces the hormones, insulin, and glucagon, necessary to regulate carbohydrate metabolism.

Pancreatic Enzyme Insufficiency

This disease occurs when the pancreas does not produce the necessary amounts of digestive enzymes the body requires. Therefore, food cannot be digested properly.

SIGNS TO WATCH FOR: Weight loss with large, bulky stools and clay-colored feces that resemble puffed rice. For birds fed seed diets, undigested whole seeds may be noted in the droppings.

DIAGNOSIS: History, physical exam, and close examination of droppings are suggestive. Definitive diagnosis requires pancreatic biopsy. Positive response to supplemental digestive enzymes can also be highly suggestive. Food allergies, stomach and intestinal disease including tumors, and fungal infections can also cause poor digestion of foods.

AVIAN VETERINARY CARE: Supplemental pancreatic enzymes will probably be prescribed. The diet should also be changed to one that is more easily digested.

Endocrine Disorders

Diabetes (Diabetes Mellitus, Sugar Diabetes)

Glucose (sugar) is a simple carbohydrate and the body's preferred fuel source. Blood-sugar levels are regulated by two hormones: insulin and glucagon. Insulin carries the glucose into the cells and thereby lowers levels of blood glucose.

Glucagon, on the other hand, stimulates glucose production in the liver and, as a result, raises the blood glucose levels.

In mammals, diabetes is the result of a deficiency of insulin and/or other factors that may prevent insulin from doing its job. In parrots, diabetes appears to be caused by an excess of glucagon that keeps sugar levels abnormally high.

SIGNS TO WATCH FOR: General Signs of a Sick Bird and, more specifically, increased water intake, increased urine, and weight loss despite increased appetite.

DIAGNOSIS: History and physical exam can be suggestive. A very high blood-sugar level, especially one that stays persistently high with repeated blood tests is another indicator.

AVIAN VETERINARY CARE: The only available treatment is daily injections of insulin. However, since diabetes is caused by an excess of glucagon, insulin is not always effective in lowering blood-sugar levels. It does help to control the severe weight loss that accompanies diabetic birds. Hospitalization with repeated blood tests is necessary to determine the proper dosage of insulin. Once that is established, injections can be given at home.

HOME CARE: The pet owner must have a strong commitment to the daily care of a diabetic bird. Dietary changes are usually necessary. Injections must be given every day, and the bird will need to be monitored regularly for glucose levels. Unfortunately, no cure exists for diabetes. However, in many cases it can be controlled with medication and the bird can live a longer and healthier life.

Hypothyroidism (Thyroid Hormone Deficiency)
The thyroid glands are located alongside the lower trachea near the base of the neck. The hormones they produce have important effects on nearly every organ in the body. In hypothyroidism, inadequate levels of thyroid hormone are produced.

SIGNS TO WATCH FOR: Obesity and feather problems, which may include delayed molt and poor feather growth. The delayed molt can cause the old feathers to appear worn out and discolored. There is an obvious lack of new pin feathers. Hypothyroidism can also cause an increased susceptibility to infections, fatty tumors, decreased fertility, inactivity, and a depressed mental attitude.

DIAGNOSIS: History, physical examination, complete blood count, and chemistry panel will often alert the veterinarian to a possible hypothyroid condition. Specific blood tests are

available to measure the level of thyroid hormone.
AVIAN VETERINARY CARE: Thyroid hormone replacement.
The medicine can be added to the drinking water or, prefer-
ably, given directly into the mouth.

Goiter (Enlarged Thyroid Glands)

Enlargement of the thyroid can occur when a bird does not
get enough iodine in its diet. See page 341 for a discussion of
this disease.

Neuromuscular Disorders

Neuromuscular disorders involve the brain, spinal cord,
nerves, and muscles. Signs associated with problems affecting
the nerves and muscles are common in pet birds. Many of the
emergency medical problems discussed in chapter 14 and diseases discussed throughout this chapter can secondarily affect
the nerves and muscles. Infections, trauma, cancer, metabolic
problems, poisons, malnutrition, developmental, and hereditary factors can all affect these particular tissues. Depending
on the cause and its severity, only a single, localized area may
be affected or the entire body could be involved.

Nervous Disorders

SIGNS TO WATCH FOR: seizures, loss of balance, paralysis,
consistent tilting of head, consistent circling of head, abnormal movement of eyes, and the General Signs of a Sick Bird.

Muscular Disorders

SIGNS TO WATCH FOR: Leg: limping, lameness, swollen
joint(s), and deformity of leg. Wing: wing droop, swollen
joint(s), deformity of wing
AVIAN VETERINARY CARE: The Medical Work-Up approach
will be followed. The above list of general problems that can
affect the nerves and muscles makes diagnosis challenging
but very important. All of these problems can present with
similar signs. Diagnostic tests are usually required. Treatment
protocol will be based on suspected or definitive diagnosis.

Hypocalcemia (Low Blood Calcium)

Calcium is known to be required for strong bones. However, it
also plays a critical role in nerve transmissions and muscle
contractions. Low blood calcium can result from unbalanced
diets (i.e., all-seed); deficiency of vitamin D, either from diet or
lack of sunshine; egg laying and certain metabolic diseases.

Although less commonly seen in recent years, young African grey parrots appear to be predisposed to this deficiency. The reason is not known.

SIGNS TO WATCH FOR: Seizures, lack of coordination, loss of balance, tremors, or simply weakness. Bone fractures from weak bones can also develop.

DIAGNOSIS: Calcium blood level and radiographs to evaluate density of bone.

AVIAN VETERINARY CARE: Birds presenting with neurological signs require immediate medical care. For long-term control, improved diet and a balanced vitamin/mineral will likely be recommended.

Vitamin E/Selenium Responsive Syndrome

This is a nutritional muscle disease caused by a deficiency of vitamin E and selenium. Cockatiel Paralysis Syndrome may be associated with this deficiency. However, cockatiels and all other species are susceptible. The lack of vitamin E can result from a dietary deficiency, a digestive tract absorption problem, or oversupplementation with oily substances.

SIGNS TO WATCH FOR: Weakness, often leading to paralysis of jaw, wings, or legs; difficulty with grasping perch, mouth hanging open.

DIAGNOSIS: No specific tests are available, however, it is important to perform blood tests and radiographs to rule out other possible causes.

AVIAN VETERINARY CARE: Injection of vitamin E/selenium can often show immediate improvement; oral supplementation is also available.

HOME CARE: Good sources of vitamin E include green leafy vegetables, corn, soy, seed oils, and eggs. Do not supplement diet with other oils (e.g., vegetable and fish oils) unless recommended by a veterinarian.

Reproductive Disorders
Excessive or Chronic Egg Laying

A female pet bird may begin laying eggs, even in the absence of a male companion. Sometimes this egg laying can become excessive, which can lead to health problems for the female bird, such as egg binding (see page 303), weak bones, and low blood calcium levels. Although any female bird can develop this problem, budgies, cockatiels and lovebirds are most commonly affected.

SIGNS TO WATCH FOR: Recurrent egg laying

DIAGNOSIS: The history is usually sufficient. In addition, radiographs can identify calcium-depleted bones, while blood tests can measure calcium levels.

AVIAN VETERINARY CARE: General Supportive Care if bird presents in a weakened condition. Improved diet and vitamin/mineral supplement is usually needed. If the bird is in good overall health and egg laying is minimal, behavioral and environmental changes as discussed below may be sufficient. However, in many instances, hormone therapy may be necessary to help control persistent egg laying. In extreme cases, surgery may be recommended, a salpingohysterectomy (modified "spay" procedure) can be performed.

PREVENTION: Birds prone to chronic egg laying should be fed a nutritious diet and, usually, a balanced vitamin and mineral supplement. It is recommended that you consult an avian veterinarian before using any nutritional supplements.

Changing the bird's environmental can also help prevent or reduce egg laying. Affected bird should be separated from other birds, especially if there is a cagemate. In addition, remove nest boxes, nesting material, toys, and any other objects bird is attracted to. Amount of light should be reduced to about eight hours a day. Changing cages or moving cage to another room may also be beneficial. Laid eggs are best left in cage, do not remove them.

Egg binding

This is a medical emergency. If a bird seems to be having difficulty passing an egg, consult your avian veterinarian immediately. (See page 303)

Dermatology Disorders

The skin and its accessory structures--the feathers, beak, cere, nails, and uropygial (preening) gland--can develop various medical problems. It is these problems that usually cause owners their greatest concern. This is not because they are the most serious, but rather, because they are the most visible! For this reason, owners generally recognize skin disorders early in the disease process.

The skin and its accessory structures have only a limited number of ways they can respond to an injury or disease. Therefore, in many instances, a diagnosis cannot be made simply by visually examining the affected area. It is difficult, and many times impossible, to differentiate one skin disease from another without a thorough history, physical exam and

This Amazon has primary skin disease. Since the head and neck feathers are also missing, this bird is not just a behavioral induced feather picker.

often diagnostic testing. The diagnosis and treatment of skin and feather disorders should follow the "Medical Work-Up" approach as discussed on page 329.

Regardless of how insignificant a skin problem may first appear, it is recommended that you seek treatment for your bird as soon as possible. First, the sooner any disorder receives proper medical attention, the easier it will be to treat. Second, birds frequently pick at wounds, and this can quickly make them worse. Third, when chewing or picking begins, the bird has learned a very undesirable habit. Once this occurs, it can be difficult to stop.

Beak Disorders

The normal beak is hard, smooth, and symmetrical. Its proper length, width, and shape varies with each species. Beak problems, regardless of the cause, can result in a permanently misshapen beak. A bird's beak grows continuously, so when the upper and lower beak are not in perfect alignment, overgrowth will occur. However, with regular beak trimming, good diet, and an ample supply of branches and other objects to chew on, the growth of the beak should be controlled and not affect the overall health of the bird.

SIGNS TO WATCH FOR:
- Misshapen (e.g., overgrown or twisted)
- Flaking, soft, or roughened surface
- Chipped or cracked
- Change in color

Beak trauma

Injuries such as puncture wounds and fractures are the most common problems. Infections are a possibility, even in the tiniest of beak injuries. Bleeding can also result when the beak is injured.

AVIAN VETERINARY CARE: If only the very end is broken off or cracked, simple filing and rounding off of the tip should be sufficient. Open wounds of the beak should be thoroughly cleaned to help prevent infections. Bleeding, if noted, will be controlled. Actual fractures of the beak may require the use of surgical glues or surgery.

Beak Infections

These most often result from an injury, but they can also be associated with more serious diseases, such as psittacine beak and feather disease (page 379). Fungal infections can occur. *AVIAN VETERINARY CARE:* Open, clean, and flush the affected area with antiseptic solution, apply topical antibiotic and/or antifungal medication; other treatment as needed.

Liver Disease

Beak problems can actually be associated with liver disease. See page 354 for more detailed discussion on diagnosis of liver disease.
SIGNS TO WATCH FOR: Overgrowth or softening of the beak (and nails).
DIAGNOSIS: Blood tests and radiographs are necessary
AVIAN VETERINARY CARE: Regular trimming and shaping of beak will be required.

Beak Tumors

Tumors involving the beak occasionally develop.
SIGNS TO WATCH FOR: Look for any lump or bump, either on the outside of the beak or along the roof of the mouth.
AVIAN VETERINARY CARE: Like any other tumor, a beak tumor should be surgically removed and biopsied. Additional treatment will be provided as needed.

Malnutrition and the Beak

The beak (and nails) can become overgrown, soft, and develop a peeling and/or roughened surface. A balanced, formulated diet will improve the health and appearance of the beak (and nails).

Mites Involving the Beak

See page 364.

Cere Disorders

The cere is the soft, rounded area behind the beak and surrounding the nares.
SIGNS TO WATCH FOR
• Swollen and reddened cere, sometimes caked with debris

- Thickened or horn-like surface
- Color change
- Change in shape or size

Infections Involving Cere

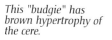

This "budgie" has brown hypertrophy of the cere.

Upper respiratory infections can result in the cere becoming swollen and inflamed. A long-standing respiratory infection can lead to a change in the size or shape of the nares. (See page 355 for information on upper respiratory infections.)

Brown Hypertrophy of the Cere

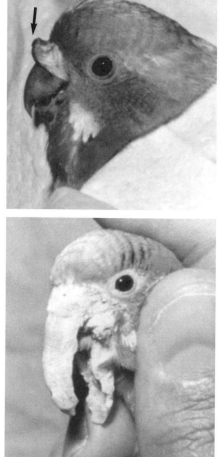

This is generally considered to be a normal occurrence in older female budgies. As the female budgie matures, her hormones influence the appearance of the cere. However, in male budgies a simple change in cere color (from blue to brown) could result from an overproduction of male hormone arising from a testicular tumor.
SIGNS TO WATCH FOR: The cere becomes thickened, almost horn-like and brown in color.
AVIAN VETERINARY CARE: In females, this condition is not serious, and treatment is usually unnecessary. Occasionally, however, the nares can become occluded. If this occurs, the buildup of the dead skin layers can be removed by gently peeling them away. Applying a little water-soluble moisturizing cream will help soften the tissue before removal. Males with a change in cere color should have a medical work-up.

Facial Skin Changes
Knemidokoptes (commonly called Scaly Face and Leg Mite)

Knemidokoptes mites caused this severe beak deformity. Early treatment can prevent such disfiguration.

Knemidokoptes (ne-mi-do-KOP-tez) is most frequently found on budgies. They can be found around the areas of the face, eyes, cere, and beak. They can also be found on the legs and feet.
SIGNS TO WATCH FOR: White, honeycomb-like crusts or growths on beak and unfeathered skin surfaces on face and legs.
DIAGNOSIS: Appearance of lesions are usually sufficient; occasionally microscopic exam of lesions are necessary.

AVIAN VETERINARY CARE: The medication Ivermectin is the safest and most effective remedy. Improvement is usually noticed within days. Many different over-the-counter medications are available, but most are minimally effective.

Facial Skin Infections

Infections involving the facial skin can result from bacteria, fungi, or a virus. Allergic reactions should also be considered.

SIGNS TO WATCH FOR: Single or multiple scabs, crusts or firm swellings, sometimes feather loss.

DIAGNOSIS: Appearance of lesions may be sufficient; additional tests such as microscopic exam of skin lesions, fungal culture, or skin biopsy may be recommended for accurate diagnosis.

AVIAN VETERINARY CARE: Medication as indicated; abscesses (accumulations of pus) require surgery.

Avian Pox Virus

Avian pox is a viral disease that requires an open wound or an insect bite for infection to develop. It's usually associated with keeping birds outdoors and usually spread by mosquito bites.

SIGNS TO WATCH FOR: Two different forms of this disease exist, the most common is the cutaneous (skin) form, in which birds develop small raised swellings that can change color from brown to yellow and become crusty. The lesions appear on the unfeathered skin around the eyes, beak, nares, and even the lower legs and feet can be affected. The wet form develops small, raised swellings in the mouth, causing swallowing and sometimes breathing difficulties.

DIAGNOSIS: Biopsy of the lesions is necessary.

AVIAN VETERINARY CARE: Antibiotics are administered orally and topically around eyes to prevent secondary bacteria infections. Vitamin A supplementation may be prescribed. Scabs should not be removed, but rather can be softened by gently applying daily, warm compresses to affected areas. The disease usually runs its course in individual birds in three to four weeks.

PREVENTION: A vaccine is available for birds at risk. It is usually not recommended for indoor pet birds. Mosquito control is very important.

> *Except for the knemidokoptes mite in budgies, and the air sac mite in canaries and finches, all other mites affecting birds are very uncommon. When skin and feather problems occur, many owners assume it is a mite problem or some other bug, when in fact, this is rarely the case. A well-meaning bird owner may then purchase some kind of mite remedy at the store. This is ill-advised. These medications are almost always unnecessary, could be harmful to the bird, and will delay proper treatment by an avian veterinarian.*

Facial Trauma

SIGNS TO WATCH FOR: Cuts, scrapes, burns, or bruises. Bruises develop a dark red to purple discoloration.

AVIAN VETERINARY CARE: Depending on the severity of trauma, treatment may include General Supportive Care, wound care and cleaning, surgical closure of wounds, and antibiotics to prevent infection.

Insect Bites

Insect bites are most common in birds kept outside. They usually involve the facial area and can be confused with trauma, allergies, or infection.

SIGNS TO WATCH FOR: Localized swelling that develops rapidly. The affected area is usually red and inflamed.

AVIAN VETERINARY CARE: General Supportive Care as needed. More specific treatment depends on severity. Medications to reduce swelling and secondary allergic reaction may be indicated. Swelling due to insect bites usually resolves within 24 hours.

Feather Loss on the Head

Feather loss on the head of birds is most commonly seen in canaries, finches, and lutino cockatiels. Possible causes are heredity, infection, thyroid hormone deficiency, and, in male canaries, a testosterone deficiency.

AVIAN VETERINARY CARE: The underlying cause dictates the best treatment; some conditions are not treatable. Hormone replacement therapy may help. Good nutrition is important.

Leg And Foot Disorders

Pododermititis("bumblefoot")

Bumblefoot is the common name for an infection occurring on the bottom of the feet. It most commonly affects heavy-bodied, inactive parrots and raptors (birds of prey). Some of the factors that can lead to the development of this disease include poor nutrition, vitamin A deficiency, unsanitary conditions, sandpaper-covered perches, and obesity.

SIGNS TO WATCH FOR: Initially, the skin on the bottom of the foot appears thinner than normal, red, and inflamed. As the disease progresses, swelling and scab formation occurs. Sometimes, ulcers or obvious wounds are observed. Eventually, the bird becomes lame and has difficulty walking.

AVIAN VETERINARY CARE: Treatment approaches vary depending on severity. For long-term control, the underlying or predisposing problem(s) needs to be corrected. Antibiotics, topical medications, and bandages are all usually needed. Changing the size and shape of perches and even padding them can also be helpful. In advanced cases, surgery is necessary to open, flush, and clean the infected wounds.

Papillomas

Skin papillomas can found on the feet, legs, wings, and eyelids. Other papillomas can also occur in the digestive tract, primarily in the mouth and cloaca (page 352). A viral cause is suspected, but not yet proven.

SIGNS TO WATCH FOR: Small, raised wart-like growths. They can become inflamed, ulcerated, and, if self-traumatized, can bleed.

DIAGNOSIS: Appearance can be suggestive, but biopsy required for confirmation.

AVIAN VETERINARY CARE: Treatment is either cauterization (application of heat, chemicals, or electric current to destroy tissue), or surgery. Supportive care as needed.

Hyperkeratosis

This is not an actual disease, but rather a descriptive term referring to the excessive buildup or thickening of the outer scaly layer (keratin) of skin. It is seen most commonly in canaries and finches. Causes can include knemidokoptes mite, aging, poor nutrition and a viral infection.

SIGNS TO WATCH FOR: Increased or heavy scaling on legs.

DIAGNOSIS: Microscopic analysis of debris and/or biopsy.

AVIAN VETERINARY CARE: Treatment depends on underlying cause. Ivermectin is the preferred medication for mites. Improvement of diet may help. Sometimes, non-greasy, moisturizing cream can be used regularly to soften and possibly remove thickened crusts.

Gout

Gout is the abnormal accumulation of uric acid in the bloodstream, and it results in deposits of this chemical in the joints and/or on the surfaces of internal organs. The metabolism of dietary protein produces uric acid. The kidneys normally filter the blood and eliminate this chemical from the body in the form of urates in the droppings.

Abnormally high levels of uric acid are most commonly associated with kidney disease. Various nutritional causes, one of which is high dietary protein, have also been suggested as possible causes.

There are two distinct forms of this disease: *articular gout* and *visceral gout*. Articular gout is the depositing of uric acid crystals in the joints, primarily involving the legs, feet, and wings. Visceral gout results in deposits of uric acid on the surfaces on internal organs.

SIGNS TO WATCH FOR:

Articular gout: lameness, difficulty walking and perching, decreased activity, painful and swollen joints

Visceral gout: General Signs of a Sick Bird and sometimes sudden death

DIAGNOSIS:

Articular gout: aspiration of joint swellings and microscopic evaluation

Visceral gout: endoscopic exam with biopsy can confirm diagnosis

For both of these forms, complete blood panel and radiographs are also helpful.

AVIAN VETERINARY CARE: Goal of treatment is to stop or slow the buildup of uric acid and reduce inflammation. Drugs are available to reduce the formation of uric acid. Anti-inflammatories and pain control medication as needed. General Supportive Care as needed

HOME CARE: Perches can be exchanged for ramps and padded to ease joint pain. Lowering the dietary protein level and feeding more fruits and vegetables may also help. Place food and water cups within easy access.

Arthritis

Arthritis is a degenerative change in one or more joints. There are multiple causes, including: infection, trauma, gout, and simply part of the aging process.

SIGNS TO WATCH FOR: Lameness, swelling in a joint, loss of function in a limb and discomfort.

DIAGNOSIS: physical exam, radiographs, and sometimes joint-fluid analysis

AVIAN VETERINARY CARE: If possible, the underlying cause will be treated. For example, a joint infection would require antibiotics and possibly benefit from surgery to open, drain, clean, and instill medication directly into the affected joint(s). Anti-inflammatories and pain medication can also be prescribed to help make the bird more comfortable. Changes in diet, especially if overweight, will be recommended. Padded perches and easier access to food and water bowls can also be beneficial.

Self-Mutilation

Self-inflicted injuries occur in birds. All of a sudden, a bird can begin chewing and picking on itself. The reason this occurs is not always known, but it can be associated with a pre-existing wound, infection, arthritis, allergies, environmental agents, a tight leg band, stress, or various behavioral problems.

This is an example of self-multilation of the lower leg.

SIGNS TO WATCH FOR: Injuries, often involving the legs, feet, wing, and chest areas, and if recent, blood can also be seen on the beak

DIAGNOSIS: History of self-inflicted injuries, diagnostic tests necessary to try and identify underlying cause of self-mutilation.

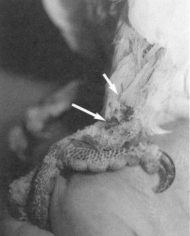

AVIAN VETERINARY CARE: If the underlying problem can be determined, treatment, if possible, will be started. Existing wounds will be treated as necessary. However, it can be both frustrating and a challenge finding a specific treatment to stop the self-mutilation since no one approach is consistently effective. Also, once injuries healed, this problem can recur at any time. Since behavioral problems may be associated with self-mutilation, long-term prevention is approached similar to that for feather picking (refer to page 374).

Mites on the Legs and Feet

See page 364 for a complete discussion.

Lumps and Bumps on the Skin

These medical problems can be found anywhere on the body.

Abscess

An abscess is a localized collection of pus, surrounded by a wall of tissue.

SIGNS TO WATCH FOR: Mammals produce a liquid pus; on the other hand, birds produce a nonliquid, cheese-like material with no odor. The most common areas affected are above the eye (look for a pea-sized swelling), along the roof of the mouth (see page 336), below the tongue, in the preening gland, or on the bottom of the foot (bumblefoot, see page 366).

This African grey has a swelling above its eye that was caused by an abscess.

AVIAN VETERINARY CARE: Abscesses cannot drain on their own. Surgery is required to open, clean, and remove the accumulated debris. Antibiotics are also necessary.

Feather Cyst

A feather cyst is a soft swelling beneath the skin caused by an ingrown feather.

SIGNS TO WATCH FOR: A thick, lumpy swelling beneath the skin and involving a feather follicle.

AVIAN VETERINARY CARE: Surgery is needed to open the cyst and remove the ingrown feather. The follicle is thoroughly cleaned and any bleeding should be easily controlled.

This canary has a feather cyst. Minor surgery is required to remove cysts successfully.

Hematoma

A hematoma is an accumulation of blood, usually clotted, in an organ or tissue and is due to a torn blood vessel. An injury is usually the cause. In birds, common sites are on the chest and top of the head.

AVIAN VETERINARY CARE: Usually not needed; they generally resolve on their own over a short period of time.

Hernia

A hernia is a protrusion of an organ or tissue through a tear or an abnormal opening in the body wall. There are two types. *Acquired hernias* result from a tear in a muscle wall, usually from an injury or straining to pass an egg. Their most common site is the abdominal wall, just above the vent. *Congenital hernias* are present at birth.

SIGNS TO WATCH FOR: The swelling should be soft to the touch. Sometimes, even the hole in the tissue surrounding the hernia can be felt. The protruding tissue may be able to be temporarily reduced, or pushed back through the opening from which it came.

AVIAN VETERINARY CARE: Surgery is needed to close the defect. Hernias can become larger over time, and early repair is recommended. If an organ should become trapped in the opening, its blood supply could be pinched off, creating an emergency situation.

Tumor

A tumor is an abnormal growth of tissue. It can develop anywhere on or in the body. A *malignant tumor* (cancerous) is the abnormal and uncontrolled growth of cells that invade and destroy the surrounding tissue. They also can metastasize or spread to other organs. Once removed, *benign tumors* (noncancerous) do not recur, and the bird will have a favorable recovery, but if left untreated a benign tumor can continue to grow and cause problems. One of the more common types of benign tumors is a lipoma (fatty tumor). It is found beneath the skin, usually on the chest or abdominal wall. It is found more often in overweight birds. *DIAGNOSIS:* Biopsy is required to determine the type of tumor and whether or not it is cancerous. *AVIAN VETERINARY CARE:* Surgical removal is always recommended. Tumors should be removed when they are first noticed because over time cancerous tumors are more likely to spread to other tissues. Also, as the tumor grows, it becomes increasingly more invasive and difficult to remove.

Pet birds can be prone to cancers and other tumors. This budgie is suffering from a tumor on its leg.

Subcutaneous Emphysema

Subcutaneous emphysema is an abnormal accumulation of air beneath the skin. It is associated with a tear in an air sac, a puncture wound through the skin, or a broken bone. Whatever the cause, air escapes into an area beneath the skin.

SIGNS TO WATCH FOR: An easily compressible, balloon-like swelling.
AVIAN VETERINARY CARE: Treatment for a torn air sac may involve making an incision, with or without placing a drain, over the swelling and keeping it open for days to weeks. Puncture wounds should be treated as needed, possibly surgically opened and cleaned, with antibiotics dispensed. A broken bone should be repaired (see page 307).

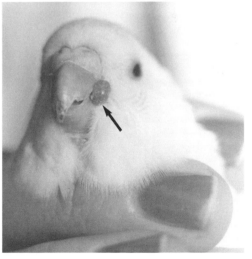

This budgie has a small tumor on the skin at the corner of its beak. Tumors can occur anywhere on or in a bird's body.

Feather Disorders

Feather problems are common in pet birds. Self-mutilation, trauma, and disease can affect the appearance of the feathers. Broken, twisted, crushed, splintered, deformed, abnormally colored, missing, or dirty feathers can result from these problems. In most instances, the feather changes are too general to actually identify the underlying

cause. It is also possible for a combination of factors to cause the feather abnormalities. For example, a disease that damages feathers could be present, along with a behavioral problem resulting in feather picking.

A torn air sac caused subcutaneous emphysema in this canary. Notice the balloon-like swellings over the back and keel areas.

Therefore, as with all medical problems, establishing the correct diagnosis is important. To accomplish this, the "Medical Work-up" approach (page 329) is recommended as the best path to follow.

Stress Bars

Stress bars can be found on one or more of the primary feathers of the wings and tail. Look for a translucent line across the width of a feather. This linear, bare area can result from poor nutrition, disease or, any other stress situation occurring during the growth phase of the affected feather(s). Assuming the underlying stress has been corrected, the damaged feather does not cause problems. No treatment is necessary.

Notice the stress bars on these macaw tail feathers.

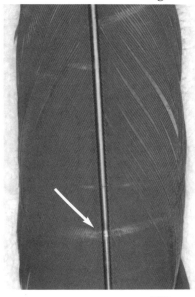

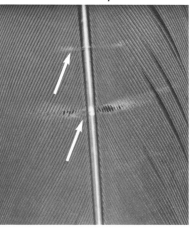

Broken Pin feather

A broken or damaged immature feather will bleed, sometimes excessively. Refer to page 289 for a more detailed discussion and appropriate treatment.

372

Discolored Feathers

Feather color abnormalities could result from poor nutrition, liver disease (page 354), or psittacine beak and feather disease (page 379).

No Feather Regrowth

Baldness or bald spots where no feathers grow can have many different causes. These can include feather follicle infection or damage, various diseases, heredity, poor nutrition, an allergic reaction, mites, and hypothyroidism.

Some birds will even have a lack of feather growth which is normal. For instance, lutino cockatiels develop a bald patch on the rear portion of their head and a brood patch (seasonal area of baldness over keel and upper leg areas). When areas of no feather growth develop, an examination with an avian veterinarian is recommended to rule out disease.

Lack of Preening

Preening or self-grooming is essential for maintaining clean and healthy feathers. If this behavior changes or stops altogether, the feathers will become unkempt and ragged. Almost any medical or behavioral problem could disrupt this normal self-grooming process. These could include injuries to the head, beak, or neck; poor vision; long-term use of restraint collars; stress and generalized weakness from any disease. When lack of preening occurs, an examination with an avian veterinarian is recommended.

Molting Problems

Molting is the shedding or loss of old feathers. An abnormal molt should be suspected when the old feathers are not replaced within the normal time frame or the new emerging feathers appear damaged in any way.

A delay in the onset of a molt or a prolonged molt can cause existing feathers to become excessively worn, dirty, and frayed. Slow regrowth of the feathers during a molt will result in a longer than normal pin feather stage. Causes are varied and could include hypothyroidism or any other disease, poor nutrition, and stress. Since molting problems could indicate an underlying disease, an examination with an avian veterinarian is recommended.

Self-Mutilation Of Feathers

Feather picking, chewing and plucking is a condition characterized by a bird damaging its own feathers. Preening (see page 131) is a normal, healthy behavior. However, when this self-grooming process becomes exaggerated and obsessive, feather damage usually results. The feathers may be chewed on or pulled out. Sometimes the skin even becomes involved. In these instances, birds may actually chew holes in their skin and into their muscle.

Feather picking is not a diagnosis, but rather a sign associated with a medical or behavioral problem. A visual examination, even by an experienced avian veterinarian, is usually not enough to determine the reason for the self-mutilation. Feather picking has many varied causes and treatments, which makes it one of the more difficult and challenging problems to treat. It can be a frustrating problem to deal with for both for owner and veterinarian.

SIGNS TO WATCH FOR: Actual picking of feathers; the feathers will appear broken, twisted, crushed, or deformed. Some birds will pick only when bored (e.g., when left alone or during the night). Birds may not pick when their owners are present. The degree of picking and its location on the body varies with each bird, but the chest, abdomen, inside of wings, and upper legs are common sites. *The head and upper neck feathers, however, will appear perfectly normal since the bird cannot reach these feathers with its beak.*

OTHER SIGNS TO WATCH FOR: Self-picking, chewing, or plucking of feathers and sometimes skin. Sometimes actual picking is not observed by owner, multiple feathers on cage floor could be suggestive.

Many different causes exist for self-mutilation of feathers. Generally these causes are lumped into two general categories--medical and behavioral.

MEDICAL CAUSES for self-mutilation of feathers:
- Skin and/or feather infections: Bacterial, fungal, viral
- Skin and/or feather parasites: mites, lice (both rare)
- Skin tumors or cysts
- Internal disease, such as liver, digestive, or kidney disease, chlamydiosis, psittacine beak and feather disease, hormonal imbalances, tumors, abscesses, intestinal parasites.
- Malnutrition (poor diet)
- Metal toxicity: lead or zinc ingestion (see page 319)

- Allergies (hypersensitivity): cigarette smoke, toxins, and other irritants
- Improper wing trim

BEHAVIORAL CAUSES of self-mutilation of feathers:

Behavioral causes of feather picking should only be considered after medical problems have been ruled out. These have been classified as follows:

- Separation anxiety--when owner is not present, boredom
- Attention seeking--when owner present but not paying attention
- Obsessive/compulsive disorder--bird interrupts other behavior to pick
- Stress associated--exhibits signs of excess fear or stress, generalized illness, major change in household
- Poor early socialization--problem starts at an extremely young age
* Reproductive related--overly bonded sexually mature bird; sexual behaviors occur out of context

DIAGNOSIS: As with all medical problems, identifying the actual cause is critical to selecting the most appropriate treatment. Birds cannot tell us they are picking because they have separation anxiety. Most clients with a self-mutilating bird assume the problem is behavioral. It's true many of these birds do have an underlying behavioral cause, but a lot of them do not. They have a medical problem instead. The approach to treatment for each cause and each bird is very different! It is not fair to the bird to be treating it for a behavioral problem, when all along some hidden disease has been causing the picking.

As listed above, there are many causes for birds damaging their own feathers. With a thorough history and physical exam, an avian veterinarian can usually narrow down the list of possible causes. But, they cannot positively diagnose the cause. Therefore, closely following the "Medical Work-up" approach, including diagnostic testing, is the only way to reach a correct diagnosis, select the best treatment, resolve or control the problem in the shortest time, and offer a realistic prognosis.

Medical causes should be ruled out first. If the results of the work-up are normal, then and only then should a behavioral problem be diagnosed. Since most clients have financial limitations, an avian veterinarian will usually begin by recommending only a few of the tests listed below:

- General health screen (blood test, radiographs): for detecting internal disease

- Disease specific tests: e.g., chlamydiosis, psittacine beak and feather disease, heavy metal (lead and zinc), giardia
- Feather and skin biopsy: microscopic exam of skin and feathers performed by an avian pathology specialist.
- Fecal analysis for intestinal parasites

AVIAN VETERINARY CARE: There are many different approaches to the treatment of feather pickers. No single treatment works consistently--even when the diagnosis is known! As mentioned, the highest cure rate will always be achieved when the underlying cause can be identified.

If a medical problem is diagnosed, it is usually treated first. Refer to Chapter 14 "Medical Emergencies" and this current chapter for a discussion of the various medical problems that can cause a bird to pick and chew at itself.

If, after a thorough workup, a medical problem has not been identified, it is appropriate to treat the bird for a behavior problem. A detailed behavioral history may be requested. Trying to place the problem into one of the categories mentioned may assist in better selecting a treatment plan.

Behavioral modification, removing the inciting cause, and redirecting the bird's attention to other things may be the first treatment attempted. The bird's social environment should also be improved (see next section). Allow several weeks to determine if these changes will help.

If the picking is severe, or if the recommendations for improving social environment are not working, medication should be considered. Psychotropic drugs (drugs that can alter behavior), hormones, sedatives, anti-inflammatories, fatty acid supplements, and topical medications all have their particular indications and benefits. Restraint collars to physically prevent a bird from reaching its own feathers is another option. Acupuncture is still another possibility.

When it comes to feather picking, there is no cookbook approach and no quick fix!

An important part of behavior modification is redirecting the bird's attention to other things. With this in mind, improving the physical and social environment of the bird is very important. Creating a more stimulating, bird-friendly home environment needs to play a part in making your bird a happier pet. Some suggestions follow.

Changes in Food: In the wild, birds spend their daytime hours with companions, searching for food and preening each other. There are many interesting things to do in the jungle, including tearing up a seemingly endless supply of leaves, wood and bark.

Medical Problems

On the other hand, life in a cage is not very exciting.

Therefore, it is important to provide a lot of different activities. Food can play an important role. Since the act of shredding is an enjoyable activity for many birds, food can be used for this purpose.

The importance of a well-balanced diet has already been discussed (chapter 4, "Nutrition"). Inadequate nutrition has been shown to be one of the causes of feather picking. In addition, feather picking puts added nutritional stress on a bird.

The simple act of eating food can be made into a game. To help stimulate our feathered friend's environment, try offering easily shreddable foods for the bird to play with. Try any or all of the following:

- Carrot sticks
- Green beans
- Corn on the cob (cut into disks)
- Spinach leaves
- Peas in the pod
- Apples
- Breadsticks
- Zucchini sticks
- Miniature bagels
- Miniature rice cakes

Although some birds may show fear or limited interest in the new foods, continue to offer them.

Changes in Caging: Since each situation is different, the owner must evaluate the effect caging might be having on their feather picker. Consider the following suggestions as only some of the possibilities, and try to think of others.

- If the cage is too small, try a larger one.
- Cover the cage or uncover the cage more.
- Move the cage to another area of the house.
- Provide a privacy box in the cage for a place to hide.
- Provide more toys--but don't overcrowd the cage.

Inexpensive, safe, and easily shreddable toys can help redirect the bird's attention. Try these suggestions, but be creative and try to think of others.

- Rope
- Straw
- Cardboard

- Toothbrushes (new)
- Toys catering specifically to feather pickers
- Safe wood
- Pine cones
- Wooden craft sticks
- Complexion brushes (new)
- Paper towels (twisted and knotted)

All these items should be clean and made of a nontoxic material. If in doubt as to the safety of any of these items, don't use them.

Changes in the Home: Birds become dependent upon their particular flock members, animal or human. Birds also become accustomed to a set routine and often do not tolerate change well. In regard to humans, adding new faces or any changes in the amount of time you spend with the bird can be stressful and disruptive to their routine. Even another animal appearing or disappearing from the scene is a disruption in routine. If any of these changes sound familiar and coincide with the onset of feather damage, consider them a possible predisposing cause. Then work to correct the situation.

These suggestions may help to fill the void or help to reestablish their routine:

- Provide lots of direct attention
- Leave the radio on when no one is at home
- Increase periods of sleep

Regardless of the reason, the longer the picking is allowed to continue, the more difficult it will be to control. In some instances, even when the original cause is long gone, the picking still continues. It can simply become a bad habit. Birds that are chronic feather pickers may damage the feather follicle and cause the new feather to grow in abnormally or not at all.

Success, if achieved, usually progresses slowly over time. Any treatment attempted should be followed for about eight weeks to provide a good evaluation of its effectiveness. Good record keeping, including the owner's and veterinarian's written observations of picking frequency and feather changes, is necessary. Photographs can be taken to better document feather appearance. Several different treatment protocols may need to be tried either together or separately before an effective treatment is found. In a few instances, birds may never stop picking.

Psittacine Beak and Feather Disease (PBFD)

PBFD affects only psittacines, and young birds are most susceptible. PBFD is caused by a virus. Although it is most common in birds under three years of age, even birds over 10 years of age or older can develop this disease. The PBFD virus suppresses a bird's immune system in a manner similar to the HIV virus, which causes AIDS in humans. Thus, birds with PBFD become very susceptible to secondary bacterial and fungal infections.

TRANSMISSION: This is a highly contagious disease, especially to young birds. It is most likely spread by preening activities, or by ingestion or inhalation of contaminated feather dust or feces. A normal, healthy appearing adult bird can transmit this disease to its offspring through egg transmission or by feeding behaviors. This virus is able to live for long periods of time outside the body and is resistant to many common disinfectants. Therefore, environmental contamination is still another possibility.

SIGNS TO WATCH FOR: The acute form (rapid onset) is generally recognized in very young birds. It is characterized by depression, diarrhea, crop problems, weight loss, and often death. The chronic form (gradual onset) show the classic feather lesions. These include retained feather sheaths, blood within the feather shaft, short clubbed or pinched feather tips, and deformed, curled feathers. The powder down feathers are usually affected first. There is an obvious loss of the normal powder these feathers produce. As the disease progresses, the contour feathers on the wings and tail become involved. On close examination, these feathers appear nearly translucent.

Beak lesions may also occur, but this does not usually occur until later in the course of disease and after the feathers

This cockatoo has an advanced case of psittacine beak and feather disease syndrome (PBFDS).

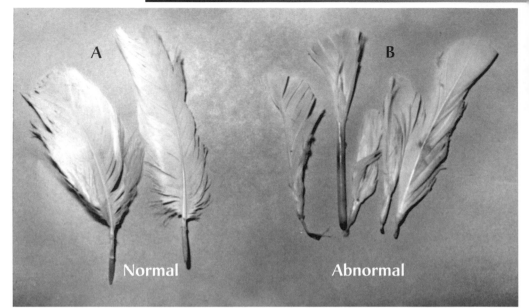

Normal   Abnormal

Notice the difference between (A) normal feathers and (B) the abnormal feathers associated with PBFD. Notice the bases of these feathers are either "pinched" or "clubbed" and deformed.

Birds with psittacine beak and feather disease syndrome often have malformed feathers, or else their feathers do not develop normally. Note the lack of feather development on these young African grey parrots.

are involved. The beak changes include overgrowth, fractures, and decay. Ulcers are sometimes present in the mouth.
DIAGNOSIS: A bird displaying many of the classic signs as described above would be highly suspect. For a definitive diagnosis, a PBFD test is necessary. A feather biopsy can also confirm the diagnosis.

AVIAN VETERINARY CARE: Unfortunately, no effective thera-py exists. This disease is generally considered fatal and most birds with classic signs do not survive longer than six to twelve months. When birds are severely affected, euthanasia must be considered.

PREVENTION: The incidence of PBFD has greatly decreased since the blood test for PBFD has become available. This test has enabled breeders to establish PBFD-free colonies of birds, thus decreasing the spread of this fatal disease. Any new bird being introduced into a home with other birds should be test-ed and found negative for PBFD. After an outbreak, the envi-ronment (i.e., walls, floors, airducts, cages) can be tested to be sure that cleaning and disinfecting has been effective in elimi-nating the virus.

Polyoma Virus

Avian polyoma virus infection affects primarily very young birds (nestlings) and also is the cause of another disease called *Budgerigar Fledgling Disease*. For this reason, aviaries raising young birds are at a much higher risk of a polyoma outbreak than homes with individually kept pet birds. It is only occasionally diagnosed in adult birds.

TRANSMISSION: Adult birds are usually carriers. These birds, having recovered from the disease, generally appear very healthy but pass the virus to young, susceptible birds. It is thought that the disease is spread through the droppings and possibly in the air and even from parent to offspring through the egg.

SIGNS TO WATCH FOR: The classic presentation is the sud-den death of a previously healthy young bird around weaning age. Signs could include weakness, appetite loss, abdominal enlargement, bleeding underneath the skin, tremors, paralysis, diarrhea, regurgitation, and sometimes feather abnormalities.

DIAGNOSIS: History and physical exam can be highly sug-gestive. A polyoma-specific test is available, however, results are not always conclusive. Analysis of affected tissue (biopsy) is recommended for confirmation.

AVIAN VETERINARY CARE: Unfortunately, no specific treat-ment is available. In some instances, General Supportive Care can be beneficial.

PREVENTION: Avian-breeding facilities should follow the guidelines for effective polyoma control measures. These guidelines are too detailed for this discussion. Readers are referred to the bibliography at the end of this book and their avian veterinarian for more information. For individual birds or small adult bird collections, risks are small. A polyoma vaccine is available and its use should be discussed with an avian veterinarian.

Zoonotic Diseases
(Diseases Transmittable From Animals To Humans)

All animals, including our favorite pets, can potentially transmit diseases to humans. For our feathered friends, specifically, the incidence of transmitting disease to us is quite low. Individuals at the greatest risk include elderly persons, immunocompromised individuals (i.e., cancer or AIDS patients), and bird breeders. To help put this discussion in its proper perspective, remember, just because a disease can be passed from birds to humans does not mean it will actually occur. In reality, pet birds pose a very low risk.

Birds can transmit a potentially large number of diseases to humans. This section will briefly discuss a few of the more significant ones. For a more complete list of avian zoonotic diseases, the reader is referred to sources listed in the Bibliography at the end of this book.

Chlamydiosis

This is the most important avian zoonotic disease. Birds can be infected with chlamydiosis even though they appear quite healthy. For this reason, it is recommended all pet birds, especially those newly acquired, be tested periodically for this disease. Fortunately, despite the high frequency of this infection in pet birds, it is transmitted to humans infrequently. Flu-like symptoms in humans are most common and include fever, headache, cough, chills, weakness, and occasionally pneumonia.

See page 340 for a discussion of chlamydiosis in pet birds.

Salmonellosis

Salmonella infection is probably the most widespread zoonotic disease in the world. Many different animals can transmit this disease to people. Human infection usually results from the ingestion of contaminated food and water. In humans, signs include those of gastrointestinal upset, such as cramping, diarrhea, and vomiting, which is frequently accompanied by fever and headache. The disease usually runs its course in a few days, but can cause more serious health problems in young children, the elderly, and those with suppressed immune systems. Scrupulous hand washing following the handling of animals and birds is a good way to prevent salmonella infection.

See page 350 for a discussion of salmonellosis in pet birds.

Allergic Alveolitis

Allergic Alveolitis, also called "hypersensitivity pneumonitis" or "pigeon lung disease", is an allergic response to a bird's feathers, feather dust, and droppings. Human signs include listlessness, chills, fever, shortness of breath, muscle pain, and coughing. This disease can occur in different forms. The acute form occurs only hours after a heavy exposure of feather dander or fecal dust, such as when a person cleans out a long-neglected pigeon coop. The subacute form can develop from long-term exposure to a moderate level of feathers and fecal dust. Signs of this form include a dry cough and progressive difficulty in breathing. The chronic form, which is irreversible, can develop after years of exposure to feather dust and bird droppings. Signs of the chronic form include weight loss, progressive shortness of breath, and a dry cough.

Avian Tuberculosis

Avian TB is usually caused by the organism *Mycobacterium avium*. Human TB is usually associated with a different type of tuberculosis-causing organism. *M. avium* has been isolated in only a few cases of human TB. In these specific cases, the organism was found to be a different subspecies than the type infecting birds. This means that pet birds are an unlikely source of *M. avium* infections in humans. In fact, confirmed transmission of avian tuberculosis from a bird to a human has never been documented.

However, regardless of the very low risk, tuberculosis is an extremely difficult disease to treat. Therefore, we should always err on the side of caution. Persons with impaired immune systems should not be exposed to birds known to have tuberculosis. Healthy individuals whose birds have been diagnosed with tuberculosis need to understand the risks associated with this disease when deciding whether to treat or euthanize their infected birds. This is a difficult decision and should be discussed thoroughly with an avian veterinarian as well as a personal physician.

See page 353 for a discussion tuberculosis in pet birds.

Giardiasis

Giardia is a widely distributed intestinal parasite. In humans, signs include diarrhea, stomach upset, and weight loss. Humans usually contract this parasite from crowded unsanitary conditions and, notoriously, from drinking contaminated water. Giardia in humans is usually caused by a different species of giardia and transmission from birds to humans has never been documented. Regardless, there is still the possibility and pet bird owners simply need to be aware of the risk. Diagnosis and treatment in humans is difficult.

See page 351 for a discussion of giardiasis in birds.

Author's Note: I would like to recognize the work of the following avian veterinarians and behaviorists, whose work has contributed greatly to the field of avian veterinary medicine, as well as to this chapter:

Dr. Branson Ritchie and his research team at the University of Georgia, who discovered the cause of Proventricular Dilatation Disease and whose research into Psittacine Beak and Feather Disease forms the basis of my discussion;

Christine Davis, avian behavior consultant, who offered many of the valuable suggestions on how to deal with a feather picker;

Dr. Kenneth Welle, avian veterinarian and behaviorist, for his research on feather picking.

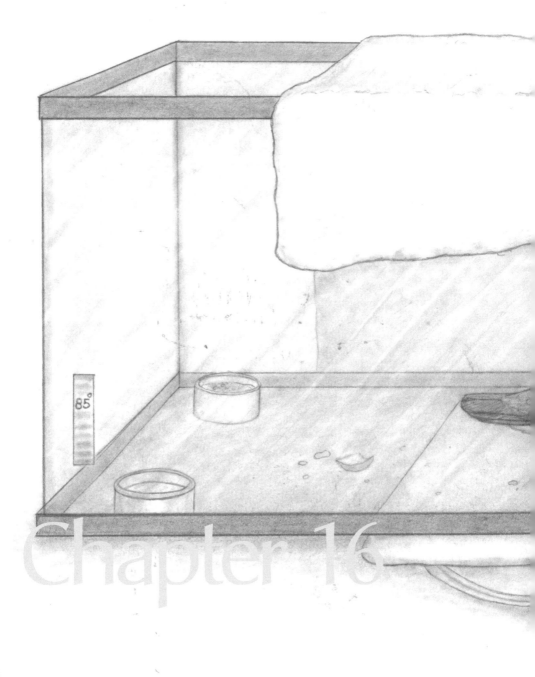

Chapter 16

Home Care for the Sick Bird

Bed rest 'n' plenty of fluids...

Home care for a sick bird involves some basic first-aid measures and good nursing care. First aid are the simple procedures owners can apply in an emergency, before they are able to obtain veterinary care. The first-aid recommendations that follow are general in nature and can be used regardless of the problem. The sooner you put these suggestions into use, the better the chances for recovery. *Remember, however, these home care procedures are not meant as a substitute for veterinary care.* In fact, the home hospital should actually be run as a partnership, with bird

387

owner and veterinarian working together.

These same home-care suggestions can also be followed when bringing a sick bird home from the hospital. However, when your veterinarian's advice is contrary to what is given in this book, always follow his or her instructions. Your veterinarian is better able to take into account the special needs of your bird.

Things To Do Before An Emergency Arises

1. Be prepared! Have all necessary supplies ready to go (see the information on a first-aid kit later in this chapter) and know how to use them. Being able to start treatment right away could mean the difference between life and death.
2. Learn how to safely and properly restrain your bird (see chapter 5, "Bird Restraint"). Administering medications or treating injuries such as bleeding require proper restraint. Practice basic restraint periodically with your bird.
3. Keep this book handy for quick reference.
4. As discussed in the "Poisoning" section on page 318, keep the phone numbers of the ASPCA Animal Poison Control Center handy and readily available for quick reference.

Basic Requirements For Sick Birds
Warmth

The importance of extra heat cannot be overemphasized. It allows the body to concentrate more of its energy on repair and recovery and less on maintaining normal body temperature. *Sick birds should be maintained in an environment of 80 to 85 degrees Fahrenheit.*

Here are a few suggested methods for providing the increased warmth:

• For small cages, place a heating pad beneath the cage or alongside it. Use a low setting. Do not allow the bird to chew on the heating pad. To prevent heat loss, cover the cage on top and on three sides with a towel.

• For large cages, an electric blanket on low setting could be suspended or tented over the cage. Be very careful--large birds are very inquisitive and could chew on the blanket.

• A small aquarium with a screen or towel-covered roof can be placed on top of a heating pad. This makes an excellent home hospital cage. If the floor gets too hot, check the setting on the heating pad. If necessary, line the aquarium with newspaper.

• A red/amber infrared 250-watt heat lamp may be the best additional heat source. Use a special fixture with a porcelain socket and clamp set-up, which you can find at most hard-ware stores. Place it two to four feet away from the cage.

A thermometer to measure temperature is strongly rec-ommended. For the most accurate reading, try to place the thermometer near the level of the cage where your bird is perching. Do not let the bird chew on the thermometer. For cages, hang the thermometer outside the cage. For aquariums,

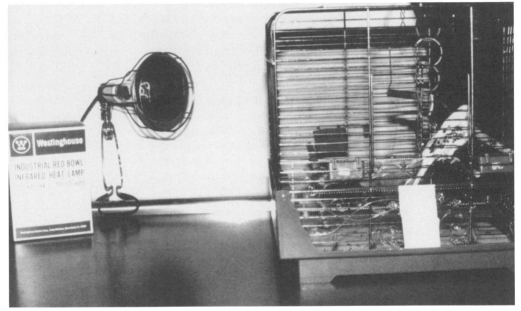

An infrared 250-watt heat lamp can provide heat for a bird recu-perating at home.

a thin wall-mounted aquarium thermometer works well. A standard light bulb is not recommended. The bright light can be stressful and can disrupt the bird's normal sleeping patterns.

Regardless of the heat source, try to focus the heat more toward one side of the cage than the other. In this way, the bird can move around and find its most comfortable tempera-ture. To be sure the bird is being kept at the proper tempera-ture, watch its appearance and behavior. If a bird becomes too warm, it will hold its wings away from the body and pant. If too cold, the bird will sit in a huddled position with feathers fluffed.

Food and Water

Food: Every effort must be made to make sure a sick bird continues to eat. Unfortunately, sick birds usually lose their appetites despite their increased nutritional needs. If birds do not eat enough, they weaken and become less able to fight off disease. Birds have a fast metabolic rate and will lose weight rapidly when they stop eating or eat less than their normal daily requirements.

Rule #1: *Make sure the food is easily accessible.* Whether the bird is perching or sitting on the cage floor, make certain the food is conveniently located. For example, if the bird is on the cage floor, place the food and water cups on the floor nearby or even sprinkle the food on the floor. This is no time to worry about proper hygiene. The less energy expended on searching or reaching for food, the better.

Rule #2: *Don't worry about a balanced diet.* Whatever a sick bird wants, feed it! Calories are more important than a balanced diet. However, a nutritious and fresh assortment of food is always preferable.

Rule #3: *Spend time trying to stimulate the appetite.*
*   Offer favorite foods.
*   Try warming home-cooked foods.
*   Soak seeds to soften and make them easier to eat, even hull them if necessary.
*   Sweeten foods slightly, with fruit juice or tiny amounts of honey or Karo syrup.
*   Hand feed.

Hand-feeding is a good approach for a tame bird or a baby bird that isn't eating from a food dish. It is not practical, however, for giving large amounts of food. In addition to a spoon, a plastic medicine dropper, syringe, or even a small piece of cardboard can be used to place the food right next to the beak or directly in the mouth. Give only small amounts at a time, and make sure it's being swallowed.

Author's Note: Tube-feeding is an excellent way to force-feed a bird. However, in inexperienced hands a bird could be severely injured. If you are going to tube-feed at home, you must do so under the supervision of a veterinarian. Follow the doctor's guidelines very carefully.

Rule #4: *Monitor weight daily.* Sick birds should be weighed each day. A scale showing weight in grams is essential because it is much more accurate and can detect very slight losses or gains. Weight losses of more than 10 percent may require force-feeding.

Home Care for the Sick Bird

Remove any grit if you have been using it. Sick birds are more apt to over-eat grit and could develop serious intestinal problems. As discussed earlier, grit is not essential for a pet bird.

Water: Sick birds frequently do not drink enough water or other fluids. In addition, their droppings usually contain increased amounts of urine. As a result, dehydration occurs and causes even more serious problems. Attempts need to be made to provide additional fluids on a regular basis. Fluids can be supplied in a number of different ways.

IF THE BIRD IS STILL DRINKING WATER: Try adding fruit juice, Gatorade®, or Pedialyte®. Use these full strength or diluted with water. Pedialyte® is an infant fluid and electrolyte replacement solution, and is available at most drug stores. Also, Karo® syrup or honey can be added to drinking water at a dilution of one tea-spoon per cup of water. These are all good, quick energy sources.

IF THE BIRD IS STILL EATING: Add more fruits to the diet. They will provide a good source of quick energy. In addition, moistened cereals or other foods, including warm soups, can be tried.

IF THE BIRD IS NOT DRINKING SUFFICIENT AMOUNTS: Use a plastic eyedropper, turkey baster, syringe, or straw with finger kept over one end to offer fluids directly into the mouth. Be careful not to give too much fluid at one time. The same fluids already discussed in this section can be used.

This cockatoo is being weighed on a gram scale. (Bonnie Jay)

Amount Of Fluids To Give

finches/canaries	4 to 5 drops
budgies	6 to 10 drops
cockatiels	1/4 teaspoon
Amazon parrots	1 to 3 teaspoons
large cockatoos/macaws	1 1/2 to 3 tablespoons

These amounts are only approximations. If the fluids are diffi-cult to give, divide the amount and give some every 15 to 20 minutes. The total amount should be given several times throughout the day as needed.

Rest and Relaxation

Less stress means more energy conservation.

- Place the sick bird in a dimly lit and quiet room.
- Each day, provide 12 hours of darkness for sleeping and 12 hours of light to encourage eating.
- Avoid unnecessary handling.
- Keep other pets and children away.

Medication as Directed (if Needed)

If the sick bird has been examined by a veterinarian, medication will probably be prescribed. Follow the veterinarian's directions closely. This includes giving the proper dosage the correct number of times each day and for the total number of days prescribed. While you are still at the veterinary hospital, be sure *all* instructions are clearly explained and that you understand them. If you have any concerns, ask *questions!*

Medications prescribed could be in the form of oral liquids, injectables, topical sprays, powders, drops, ointments, and food or water additives. With a little practice, all of these medications are easy to give. Proper restraint (see chapter 5, "Bird Restraint") is usually the most difficult part. The veterinarian or a staff member should offer to demonstrate the correct method of restraint and medication administration before your bird leaves the hospital.

Owner with an "Observant Eye"

While a bird is sick, its owner needs to look, listen, and pay special attention to the patient. In other words, is the "little guy" getting better or worse?

DROPPINGS: Continue to observe their number, volume, color, and consistency. They provide an excellent indicator of how things are going inside the body.

BREATHING: Look and listen to the pattern and rhythm of respiration. Is it smooth or forced? Is it getting better or worse?

FOOD AND WATER CONSUMPTION: Has it changed? Is more or less being consumed?

BODY WEIGHT: Is it increasing, staying the same, or decreasing?

BODY TEMPERATURE: Does the bird appear too hot, too cold, or just right?

GENERAL APPEARANCE: More alert and responsive? Standing up straight or hunched over? Feathers being groomed?

First Aid:
Urgent Care Don'ts
Birds are more sensitive to medications than other animals and humans, so:

* Don't give a bird human medications or medications prescribed for another animal unless so directed by your veterinarian.
* Don't give your bird medications that are suggested by a friend, a store employee, or your personal physician.
* Don't give a bird alcohol or laxatives.
* Don't apply any oils or ointments to your bird unless your veterinarian tells you to do so.
* Don't bathe a sick bird.

The Well-Stocked First-Aid Kit

* Emergency care instructions (keep a copy of this book handy, or make copies of the chapters on restraint, emergencies, diseases, and home care for the sick bird)

A well-stocked bird first aid kit should include a variety of items (see text).

* Address, phone number, and office hours of your avian veterinarian's office, along with address, phone number, and office hours of your closest animal emergency hospital
* Appropriate-sized towels for catching and holding your bird
* A heating pad, heat lamp, or other heat source
* A pad of paper and pencil to make notes about bird's condition
* Styptic powder, silver nitrate stick, or cornstarch to stop bleeding (use styptic powder and silver nitrate stick on beak and nails only)
* Blunt-tipped scissors
* Nail clippers and nail file
* Needle-nosed pliers (to pull broken blood feathers)

- Blunt-end tweezers
- Eye irrigation solution, such as a saline solution or wetting solution for contact lenses
- Basic bandage materials such as gauze squares, masking tape (it doesn't stick to a bird's feathers like adhesive tape), and gauze rolls
- Pedialyte® or other energy supplement, such as orange juice or Gatorade®
- Eye dropper
- Syringes to irrigate wounds or feed sick birds
- Penlight
- Cotton swabs to apply medication and clean wounds
- Betadine scrub, which is an anti-infective soap

Keep all these supplies in one place, such as in a fishing tackle box or toolbox. This will eliminate your having to search for supplies in emergency situations, and the case can be taken along to bird shows, on trips, or left for the bird-sitter if your bird isn't an adventurer.

Gatorade® is a registered trademark of Stokely-Van Camp, Inc. Stokely-Van Camp, Inc. is a subsidiary of The Quaker Oats Company, a wholly-owned subsidiary of PepsiCo, Inc.
Pedialyte® is a registered trademark of Abbott Laboratories
Karo is a registered trademark of ACH Food Companies, Inc.

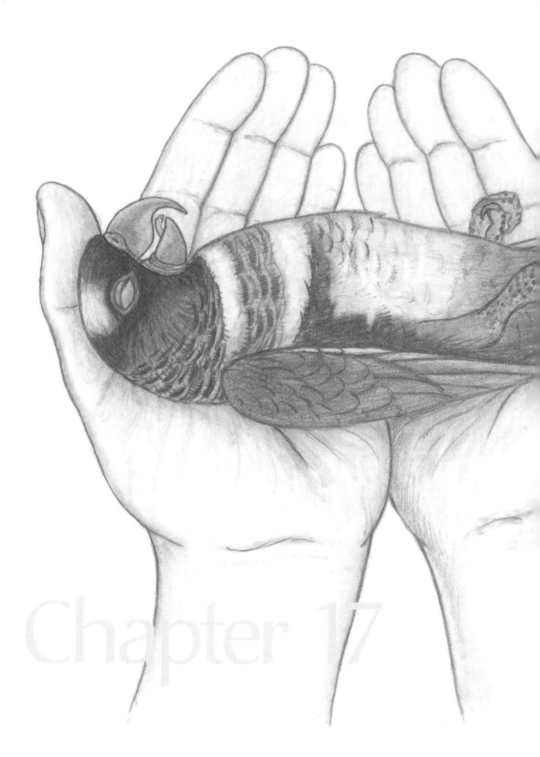

Chapter 17

When Bird and Owner Part

When the bond is broken...

"'Neath this stone doth lie more love than could ever die."
This beautiful tribute is carved on a granite headstone at a pet cemetery. These words demonstrate the depth of emotion people feel for their pets. This chapter addresses the issues and feelings involved when a pet bird and its owner must part, either through the death of the bird or the death of the owner, and some of the ways to cope. The issue of rehoming a pet bird will also be addressed.

The Loss

Sooner or later, most pet owners will face the loss of a beloved pet. Whether due to natural causes, accidents, disease, or whatever reason, the fact is the pet is gone, and you're left with the emptiness. Mental health professionals have only recently realized the impact that losing a pet can have on people. Many books are now available to help people more effectively deal with this difficult problem. These are available at your local library or bookstore. Your avian veterinarian's office may know of additional resources, such as pet loss support groups or hot lines in your area. Finally, some pet-loss support groups are available online through the Internet.

Helping Children Cope

Although birds are relatively long-lived pets, eventually, when the bird dies, the wonderful relationship between bird and owner ends. While no one has an easy time accepting the death of a beloved pet, children may have more difficulty with the loss than adults. To help your child cope, consider the following suggestions.

397

Let your child know that it's okay to feel sad about losing the family bird. Encourage your child to draw pictures of the bird, to make a collage using photos of your pet or pictures of pet birds from magazines, to write stories or poems about it, or to talk about the loss. Also explain to the child that these sad feelings will pass with time.

Depending on your child's age, he or she will have varying reactions to the loss. Children under the age of five may not understand how final death is. They may think that something they did or thought caused the bird to leave. Explain what happened as clearly as you can.

Grade-school-age children (from about five to twelve) may seem to want to know all the details surrounding the bird's death. Straightforward answers seem to satisfy this age group's need to know and help them cope.

Teenage children may have the hardest time dealing with the loss of a pet, especially if the bird was a member of the family for many years. Let teens have as much say in the decision-making process as they want to. Include them in visits to the veterinarian's office so they can discuss the bird's condition with the doctor and hospital staff.

Regardless of a child's age, being honest about the loss of your pet is the best approach to help all family members cope with the loss.

While helping their children cope with the death of a pet, parents need to remember that it's okay for adults to feel sad, too. Don't diminish your feelings of loss by saying "It's only a bird." Pets fill important roles in our lives and our families. Whenever we lose someone close to us, we grieve.

The agony suffered when a pet is lost can seem unbearable. The grief process can linger for months, even years, unless a certain progression of emotions occur. Elisabeth Kübler-Ross, a front-runner in grief acknowledgement research, found that the grieving process is divided into five distinct stages: anger, denial, sadness/depression, bargaining, and acceptance. She also discovered that, unless a grieving person traverses each of these stages, he or she can remain stuck in the grieving process. This discovery confirms the normalcy of the emotions, pain, and thoughts suffered when someone dear to us has been lost. Therefore, it is important to work completely through each of the phases.

Pet lovers have been told by well-meaning people, "It's only an animal." For years, many pet owners would not allow themselves to grieve over the loss of a pet. They could not find the acceptance and support of friends who understood what they were going through. Strong support of close family and friends can be critical in allowing the grieving process to become complete. Fortunately, attitudes about pet loss are changing. Major greeting card manufacturers now routinely offer pet-loss sympathy cards, and support groups are now available for people who have lost a pet.

The sections that follow discuss some important issues regarding pet loss: euthanasia for pets; options for the body after death; and options for survivors, including books and support groups.

Euthanasia

Fortunately for many bird owners, they never have to make a decision regarding euthanasia (humane death). Birds often die so quickly that they take this difficult decision away from us. However, if you are faced with a situation where your pet is suffering, and all hope has been exhausted, you may have to consider the euthanasia option.

It is important to understand what will actually happen during the euthanasia and what method will be used. Usually, a lethal injection of a potent and concentrated anesthetic agent is given. The pet goes into a very deep anesthetic sleep, and the drug stops the heart. It takes less than five seconds for death to occur. The only sensation is the needle prick.

Euthanasia must be performed by a veterinarian. Discuss the options your veterinarian can offer and listen to his or her opinion. Other considerations include where it will be done--in hospital or in the home? Do you want to be with the animal? Do you want to view the body afterward? There are no right or wrong answers. Each situation is different. Most owners do not want to be with their pet during euthanasia. This is usually the best decision, providing there is a trusting relationship with your veterinarian. Most owners want to remember their pets as they were in life, not in death. A caring and sensitive veterinary staff will understand that everyone has different needs, and they should make every effort to meet those needs.

Options for the Body

What options are there regarding care of the body when a pet dies? Many people are not aware of the choices available to them.

Some people want to bury the pet in the backyard. However, this is not legal in many areas. If it is legal in your community, make certain you dig a deep enough grave to prevent other animals from disturbing it.

Cremation is another very accepted option. Private pet crematoria, cemeteries, and some veterinary clinics have the ability to cremate an animal. The body is turned into "cremains," (not really ashes) by heat approaching 2,500 degrees Fahrenheit. The term cremains is preferred because ashes are thought of as powdery. Cremains still have bone fragments in them and are a different consistency from ashes. The cremains can then be scattered, buried or placed in an urn for safekeeping. Pet cemeteries may even offer mausoleums where the cremains can be interred.

Burial at a pet cemetery is a third option. These areas are specifically zoned for burial of pets. They provide a quiet, beautiful surrounding to help ease the loss and emptiness. Since there are many options to choose from, costs vary widely. The process can be as simple or as elaborate as personal preferences dictate. Any choice made is perfectly acceptable. After visiting the cemetery, it will be readily apparent that you are not alone in your feelings for your pet.

Your final option is to leave the body at the veterinary hospital. This option is the one most frequently selected. Every clinic is a little different, but most have a service pick up the bodies and either bury or cremate them. The animals are not cremated individually. The remains will then be returned to the earth. It is okay to ask how the clinic handles this. The staff should be prepared to discuss it.

Easing the Pain: Support Groups and Books

Talking about your pet and the loss you feel can be the quickest way to lessen the hurt. Choose appropriate people to talk with because you don't want to hear, "It was only a pet!" Your veterinarian or clinic staff may be the best resource to assist with this. Remember, these professionals also love animals or they wouldn't be in this field. They have dealt with this type of problem before, both with their own pets and with their clients'. As difficult as it is to talk about the death of a pet, the more you do so, the easier it will become.

Another option is attending a pet loss support group run by qualified individuals with psychology backgrounds. Many pet owners feel they could not have handled the grieving process on their own. Without the support group, they would have been lost. It is very comforting to know others have gone through similar circumstances. To locate such a group, contact your veterinarian or local veterinary association.

As previously mentioned, many great books are available on the subject of pet loss. Reading can help you better understand and ease the hurt. This can be extremely important if children are involved. Some wonderful books on the subject have been written especially for children. For them, these books can help make sense of what has happened to their pet.

As strange as it may seem, the following, final suggestion can sometimes be the best: Get a new pet. For some people, it's better to work through the grieving process before a new pet is introduced, while others find that a new pet helps them work through the process more quickly.

No disrespect is shown to your previous pet by adding a new family member. The intent is not to replace your old friend in your heart; it is just to make room for a new one. Turning your mind to life and renewal can really help ease the emptiness. Think of this as a memorial to your old friend, since the love and companionship it provided you was so special. Also, helping another homeless bird find a home is comforting to some people.

Don't be surprised if other pets in the family react to the loss as well. Plenty of evidence exists to suggest that animals mourn the loss of other animals. Therefore, be a source of consolation for the other pets in the family. Spend time with them to help ease their loss, too. Lack of appetite, incessant vocalization, poor potty habits, and other abnormal behaviors may begin. Encourage interaction between family members and existing pets. It will make everyone feel better.

Despite the pain and sadness that occurs when the bond is broken, the incredible joy that pets bring to our lives makes us willing to go through it again and again.

When a Bird Owner Dies

In some cases, the relationship between bird and owner ends with the death of the owner rather than the bird. Many bird owners make provisions in their wills for their pet birds. This is important since many pet birds have long life spans, and many bird owners adopt their pets relatively late in the owners' lives.

Because they are considered "property" in the eyes of the law, pets cannot be named as beneficiaries in wills. In other words, you can't leave all your possessions to your pet bird. You also cannot make pets direct beneficiaries of trusts. This

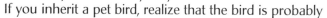

doesn't mean you shouldn't make provisions for your pet bird in your will; in many cases, pet birds can outlive their owners, which means that you will want to make arrangements for your pet's care after your death.

To do this, legal experts suggest creating a trust into which you place the bird and some money for its care. Make the beneficiary of the trust a friend or relative who you trust to care for your feathered friend. Of course, you should discuss such plans with your chosen beneficiary well in advance of making the arrangements.

Discuss the legal requirements of wills and trusts with your attorney because they vary from state to state.

If you inherit a pet bird, realize that the bird is probably grieving and may not be itself for awhile. The bird may have a poor appetite, it may act depressed, or it may exhibit behavior problems, such as feather picking. Be patient and understanding as the bird adjusts to life in your home. Realize that not only has the bird lost a very good friend, its whole world and routine have been turned upside down, and the new situation with you will take some getting used to. Offer it a healthful diet and pay attention to it in order to win its trust and begin building a bond between the two of you.

In time, a bird that has lost its owner can form bonds with other members of the family.

In time, the bird should be able to form a bond with you or with someone in your family, but it has to mourn first. While the bird is mourning, make sure it doesn't spend excessive amounts of time in its cage because this can create additional problems relating to territory and space.

Birdie Retirement Homes

If you don't have any friends or relatives willing to take on the responsibility of your pet bird after your death, you may want to look into a "retirement home" or sanctuary for your pet. Around the world, bird lovers operate these facilities, which are dedicated to lifelong care for your pet.

402

The Rehomed Parrot

Although the decision to adopt a bird is ideally a lifelong commitment, sometimes circumstances arise that require you to find a new home for the bird. Remember, the goal of an owner who is also an animal advocate is to keep the bird's best interests at heart.

Here are some of the reasons that pet birds go to new homes:

- Owners get tired of birds
* Birds develop behavioral problems that owners can't cope with
- Owners undergo significant life change--marriage, par enthood, divorce--and don't have time for the bird
- The owner dies
- The owner or a member of the owner's family develops a severe allergy to bird
- The owner becomes seriously ill and cannot care for bird
- The owner moves to a facility where pets aren't permitted

So what do you do to help your family cope if your beloved pet bird needs to be placed in a different home? You should be honest with your children when explaining that the pet needs to live elsewhere. Don't put the blame on the pet, and don't try to convince your children that the animal will be happier with another family.

Take the responsibility as the parent for making the decision that the pet must go and let your children express their emotions over the pet's departure.

Realize that your family will grieve a bit over your pet's departure, even though the animal will be alive and in a new home. To help your family ease the pain of parting, discuss how you want to remember the pet: Do the children want photos taken with the pet before it goes to a new home? Next, involve the entire family in the rehoming process. The children may want to be in charge of making a list of what criteria the pet's new home should have. The children may also want to gather up all the pet's toys to take with it to its new home.

Get together to decide how to best find a new home for the pet, such as putting up an advertisement at your veterinarian's office. Many offices have bulletin boards that clients can post messages on, and what better place to find a good home for your pet than among a group of animal lovers? Some pet supply stores may also allow you to post an adoption notice in their establishments. If you've been a regular customer, ask the manager if he or she will allow you to advertise the need for a new home for your pet in this way.

Let your children check out the bird's new home before you place the pet with its new owners. This can help bring them closure on the pet's departure. Let your children talk about how they feel about the new home and listen carefully. Your chil-

Birds are sometimes rehomed when they develop serious medical problems. This female Eclectus was found in the street and brought to a bird rescue group. She is blind, deaf, and prone to seizures. (Parrot Education and Adoption Center)

dren may notice things that you do not and bring up some valid concerns, or they may say that a home seems unsuitable because they fear losing their beloved pet.

If you would like to open your heart and home to a rehomed parrot, consider the following sources: A parrot adoption center, a breeder who may be seeking new homes for birds that have retired from breeding, an aviary or a multibird private home.

Appendix A

Bibliography

The following references are listed by category as a helpful guide for additional reading.

General Bird Care

Forshaw, Joseph. *Parrots of the World*. Neptune, NJ: TFH Publications Inc. 1977.

Freud, Arthur. *The Parrot: An Owner's Guide to a Happy, Healthy Pet*. New York: Howell Book House. 1996.

Hanna, Jack and Hester Mundis. *Jack Hanna's Ultimate Guide to Pets*. New York: G.P. Putnam's Sons. 1996.

Higdon, Pamela Leis. *Bird Care and Training: An Owner's Guide to a Happy, Healthy Pet*. New York: Howell Book House. 1998.

O'Neil, Jacqueline. *The Complete Idiot's Guide to Bird Care & Training*. New York: Alpha Press. 1998.

Spadafori, Gina, and Brian Speer, D.V.M. *Birds for Dummies*. New York: IDG Books Worldwide. 1999.

Pet Bird Behavior

Doane, Bonnie Munro, Quakinbush, Thomas. *My Parrot, My Friend: An Owner's Guide to Parrot Behavior*. New York: Howell Book House. 1994.

Rach, Julie Ann. *Why Does My Bird Do That? A Guide to Parrot Behavior*. New York: Howell Book House. 1998.

Short, Lester L. *The Lives of Birds: Birds of the World and Their Behavior*. New York: Henry Holt and Co. 1993.

Sparks, John, and Tony Soper. *Parrots: A Natural History*. New York: Facts on File Inc. 1990.

Pet Bird Health

Altman, Robert B., D.V.M., Susan L. Clubb, D.V.M., Gerry M. Dorrestein, D.V.M., Ph.D., Katherine Quesenberry, D.V.M. *Avian Medicine and Surgery*. Philadelphia: W.B. Saunders Co. 1997.

Hawcroft, Tim, B.V.Sc., M.A.C.V.Sc., M.R.C.V.Sc. *First Aid for Birds*. New York: Howell Book House. 1994.

Rach, Julie Ann, Gary A. Gallerstein, D.V.M. *First Aid for Birds: An Owner's Guide to a Happy, Healthy Pet*. New York: Howell Book House. 1998.

Ritchie, Branson, W. D.V.M., Ph.D., Greg J. Harrison, D.V.M., Linda R. Harrison. *Avian Medicine: Principles and Application*.

Lake Worth, Fla.: Wingers Publishing Inc. 1994.

Rosskopf, Walter J. Jr., D.V.M., Richard W. Woerpel, M.S., D.V.M. *Diseases of Cage and Aviary Birds*. Baltimore: Williams and Wilkens. 1996.

Rupley, Agnes, D.V.M. *Manual of Avian Practice*. Philadelphia: W.B. Saunders. 1997.

Schoen, Allen M., D.V.M., M.S., Susan G. Wynn, D.V.M. *Complementary And Alternative Veterinary Medicine: Principles And Practice*. St. Louis: Mosby Inc. 1999.

Pet Bird Training

Athan, Mattie Sue. *Guide to a Well-Behaved Parrot*. Hauppauge, N.Y.: Barron's Educational Series Inc. 1993.

Hubbard, Jennifer. *The New Parrot Training Handbook*. Fremont, Calif.: Parrot Press. 1997.

Toxic Plants

Alber, John I. and Delores M. *Baby-Safe Houseplants and Cut Flowers*. Highland, Ill.: Genus Books. 1990.

Morelli, Jim. *Poison!* Kansas City: Andrews and McMeel. 1997.

Magazines

AFA Watchbird. P.O. Box 56218, Phoenix, AZ 85079.

Bird Talk. P.O. Box 57347, Boulder, CO 80322-7347.

Bird Times. 7-L Dundas Circle, Greensboro, NC 27499-0765.

Pet Bird Report. 2236 Mariner Square Dr. #35W, Alameda, CA 94501

Appendix B

National Bird Clubs

These bird clubs and societies and their addresses are subject to change

African Lovebird Society, P.O. Box 142, San Marcos, CA 92069

African Parrot Society, P.O. Box 204, Clarinda, IA 51632-2731

Amazona Society, P.O. Box 73547, Puyallup, WA 98373

American Border Fancy Canary Club, 348 Atlantic Ave., East Rockaway, NY 11518

American Budgerigar Society, 1704 Kangaroo, Killeen, TX 76541

American Cockatiel Society, P.O. Box 609, Fruitland Park, FL 34731

American Federation of Aviculture, P.O. Box 56218, Phoenix, AZ 85079

American Norwich Society, 113 Murphy Rd., Winter Springs, FL 32708

American Singers Club Inc., Rt. 1, Box 186-B, Ridgeley, WV 26753

American Waterslager Society, 14750 Carolcrest Dr., Houston, TX 77079

Asiatic Parrot Association International, 734 S. Boulder Hwy., Suite 400, Henderson, NV 89015

Aviculture Society of America, P.O. Box 5516, Riverside, CA 92517

Bird Clubs of America, P.O. Box 2005, Yorktown, VA 23692

Cockatoo Society, 26961 N. Broadway, Escondido, CA 92026

Confederation of All Type Canaries, 2801 Mayfield Dr., Park Ridge, IL 60068

Fig Parrot Group, 8023 17th N.E., Seattle, WA 98115

Forpus Fanciers, P.O. Box 804, Jamul, CA 92035

International American Singers Club, 3584 Loon Lake Rd., Wixom, MI 48096

International Aviculturists Society, P.O. Box 2232, La Belle, FL 33975

International Border Fancy Club, 1888 Mannering Rd., Cleveland, OH 44122

International Columbus Fancy Association, 305 Grosvenor Ct., Bolingbrook, IL 60439

International Fife Fancy Club of America, 11614 January Dr., Austin, TX 78753

International Gloster Breeders Association, 1816 Trigg Rd., Ferndale, WA 98248

International Loriinae Society, P.O. Box 4763, Plant City, FL 33564-4763

International Parrotlet Society, P.O. Box 2428, Santa Cruz, CA 95063-2428

Lizard Canary Association, 26295 W. 315 St., Paola, KS 66071

Macaw Society of America, P.O. Box 90037, Burton, MI 48509

Milo Wells German Roller Canary Club, 2040 N.W. 20th, Oklahoma City, OK 73106

Mynah News, 641 Invader, Sulphur, LA 70663

National Cockatiel Society, 286 Broad St., Suite 140, Manchester, CT 06040

National Color-Bred Association, 236 Lester St., Burleson, TX 76028

National Finch and Softbill Society, P.O. Box 3232, Ballwin, MO 63022

National Gloster Club, 58 Joanne Dr., Hanson, MA 02341

National Institute of Red Orange Canaries, P.O. Box 93, Mokema, IL 60448

National Norwich Plainhead Canary Club, 21 Maple Ave., Niles, OH 44445

National Parrot Association, 8 N. Hoffman Ln., Hauppauge, NY 11788

North American Border Club, 36051 S. 545 Rd., Jay, OK 74346

Old Varieties Canary Association, 5513 Manor Rd., Austin, TX 78723

Parrot Rehabilitation Society, P.O. Box 620213, San Diego, CA 92612-0213

Society of Parrot Breeders and Exhibitors, P.O. Box 369, Groton, MA 01450

Society of Parrot Breeders and Exhibitors, P.O. Box 369, Groton, MA 01450

Stafford Canary Club of America, 981 West Glen Oaks Blvd., Glendale, CA 91202

U.S. Association of Roller Canary Culturists, 533 Beach Ave., Bronx, NY 10473

U.S. World Parrot Trust, P.O. Box 341141, Memphis, TN 38184

Waxbill-Parrot Finch Society, 6419 N. 15th St., Philadelphia, PA 19126

Yorkshire Canary Club of America, 7616 Carson Ave., Baltimore, MD 21224

Appendix C

Web Sites of Interest to Bird Lovers

The Internet can be a wonderful resource for bird lovers. You can use the World Wide Web to shop for bird supplies, books, and videos; you can network with other bird lovers around the world; or you can gather information on a particular species that interests you. You can even send pet-themed electronic greeting cards to family and friends online.

Bird-specific sites have been cropping up regularly on the Internet. These sites offer pet bird owners the opportunity to share stories about their pets, along with trading helpful hints about bird care. You may, however, not want to use the Internet as your sole source of bird care information. You should "consider the source" when using information off the Internet because it may be someone's opinion rather than proven factual information.

If you belong to an online service, look for the pet site (it's sometimes included in more general topics, such as "Hobbies and Interests," or more specifically "Pets"). If you have Internet access, ask your Web browser software to search for "pet bird health" or "parrot health."

Here are a few Web site addresses to get you started. Happy browsing!
Please note: these websites and their addresses are subject to change.

General bird information

Acme Pet: http://www.acmepet.com/bird
Avian Health and Disease Prevention:
http://members.tripod.com/avianweb/index.html
Avian Yellow Pages: http://www.skyeweb.com/ayp/
Bird Talk, Bird Breeder and Birds USA magazines:
http://www.animalnetwork.com or http://www.petchannel.com
Bird Times magazine: http://www.birdtimes.com
Birds n Ways: http://www.birdsnways.com
Bittacus Pet Bird Page:
http://www.mindspring.com/~mintz/coverpg.html
Cagebird.com: http://www.cagebird.com
Exotic Birds: http://www.keyinfo.com/birds
NetVet/Electronic Zoo: http://netvet.wustl.edu/birds.html
Old World Aviaries: http://www.oldworldaviaries.com
Pets.com: http://www.pets.com
The Aviary: http://www.theaviary.com
The Lexicon of Parrots: http://www.arndt-verlag.com
The Pet Bird Page: http://www.aloha.net/~granty
The Pet Bird Report: http://www.petbirdreport.com
Up at Six Aviaries: http://www.upatsix.com

Grief and Bereavement

Association for Pet Loss and Bereavement:
http://www.aplb.org
Pet bereavement links: http://www.vetmed.iastate.edu/support/weblink.html
Rainbows Bridge: http://www.rainbowsbridge.com

Health issues

Academy of Veterinary Homeopathy: http://www.acad-vethom.org/index.html
American Holistic Veterinary Medical Association: http://www.altvetmed.com/AHVMA_brochure.html
Association of Avian Veterinarians: http://www.aav.org
International Veterinary Acupuncture Society: http://ivas.org/index.html

Purdue University's toxic plants for pets list:

http://vet.purdue.edu/depts/addl/toxic/cover1.html
Import/Export Requirements
United States Department of Agriculture: http://www.usda.gov/aphis

Rescue groups

NetVet Animal Welfare/Rights/Humane/Rescue Organizations: http://netvet.wustl.edu/welfare.htm
Pet Rescue Clearinghouse: http://homearts.com/depts/pas-time/shelters/shelters.htm
Shelters and All-Breed Rescue Organizations: http://www.ecn.purdue.edu/~laird/animal_rescue/shelters
PEAC: http://www.peac.org
The Gabriel Foundation: http://www.thegabrielfoundation.org
The Oasis: http://www.the-oasis.org/st-lory.php

Specific species information

African parrots: http://www.wingscc.com/aps
Alex the African Grey: http://www.cages.org/research/pepper-berg/index.html
Budgerigars: http://www.budgies.org
Canaries: http://www.canaryfinch.com
Cockatiels: http://www.cockatiels.org
Eclectus: http://www.landofvos.com
Finches: http://www.finchworld.com
Macaws: http://www.exoticbird.com
Parrotlets: http://www.parrotletranch.com
Pionus: http://users.aol.com/apionus/PBAPAGE.HTM
Quakers: http://www.QuakerVille.com
Softbills: http://www.softbills.com

Appendix D

Weights and Measures
METRIC CONVERSION TABLE
Abbreviations

oz.	=	ounce
lb.	=	pound
fl.	=	fluid
tsp.	=	teaspoon
tbs.	=	tablespoon
qt.	=	quart
gal.	=	gallon
g.	=	gram
kg.	=	kilogram
cc.	=	cubic centimeter
ml.	=	milliliter
L.	=	liter/litre

Volume

1 cc   = 1ml.
1000 cc = 1 L.
8 fl. oz. = 1 cup
4 cups = 1 qt.
4 qt.   = 1 gal.
1 tsp.   = 5 cc.
3 tsp.   = 1 tbs.   = 15 cc. = 1/2 oz.
2 tbs.   = 30 cc.   = 1 oz.
1 qt.   = 946 cc. = 0.946 L.
1 gal.   = 3785 cc. = 3.785 L.

Weight

16 oz.   = 1 lb.
1000 g. = 1 kg.
1 kg.   = 2.2 lb.
1 oz.   = 28 g.
1 lb.   = 454 g.

Appendix E

A Brief History of Birds

As a bird owner, you're in good company. Some 12.5 million pet birds are kept in American homes, and birdkeeping is a popular pastime around the world.

Birds have been kept throughout history. Historians give credit to both the ancient Egyptians and the Chinese as being the first birdkeepers. The Egyptians kept pigeons, while the Chinese trained falcons to hunt and cormorants to fish. Egypt's Queen Hatsheput (1504 to 1482 BC) is credited as being the first monarch to create a royal zoo, which included exotic birds. The ancient Persians also knew about talking birds as early as the fifth century BC, when a court physician and naturalist wrote about talking birds that were described to him by Indian merchants.

From Egypt, birdkeeping spread to Greece and Rome.

Alexander the Great receives credit from some historians with discovering the Alexandrine parakeet, and the Greeks are credited with popularizing parrot keeping outside of the birds' native lands of Africa and Asia. Aristotle authored many works on the fascinating world of birds. These were based on descriptions of birds brought back by Alexander the Great. Psittace, the name of a pet bird that Aristotle wrote about frequently, formed the basis of the scientific name of the parrot family--Psittacine.

Wealthy Romans also built extensive garden aviaries, and they also employed mockingbirds in the entryways of their homes as feathered doorbells that would announce visitors. The Romans are also thought to be the first bird dealers, bringing different types of birds to Great Britain and the European continent.

Until the Renaissance, birdkeeping was considered a hobby that only the wealthy could pursue. After canaries were introduced to Europe by Portuguese sailors, birdkeeping began to take off as a hobby, although it was still confined largely to upper class fanciers. (Some credit Christopher Columbus with bringing Queen Isabella a pair of Cuban Amazons from the New World and introducing Amazon parrots to European bird fanciers.)

Birdkeeping spread beyond Europe during the Victorian era. At that time, British bird sellers offered common European species, such as goldfinches and larks, to the captains of ships bound for the West Indies. The captains would trade their feathered cargo for common Caribbean species, and bird-keepers on both sides of the Atlantic began to develop interest in new species of birds.

Explorers to the South Pacific did their part to popularize birdkeeping, too. Naturalist John Gould brought budgerigars and other Australian species to Europe, and he was one of the first aviculturists, setting up breeding colonies of budgies in the late 1800s.

At least nine U.S. presidents shared the White House with pet birds, although in many cases, the birds were described as pets of the First Ladies rather than the presidents.
Martha Washington was said to have doted on her pet parrot, but the first president did not share her opinion of the bird. He once wrote to a friend, "On the one side I am called upon to remember the parrot, and on the other to remember the dog. For my own part I should not pine much if both were forgot," according to the book Presidential Pets by Niall Kelly.
Dolly Madison took her green parrot with her when she evacuated Washington during the War of 1812. She gave the bird to a servant with instructions to take it to the French ambassador's residence. After the British left Washington, the Madisons lived in the French ambassador's residence for the remainder of his term of office while the White House was rebuilt.

Andrew Jackson found his parrot, Poll, in a Nashville candy store. The bird stayed in Tennessee when Jackson became president, but he often asked about it in letters home. Reportedly, the bird had to be removed from Jackson's funeral service because it began screaming obscenities.
Frances Cleveland kept a canary in the White House, but it was her pet mockingbird that caused a minor uproar one night. The bird's song disturbed the president while he was working, so he requested that an aide move the bird to another part of the house. The aide spent the better part of the night moving the bird from room to room because Cleveland worried that the bird might catch cold from being left in a draft.

William McKinley's double-headed Amazon, Washington Post, was quite a talented bird. He often commented "Look at all the pretty girls" whenever a group of women passed his cage. He was also a good whistler and frequently finished the tunes that the president would start whistling to him.
During the Coolidge administration, the White House must have seemed like a small aviary. Grace Coolidge had an

assortment of birds, including Hartz Mountain canaries named Nip and Tuck, a white canary named Snowflake, a thrush named Old Bill, a mockingbird and a parrot. She allowed the birds to roam free in the White House, although this habit made housekeeping difficult for one of the maids because President Coolidge's mynah bird enjoyed riding on her head. The mynah's vocal talents were also used to help fund the National Zoo. During a meeting between the zoo's director and the president, a maid prodded the mynah into saying "What about the appropriation?"

In the United States, birdkeeping began to boom after World War II. The budgie rose to its position as most popular pet bird in the 1950s, and the bird care industry began to grow steadily and significantly in the 1970s. The interest in keeping pet birds continues to grow today, and it shows no signs of stopping!

The Origins of Birds

The earliest recognized bird was *Archeopteryx lithographica*. In 1861, quarrymen near Pappenheim, Bavaria found a fossil of a crow-sized reptilian animal with a long tail and obvious feathers that they passed along to a local museum. The slate was from the Jurassic period, about 150 million years ago. Other, more recent, archaeological discoveries have strengthened the possible connection between birds and reptiles. A fossil of a dromaeosaur found in China in 2001 shows evidence of well-defined feathers along the animal's forearms and hindlimbs.

Today, scientists recognize 28 orders, 163 families, 1,975 genera, and about 8,805 species of birds. In the eyes of science, all animals are classified by kingdom, phyllum, class, order, family, genus, and species. All birds are classified as members of the kingdom *Animalia*, the phylum *Vertebrata* and the class *Aves*. Pet birds are further classified into the order *Psittaformes* (if they are parrots), *Piciformes* (if they are toucans) or *Passeriformes* (if they are canaries or finches).

Let's take a taxonomic look at a fairly common pet bird species: *the African grey parrot.*

Animalia

Vertebrata
   Aves
      Psittaciformes
         Psittacidae
            Psittacus
               erithacus erithacus (Congos)
               erithacus timneh (Timnehs)

For comparison sake, let's look at the taxonomic grouping of two mammals: a house cat and a person.

The house cat's taxonomic grouping looks like this:

Animalia

Vertebrata
   Mammalia
      Carnivora
         Felidae
            Felis
               domesticus

While a human's taxonomic grouping looks like this:

Animalia

Chordata
   Mammalia
      Primates
         Hominidae
            Homo
               sapiens

Index of Signs

Note: page numbers shown in boldface contain detailed coverage of the subject. If your bird is having a medical emergency, refer to chapter 14 of this book and call your avian veterinarian's office immediately for further instructions.

A

Abdomen

    distended/swelling, **238, 244, 246, 303, 343, 354, 356, 381**

Activity

    less active, **238**, 240, **285**, 286, 290, 292, 297, 311, 319, 322, 323, **333**, 338, 340, 355, 356, 358, 368, 379, **402**

    less responsive, **238**, 240

    less talking/vocalizing, 174, **238, 285**, 333

    sleeping more, 174, **238**, 285, **333**

    sitting on the bottom of the cage, 174, **238**, 303

Appearance

    change in posture, **238**, 240

    fluffed, 174, **238, 285**, 286, **333**, 389

    hunched over, 174

    poor feathering, 340, 356, **358**

    ruffled feathers, **238**, 242, 243

    shredded feathers, **175, 239**

    squatting, **246, 303**

    tail bobbing, **238, 244**, 287, 335, 338

Appetite

    excessive eating, **239**, 241, 358

    less eating, 174, **239**, 240, 242, 249, **285, 293-294**, 297, 319, **333**, 336, 340, 342, 345, 354, 355, 356, 381, 389, **402**

B

Balance difficulties,

    loss of balance, **240, 241**, 242, 292, 293, 298, 311, 319, 322, 348, 359, 360

    difficulty perching/not perching, 92, **238**, 360, 368

    falling off the perch, **241, 292-293**, 319

C

F

Facial swelling, **335**, 365
Feather
blood in feather shaft, 379
chewing, **175**, 239, 362, 374
curled, 239, 374, 379
discolored, 358, 373
loss on the head, 366
picking, 23, 41, 42, 43, 57, 72, **174**, 180, 181, 192, **239**, 243,
275, 319, 321, 351, 362, 369, 372, **374-378**, 402
poor feathering, 340, 356, 358
retained feather shaft, 379
short clubbed feather tips, **379-380**
wet appearance, 243, 296, 305, 315
Feet
raw feet, 92, 366
sore feet, 92, 306
swelling, **301**, 306, 366, 368

H

Head
abnormal movements/position, 240, 242, 311, 319, 342,
346, 359
shaking, 334, 335

I

Inability to vocalize, 307

J

Joint swelling, **313**, 359, 368

L

Lameness, **238**, 240, 241, 298, 306, 313, 356, 359, 366, 368
Leg
see also lameness, limping
swelling, 307, 313-314
Lethargic, see activity
Limping, 174, 359
Loss of consciousness, 292, 309, 311

M

Molting
  delayed molt, 358
  prolonged molt, 239
Mouth
  blunted papilla in the mouth, 345
  growths/masses, 345
  hanging open, 360
  odor, 246, 346
  problems, 246, 336, **344-345**
  redness or burns around the mouth, 317, 323
  scabby lesions in the mouth, 345
  swelling, 365
  white cheesy patches in the mouth, 246, 336, 345
Muscle wasting, 343

N

Nails
  bleeding, 289
  overgrown, **139**, **239**, 243, 356, 363
Nares (nostrils)
  congestion, 345
  discharge, **238**, **245**, 287, 306, 335, 339, 340
  plugged, 242, **245**, 335, 364
Nasal, see nares
Non-weight bearing, 92, 306, 307

O

Obesity, 34, 186, 241, 243, 244, 303, 351, 356, 358, 366, 371

P

Paralysis, 240, 241, 303, 309, 317, 319, 341, 359, 360, 381
Preening excessively, 174

R

Regurgitation/vomiting, 164, 189, **238**, 246, **295-296**, 317, 319,   323, 341, 344, 346, 348, 354, 381

S

Scratching, 242, 351
Seizures, see convulsions
Self mutilation, 57, 189, 323, **369**, 371, **374-378**

Skin
  crusting, 243, 364, 365
  excessive flaking/scaling, **239**, 351, 367
  lesions, 365
  lumps and bumps, **239**, 243, 365, 370
  masses, 243, 253
Slow weight gain, 302
Sneezing, **245**, 335, 339, 340
Stiffness, 313
Straining, **238**, 246, 247, 303, 344, 351, 352, 370
Stretching of the neck, 287, 335
Swallowing difficulties, 246, 341, 365

T

Tiring easily, 244, 306
Tremors, see convulsions

W

Weakness, **174**, **238**, 286, 289, 290, 292, 299, 303, 309, 311, 319, 342, 348, 355, 360, 361, 381
Weight loss, also see muscle wasting, **239**, 285, 293, **333**, 340, 348, 350, 351, 354, 357, 358, 379
Wing(s)
  deformity, 359
  drooping, **174**, **238**, **244**, 298, **307**, 309, 313, 359
  held away from the body, **224**, **244**, **245**, 311, 389
  inability to move wing, 307
  swelling, 307, 359

General Index

Note: *Page numbers in boldface contain detailed coverage of the subject*

A

B